THE DEATH Q

An unusual guide to an 811 mile thru hike
circling Death Valley on abandoned railroads.

By Steven "Blast" Halteman

Vol. 1 of "Stories from Steve," an Adventure Series

May the miles on your "Q" be filled with wonder and joy!

Written by Steven Halteman
Editor Cirina Catania
Cover design by Ashley Hubbard
Additional Copy Editing Klaire Odumody

The author of this book is not responsible for any damage, personal
injuries, or death as a result of the use of any advice,
gear, or techniques discussed within this book.
Hiking and backpacking can be dangerous activities.
Please use caution and common sense as you proceed.
All outdoor activities discussed in this book
are carried out at the reader's own risk.

For further information visit www.storiesfromsteve.org

To Myrna Halteman, a.k.a. Mom,
who genetically wouldn't allow me to sit still when there were un-
knowns around the corner.

To Jim O'Donnell, who taught me the necessity of seeing the desert
through the right eyes.

YODO

You Only Die Once.

And that death matters much less than the life you live.

But an acquaintance with death and the valley it resides in,
is perhaps a prudent approach to that inevitability.

I wonder if anyone on their deathbed has ever said,
"I should never have gone on so many hikes."

Table of Contents

PART ONE

Chapter 1

A Hike Has to Start Somewhere

I found myself at a place called China Ranch. Sitting in the shade of palms that provided the dates for the shake I was sipping. It was all about to begin, though I had not an inkling. Halfway through the date shake, I noticed a signboard for a trail. I reverted my eyes to my wife and young daughter. Then refocused on my shake. Taking off down trails disrupts domestic harmony. I knew this. But shakes come to an end. Without the straw as diversion, my thoughts strayed again to the trail. Where did it go?

Somebody probably once said that human beings are divided into two groups. Those who are content to stay where they are, and those who have to see what's around the corner. I suspect the majority of people who have picked up this book, to be guilty of the latter. I am certainly a victim of the urge.

Delicate marital negotiations ensued. Future promises were made. I was given an hour. I took off with the foresight not to bring a watch. I passed old cars. Followed by a ruined stagecoach stop. Then some forgotten mining works. I spotted more mines in the hillside. My hour began a slow drown. Then a trail 'T.' I turned left for no particular reason. The trail struggled through thick brush before dropping into a dry riverbed. The struggle turned into tunnels of green. In the dry riverbed, a strangeness. A small river. Which, due to my proximity to Death Valley, was akin to a cactus sprouting in Yankee Stadium.

I exited the green and climbed to the base of the cliffs that lined the canyon. The trail suddenly widened, straightened and flattened. Right away, I missed all the clues to what I didn't know I was looking for. But in my defense, the view was incredibly distracting. The kind of view you flip through in other's photos but stop still when you're there. I wanted to be in that view. The chase was on. Maybe you can't catch a rainbow, but I firmly believe you can hike down a view. Perhaps even get to its other side.

The canyon narrowed. The trail stayed straight. A tapping started in a forgotten section of my brain. I ignored it. It became more persistent. I assigned it an identity. It must be the thirty-minute turnaround alarm. I ignored it more. The marital price to be paid climbed steeply.

The trail sliced through rises and jumped ravines. At each ravine, there was a scramble, down and up. The tapping became knocking. Ten more minutes is all I ask. A revelation came to me, once there were bridges on this trail. This was a road at one time. A narrow road. The knocking turned to hammering. (At the time, I had no idea the hammering had nothing to do with time and turnarounds. No, the hammering had everything to do with the obvious struggling to be observed.) I rounded a curve. The trail came to an end. I was looking back down at the river from up high. The trail was no more. Time to turn around. The hammering did not stop, it turned furious.

Sometimes we must turn inward before we can turn around. An internal dialogue.

"Look across."

"OK."

"What do you see?"

"Hey, the trail continues over there."

"So, what was once here?"

"A bridge!"

"What do you notice about this bridge?"

"It's gone."

"Other than that?"

"It's strange."

"Why?"

"It's narrow."

"And that means?"

"It was a horse trail?"

"I hear the train a comin' - It's rolling around the bend..."

"Johnny Cash is the greatest."

"I give up."

12

I turned back and walked 20 feet. Then stopped. Light. I spread my arms wide, looked to the sole cloud and shouted "It's a railroad! I'm standing on an old railroad!"

Apparently, the job title of detective would not be appearing on my resume. The obvious that had been hammering to be observed immediately relaxed. I hurried back, secure in the fact that my discovery of a railroad would eliminate any penalties for doubling my contractual return. Negative.

A botfly, or torsolo in Spanish, is a big hairy fly. It lives in Mexico and Central America, and possesses a singular, unsettling opinion of the human species. It considers us incubators. In short, the botfly's life goes something like this. The female botfly heads out on a flight. Along the way, she ambushes some poor mosquito and tackles them. Dominance is established by holding the mosquito's wings down. She then lays eggs on the mosquito, and finishes the catch and release. The mosquito is free to continue their business. Which is biting humans, among other pursuits. A by-product of such a bite is the depositing of a botfly egg in the human's bloodstream. Where it is warmed and eventually hatches into a maggot. That wants to grow. For which it needs food and air. The food is you. Your meat is carved by two oral hooks. The air comes from a breathing hole, or volcano pimple, depending on perspective. The little one keeps growing. Anchored in your flesh by those hooks. After a while, that little one is ready to return through the air hole into the world. A certified botfly. Ready to continue the cycle.

The relevance? Somewhere on that day-hike I picked up a botfly egg. And like many hosts, I didn't realize I was a carrier. After a few hours, the contentedness of my two-hour walk dissipated. While sitting in some nearby hot springs, my railroad find floated elsewhere. By the next day, life pushed me in the next direction. And that was that.

Only it wasn't. My private botfly was feeding and growing. I'll call him Fred. Fred first made his presence known a couple of weeks later with a simple question between bites. "Why would someone build a railroad through a canyon?"

Easy answer. "I don't know." Nor did I have time to ponder it as I was reapplying myself to capitalism.

Another couple of weeks passed. Fred, maturing and now with a little more confidence.

"Don't you at least want to know its name?" "If you quit bugging me, yes I do."

To answer a life mystery, I picked up my first-string brain and asked the appropriate search engine. Fred had a formal name. The "Tonopah and Tidewater Railroad" built by "Borax" Smith.

The next day Fred was eager.

"Don't you wonder where it goes?"

"I was wondering the same thing."

"Hey, Fred, it goes from Ludlow, California to Beatty, Nevada."

"How long is it brother?"

"Looks like about 200 miles."

"Bet it's never been hiked."

"Doesn't matter. It's old, probably long gone."

"Why don't you go check it out?"

"Because I'm dedicated to financial responsibility, old friend."

"Sure you are."

Two nights later, at around 2 a.m., I was awakened by an incessant buzzing. I contemplated the location of a flyswatter. Then words from the dark. "I'm off amigo. Thanks for the hospitality. And the excellent dining." But a final thought.

"Bet you couldn't hike it."

"Could too."

"Could not."

"Could too."

"Later."

And that is how it started. By 3 a.m., the hike was my own. Fred departed. His mission accomplished. Secure that his metaphor was enshrined.

Chapter 2

The Process of Discovery

The start of an idea is often different than its end. When it comes to hiking, that difference is often measured in miles. Many miles. As in, many more miles. Thus, I started with the idea of hiking the Tonopah and Tidewater Railroad (TTR) from start to finish. Early research indicated that the railroad started in Ludlow, California and ended in one of the following: Beatty, Nevada; Goldfield, Nevada; or Tonopah, Nevada. Depending on one's choice, it was either 169, 210, or 250 miles long. The TTR was built around 1907 and pulled up sometime in 1940. My thought, was it could be a cool ten-day hike for someday. So, I gently placed the TTR someday hike on the someday shelf with all the other ideas in waiting.

Then a gift of a 1929 World Atlas came from a fine friend. While thumbing through it, I came to the California map. Lo and behold, there was the TTR. Barreling north from Ludlow, skirting Death Valley and then coming to rest in southwestern Nevada. But the mapmakers weren't satisfied with a black line alone. They planted a hook. A hook that caught 85 years later. Because on that black line there were over 20 towns listed between Ludlow and Beatty. I pulled out a modern Atlas. Only six of the towns remained. That meant ghost towns. Which meant ruins. Which meant abandoned mines. Which meant exploration. Which meant discovery. Which meant hiking into history. Which meant chasing ghosts. Motivation uncut. Sure, I thrashed around a bit, maybe, but there was no way I was getting off that hook.

Everyone has their pleasures and their avoidances. For myself, pleasures would include hiking, natural scenery and history. The first two are self-explanatory. But history is vague. Specifically, I'm talking about where man has been, then given up and left for greener horizons. The life that occurred. Why they gave up. What they left. And how nature reasserted herself. All extend their pull. When all three pleasures coincide,

15

there exists a potential for special. The first-string brain was full of information. There were websites. Others were interested. Primarily railroad enthusiasts, or off roaders, who knew certain sections of the TTR. Nobody mentioned hiking it. No surprises there. With time, the veins of the Internet revealed the TTR's fascinating story. Now I could tell it. But could I walk it? Was it even there other than the short section I had stumbled upon?

According to the Internet, the town of Ludlow still existed. But barely, with a total population of around ten people. Businesses included a motel, cafe and two gas stations. Ludlow's most recent claim to fame was an 18-wheeler carrying 75,000 pounds of beef ribs that caught fire near town. In local lore thereafter known as "The Big Barbecue." A fine place to look for a railroad. What was needed were eyes on the ground.

Which is why I jumped in the truck and drove away from the Pacific Ocean to Barstow, California. Then turned on I 40 towards Needles. Fifty-seven miles out from Barstow lay Ludlow. Passing through this part of the Mojave Desert, one is not struck by local overpopulation. Arriving late, I wanted my railroad. I checked into the motel at the gas station. My first question, "So where does the TTR start?"

"Come again?"

I immediately provided way too much information to the woman behind the cash register. "News to me. Sorry." Was all I got.

Maybe there were answers in the café. Outside of which I read two plaques by phone light. One commemorating the TTR. And the other memorializing Operation Plowshare, which was a federal brainstorm to use nuclear weapons to advance major infrastructure programs in the area through detonation. For example, there's a mountain where that road should go. Nuke it. Fortunately, the Feds lost interest in plowsharing before they started pushing local buttons.

Dinner. A new tact with the waiter. "How long you lived here?"

"A little over 20 years."

"Seen a lot of changes I bet."

"Not really."

"Ever heard of the Tonopah and Tidewater Railroad?"

"Nope. But the cook knows about an old railroad around here."

16

With that a name was called, followed by an appearance from the grill. "Where's that old railroad you were talking about the other day?"

"It's gone."

Followed by a return to the grill. "Oh well, you can't win all of them" she said. "But that was what Ludlow looked like back in the day." She swept a series of photos with her index finger.

I ordered a burger. And then gave each photo its due. When photos were black-and-white, Ludlow was a hopping place.

My head hit the pillow and I settled in for a Christmas-morning-style wait. With light, it was bike to pavement. Breakfast understanding of its dismissal.

Here's what I found. Ludlow presents its history in three acts. Act I was the early town along the still active BNSF railroad train tracks. Ruins, and the old cemetery were the last of the audience. Act II is a more recent town that lines Route 66 of nostalgic cultural fame. The "get your kicks" road. Built in 1929, it quickly became the escape route out of the drought-stricken Midwest, a.k.a. the dust bowl. Escapees fled to the California of promised land fame. Some of Ludlow that lines Route 66 still functions, and some has passed to ruin. California seems to be low on affection for Route 66, as the road appears permanently washed out in either direction out of Ludlow. Act III is the modern incarnation along the freeway. It lacks charisma but provides income.

But, I was here for a railroad that was hiding. I knew the TTR headed north. So, I passed under the east-west freeway and tried to think like an engineer. Engineers are passionate about straight lines. I found a straight dirt road and followed it north. Nothing looked railroady. I did stumble upon a few acres of Peruvian Nazca lines. The kind that make sense from an airplane's perspective but seem nonsensical on the ground. I followed the rock lines here and there. Grids became apparent. Someone had deliberately carried rocks to this particular patch of desert and lined them up for a purpose.

Later, my favorite waiter confirmed that it was an Army camp in World War II. Part of General George Patton's desert training center. Where over one million men trained to prepare for the North African campaign against Germany's Erwin Rommel (a.k.a. "The Desert Fox") and his

17

Afrika Corps. Of course, it would make sense to the Army to have recruits line up rocks to highlight their tents. Seventy-five years later, I appreciated the grunt work.

Ludlow had its distractions, but so far, no TTR. I returned to Act I. And noticed a series of earthen dams that appeared to be designed to protect Ludlow from flash floods. I bypassed them and focused on the area around the BNSF tracks. Knowing these tracks existed at the same time as the TTR, it seemed reasonable to conclude a connection. I moved west.

I came across a white brick with "snowball" stamped on it. My first-string hand-held brain told me it was a firebrick, made in England at the end of the 19th century by the Snowball Firebrick Company. (To your question, the owner's name.) They were used as ship's ballast for the trip around the horn at the bottom of South America. Then exchanged for wheat in California. One brick apparently destined from London for Ludlow. Perhaps a clue, but I was not proving the heir-apparent to Sherlock Holmes, as I searched the ruins. I poked around mining works. I saw another dam in the distance.

Ignored during the search was a large pile of desiccated railroad ties. When I turned to them, I found the X on the treasure map. Because just beyond the ties were the ruins of forgotten railroad works. The first things I saw were a number of concrete pits where the workers could comfortably address the train's running gear needs from underneath. Scattered machinery and smelters lay about. But most importantly, the grail. Multiple rail-beds heading out of town. Distinguished by sections of rail ties sunk deep in the desert sand. Eventually the multiple lines became one. The TTR headed west. I believe I danced a little. Gotcha. A botfly buzzed triumphantly by my ear. We both win, Fred.

There was no restraint. I took off. The TTR began a gentle swing to the north. I passed a bucket of relics and came to the earthen dam. It was no dam. It was a raised railroad bed passing through a wash. Flash floods had taken out sections of the railbed. (Later I learned that the other earthen dams were yet another abandoned railroad, the Ludlow and Southern, which headed south. As well, the earthen dam within Ludlow proper was the TTR balloon track, a circular track that looped through Ludlow. That track allowed the TTR trains to loop around and head in the opposite direction.) I continued along the TTR until it crossed Route 66 and was guillotined by the 40 freeway. An irreligious advertising trailer squatted upon the dead-end of my grail.

I passed under the freeway for answers. Did it continue? The trailer oriented as a marker. I trooped out into the desert, knowing trains take a while to alter course. And there she was again. Another raised bed, with railroad ties as confirmation. This time the kind of big dance you do when you know no one's watching. Hello, old girl, we're going to get acquainted. And we're going to get along just fine. It was a trail and the hiking of it was necessary.

Chapter 3

The Death Q

As mentioned earlier, the start of an idea can look very different than its end. That first day in Ludlow the thought was compact and straightforward. Hike from Ludlow to at least Beatty for the simple pleasure of doing it. Or at least trying to do it. And if it couldn't be done, then a retreat to a beer and a laugh.

Well, it turned out that it could be done. And it was amazing. A hike existed where there wasn't one. It was repeatable. It had views. It had history. It had challenges. It had solitude. It had food. It had water. And it was a mass of laughs. In sum, the TTR had all the elements of a great hike.

More importantly, Beatty turned out not to be the end. In fact, it presented an entertaining proposition. At one time, three railroads passed through Beatty. Now, not a one. All three of those railroads are defunct and abandoned. Their bleached bones still extended out into the desert. Where did they go? And what about all the railroad spurs (offshoot railroads) we passed along the way? Just where did they go? Worms can still leave a half-opened can. I returned to the books and the trail. Completely opening the can.

The end of the puzzle looks like this. The Death Q is an 811 mile thru hike that follows part, or all, of ten different railroads. Nine of them abandoned. Those railroads encircle Death Valley. So, in effect, any hiker who hikes the Q in its entirety will completely circle Death Valley National Park. Hence the Death in Death Q. The Q is derived from the shape of the trail. (And I wanted to do my bit for the unloved Q, which is the second least used letter in the English language.)

You can park your car at any point along the Q and walk away. Thirty-five days later, more or less, you walk right back up to your car and get in. The Q your hiking memory. It needs to be said that 35 days is how long it took us. You can certainly speed up, or slow down, to your desire and ability. But 35 days means averaging 23.17 miles a day. A respectable average.

If you leave Ludlow and hike counterclockwise, the form in which this book is written, you will touch base with the following railroads in order of appearance. The Ludlow Southern Railroad, the Tonopah and Tidewater Railroad, the Tecopa Railroad, the Death Valley Railroad, the Las Vegas and Tonopah Railroad, the Bullfrog and Goldfield Railroad, the Carson and Colorado Railroad, the Los Angeles "Jawbone" Aqueduct Railroad, the Randsburg Railroad, and the Burlington Northern Santa Fe Railroad. A rail tour de force. Railroads that all started in the era of the steam locomotive. A few of which survived into the age of the diesel locomotive. All but the last, long abandoned.

What is out there? Here's a taste to entice your own botfly. An opera house, a Greek restaurant, marooned boats, wild burros, a bathtub, oases, stagecoach stops, hot springs, salt flats, forgotten health resorts, plane crashes, date shakes, pool tables, cave dwellings, sand dunes, disappeared villages, brothels, wild horses, ruins, endless mines, relics, tramlines that summit mountains, museums, canyons, cemeteries, a place called Zzyzx, dry lakes, a town where 20,000 once lived and now 268 do, the grave of a prostitute that became a shrine, fine dining, casinos, peak bagging, no permits, cold beer, no crowds, mystery, an outdoor sculpture garden, ghost towns with the life sucked out of them and ghost towns that live on, rail tunnels, Punjabi food and some more beer. Feel the wiggle.

Chapter 4

Death Valley

The Death Q completely circumnavigates Death Valley. At a few points along the Q you will be able to look down into Death Valley. At other times, you cross through remote sections of Death Valley National Park. But, at no time do you actually enter the valley itself. Still, it's nice to know who you're dancing with.

Perhaps the Park Service describes Death Valley best. "You are entering the hottest, driest, lowest spot in North America." The lowest point they speak of is Badwater, some 282 feet below sea level. Eighty-five miles away is Mount Whitney. The highest point in the lower 48 at 14,505 feet. At Furnace Creek, in the heart of Death Valley, a thermometer once topped out at 134°F. The highest temperature ever recorded on earth. The Shoshone word for Death Valley is, "Tomisha," which translates as "ground on fire." A pretty good argument for circling Death Valley on the Q during winter. Ironically, the same place and same year that saw 134°F also witnessed the lowest Death Valley temperature ever recorded of 15°. That year was 1913. Though a small section intrudes into Nevada, Death Valley lies mostly in California. The valley is 140 miles long. To the east is the Armagosa Range of mountains. To the west, the Panamint Range. Which acts as a rain block, discouraging rain clouds from the Pacific Ocean from passing over Death Valley. The Panamints are effective in their work. Average rainfall in Death Valley is less than two inches a year. That's phenomenally low compared to other deserts in the region. There have even been a couple of years where no rain was recorded in Death Valley at all.

The weather spectaculars go on and on. Between 1931 and 1934, in a 40-month span, there was 0.64 inches of rain. But when the Panamints fail, rain can dump hard and fast. The steep mountain walls funneling avalanches of water down across alluvial sediment fans to the valley floor below. These flash floods have killed. And, inevitably, will do so again. June 2005 is the wettest month on record with a total rainfall of 4.73

inches. That year, Badwater became Lake Badwater. It took a year and a half for the sun to evaporate it back to Badwater.

The total area of the park is 3,000 square miles. It is basically a basin and range set up. The steep mountains on either side tend to trap whatever ends up on the basin floor below. Air is one victim. When air is trapped near the valley floor it becomes superheated by reflected sunlight, clear air, and a lack of groundcover. This process leads to temperatures that set records. Water is also unable to escape. Furnace Creek and the Armagosa River both bring water into Death Valley. Once there, the water courses are unable to move on and must accept a return to the sand.

This has been the case for a very long time. Even during the much wetter Pleistocene Era (which ended some 11,000 years ago) the same fate awaited the many rivers and streams that flowed into Death Valley. A valley without exit. Eventually those Pleistocene rivers gave up and decided to call the Death Valley region home. They formed Lake Manley, Owens Lake, Searles Lake, China Lake, as well as a number of others. All of which are now dry lakes, due to the climate change that brought desert to the region. Many of those dry lakes you will traverse, or at least see. Lake Manley was the lake that formed in Death Valley itself. When Manley eventually evaporated, it left the massive salt pans you see today at Devils Golf Course and Badwater. The salt pans contained more than salt. Other chemicals were left behind, including borax, which is central to our story.

Borax is a naturally occurring mineral. To the untrained, which would be myself, it looks like an unexciting version of white powder. When researched, however, its properties become heroic. Here's a short list of its capabilities. Borax is used as a laundry detergent (the 20 Mule Team brand is still available), as a fungicide, a preservative, a multipurpose cleaner, an insecticide (it even kills cockroaches), an herbicide, a disinfectant, an antiseptic, a fire retardant, flux in metallurgy, and it can be used to remove gold from other minerals. It is a component of fiberglass, cosmetics and is even used for making neutron-capturing shields for radioactive sources. Impressively, borax is used in over 300 high-tech products. One hundred years ago, borax was the primary material women used to shampoo their hair. An activity they performed about once a month. I remember Boraxo quite clearly as a kid. It came in round, blue cardboard canisters and we would sprinkle it on our hands after working on cars or bikes. With water, the borax-saturated grease lost interest in staining our hands. A quick Internet check revealed Boraxo is still available and remains highly thought of.

Borax was first discovered on the dry lake beds of Tibet. It was brought east to Arabia along the Silk Road. Where it was given the Arabic name, "Borax." But it was "Borax" Smith who truly popularized borax. With his marketing campaign showing 20 Mule Team wagons hauling the borax ore out of Death Valley from his Harmony Borax Works. Those mules followed a six-foot-wide path, built by Chinese laborers, straight through the four-mile-long Devils Golf Course. Hacking down the salt pinnacles of the golf course, in the oppressive heat, probably made those laborers reconsider their emigration. The 20 Mule Team image popularized borax throughout the United States. Where it was initially used as a cleaning agent. But soon, the creativity of the human mind discovered other uses for borax and demand increased. Borax Smith started looking around for other sources. Which he found. Which led him to build the Tonopah and Tidewater Railroad. Which led to this hike. History, as always, creating the future.

Death Valley is getting on in years. Some of the oldest rocks are estimated to be 1.7 billion years old. The valley itself, perhaps five million years old. Lake Manley was around for about 230,000 years before drying up 10,000 years ago. Which all sounds very old, until you compare it to the Earth's estimated age of 4.6 billion years. Native Americans have been present in Death Valley since the receding of the Ice Age. Their descendants still in residence today.

The first Anglos to pass through didn't fare well. Their journey not promising, when you learn the Valley is named after them. They were 49ers headed for the promise of gold in California. Approaching the Sierra Nevada Mountains in winter, and wishing to avoid the fate of the Donner party, the group elected to take the southern Old Spanish Trail. (The Donner party had been trapped by early snows in the Sierra Nevada Mountains three years earlier in 1846. Thirty-eight of the 83 members of the party perished. Cannibalism proved necessary to survive.) When some of the group became impatient with the Old Spanish Trail, they decided to take a shortcut through Death Valley. A major miscalculation. After four months of wandering lost, and the death of one of their members, the wagon train finally escaped the valley. As they left, two members of the party were said to have turned around. They took one last look down on the valley where they thought they would be buried. One was heard to say, "Goodbye Death Valley." Some things just stick.

In the mid 1800s, mining came to Death Valley, primarily gold and silver. By the 1880s, borax had taken over as king. Along the way, mining camps such as Harrisburg, Panamint City and Skidoo sprung up. (Harrisburg was named for Shorty Harris, a prospector responsible for the original strike in the area and a character you will learn more about later.)

Life could be wild in these remote camps. A tale from Skidoo and 1908 illustrates this. It seems that, one day in that year, a no-good showed up in town. He took a stab at robbing the local bank. But failed. What he didn't fail at was killing a popular local man in the process. Soon after, he was arrested by the town sheriff. The good citizens of Skidoo were understandably enraged. They impatiently decided to substitute in for the judge, who was away at the time. Once the sheriff was relieved of custody, the no-good was promptly hanged without the inconvenience of a trial. The next morning, his body was taken down from the telegraph pole gallows and buried without fanfare. Which was not the end of the story.

Five days later, a reporter from a Los Angeles newspaper showed up to report on the attempted robbery. His disappointment at missing the hanging stirred the hospitality of the local populace. Who, quite considerately, dug up the no-good and hung him again. So that the event could be properly photographed.

Panamint City also did not lack in wildness. At its height, 2,000 people called the city home. Their pursuit was silver. Getting the silver out of the ground did not prove to be the challenge. Getting it out to markets through the remote, narrow canyons did. Primarily due to the highwaymen (robbers) who found ambushes in canyons the best way to steal that silver. And they were very good at it. The thievery was so bad that Wells Fargo gave up, and refused to carry silver out of Panamint City. Which threatened the town's very existence. Luckily, desperation caused genius to surface.

Someone came up with the idea of casting the silver into 750-pound cannon balls. A test wagon full of them left camp on the appointed day. The bandits were not far down the canyon. The scene pleasantly comical, as they took turns courting hernias while trying to hoist 750 pounds. When they finally gave in to the inevitable failure, the thieves rode off, "frustrated and mad as hornets." After that the cannonballs were regularly transported without molestation. Guards no longer even necessary.

In 1933, President Hoover, recognizing the uniqueness of the area, declared the valley a National Monument. This spelled doom for mining in Death Valley. One by one the grandfathered valley mines were phased out. In 1994, Death Valley became a National Park. The last mine closed in the early 2000s. But mining was replaced by visitors. Lots of them. In 2015, over one million braved the heat. Dropping a cool $75 million throughout the area in the process.

Chapter 5

A Modest Little Thru Hike

Thru hiking is commonly accepted to mean hiking a long-distance trail from its beginning to its end. The concept has become fairly well known due to the popularity of the Pacific Crest Trail, the Continental Divide Trail and the Appalachian Trail. All 2,100 miles plus trails. Which is an admirably long way to carry a backpack. But thru hiking is not limited to the "Big Three." It exists around the world, and in your backyard. Surprisingly, the ones in your backyard are often the hardest to see.

To be considered a thru hike, then, it just needs to be a long-distance trail. I'm sure somewhere there is an edict setting out how long "long-distance" is. But I figure 811 miles surely qualifies. It certainly felt long-distance. So, I declare the Death Q a thru hike. But to be safe, I'll call it a modest little thru hike.

Since it is, hopefully, an official thru hike, it qualifies for section hiking. Section hiking involves hiking sections of a long-distance trail over time. In no particular order. The goal being to eventually complete the entire trail over the seasons of one's life. The Death Q welcomes this approach. So, have at it. In one big go, or in bits, but have at it.

Chapter 6

Why Thru Hike?

As previously claimed, humans perhaps fall into two basic categories. Those who are content where they are and those who have to know what is around the corner. Neither approach is superior to my eyes. Both are laden with pluses and minuses. But in the end, we're not what we're not.

Thru hiking is a soul aphrodisiac to the peek-around-the-corner crowd. Point A to Point B. Weeks bleed into months. Every day containing endless corners to explore. An infinity really. No repetition. Every step a greeting. More newness than your brain can crave. Saturation by so many visuals swept away by sleep. Fresh for breakfast and more rounded corners. Until you reach point B and take off your pack. And start planning for your next hike. For addiction isn't always a bad thing. And chasing that addiction, perhaps, even healthy.

But, why do it? The standard answer is, "If you have to ask, you'll never understand." There is truth in that. And possible arrogance, if care is not taken. For that answer reflects onto the questioner. To me, thru hiking is so intensely personal that the answer can only reflect me. For others, I cannot speak. And unfortunately, for me, thru hiking is a complex subject. A selfish act in the most positive sense. A search for the tangible and intangible within a whole. Such an answer, by its nature, must contain multiple depths.

On the surface, my answer is simple. One word in fact. Reduction. Thru hiking offers one the opportunity to reduce life to its simplest components. Some components are reduced because of necessity. While others are reduced by time, thought and lack of distraction. Everything is reduced to its minimum. Physically, mentally, spiritually, possessions, lists, priorities all reduced to what is needed. Excess discarded by the end. Lighter, faster, freer through the process of the thru.

Below the surface, as always, lies complexity. Trying to describe what the eye, heart and mind take in during a thru hike. The great reward for putting in the miles. Or the inner transformations of where one stands. The value of attempting to reach the end of oneself through a very long, uninterrupted self-conversation. The creation of a story that wholly forms between the first and last day of a hike. Are there words that properly bring these thoughts into commentary? Perhaps not.

So, how to convey all this endless through a simple answer? I know I can't, but I do know this. I have always failed poetry. My struggles never sustained, due to a deficit of appreciation. I pick up a poem and I put it down, rarely at its end. My shortcomings acknowledged. Hopes dashed. My mother, a poet, once said the goal of a poem is to shift the soul just a little bit. That's a tall order for a bunch of words. Maybe the bar was set too high, too early. I would read a poem in school and might get it, but more often not. My soul though, always stationary.

Then I discovered three mph. The speed at which a hike seems to settle down to after a couple of weeks. When movement is smooth and all is blank. A slow fluidity. Then a sudden shift in perspective. Working backwards to the poem by simply looking around and being swept with tingling. Realizing that maybe words aren't necessary for poetry when you're in it. That they may actually get in the way of a poemscape that reveals itself at the right pace. Your soul subject to a gentle shove, while arriving at Mom's wisdom by way of the trail.

To walk through poetry is a lot of answer for a simple question. And some readers, I imagine, might prefer a more concrete answer as to why thru hike. How's this? Grit. Which is the ability of a human being to demonstrate perseverance and passion to achieve a long-term goal despite significant obstacles. That is pretty much the textbook definition of a thru hike. In other words, a thru hike will test the grit of anyone who attempts one. But it will do more than that. Succeed or fail, a thru hike will significantly build your reserves of grit. Which turns out to be incredibly beneficial. As grit has been shown to be the single greatest predictor of a person's success in life. Above wealth, IQ, looks, background and education.

Or we can continue the process of reduction and give a simple answer. Why thru hike? It's a blast!

So, take your pick. Poetry, a full tank of grit, or a hell of a good time. Or choose all three. Regardless your trail awaits.

Chapter 7

Questions

What is it?

    The Death Q is a loop thru hike. My challenged math figured it at 811 miles long, if one completes all the side trails. This guide starts and ends in Ludlow, California. It moves in a counterclockwise direction. Why? Because that's the way we hiked it. Since we were walking back into history, it seemed appropriate to hike against the clock, though there is no startling reason that it can't be hiked in the opposite direction. Nor, for that matter, started at any point in the loop. Other than the mental dexterity required to reapply the guidebook.

Where does it go?

    The Death Q starts in Ludlow, California. Ludlow is located on I 40 about 57 miles east of Barstow, California. The Q follows the Tonopah and Tidewater Railroad north from Ludlow passing through the Mojave National Preserve. Then it slices, or rather gets sliced, by I 15 and its dreamers headed to the shortcuts promised by Las Vegas. The slice happens at Baker, California. The Q then begins a long, oval circumnavigation of Death Valley National Park with occasional side trips. Significant atlas-qualifying towns on the eastern half of the Q would be Tecopa, Shoshone and Death Valley Junction in California. As well as Beatty, Goldfield and Tonopah in Nevada. At Beatty, hikers transition to the Bullfrog Goldfield Railroad and then quite quickly to the Las Vegas and Tonopah Railroad. Next up is the Tonopah and Goldfield Railroad which is joined at Goldfield, Nevada. At the height of the northern curve, the Tonopah and Goldfield Railroad is left and the Carson and Colorado Railroad is joined. From there, the northern curve of the Death Q crosses back into California over

Summit Pass. There it finds the Owens Valley. The Q hugs that valley's unpopulated eastern half. Skirting the towns of Bishop, Independence and Lone Pine along the way. When Keeler is reached, the trail turns west, hugging the southern shoreline of Owens Dry Lake. At the western edge of the dry lake, the Q joins the Los Angeles "Jawbone" Aqueduct Railroad. Turning south toward Searles, the Q mirrors the 395 as far as Johannesburg. There, the connection is made with the Randsburg Railway and a taste of South Africa. Then onward south to Kramers Junction. A turn east at the junction, along the Burlington Northern Santa Fe tracks, brings you to Barstow. At 22,000, the biggest enclave on the Q. Two more days east, closes the Q at Ludlow. Where the fun begins and ends. Memorable side hikes occur at the following step off points. At Ludlow on the Ludlow and Southern Railroad. At Tecopa on the Tecopa Railroad. At Death Valley Junction on the Death Valley Railroad. And at Swansea on the Saline Valley Tramway.

Why is it still there?

The Death Q exists as a hikable trail for a number of reasons. First and foremost, it is entirely located in the desert. Remote desert. No one is plotting out subdivisions anywhere along the Q. This is forgotten and abandoned territory. Its beauty subtle, like a black-and-white photograph. Most are rushing through it on their way to somewhere else. Certainly no one is developing it. And therein lies the blessing. While other regions bulldoze their history, or manipulate it, the ex-railroads of the eastern Mojave are just there. As is the desert that surrounds them. Left alone, mostly, by man, coerced only by Mother Nature.

Second, for the most part, these railroads followed the logic of wealth extraction. And desert wealth at the start of the 20th century came from mines. Towns pursued the same logic. Springing up around those mines. Again, and again, the illusion of permanence was shattered. The mines would play out. The next boom would appear on the horizon. Populations would scatter. Towns would fill with ghosts. And railroads would pull up and haul off their rolling-stock. With no one left around, succeeding generations that would have obliterated railroad remains weren't born. The railbeds were left alone. But not quite.

Third, an old railroad consists of three parts. Its metal rails, its wood ties and its raised railbed. The rails are valuable, the ties have some value and the railbed has no value. Except, of course, to hikers. The abandoned railroads were mostly left alone until World War II. Then, the war effort created a massive demand for scrap steel. Any abandoned railroad along the Q saw their steel rails seized for war recycling. Which left the wood ties. In remote sections, they are still there. In accessible sections, they were claimed for fencing, landscaping, and in two cases, they were used to build hotels. Elsewhere, there are sections of ties buried and yet other sections carried away by flash floods. Which leaves the railbed. Old faithful. There for the hiker because of its lack of value to the economy. At times, carried away by flood or submerged by road. But always reappearing with detective work.

Finally, the old railbeds carry on because they are unattractive to off-road vehicles. The presence of old railroad spikes and other sharp objects that litter the ground, the constant washouts (only one wooden trestle bridge remains on the Q) and the ongoing presence of ties, make off-roading on the old railbeds an inconvenient proposition. It occurs in areas, but is not devastating.

What does the trail look like?

Quite rapidly, you will become expert at spotting railbeds. They are narrower than roads. They often appear to be built of materials brought from someplace else. Clues such as spikes, ties, rusted cans, colored glass and sheared bolts litter their surface. But most importantly, they are raised. Because they had to be. A train's course must be flat, gradual and true. Hills must be leveled. Valleys filled in. Water kept from pooling on the tracks. There is little surrendering to the vagaries of terrain. And that makes the Q easy to follow, until it is not.

do I follow the Death Q?

Most of the Q is easy to follow. But there will be times out there when the Q loses its continuity. It happens in basically one of three ways. Flash floods swept away portions of the railbed, roads were built for cars over the railbed and towns bulldozed their immediate railroad sections.

This guidebook is designed to navigate you through the major flood breaks, road breaks and town breaks. As for the minor flash flood wash-outs, the approach is simple. Think like a railroad engineer. Follow their truisms. A straight route is best. A flat route is happiness. Avoid sharp turns. And build along the path of least resistance. For your purposes, if the railbed is interrupted, stand on its last known point. Make a narrow outward V with your arms in the direction of travel. Know that the railbed continues within that V, somewhere in the near distance. Unless a hill or mountain lies in your path. Then become the engineer. Where would you put your railroad? And head there. The Q will be waiting.

When to hike it?

The Q is a strongly-suggested winter hike. We hiked the first half in early December. The highs were in the 60s and 70s. The lows in the 40s. That is fine hiking weather. The second half was completed by the end of March. Already temperatures were climbing and reptiles were out, though the 80s were not surpassed as a high. A general weather chart for five points along the Q is included in Chapter 20. Please use it to plan according to your comfort zone.

For example, hiking in January/February, on the northern half of the Q, would take me out of my particular comfort zone. Due to the low temperatures and possibility of a real snowstorm. Others, like my hiking partner, Orbit, who grew up in the Arctic tundra around Albany, New York, might relish those conditions. In the end, to each their own.

Why a winter hike? Because a hiker is able to avoid two migratory killers that take up residence in the desert every summer. Namely, thirst and heat. In winter, five liters of water was sufficient for 48 hours. For myself anyway. In summer, you would be talking gallons. Likewise, at 70°

your body is at full function, while at 115°, it is seeking survival. So, stick to winter, unless suffering is of importance to you.

Isn't a desert hike boring?

This is an important question for a potential Q hiker. If one is not fond of a specific terrain, it is logical to avoid hiking through it. When I hiked the PCT, many northbounders complained about the early desert sections. "I can't wait to get out of the desert," was a common refrain. Or take the documentary I watched the other day about a trip through the western deserts of the United States. In it, the commentator constantly referred to the desert as a wasteland and grotesque. The term "Godforsaken" was tossed around a lot. I checked out the dictionary. Godforsaken translates as a place not containing anything interesting or attractive. Or, a place ignored by God. I would argue the opposite. That the desert demonstrates some of the very best that God, or the Gods, could come up with. But if you personally lean toward Godforsaken, then perhaps the Q is not for you.

For other than the mountain sections, this is pure desert. It's subtle, stark, confident, shadowed and crushingly beautiful. As are many things where the primary motivation is survival. But its vistas and muted coloration aren't for all. Consider yourself before embarking. Likewise, the trail is sometimes straight and flat, occasionally visual for miles due to the lack of trees. A hiker can see where they're going. They can also see where they've been. An angle on life that some are drawn to, others not. If such a perspective is not for you, consider other hikes. Finally, the solitude. You're on your own out there. There were almost never encounters of others. Does being alone in the middle of it all put you off?

All answers that should be answered before departure. But if you are drawn to the above, rather than repelled, then by all means, have at it. And if at some point it doesn't suit you, just hike away. Though I must say, a Ludlow reunion with month-old footprints is sweetness itself. Regardless, whether zero or hundreds of hikers tackle the Q, it really doesn't matter. The Q seems content to exist and I suspect it will stay that way.

And if you're on the fence about the desert? Why not give it a chance? The desert's natural inclination is to grow on you as you spend more time with her. Perhaps, at the end of 35 days, you'll have fallen in love. If you find yourself at the other end of the reaction spectrum, at least you'd be able to divorce with certainty.

Chapter 8

Nuts and Bolts of the Death Q

Hiking Partner

I've hiked alone. I've hiked with others. Both have their attractions. Both carry burdens. But few would argue that in a fucktuation, it's good to have a buddy. The truth of this becomes biblical in the desert. If you're incapacitated on the majority of trails in the States, someone will eventually come along. Or, at least, hope is reasonable. In the desert, it is not. Human density is thin and isolated. Humans on the move, rare. Fellow hikers nonexistent. In fact, we saw but one other hiker in 811 miles. If you go down, it's nice to look up and see your buddy coming. If you go down without a buddy in the desert, you're just down.

Strangely, I followed my own advice. Throughout this book "we" is sometimes used. That would be Orbit, a.k.a. Jessica Mencel, who hiked the vast majority of the Q with me. (During the solo bits, I revert to "I" in the narrative.) Orbit and I met one day removed from Mexico while hiking the PCT in 2013. Our meeting involved an Orioles obsession, umbrellas and caffeinated misdirection. In other words, a tale for another time. Of relevance is the friendship that developed. A friendship possible in the micro society of the hiking fraternity that odds would have been against anywhere else. Four months after that meeting, we stood on the Canadian border, stories exhausted, tests passed and easy in each other's presence.

When the idea to hike an abandoned railroad had gnawed at me long enough, I sent a paragraph to Orbit detailing my thoughts and approaches. Back came a line. "I'm in. When?" Orbit, one of life's great finds. And while I'm at it, congratulations, Orbit, on your recent coronation as a "Triple Crowner." (A Triple Crowner is one who has hiked the PCT, AT and CDT in a lifetime.) A feat she accomplished in just under a year total.

Miles

What worked well for us was around twenty-three miles a day. Or seven to ten hours a day. At that rate there was water, food and restaurants pretty much every two to four days. The miles are often easy desert hiking. Then again, they are not. Railroads tend toward flat. With gentle up-and-down grades. On paper this sounds like smooth sailing. In reality, it makes for an assault on the same muscles all day long. Normal trails provide a respite of up, down and flat. Alternating the taxing and relieving of muscles allows the body to recover throughout the day. The Q, not so. Still, there are climbs. And if summit fever seizes you from above, there are endless obtainable peaks along the way.

Another challenge, when it comes to miles, is the illusion of distance. On the ocean, the human eye can see 2.9 miles. At that point the horizon takes over, and the earth's surface curves downward and out of sight. On the other end of the spectrum is the highest point on earth. Theoretically, from the top of Mount Everest, one could see 211 miles on the clearest of clear days. Its height creating the opportunity for such distance. I believe the desert to be toward the upper end of that spectrum. As it is often free from both obstruction and pollution. But more than that, the desert seems to enjoy a good tease. Always presenting things as closer than their actual distance.

An example. Railbeds are often long, flat and straight. The ability to see a town in the distance morphs the eyes into optimists. You square up and eyeball the water tower. The brain figures a couple of miles, 45 minutes, an hour tops. Four hours later you're still humping down that oblivious railbed. Still taking in the water tower. Tortured by the unobtainable promise. Humiliation, awe, an inducement to scream at the silence, it doesn't matter. The miles still have to be put in if you truly care about that burger. But that clarity has a bonus. Under perfect conditions the human eye can see roughly 2,500 nighttime stars. Unfortunately, the activities of humans have blotted out the majority of those stars. In the desert, those 2,500 will welcome you back.

It would be remiss not to mention the counterpoint to miles. Rest rarely hurts anyone. Neither do rest days. In fact, they contribute to the success of a hike. Unless they become the preferred alternative to the hike itself. So, take rest days, or shortened days, as you need them. In Part Two of the book, a rest day on Day 25 is suggested in Lone Pine. But, really, take rest days as you need them. Wherever you need them. There are plenty of towns along the way that would suit. Alternatively, a rest day in the desert, without distraction, makes for a fine meditation.

Finally, putting in miles at night. We tried it. It wasn't fun. If you hike on the railbed, the leftover ties become foot traps. A face plant, with splinters, not a cause for rejoicing. The alternative, hiking alongside the railbed, too often involved veering off goal into the dark. Best to stick to the day. Unless, of course, there is still beauty to be found in such suffering.

The Basics of Food, Water, and Shelter

This book is laid out in a days-hiked format. If, on a particular day, the trail passes through a populated town, any essential services available from the list below will be noted.

1.	Food resupply
2.	Restaurant
3.	Water
4.	Hotel
5.	Beer
6.	Pool table
7.	ATM
8.	Post office
9.	Casino

Some thoughts about the "big three" when it comes to backpacking. First, food. The towns you will be passing through are small or geared for motorists. In other words, low demand. Supermarkets are rare. Convenience stores and a grade above are the norm. There, your shopping efficiency will skyrocket due to the absence of choice. And buying as you go keeps you light and adaptable. Resupply every couple of days is possible. However, your special diet or preferences are not their concern. Thus, if there are foodstuffs you're incapable of life without, arrange accordingly. Through drop-offs or packages mailed to post offices. For the latter, call ahead, but most post offices will hold packages for free until your arrival.

I've provided contact info for the post offices along the Q, should you decide to mail your necessities. But confirm with each individual post office, as their policies seem to vary. Restaurant menus are available in a surprising number of locations. All delicious, because their anticipatory build up usually consists of a prior diet of cup of noodles. A few of the restaurants would be outstanding whenever they opened their doors.

Second, water. Every two or three days we came to a man-made water source. Natural water sources exist in the desert but are very unreliable. If it has rained recently, water will collect. But wet skies are not native to the desert. The only year-round rivers on the Q are the Armagosa River near Tecopa and the Owens River in the Owens Valley. Personally, I carried 2.5 liters of water for each day. When leaving a water source, I would down a lot of water. Then stretch out my carried water through the hiking day. As the weather was cool, sweating was minimal. At the end of the day, there was always sufficient water to cook with. This system worked for me. But needs are individual. And 2.5 liters of water per day would be considered insufficient by many. Knowing your needs makes hiking easier. Simply hump more water if you tend toward thirsty.

Third, shelter. In the bush, I carried a tent. But 90% of the nights we cowboy camped (didn't set up a tent.) If stars were out, we got to see them all night. If the weather indicated rough, i.e., no stars, the tent went up, or better yet, we slept in the entrance to a mine. The lack of interest/population in the desert ensures quiet nights. In towns, hotels are common. $40-$75 for a double seemed to be the norm. If you prefer your stars, the bush is never far from Main Street when the population is counted in the hundreds or less. And your credit card remains unburdened.

Chapter 9

Fauna of the Death Q

Upon return from any extended hike, there is a period of time when answers are given to questions. Most questions are curious about wild animals and the fear associated with them. On the Q, the winter animal list is fairly short, as most reptiles are in hibernation. Thus, no snakes. And only one species of lizard, known as the uta or side-blotched lizard, is out and about. For reasons they keep to themselves, utas prefer all the seasons. So, when you see a little gray lizard running around in winter, it's a uta. And you are a master winter herpetologist.

Other than that, we saw tarantulas, foxes, kangaroo rats, jackrabbits, cottontails, pronghorn antelopes, wild burros, wild horses, coyotes, bats, desert tortoises, roadrunners, scorpions, vultures, hawks and many small birds I am hopeless at identifying. Certainly, there were a few ghosts, so to be inclusive I include them here. Other animals were about, I'm sure, but they kept to the shadows.

Should your hike stretch into spring, as ours did (3/23), or should spring arrive early, as ours did (2015), then the desert repopulates. Primarily with reptiles. Here are the reptiles we crossed paths with. Using the colloquial reptile names, I was taught as a kid by my science teacher, Jim O'Donnell, rather than the tongue-mangling, scientific names. There are other reptiles out there. I limited the list to those that we actually saw.

Horned Toad

Horned toad lizards are wide-bodied and slow moving. Their predominant features are their spiked head and studded back. Which brings to mind dinosaurs and Godzilla feuds. They are known to frequent ant buffets, where they plop themselves down amongst frenzied attackers. Grin.

42

Close their armored eyelids to shut off their only vulnerability. And proceed to blindly radar-tongue those attackers down the hatch, one by one. When threatened, horned toads do one of three things: bury themselves in the sand to avoid the humiliation of trying to run, squirt blood out of their eyes, or puff themselves up to make predator swallowing difficult.

Whip Tail Lizard

Whip tail lizards have a long, bluish-orange body, which is followed by a very long tail. They are easily identifiable by their continuous, jerky movements and tongue sensing. They seem unable to stand still. Veterinarians have prescribed sedatives in the past.

Chuckwalla

Chuckwallas are the largest lizards you're likely to encounter. (The poisonous Gila Monster is larger. But extremely rare. In all my years of tromping around the desert, I have never come across one in the wild.) On average, chuckwallas are over a foot long. They are seen primarily in rocky areas, especially lava flows. Chuckwallas are solidly vegan. They spend their day as they like. Which means basking in the sun, munching the occasional flower and threatening intruders with a ferocious display of push-ups. When overwhelmingly threatened, things get interesting. The chuckwalla makes a mad dash for the nearest rock crack and crawls inside. There they start sucking air, ballooning their stomach to comic book proportions. This causes a wedging affect. Rendering predator extraction a daunting challenge. Chuckwallas exist only in the southwestern U.S. and Mexico. Their altitude range caps out at 4,500 feet.

So, imagine my surprise some years ago, as I made my way across an alpine valley in India. The valley, set at a bit above 10,000 feet, was in the Indian Himalayas. Tired, I sat down for lunch. Then looked over at a rock and saw a chuckwalla doing push-ups. Now, I grew up in the Mojave Desert. I am on very familiar terms with chuckwallas. Seeing that chuck there was akin to seeing a rhino traipsing across the Arctic. Perhaps there was a questioning profanity. I got up, went over and put the grabs on it. Same color, same size and a mouth stained yellow with flowers. As I held it, the belly inflated with air. A chuckwalla, sure as a beagle is a beagle. What geological shift could possibly have landed chuckwallas in the Himalayas? I put the chuck back down, and it made a beeline for a rock crack. I, in turn, made my way out of the valley without answers I thought were my right.

Zebra Tail Lizard

Zebra tails are medium-sized, tan lizards with black and white horizontal stripes on their tail. They are known for their speed. Think beep beep roadrunner, now you see 'em, now you don't, speed. Their best party trick is ejecting their tail when grabbed. Many a zebra tail predator has ended up with a twitching black-and-white tail and a cloud of dust for lunch. Other than speed, a zebra tail will bury itself in the sand to avoid consumption. When you come upon a zebra tail in the heat of the day, still yourself. If lucky, you'll see the hotfoot dance. Basically, a zebra tail will stand on opposite front and rear feet while the heat builds. At the pain point, the zebra tail switches to the other two feet. An endless cool-and-cook waltz.

Collared Lizard

The collared is a tan lizard with white spots. Its name is based on two black rings that encircle its neck. Almost always spotted in rocky terrain. A charismatic lizard due to two traits. First, collared lizards are cannibals. More than content to consume other lizards as well as their own. Rounding out their charisma is an ability to run vertically on their two back legs. A stunt they pull off with considerably more élan than a human running on all fours. If you eyeball one covered in orange spots, it means she's pregnant.

Desert Iguana

The desert iguana is a longish gray/tan lizard with faded spots. It is a muscular lizard whose head seems disproportionately small. Looking at iguanas makes you think that they have multiple cousins in the dinosaur families. The iggy fears no heat and is comfortable moving around on the sands when other lizards have sought the shade. When it comes to meals, desert iguanas are strict vegetarians. Their mouths often stained yellow by creosote flowers.

Scaly Swift

Scaly swifts are lizards that tend to hang out on rocks or in trees. Usually at higher altitudes. When you spot one, their scales will be very pronounced. They look rough. Running your fingers against the grain on a scaly swift might be a bad idea. Their color scheme spans the black/brown/grey spectrum. But, their bellies will often reveal a violent turquoise bloom. The perfect trail lunch spot is opposite a vertical boulder populated by swifts. Their free-climbing skills are endlessly entertaining. Approach too closely and you will be intimidated into retreat by a ferocious push up display. Grab one and they will put a blood drawing bite on you, if given an opportunity.

Alligator Lizard

The alligator lizard likes grassy areas and places with downed logs. Preferably near water. Their name is accurate, as they could easily pass for a baby alligator. Alligator lizards are muscular, have very smooth scales and are slippery to the touch. Another lizard capable of dropping its tail when threatened. Extremely hostile to being caught. If in hand, they will bite hard and defecate on you simultaneously. Best left alone to go about their business.

Mojave Green Rattlesnake

The sizzling rattle rises from the ground. No break in the sound means the snake is angry. I've come too near, too fast. A surprised Mojave is disappointed in themselves and you. Its gut is to lash out. At the same time, your brain has gone primordial. Adrenaline river. Which causes you to jump straight up. While moving toward the sun, your ear tries to triangulate the sound source location. My ear told me the Mojave was ever so slightly to the left. In the meantime, upward momentum is finite. At the top of the arc one feels like a cartoon character. The descent is accompanied by a sharp closing of the eyes and sphincter. The rattle booming its displeasure at your nearing return. Your feet hit Mother Earth. The strike a snake's choice. I pogo right. Another landing. Pivoting to see the Mojave with its head elevated and strike ready. A quiet thank you whispered for the tolerance of another creature. My footprint six inches from the Mojave's camouflaged body.

Thus, my introduction to the first and last Mojave green on the Death Q that spring. The Mojave is an impressive snake. It doesn't yield easily. And its venom is a complex brew of toxins that is vastly more powerful than any other poisonous snake in North America.

Unusually, its young are born live, while most snakes lay eggs. Diamonds decorate their back, while black and white bands often neighbor their rattle. They have a slight greenish tinge but not always. Their head has the characteristic triangular shape of a pit viper. Meals include rodents and lizards.

And finally, a clarification. The number of rattles does not bear any relation to the age of the rattlesnake.

So, what to do if bit? A statistic first. Of the thousands of snakebites each year in the States, less than ten are fatal. For perspective, your chances of being struck by lightning or killed by your spouse are much higher. Armed with that comforting knowledge, panic is confrontable.

More cause for hope. In one of four bites, the rattlesnake decides to withhold its venom for smaller things the snake knows it has a chance of swallowing. So, you have a 25% chance of dodging the bullet.

The first step to avoid being bitten is to suppress your tactile urges when you see a Mojave or any snake. Not messing with a Mojave green or Mojave green look-alike, ensures you leave the encounter without puncture marks. If you're ambushed, well, that's the way it goes sometimes.

Back to the original question. If bit, calm down to Buddha levels. The less your heart is pumping, the slower the venom makes its way into your system to do its havoc. Remove anything that constricts the wound, including jewelry. Then wash the bite with soap and water, if that is feasible. Also circle the bite with a marker, if that is feasible. This will assist the medical professionals in locating the puncture marks. Then make your way to a medical facility however you can.

Antivenom is the cure. Everything else, including cutting and sucking the wound, are the tales of elderly wives.

On your way to that medical facility, try and keep the wound immobile and below the level of your heart, if that is possible. Now, if it is more than 30 minutes to medical care, there is one more step you can take. If you have a bandage, wrap it two to four inches above the wound. But not too tight. A good rule of thumb is loose enough to slip one finger under the bandage. This might slow down the spread of the venom.

Don't try to kill the rattlesnake so that the hospital can identify it. It's a good way to get bit a second time. And a dead snake can still reflexively bite an hour or two after its passing. Making it dangerous to carry. Much better to take a photo for identification purposes and then hightail it calmly to that medical help. There, the current incarnation of antivenom covers most species of rattlesnake. The bite will hurt, just keep your focus on getting to a hospital.

A final reminder that should put you much at ease. If you hike the Q during winter, your chances of getting bit by a rattlesnake are close to non-existent. For rattlesnakes and all other snakes for that matter, are underground and in hibernation. It's only during the shoulder seasons you need to pay attention.

Gopher Snake

Gopher snakes are large, non-poisonous, yellow/brown snakes with dark brown/black spots decorating their backs. Large, as in up to eight feet long. They are often mistaken for rattlesnakes. Look at the head and tail. A narrow head, and no rattles, leads to friendship on the trail. Humans aren't the only ones to notice the rattlesnake similarity. Long ago, gopher snakes came to the same realization. Figuring it was to their advantage, they adopted the quivering tail and the coiled body/aloft head strike of their rattlesnake cousins. Though when they strike an attacker, it is often with a closed mouth head butt, rather than fangs.

Prey includes lizards, rodents, small rabbits and sometimes other snakes. Takedown is accomplished by an initial biting seizure, followed by constriction and suffocation of the victim. (Which sounds an awful lot like a police report.) The gopher snake monitors the prey's heartbeat through its own body. When the heartbeat ceases, it is time for the gopher snake to begin swallowing the deceased whole. When cornered by something that bothers them, gopher snakes will defensively hiss their displeasure.

Red Racer Snake

Red racers are aptly named. They are red, long, thin and very fast. Reminiscent of a whip. The fastest snake in North America, capable of short bursts up to seven mph. If someone claims to have been chased by a snake, then it was probably a red racer. A highly suspect claim, as the snake was probably headed in the opposite direction. Red racers have a healthy appetite that includes other snakes. Even baby rattlesnakes. Finally, red racers have a reputation for being foul humored when cornered. Biting hard and often. Best left alone, as are all the reptiles on this list. And please forgive the urges of my youth to catch and hold everything that moved in the desert. I've since, mostly successfully, purged such urges.

California Kingsnake

The California kingsnake is decorated in horizontal black and yellow or white body bands. And it is a beauty. That, and its mild temperament when acclimatized to humans, make it a popular pet. Their appeal is not limited to the States. In the Grand Canary Islands, off Africa, a number of albino kingsnakes were imported from California as pets. The inevitable escapes followed. And now thousands of the snakes are king of the island. With authorities at a loss as to how to eliminate their invasion.

It should be mentioned that California kingsnakes are a protected species in California. So why are kingsnakes so named? Because they are at the top of the snake pyramid in the Mojave Desert. Not only do they not fear rattlesnakes, they actually eat them. Rattlesnakes are aware of this. When a rattlesnake chemically senses a kingsnake, they will attempt to escape. The nonvenomous kingsnake confident because they are resistant to rattlesnake venom. If the muscular kingsnake can get a hold of the rattlesnake, it will kill it by constriction. Once the rattlesnake is suffocated, the kingsnake will swallow it whole. Other snakes are not immune to this treatment. Thus, the moniker, "King of Snakes."

The California kingsnake can grow to four feet. It is out day and night. Though in winter it hibernates. When mating, a male will slither up next to a female and vibrate uncontrollably. This usually accomplishes the desired seductive effect and follow up activity. After which the female eventually lays eggs, rather than delivering live. When annoyed, kingsnakes imitate the body language of rattlesnakes. If picked up annoyed, they will simultaneously put the bite on you and poop on you. As well as coat you with an unpleasant musk.

Kingsnakes will basically eat any animal they can suffocate and swallow. Other than snakes, this list includes lizards, rodents, small turtles, frogs and birds. And once, in a time of need for my pet kingsnake (prior to their protected status), my sister's hamster. A crime I was tried for and found justly guilty of in family court.

As spoken of earlier, we saw other non-reptile animals during our hike. Which represent but a small fraction of what is actually out and about. Very large books have been written about the fauna of the Mojave

Desert. I won't try to replicate that here. As it is beyond my abilities. I will, however, give a brief description of the animals I did note when they appeared along the Q. My apologies upfront for my limitations.

Tarantula

Tarantulas crawl much of the earth. Those in the know, claim more than 800 species worldwide. Four species alone in the deserts of the Southwest. Those without knowledge, myself, know the tarantula to be the big, hairy spider one occasionally comes across on a hike. Friendly, but with a destination in mind. Here's what I learned.

Tarantulas have eight legs, eight eyes and two large fangs. And I wasn't wrong. They are hairy. Thousands of tiny hairs cover the skeleton that exists on the outside of their body. In length, adults can reach three to four inches. Males live up to ten years, females twenty. Home is generally a burrow in the ground, rather than a web. That home is lined with a silk webbing. This webbing provides a structural integrity to the burrow that limits cave-ins. As the tarantula grows, it enlarges the burrow to accommodate new bulk.

Tarantulas find themselves in the middle of the food chain. They hunt and are hunted. Since there is no web to snare anything, tarantulas hunt by ambush or pursuit. This hunting takes place at night. Meals include insects, lizards, grasshoppers, beetles and other spiders. Death comes to the above through those two large fangs which produce a mild venom. This venom liquefies the innards of what has been caught. Once this process is complete, the tarantula ingests the innards by sucking them in. The venom is not harmful to humans per se (roughly equivalent to a bee sting), but it is best not to tempt the tarantula by harassing them. After a good meal, a tarantula can wait up to a month before the next one.

Tarantulas are eaten by a variety of animals that include snakes, lizards, birds and humans. During the Khmer Rouge reign in Cambodia, when starvation was the norm, people learned to consume tarantulas. The habit continued after the Khmer Rouge were deposited into the history bin. The popular method is to grill tarantulas over charcoal on a skewer. To put off the above predators, tarantulas will attempt to shed those thousands of fine hairs into the eyes of the potential diner. Irritated eyes hopefully leading to a sudden lack of interest.

Perhaps the tarantula's most daunting opponent in the U.S. is the tarantula hawk. Which is not a bird, but a large wasp. Tarantula hawks are generally blue/black in color with orange wings. They deliver an incredibly painful sting to humans. But for tarantulas, it's much worse. Pregnant tarantula hawks have a particular knack for locating tarantula burrows. When they find one they pay an unwelcome visit. If a tarantula is home, the wasp will sting them. Which paralyzes the tarantula. The wasp then lays her eggs on the tarantula. After which Mom departs. On her way out, she seals up the burrow. Then flies away. The paralyzed tarantula and eggs then begin a waiting game. When the eggs finally hatch, their bed is fresh, non-moving meat. After their nourishing tarantula meal, the baby tarantula wasps dig themselves out of their sealed tomb and get on with life. At other times, tarantulas provide a pleasant meal for a tarantula hawk.

The mating process of tarantulas is rough on males. First, they have to go walkabout searching for female burrows. Where the females wait during mating season. Males can cover up to 50 miles during this hike. Once they find an acceptable burrow, a male crawls down to an uncertain reception. If a female doesn't approve of this or that, she kills and eats her prospective suitor. But even successful suitors don't escape cannibalism. As a hungry female just might eat the successful applicant after sex. Accomplished unions produce between 500 to 1,000 offspring.

Fox

There are two kinds of foxes making appearances in the Mojave Desert. If you see a fox, odds are it's a gray fox. As gray foxes don't mind being out in the daytime. Their brethren kit fox does. Gray foxes first.

Gray foxes, as all foxes, are members of the dog family. They're the only members of that family that climb trees. Peculiarly curved nails allow this ability. This comes in handy when being pursued by a hungry coyote. And a tree is handy. Not so much if the pursuer is a bobcat or mountain lion, which can climb trees very well, thank you very much. A gray fox's top speed is 28 mph. They are 32 to 45 inches long and weigh 7 to 11 pounds. Which makes them significantly larger than the elfin kit fox. Their dens are impressive, reaching up to 75 feet in length. For convenience, and predator avoidance, they create multiple exits. Sometimes more than ten in total.

Gray foxes are omnivores in the extreme. Anything live or dead is not turned away from their stomachs. Plants are also welcome. When annoyed, gray foxes bark. Other than predators, rabies is the great nemesis of gray foxes. Periodic outbreaks devastate the gray fox population. High pup mortality, combine with small litters to significantly slow rebounds from such rabies reductions.

The kit fox is a creature of the night. They are shy, so your chances of seeing one are slim. As mentioned, they are smaller than the gray fox, weighing in at around 4 pounds. Their main predators are coyotes and cars. To discourage coyotes, kit foxes sculpt the entrances to their dens too small for a coyote to crawl through. In an act of sensibility, they dig those dens roughly two miles apart. Which just happens to be their hunting range. Overhunting is thus avoided.

A day in the life basically finds a kit fox lying around all day in their den and then hunting at night. Kit foxes are mostly carnivores. Their druthers meal is kangaroo rats, but reptiles, birds, rabbits and insects will serve. Very large ears enable attentive hunting, as well as heat dissipation. Top speed for short distances comes in at 25 mph. Life spans generally reach about eight years. Around this time their teeth give out. Which spells doom for a carnivore. Up to three quarters of a litter will die in the first year. Two biological curiosities about the kit fox. They rarely drink water, as they are able to derive moisture from their prey. And they have fur on the bottom of their paws, which creates a very effective sand shoe and heat protector.

Kangaroo Rat

The kangaroo rat is all charisma. Think a hamster that hops. Everyone loves kangaroo rats. Unfortunately, for K rats, most of that love is expressed by eating. As in most bigger animals in the desert love to dine on

K rats. Of which K rats are well aware. To avoid this, the K rat has developed some defense mechanisms based on anatomy. Very long, hinged back legs allow a springing run. A top speed of six mph does not intimidate predators. But the ability to leap a distance of nine feet does. On top of that, the K rat has a very long tail. One and a half times its body length. Which gives the K rat incredible balance and steering capability. Resulting in multi-directional pivots at speed. All this combines to make dining on a K rat a challenging proposition.

The kangaroo rat has a curious relationship with heat. They live in the desert but don't like to be hot. Biology created this distaste. K rats don't dissipate body heat by sweating or panting. Nor do they take in much water. Obtaining just enough water to survive from the seeds they live on. So, to adapt, they simply avoid the heat. That is why you see K rats only at night. During the day, they stay in their dens sleeping. To avoid moisture loss while sleeping, they tuck their noses in their fur. This creates a small pocket of moistened air. A mini air conditioner, if you will. On particularly hot days, they plug the entrance to their den with dirt. This prevents the heat of the day from raising the buried den's cooler temperature.

Kangaroo rats live from two to five years. Their dens follow the standard suburban layout of bedroom, living room and kitchen. The kitchen is where seeds are stored for hard times that may come. The living room is where K rats hang out. And the bedroom is where they sleep. The dens exist in colonies, which can run into the hundreds of dens. K rats keep their seed gathering ranges small (200 to 300 feet) to avoid needless moisture loss. Reproduction rates depend on climate. In times of drought, they plummet. In times of plenty, the opposite. Their mating dance is a joy to behold. The dance consists of a male and female running in tight anal/nasal circles, until the female declares a readiness to end the cardiovascular foreplay.

Rabbit

As you hike, an explosion. Your body jerks in reaction. While your reptile brain begins issuing commands. False alarm. Stand down. Just another jackrabbit bursting from a bush. Jackrabbits are everywhere in the

Mojave Desert. Waiting until the last moment to escape your closing footsteps. When you spot one, there is no mistaking them. Their very long ears give them away immediately. Those ears are custom designed for maximum hearing and heat dissipation. They provide warning of a predator from a long way off. If a predator is in the neighborhood, the jack waits and waits, hoping to be missed. If spotted, the chase is on. But it's not an easy chase. Jacks can reach 40 mph and turn on coins, smaller than dimes, with ease.

Jackrabbits are around two feet long and weigh between three and six pounds. They are very adaptable. Living from sea level to 10,000 feet. They move about during the day or night. But prefer to relax during the more intensely heated parts of the day. Jacks are strictly plant eaters. From which they derive all the water they need. Mother jacks don't build nests. They just lay live young, in a shallow depression, under a bush. The newborns are able to move about within minutes of birth. And are born with their eyes open. Predators a threat from the first seconds.

Cottontails are the smaller, cuter rabbits. The big puff of white cotton on their butts is the identifying clincher. Bonus is a laundry list of fascinating traits. For starters, cottontails can swim and climb trees when pursued. When hungry, they're not put off by consuming their own poop. A cottontail's tracks resemble the number seven. And their teeth never stop growing. This enables them to eat tougher items like twigs without permanently dulling their teeth. Mother cottontails line their nests with grass and fur pulled from their own bellies.

Some other trivia. Cottontails have very large eyes that enable them to see predators from far off. When pursued, they can hit 20 mph and tend to elude using a zigzag pattern. Riffs on fleeing include being able to jump eight feet and change directions quickly. Their light fur reflects the sun quite well. Thus, keeping their body temperature low. The harshness of a cottontail's life is indicated by the fact that only 15% of newborns survive their first year.

Pronghorn Antelope

Between Beatty and Goldfield, I spotted some deer. But I didn't. As my pace brought me closer, I saw antelope instead. Which I knew nothing about. Here's what I know now. I didn't see antelope either. I saw pronghorn antelope. Which aren't antelope at all. Though the "Home on the Range" song refers to them as such. Confused? So was I. Here's the skinny.

Pronghorns are a species of mammals. They belong to the family Antilocapridae. Way back when, there were 12 different species of Antilocapridae running around North America. Enough to make up a family. Now we're down to one. Whose closest living relative is, of course, the giraffe. So back to the confusion. Lewis and Clark stumbled upon the pronghorns when they explored west. They decided it was an antelope. Then along came the lyrics: "Where the deer and the antelope play." Now the concept of antelope was cemented. Then the scientists weighed in and said "No, it's not an antelope. There are none in North America, nor have there ever been. It's a pronghorn." The compromise seems to be "It's a pronghorn antelope." Everybody, and nobody, is happy.

The pronghorn is a fantastic animal. First and foremost, it is a speedster. Top end is 60 mph. Which makes it the Western Hemisphere's fastest land animal. The pronghorn can also go the distance. They can maintain 55 mph for a half-mile and incredibly, 35 mph for four miles. No animal around is that fast for that long. Though the cheetah is faster for short bursts. Why is the pronghorn so fast? Some clever scientists figure that, at one time in North America, there was a cheetah that could run down a pronghorn. So, the pronghorns evolved the speed in response. Then the North American cheetah went extinct. And the pronghorns were left with the somewhat obsolete relic of lightning speed.

Pronghorns weigh in between 75 and 143 pounds and live 10 to 15 years. Subsiding on various plants that please them. Given an opportunity, mountain lions and coyotes will eat them. As do humans. Too much so early in the 20th century. Excessive hunting, combined with fencing, looked to wipe out the 12th of the 12 species. The fencing was a problem for the pronghorns for a couple of reasons. One, they are migratory. Their

300-mile round-trip migration across the western United States is, even today, the longest on the continent. Early century fencing threatened this migration. Two, pronghorns are runners, not jumpers. When they come to a fence their instinct is to go under, not over them. The lowest strand on a traditional barbed wire fence prevented this maneuver.

Without access to their traditional ranges, pronghorns looked to join the long list of the extinct. Until a private conservation group stepped in and began preserving ranges and migration corridors. They also tried to convince ranchers to raise the lower strand of their fences. Then the Feds joined the effort. Eventually, the pronghorn rebounded from an estimated 12,000 in the early 1900s, to a current range of 500,000 to 1,000,000.

Pronghorns are tan with white necks, bellies and rumps. Their horns are actually big, flattened bones growing out of their skulls. The horns look like a reversed, black origami swan. Pronghorns have the largest eyes versus body weight of any mammal in existence. Remarkably, their eyes are capable of seeing 320°. One almost feels a sympathy for their predators. Can't sneak up on them and can't catch them anyway.

Wild Burro

Another day of silence and solitude on the Q. A sudden explosion of sound shatters the tranquility. The inhale/exhale hee haw immediately familiar. Is that donkey in great pain or pleasure? Could be either, as they sound-off for both. One thing for sure, the braying seems out of place. And it is. Therein lies the problem. The wild burros of the Mojave Desert are a non-native species. They were introduced to the area in the 1500s by the Spaniards. For the most part, the burro/donkey/jackass (the three labels interchangeable) stayed domesticated, until the mineral rushes of the 1800s. Prospectors quickly realized no better animal existed for hauling supplies. Soon their use spread, just as mining did. Inevitably, some burros escaped. Their descendants still roam wild.

And it is that roaming that causes problems. For burros compete for food and water resources with animals that are supposed to be there. Especially the bighorn sheep. Every year, the Bureau of Land Management captures 9,000 horses and burros and puts them up for adoption. The National Park Service has pretty much a zero tolerance for burros on Park Service land. In the past, hunts have been sponsored by that same Park Service. If interested, at the time of this writing, the fee for adopting a wild burro is $125. Regardless of your position on non-native species, it is impossible to deny the pleasure of a burro shout out during a desert ramble. Keep your eyes especially peeled around Beatty, Nevada, where they seem to be most plentiful. Sometimes even socializing on Main Street.

Burros are originally descended from African wild asses. Being introduced, they have no natural predators. They grow to about 350 pounds and live an average of 25 years. Burros are herbivores. Since they can't get enough water from the plants they eat, burros must live within 10 miles of a reliable water source. They are legendarily tough. Being able to lose up to 30% of their body weight in water loss and survive. A human would be very dead in that scenario. But a burro would need just five minutes of drinking to replace that 30%.

On a recent hike down a remote desert canyon near the Q, Orbit and I surprised a young male burro. We were perhaps his first humans. His bray of shocked terror was deafening. It seemed to scream "Oh, the horror of these forms! Their homeliness, invasion of my space and inability to communicate!" It was all too much for him. He fled down the canyon with agonized hee haws trailing. Unfortunately, he fled in our desired direction. Around the bend, the same terror played out. "Gawd! They're back and uglier than ever! Run far to recover a life without them!" We tried to hee haw our harmlessness but failed miserably. And so it played out over the next mile, for all of us were of the same direction. A rounding of a bend, followed by profane braying. "For the love of God, stop haunting me!" Finally, a break in the canyon wall allowed the burro to scramble up to a vantage point. From there, he rained down a rude tirade until we passed over the horizon. Leaving a traumatized burro to contemplate, "Was it just a dream, or are they capable of returning?"

Wild Horse

A band of mustangs moving across open desert. Who wouldn't be happy to see it? With luck, you will be happy on the Q. We spotted herds of wild horses near Death Valley Junction, Goldfield and Candelaria. The mustangs you might cross paths with are the result of both evolution and interference. Horses have been around for 55 million years. They first made their appearance in North America. Then, about 10,000 years ago, they disappeared from that same continent. Luckily, in all those millions of years, horses made their way to the rest of the world across the Bering Straits land bridge.

The ancestors of those migrants were reintroduced to North America, by the trusty Spaniards, in the 1500s. Occasionally, Native Americans would help themselves to the Spanish stock. And use of the horse spread. Inevitably, escapees formed their own herds. The descendants of whom still manage to hang on in the west today. Where it is estimated there are currently 30,000 to 50,000 wild horses. Roundups of which occur every year to control populations.

All wild horses are mustangs, which is the generic term for wild horses in the western U.S. Though scientists would prefer a genetic name differentiation between feral horses and escaped domesticated horses. Mustang comes from the same Spanish word meaning "have no master." They are usually spotted in a band of around 10 horses. The band is led by an alpha stallion, who might have one or two junior stallions. The rest of the band is comprised of mares and colts. When stallions get old, they tend to leave the band for a life of contemplative solitude. Often with the unsubtle encouragement of younger, upcoming stallions.

Wild horses are herbivores. Though they will eat dirt or lick minerals when they perceive an internal deficiency. Mustangs prefer an open range to keep an eye on predators. Mountain lions being the sole member of that club. They move about day or night and tend to range 10 to 30 miles. When ranging they prefer walking in single file. Often, they follow the same path. Which makes their trails very distinct. You can't miss them as you descend out of Candelaria. Wild horses do sleep. But not much. Averaging around three hours a night.

Coyote

They are everywhere but rarely seen. One of America's great wildlife success stories that few seem happy about. In reality, for 200 years, humans have tried to eliminate the coyote. All for naught. The coyote just keeps expanding its range. They are now present in every state but Hawaii. And I'm sure they are making plans for that final invasion. From New York City's Central Park, to suburbia where I once saw a coyote running down the street with a live chicken in its mouth, the coyote is here to stay. In fact, there are more coyotes in the U.S. now, than when the country was declared.

The coyote is successful because it can live anywhere and will eat anything. An omnivore without limits or snobbery. This adaptability has evolved to deal with the threat of humans as well. Coyotes have always been able to see well, hear well and smell well. Both to hunt and avoid being eaten. But the concerted effort to eradicate them by humans seems to have elevated the coyote's game to the next level. They have become smarter, wiley even, at surviving and flourishing.

Coyotes run anywhere from 15 to 45 pounds. Average lifespan is 15 years. The first year of the coyote's life is fraught with danger. Mortality ranges between 80 and 95%. Big litters offset this. Coyotes can breed with domesticated dogs, as well as wolves. As I said, they are adaptable. Offspring of dogs and coyotes are known as coydogs. Coyotes are fast when they need to be. Topping out at 40 mph. At the same time, they can clear an eight-foot wall. Other than man, predators include golden eagles, great horned owls and mountain lions. When annoyed, their tail gets big and bushy. Like every other dog there ever was, coyotes mark their territory with urine.

Along the Q, you're more likely to hear coyotes then see them. Especially at dawn and dusk. From the quintessential howl of the desert, to barks, to intimate yipping. Coyotes in the Mojave are vocal. It's considered rude of humans not to respond. If you are lucky enough to see one, they are generally moving in the opposite direction. Coyotes in the Mojave Desert get most of their moisture from what they eat. If really thirsty, they will bite into a coyote melon. You will see this melon along the Q. They sometimes look like round squash, other times little watermelons. Don't mimic the coyotes in this regard. The coyote melon is incredibly bitter to humans and would tear up your insides. For days.

Bat

There are over 900 species of bats worldwide. In the Mojave Desert, there are at least five. The leaf nose bat, pallid bat, Yuma mytosis, spotted bat and big-eared bat. Perhaps there are more. I am unable to differentiate them in flight. So, my ignorance allows me to simply point as the sun goes down and say, "Look, a bat!" I know it's a bat because they fly jerkily, unlike a bird. If you want to see bats begin their commute, hang out by any mine entrance around sunset. As many desert bats make abandoned mines their homes.

Bats are the only mammals that take flight. Their bodies are covered in hair. Their ears large for hearing during night flights. They regularly clean those ears with pointed thumbs. Contrary to popular belief, bats are not blind. Though they only see in old-fashioned black-and-white.

The bat's most amazing attribute has to be their vocalizations. Which they accomplish with soundwaves. Very much similar to dolphins. Basically, bats emit high-pitched sounds at a rate of 30 vocalizations per second when flying. Most of the sounds are above the range a human can pick up. Those sounds bounce off objects that orient the bat and allow it to avoid danger while flying. They also bounce off prey insects. As well as communicate with other bats. Those sounds were also why we were never able to hit a bat with a basketball as kids. Forgive us, for we knew not the error of our ways.

If standing water is about, hang out at dusk, and you might see a bat stop by for a drink. Though they don't drink in the traditional sense. More like skim the surface with their jaw lowered. A slight dip, then a scoop of water. This process is repeated until the bat is hydrated. After a dinner of insects is over, bats return home and climb into bed upside down. The upside-down slumber is for a few good reasons. First, hanging from a roof makes it tough for predators to get to them. Second, hanging upside down turns out to be the bat's most relaxed state of being. And third, a bat's most efficient take off is falling into flight. As bats find it a great challenge to take off from the ground like a bird. Their wings simply don't have enough lift. Before sleep, they spend 30 minutes giving themselves a good tongue cleaning. If they can avoid being eaten by large birds, bats will generally live between 10 and 20 years. As with many, man is enemy number one. Through both habitat loss and insecticide-laden insects.

Desert Tortoise

Desert tortoises are a treat to behold. Unfortunately, they are a rare treat due to declining populations and their habits. Some explaining about those habits. Tortoises can handle surface temperatures up to 140°. But they don't particularly like it. For that reason, they spend 98% of their time underground in burros dug from sandy soil. This keeps their body temperature down and their water retention up. Which is why you don't often see them.

Water is a desert tortoise's fickle dance partner when it comes to survival. And the tortoise is responsible for doing all the wooing. Tortoises are able to obtain some water from their herbivore diet. But not enough. In times of drought, a white paste will replace tortoise urine. As the tortoise tries to retain all its body water. To that end, a tortoise can survive a year without drink. Through these hard times, the tortoise patiently waits for rain. They even dig shallow water holes for the hoped-for deluge to fill. When the heavens do open, tortoises storm out, relatively speaking, from their burrows and swallow the plenty. They can hold up to 40% of their body weight in water. This occasional abundance allows them to thoroughly flush their urinary tract.

When satiated, tortoises go on the move. They can cover up to 660 feet a day. If you want to see a desert tortoise, the time after rain is the best time. But don't pick them up. Ever. As peeing is a defense mechanism, and tortoises can't afford the water wastage. As previously stated, after a rain, tortoises go crawl about. They check on their home range, which can cover from 10 to 100 acres. They gorge on flowers. Then it is time to return to their burrow. Which is often shared by a variety of other desert dwellers. As well as other tortoises. Up to 23 tortoises might reside in a large burrow. When winter arrives, tortoises stay underground in full-time hibernation.

Tortoises might live to be 80 years old, though 50 is more likely. They can grow to be 14 inches long and 6 inches high and weigh in at up to 15 pounds. They live from below sea level in Death Valley up to 3,500 feet in the high desert. (Low desert in California generally refers to any desert below 2000 feet. And high desert any desert above that altitude.) Unfortunately, up to 98% of tortoise hatchlings don't make it.

Tortoises take their time in everything they do. Whether it be moving, growing, eating or reproducing. Even the butting battles between males at mating time seem to take place in slow motion. The goal of which is to flip the other tortoise onto its back. And if it's too hot, the two males will postpone the shell slamming for another day. All of which saves water. Predators include ravens, foxes, coyotes, road runners and humans. Especially human off-roaders and pet seekers. Finally, if you see a tortoise eating dirt, they are trying to make up for a deficiency in calcium. And that particular patch of dirt pharmacy is rich in the needed calcium.

Roadrunner

The roadrunner lives large in the American imagination. Older generations know the reason well. For the younger generations, I can only say, there once was a cartoon... In the desert, if you see a long bird, running fast, it's a road runner. That's not to say they can't fly. But their flying, as it is, takes place over very short distances. Then it's back to earth and running. Which roadrunners do at speeds up to 20 mph. The flying is generally reserved for escaping predators. Those predators are numerous and include hawks, snakes, skunks and coyotes. The latter, much faster than roadrunners when not appearing in cartoons.

A snake the roadrunner does not fear is the rattlesnake. A roadrunner will approach a coiled, annoyed, smaller rattlesnake using its wings as a shield. When positioned, it will grab the rattlesnake with its beak and ground slam the snake to death. Then it will swallow as much of the snake as it can. The excess hangs out of the roadrunner's beak like a grotesque tongue. The roadrunner then goes about its business, while stomach acid creates more room for further consumption.

Roadrunners can grow up to two feet long. They are primarily meat eaters who prefer moist animals with high water content. Such as lizards, snakes, rodents, birds and tortoises. Though they don't mind a scorpion now and then. In winter, when many animals are in hibernation, roadrunners will turn to plants to make up for shortages. Roadrunners rely on their lightning reflexes to hunt. They can actually snatch a dragonfly or hummingbird from midair. During the midday heat, roadrunners will cut their activity by half. A couple of curiosities: Roadrunners rid themselves of excess salt through their nose, rather than their urine. And internally, they ring out all the moisture from their feces before discharging it. Beep, beep!

Scorpion

Scorpions are seen and immediately the judgment is unkind. Their aesthetics, a threat. But with two pincers upfront and a curved stinger outback, it's a fair assessment. Still, if you can get past looks, you'll discover a neat little critter. Let's talk about the threat first. There are 1,500 scorpion species worldwide. Only about 25 of them could seriously threaten a human life. In the Mojave Desert, there are three main types of scorpions. The stripe tailed scorpion, the hairy scorpion and the bark scorpion. The first two deliver stings akin to honeybees. Painful but not life-threatening. Unless you are allergic. The latter bark scorpion can cause serious problems. Fortunately, the Q is out of their range. Even then, there has not been a U.S.-reported fatality from a scorpion sting in the last 20 years. So all can breathe easy.

Well not all. Let's concentrate on the hairy scorpion. It is big, capable of reaching 5 inches in length, and it is predatory. Even cannibalistic. Victims include fellow scorpions, spiders, centipedes, insects, smaller lizards, snakes and even mice. The hairy scorpion prefers to hunt by ambush. A method they are very successful at, due to their extreme sensitivity to ground vibrations.

A case study: So, our hairy scorpion is hanging out behind a cactus and along comes a centipede. The scorpion can easily sense the march of a hundred legs. The scorpion springs out. With four pairs of legs they can move quickly. The scorpion seizes the centipede with its pincers. It prefers to subdue the centipede with pincers alone. If not, the scorpion must use their stinger to inject venom. A scorpion will try to avoid this because it takes two weeks to replace that lost venom. Once the centipede is immobilized, the scorpion will either tear small bits off and eat them. Or, it will coat the centipede with an acid spray that turns the unfortunate victim into a kind of goo. The scorpion then slurps up that fine goo at its leisure.

Of course, it being the desert, the eaters are also eaten. Predators include tarantulas, lizards, birds, mice and bats. Scorpions have been around for over 400 million years. They are related to spiders and ticks. In the Mojave, they live in burrows that can reach eight feet long. Roughly, their lifespan is three to five years. Scorpions are nocturnal. That is when they hunt and search for mates. During the day, they hide. Sometimes in empty shoes or clothing. For that reason, you should do a little check each morning after ground camping in the desert. And give those shoes a good knock. I once carried a scorpion for five hours, between my hat and head, on the desert aqueduct section of the PCT. On a break, I removed my hat. A fellow hiker pointed out my passenger. Unfortunately, the poor thing had cooked to death.

Some endearing traits to help you bond with scorpions. During mating season, scorpions hold each other's pincers and dance. This frolic is known as the "promenade a deux." When put under a backlight, scorpions will glow due to chemicals in their exoskeleton. Mama scorpions give birth to live young. The young then climb aboard mom's back for a week-long piggyback. After that week, they jump ship one by one and begin their own adventures.

Turkey Vulture

Another of the unloved. The ugly tag gets thrown around a lot. Especially that featherless head. But the turkey vulture's appearance is the result of a long and carefully considered evolution. Let's chat about that head. The lack of feathers serves two critical purposes. First, it dissipates heat. Second, the lack of feathers prevents harmful bacteria from accumulating. This inhibits the transmission of disease. A concern of any scavenger who spend their days sticking their head into rotting carcasses. A powerful immune system further combats disease.

If you are hiking the Q in the dead of winter, you won't see turkey vultures as they hang out elsewhere. But if you hike either shoulder season, you will probably spot some. Whether it be soaring high above on six-foot wingspans, or busy with a roadkill. An often-chaotic scene whose visual will stay with you for a while. If you do come across a vulture, here are some things to keep in mind. Vultures have those large wings so they can glide long distances without flapping their wings. Which preserves body moisture content. Most of which comes from the dead animals they consume.

Another neat water retention trick occurs when vultures urinate. Which they do on their legs. Their legs then absorb the urine, which effectively cools them. Probably not a trick to try on the trail. Vultures live in large groups but hunt independently. Their strong sense of smell directing them to the dead. Where they provide a sanitation service, which keeps the Mojave free of unsightly remains. Finally, if a vulture begins circling you as you hike the Q, it is considered polite to inform them, "Not today my friend." This prevents them from wasting anticipatory time.

Red Tailed Hawk

Red tailed hawks have feathers on their head, so they are considered beautiful. And rightfully so. They are big. Their wingspans can reach five feet. Though their body weight is only two to four pounds. Interestingly, the female is usually one third larger than the male. The red tailed hawk is a raptor, which basically translates as a bird of prey. They are exclusively carnivores that prefer to dine on small rodents and the occasional snake. Multiple times, I have observed a red tailed hawk zipping along with a panicked snake in its talons.

A red tailed hawk begins its hunt by soaring high above the ground. The long scream of a red tail, when it is hunting, is quite unforgettable. Once you've heard it, you become a lifelong identifier of the red tail.

While gliding, the red tail is taking in the landscape. With eyesight eight times more powerful than a human's, it doesn't miss much. When it spots something, say a mouse on the move, the red tail will dive toward it. The dive can reach 100 mph. Meanwhile the mouse goes about its business. Unaware of the terror descending into its world. The red tail will pull up at the last second and seize the mouse with its powerful talons. These talons are long and razor sharp. And deliver death to the mouse. The mouse is then eaten whole or torn apart, depending on its size. Red tailed hawks are also called chicken hawks for guessable reasons.

Dating between red tailed hawks is mesmerizing. The male and prospective female soar to great heights. Then, the male folds its wings and plummets toward the ground at high speed. At treetop level, they pull out of the dive and rocket upward back to the female. After a few repeat performances, the male checks in with the female. If she is buying into the program, they might lock talons and spiral down to earth together. Where they proceed to build a nest high in some tree. It is thought that red tails mate for life. Which can extend to 20 years in the wild.

Human Being

With certainty, you will encounter human beings (humans) on the Death Q. At times, their presence will be commonplace. Especially when their dens are in close proximity to each other. Which they often, but not always, seem to prefer. Other times along the Q, the species becomes infrequent and spottings are rare. Though sometimes in the far distance, humans can be seen moving toward a chosen destination in or on a wheeled conveyance.

When humans are closely observed, your impression is one of variety. As they tend to present in a broad range of size, coloration, coverings and behavior. In fact, hard and fast rules about humans are much debated within the scientific community. Here are some generalizations should you encounter a human during your hike. But keep in mind, these are only generalizations.

Humans are first and foremost unpredictable. Their reactions to hikers are varied and can run the gamut from accepting to hostile. Best to approach with kindness, caution, or not at all, depending on your read of the situation.

To get around without assistance, humans move on foot. Some of the species are quite slow and have a very limited range. While others are capable of speed (top speeds of 28 miles an hour have been recorded) and great distances.

Humans have quite long lifespans. Ages of 120-plus years have been documented. But diet, environment and behaviors significantly reduce the average lifespan to around 79 years old.

Young are born after a gestation of 40 weeks (more commonly referred to as nine months). But are not ready to survive on their own for a number of years or even decades. Humans can mate for life. Though more typical are pairings of far shorter duration.

Communication is accomplished through a broad variety of vocalizations. Some are quite pleasant to the ear. Others can be grating and will cause a longing to return to the trail for the average Q hiker. Much of this communication, resulting from evolution, is accomplished through devices of the species' own invention.

Humans are adaptive omnivores. And can survive on an array of plants, animals and animal by-products. The varied preparation of which seems limited only by the human imagination itself. Often the food groups are eaten in conjunction with each other.

Water satisfies all thirst needs of the species. But various water-based liquids are generally much preferred by humans.

As said, humans tend to live in dens. Which they either construct themselves or with the assistance of other humans. They can be quite territorial about these dens. Therefore, a hiker should not disturb human dens whenever possible.

Predators of humans in the Mojave Desert are almost exclusively other humans. Though this predation tends to be a result of intra-species interaction and not a result of food acquisition. As well, the behavior is considered somewhat uncharacteristic by those who study the species extensively.

Now that you've been introduced to the fauna of The Death Q, it's time for you to go out and make their acquaintance.

Chapter 10

Flora of the Death Q

Opening this chapter with a confession of ignorance is appropriate. I know little about desert plants. But I see them. Many don't. Commentary on desert landscape is replete with descriptions of monotony and barrenness. "Stop and really look," as my dad used to say. You'll see the desert floor thick with a mass variety of grasses and shrubs. Their failure to be colored or designed in eye-catching manner, inconsequential. Some, when they die, become tumbleweeds. Others grow in rings that date back hundreds or even thousands of years. Neat names like Mormon tea and cheese bush abound. All of them will get stuck in your socks, at one point or another.

And maybe, just maybe, the springtime conditions will be just right. As they were in the spring of 2015, when plentiful winter rains caused rainbows to ground. Lupines, asters, primroses, indigo bushes and prince's plumes came out for display. The mad riot of wildflowers that year neutered all adjectives. And I bet all alive could not help loving the desert that spring.

Hurdling my ignorance, I can at least identify and describe the easily distinguishable plants and trees of the Death Q. When altitude is reached, on a couple of sections of the Q, a hiker will encounter pines and junipers, etc. These are well known. I'd like to focus on the lesser-known desert species. To start, a general truth about desert plants. They grow slowly. Plenty of sun, but not much else to speed up growth. So, a safe guess is that most of what you're seeing is probably older than you think it is. And it has put in a lot of hard work and effort to stay alive. Please try to avoid ending all that work and effort prematurely.

Joshua Tree

The tree of U2's affection. A tree beautiful but not huggable. Rough bark covers the trunk. Higher up, thick, irregular branches are crowned with bunches of spear-like leaves. The tallest Joshua trees can reach over 40 feet. Making them prime desert shade options for meals and naps. There is a lot of debate as to how old Joshua trees can reach. This is due to their fibrous core, which doesn't capture annual ring growth. The consensus seems to be that 200 years is about the average lifespan. As to the name, the tree was christened Joshua by early Mormon pioneers. The branches stretching upwards reminded them of the biblical Joshua, with his arms raised beseechingly to his God. Interestingly, a common Native American petroglyph has a human performing that same beseeching effort to the heavens.

Creosote Bush

The creosote bush is everywhere to be seen. It grows in a tight bunch, having long slender limbs, capped by small, green, resin-coated waxy leaves. Often there are fuzzy white balls amongst the leaves. In spring, yellow flowers decorate. The creosote can reach ten feet high. Basically, in the Mojave, look anywhere and you will see one. It is a bush that sprouts fun facts. To begin with, it is the most drought resistant plant in America. Mature creosotes can go two years without rain. This is because they have two root systems. A shallow one to collect water and a deep one to store it. The leaves are waxy, so all that stored moisture doesn't escape easily. When conditions are good, creosotes allow plants to crowd around them, including other creosote bushes. But when tough times are the norm, creosotes produce a toxin around them that keeps the competition from growing near.

Staying with toxins, the creosote on railroad ties was at one time derived from creosote bushes. The creosote naturally prevented bugs from munching on ties, which extended their usability. The process was expensive, though, and many of the railroad constructors on the Death Q skipped the process. Preferring to focus on the short-term cost savings rather than long-term profit. A not so novel concept in capitalism. And an explanation of the advanced decay of many of the ties you will traipse across. Medically, extracts from the creosote bush have shown promise fighting cancer and HIV.

Creosote bushes replicate through a cloning process. Some creosotes end up cloning into large rings, the oldest of which has been estimated at 11,700 years old. Which would make it arguably the oldest living organism on Earth. Hail the creosote bush! And if it rains in the desert, a hiker will be engulfed in creosote perfume. Don't worry, you'll know it. And enjoy it. Finally, at the end of all those hiking miles, the creosote kicks in some refreshment. A tiny sprig of creosote leaves dropped in a pot of boiling water creates a fine tea. Throw in a couple of lemon drops to soften the hardness. Elevate the feet, sip slowly and let your eyes drink stars.

Mojave Yucca

The Mojave yucca looks like a Joshua tree with its limbs amputated. No beseeching here. Same rough bark and spiked leafy head though. Which is the reason, at one time, yuccas were called Spanish daggers. Yuccas grow from seeds, but after 100 years or so, a shoot will grow out the side of a mature yucca. This jump-starts a new yucca. Though, genetically, it remains the same plant. This continuing process can result in yuccas over 1,000 years old. The yucca can grow up to 15 feet high and its flowers are white. To the Native Americans and their ingenuity, the yucca was a mall. Its parts were used to make soap, medicine, shoes, flour, rope, shampoo, hats, hairbrushes, mattresses, clothes and saddle blankets.

Cholla Cactus

The cholla cactus is a tall, thin cactus with multiple branches. It grows in short segments. Each segment is armored in fierce looking yellow spines. Their usual height is about 3 feet, but they can grow much closer to the heavens. As the branches grow, heavy segments will fall to the ground, creating new plants. In this way, cholla cactuses end up being hundreds of years old. Their siren call is a pretty pink flower. "Come on over for a close-up, friend." Meanwhile the spined segments lay in mute ambush. For the cholla has another name. "The jumping cholla." Get near one and a segment tends to latch onto what it can. The spines are hollow and razor sharp. The lucky only have to remove the spines from their pants or shoes with pliers. Time spent, but no pain.

I would be one of the unlucky. While running through dunes barefoot in Mexico, I came down hard on a cholla segment. It went deep into the arch of my foot. When the cholla spines come into contact with moisture, a.k.a. flesh, they tend to curve for better grip. This curvature inhibits successful removal. In my case, my foot's reflexive embrace of the cholla invader further strengthened their bond. The pain of that day, 30 years ago, is recalled easily. I committed every capitulation to agony imaginable, as the spines were yanked out one by one. But there is solace if you get jumped. As you run down the path screaming, with your body hosting a cholla, know this: you are participating in the biological process by propagating a species. Because wherever you yank it out, there it will grow.

Barrel Cactus

Barrel cactus on the Death Q are short, squat and barrel shaped. They are usually green and covered in red or yellow spines. Rings of flowers crown their top when the barrel is in the mood. Some barrels have spines shaped like fishhooks. Legend has it that Native Americans used them as such. And the Native Americans didn't stop there. At the end of the day, they might pick out a barrel cactus and cut the top off. Then they would carefully remove the pulp. Which they would wring water out of for a drink. The remainder they would stew into a soup. Then, if they had other food that needed cooking, hot stones would be placed in the hollowed-out barrel. In that way, a barrel oven would be created.

Tamarisk Tree

Tamarisk trees are barked brown/red with green, wispy leaves. The leaves are fine and hairlike. They can grow up to 25 feet tall and prefer real estate that is wet and salty. When you shake a tamarisk, you tend to end up covered in yellow powder. Tamarisks originated in the Mediterranean zone and were brought to the States in the 1800s to be planted as ornamentals. Soon, they escaped their gardens and invaded wildlands. Each tree produces about half a million seeds annually, so their spread was rapid. Their immigration preference proved to be the Southwest where they quickly muscled out the locals. Growing in dense thickets, they choked riverbeds and changed eco systems. You'll appreciate their density when you pass through them on the Armagosa River. Which is strangled by them. Catastrophically, they lowered water tables due to their thirst. Each tree capable of consuming 200 gallons of water a day. A significant amount in the desert.

These days, the tamarisk finds itself powerful but unpopular. The Feds have declared war on the tamarisks. Trying a variety of methods to eradicate, or at least minimize, the spread of tamarisks. The latest incarnation is introducing beetles from the tamarisk's original homeland. These beetles have an appetite for tamarisk flesh. But are yet another invasive species. I can't remember whether two negatives make a positive.

Cottonwood Tree

Chances are, if you see a significant tree growing near a dry or wet streambed along the Death Q, you are looking at a cottonwood. In mature trees, the bark is rough and quite white. The leaves are green and heart shaped. Depending on water availability, they can grow up to 100 feet high. But the cottonwood does not live long.

Average lifespan is between 50 and 75 years. While they are around, though, cottonwoods make the loveliest shade. One Native American tribe figured the rustle of wind through cottonwood leaves to be Gods trying to speak to people. I'll leave it there.

Chapter 11

Mines

Mines are thick along the Death Q. Their dark mouths yank your attention. Their histories largely unknown. But this is known. Without them, the Q would not exist. Simply put, mines brought railroads and railroads brought more mines. It was a romance that lasted well into the last century. Undercut, finally, by ever more powerful trucks. But while it lasted, the story went something like this. Prospectors would scour the hills looking for promising mineral outcrops. (A group of people solidly in the "what's around the corner" grouping.) With time, such a mineral outcropping would be discovered in a back-of-beyond location. Claims were then taken out. And mining begun. The minerals extracted would be transported to the nearest railroad by wagon. There it would be loaded and transported to the nearest mill. At the mill, crushing and sorting would take place. If the mineral was high-grade (valuable), other mines would open in the area.

The wagons almost always were the weak link, as they were expensive and slow. Eventually, the mine owners would get together and discuss a railroad spur with the railroad barons. Sometimes the barons would build and sometimes the mine owners financed. Often the mines played out before the rails were laid. Or the mine owner would build his own stamping mill. Thereby eliminating the need for a railroad to haul bulk ore. But these mills were often plagued with power or lack of water issues. So, often a railroad spur to the mine was needed.

But every spur was a gamble. Would the mineral veins end before the railroad justified the investment? If a spur was laid and the trains were chugging, the smaller mine operators moved in. With transport costs low, their strikes need not be as stunning. A profit was viable on smaller margins. Even a solo miner with a pick, shovel and burro had a shot at dreams. Everyone was digging a hole looking for the big strike.

That is why, most everywhere you scan, tailings will be present. Tailings are the debris removed from the inside of mines and dumped in front of them. Often a different color from the hillside. Spot a tailing and a mine is nearby. The larger the tailings, the more extensive the mine. The other telltale signs of a mine are structures themselves. Outbuildings, chutes and holding tanks often crowd a Death Q mine.

But the most dominant feature of larger vertical mines was their head-frame. Many of which are still in place. A headframe is a wooden (in those days) tower, built over an underground mine shaft. Somewhere nearby would be a motor or a hand-operated winch that ran a hoist. A cable would run from the hoist up to a wheel located at the top of the tower. From there, the cable would descend vertically down the mineshaft. Attached to the cable would be a bucket. Buckets hauled the minerals up and out of the shaft. Buckets also operated as elevators. Starting shift miners descending in the bucket and ending shift miners returning to the light in that same bucket.

When the mine ended its run, it was often more economical to leave the headframe in place, rather than disassemble and remove it. Wood doesn't rot in a rainless desert. So, bygone sentinels remain, as long as vandals can avoid the charisma of stupidity. Headframes are visual mag-nets along the Death Q. That's because, in a treeless desert, they are often the only significant horizon event. The reward of their company only after your miles of effort.

What was mined? The heavy hitters, as always, were gold and silver. Other significants were borax, copper, lead, zinc, talc, tungsten, clay and gypsum. Why so many minerals? Geologists will tell you it is because the Mojave region is very active geologically. All the shifting around of plates, and subsequent earthquakes caused various mineral deposits to pepper the area. Why was so much found? Miners say that without thick vegetation and groundcover, rock outcroppings are much easier to spot. Many mines were started with this conversation. "Hey what's that over there? Let's go have a look."

Another reason so much mineral wealth was discovered might be sat-uration. Back in the day, a young man on the east coast opens the newspa-per. Maybe he has little or no prospects or is employed in an unrewarding manner. Or maybe he is well-off but bored. One day all of these young men read the same article about a gold strike out west. About the boom that follows. Fortunes are being made overnight. Excitement is around every corner. Why not head toward the sunset? Life is lived but once. So, they made their own way. Others were grubstaked.

Grubstaking meant one or more individuals financially backed the aspiring miner's quest. In return, the investors got a piece of the action when pay dirt was struck. On arrival, a few made their fortune. Most did not. But they all were looking. Covering every nook and cranny for the big strike. That is how the surface got picked over in the west.

So, who did get rich? Usually not the guy running an ore drill or placing dynamite hundreds of feet underground. Or the guy dry panning for gold in some gulch. Or the guy laying rail across the expanses of open desert. Nor the prostitute in the brothel or the clerk in a store. As always, in the storied history of capitalism, it is the people who had money to begin with that raked it in.

At the lower end of the profit spectrum were the shopkeepers, hotel owners, and saloon owners who supplied the miners. Money flowed from the mines to their pockets. The miners were simply conduits.

At the upper end were individuals with capital in the bank and capacity to obtain more when needed. These people built the railroads. They ran the mines and signed the paychecks. How they generally obtained the mines provides insight into the times. A typical tale: Hard luck miner strikes it rich. Wealthy individual or syndicate hears the news. They ride out to the camp. There they review the assay reports, which indicate the mineral value of the samples. Hard luck miner is between a rock and a hard place. (An expression that possibly originated in the copper mines of Arizona.) He knows he doesn't have the capital to exploit the mine, and he knows he is going to get lowballed. What to do? In the end, hard luck miners often took the thousands offered and headed for town. While the new mine owners went on to add to their millions.

Mining's glory days along the Death Q are distant in the rearview. Small-scale mining operations putter on here and there. Dreamers with metal detectors search for the big nugget that escaped earlier detection. And every once in a while, a strip pit operation will gouge a hole deep in the Earth. Or a new method of working old tailings will pop up. But for the most part, things are quiet. In Death Valley National Park, the last grandfathered-in mine closed in 2005. Now all that remains along the Q are the relics and debris that were walked away from. Along with sometimes significant environmental degradation.

Now you are walking by all those leftover mines. Levels of accessibility vary, depending on remoteness. Where there is tourist traffic, many of the mine entrances have been sealed with metal bars. The bars keep you out, but allow the bats to move back-and-forth. This is the case around Johannesburg and Randsburg, where I spent a portion of my youth exploring miles of tunnels in pursuit of the forgotten. As remoteness increases, perhaps some fencing or barbwire guard a mine entrance. Usually with a sign saying, "Stay out, stay alive." Then in fine print the list of gases, collapses, and other threats that will surely befall you should you enter. Finally, when you're really out there on the Q, it's just you and a hole. Horizontal into the hillside or vertical down an old ladder in an endless shaft. Do you go in or pass? Every individual is responsible for their own counsel. But I will say this, "Stay out, stay alive" is true and certain. Going in erases certainty. Is the risk worth it?

Chapter

Ghost Towns

The beauty of what once was. In modern times,
donment has a negative connotation. Whether it be a tc
son. The word abandonment leaves a sour taste. But this w.
In the late 1800s and early 1900s abandonment, of mines and
the Q, was an acceptable tactic. The mine played out. Walk away
the next. Which is logical when examined. A mine becomes just a .
the ground when its value departs.

A town, on the other hand, has structures and infrastructure. Wh,
abandon it? Part of the answer lies in the level of development. In the early
stages of a boomtown, most of the structures were either tents with rock
base walls, dugouts with roofs, or wooden buildings. Two of the three were
transferable to the next boom. So, the town itself would move when the
mine played out. Leaving just a few scars. The remaining part of the answer
addresses towns that were more established.

A town is usually situated for one or a combination of three reasons.
Convenience, beauty or purpose. All of the ghost towns along the Q were
about purpose. And that purpose was mining or railroading. A mining town
was once described by a local newspaper as such: "It grew up in a flat little
hollow but it did not nestle because a mining camp does not nestle. Like a
tin can, it lies where it is thrown." Where the minerals were dug or the
railroad built, was where the town needed to be placed. Often, it was not a
good place. Too hot, too remote, too many flash floods, and so on.

But the biggest problem was the scarcity of water. Strikes didn't often
happen near high water tables. So, water was either piped in, or brought
in. Which made water and life expensive. People endured for the profit to
be made. And when that profit was high, optimism was a contagion that
infected the future. Which caused the vision of ever escalating riches to be
projected far into that future. Based on that optimism, permanent structures were built. But when profit inevitably departed, because the mine or
railroad shut down, the purpose was lost. Without purpose, the townsfolk

the fleeing profit prophet toward the horizon. With their custom-
e, the business owners had no choice but to follow suit. Leaving
tructures as testaments to the frailty of the future.

A range of these ghost towns await your exploring pleasure on the
th Q. At the low end, there will be nothing more than a few piles of
tal cans. To the knowledgeable, age specified by their soldering tech-
iques. Moving up the range brings one to foundations and perhaps street
grids. Escalating to cemeteries and ruins. And finally, identifiable towns
with buildings still in place. Towns that once had swimming pools, golf
courses and operas. But which are now home to confused winds.

That is one kind of ghost town. Where people are no longer in residence. A second type are ghost towns that died and revived. Towns whose
allure was too strong. Repopulated by a wide range of folk, motivated by
an equally wide range of motivations to live in a place that others walked
away from.

The final classification of ghost towns is those that were never fully
abandoned but lived on. Depleted to skeleton populations. Content to function in the shadows of former glory. Every view soaked with a grander
history.

Chapter 13

Railroad Archaeology

As a hiker collects miles on the Q, the detritus of abandoned railroads will always be underfoot. These remnants began in the era of steam engines. Whose initial development caused great fear among some members of the public. For instance, it was thought by some, that human bodies would melt at speeds higher than 50 miles an hour. Or that women's uteruses would fly out of their bodies at such speeds. Luckily, neither occurred. Other remnants you step over will be from the later era of diesel locomotives. All these parts and pieces bring to mind a question. What was all that stuff's original purpose?

Some answers, starting with railroad construction. A railroad proposal begins with an idea of connecting point A to B. Engineers would sally forth and determine if a route was possible. The enemy was too much ascent or descent. (Though I once rode a small train in India that climbed multiple freestanding, ascending, corkscrew shaped loops to summit a cliff. It was quite novel to look directly across at the engineer going in the opposite direction.) Determining if a route was feasible was the first step.

The second step: Was it economically feasible? Too many bridges or tunnels needed or a surplus of rolling terrain encountered could be economically fatal.

If both hurdles were cleared, the construction process would begin. The first step was the railbed. A graded, flat, built-up bed with minimum curves. The fewer curves, the faster the train could go, and the less engineers used their brakes. All money savers. The bed was raised to keep water from collecting on it. Preferably made with crushed stone, so that it drained easily. But in the days of the Q, whatever materials were close at hand became the bed. At times, you will be staggered by the sheer volume of hand-moved earth used to push a flat line across a deep canyon. At other times on the Q, you will be frustrated when that deep canyon has reasserted itself in the middle of that flatline. Thus, necessitating a side-slide and climb.

Once the railbed was established, the tie-laying commenced. Ties are the wooden beams laid horizontally across the railbed. They were there to stabilize the rails, distribute weight and hold the rails at the correct width. Widths were referred to as the gauge of the railroad. In the glory days of railroading, long before the creation of the Death Q, there were generally two gauges. Standard gauge, which was approximately four feet nine inches between the wheels on each side. (This gauge has witnessed it all. From the old steam engines to the most modern diesel locomotives.) And the more economical narrow gauge, which was three feet between the wheels. Both gauges existed on the Q. There was even a two-foot baby gauge railroad at New Ryan. At points where a narrow gauge would intersect a standard gauge railroad, a third rail was sometimes laid. The third rail would lie inside the standard gauge rails. This would allow the narrow gauge train to be switched onto the standard gauge rails for short distances.

These same switches allowed trains to be diverted onto spur lines, sidings and maintenance lines. An excellent example of a modern switcher is located just before the Searles tunnel as you approach Johannesburg. Ties were generally made from pine on the Q and not treated with bug repelling creosote, due to the cost. In modern times, ties are made from concrete and laid down mechanically. But in the days of wood, a tie traveled far from the forest to the desert.

Ties were an expensive investment. Railroads were cost-curious about how long their tie investments would last. To measure aging, they came up with an ingenious solution. The date nail. Which was basically a nail with two numbers stamped on their head. Thus 08 would be 1908, and 17 would be 1917, and so on. These nails would be driven into a selected tie along the Q. Their head number would reflect the year the tie was installed. When the tie deteriorated to the point that it needed to be replaced, the date nail would provide a record of the installation date. As well as explain the duration of the tie. Keep your eyes downcast on the Q, and you're bound to come across a couple of these date nails.

The rails themselves, were laid end to end on the ties. Originally, they were simply spiked directly to the ties. The spikes were driven in with an elongated sledgehammer. Each new rail was butted up to the previous rail but not tightly. Room was left for expansion and contraction caused by heat and cold. Which explains that click clack of a train coming down the line in past times. Nowadays, rail is seamless, each rail welded to the next. As technology advanced, so did the method for securing the rails to the ties. Eventually, joint bars and tie plates entered the picture. These created a more secure bond between rail and wooden tie and will be discussed in the next paragraphs.

Back to the detritus. What will you see as the miles slide past? First, not a lot of rails. All rails on abandoned Q railroads were removed. Either to create weapons of war during World War II or for scrap metal value during other times. When access was convenient, ties disappeared too. As stated earlier, two hotels were built with them. Others became fences or firewood. Still others were stacked and forgotten. But thousands remain. Beautiful to see. Confirming, when doubt creeps in, your direction. Cursed, when they trip you up.

Also in the thousands are railroad spikes. In various degrees of rust separation, depending on the area's level of humidity. In the thousands, also, will be carriage bolt heads and nuts. These bolts were used to hold the joint bars on the rails. A joint bar was basically a splint between two rails. It secured one rail to the other. When the rails were taken up, these carriage bolts were sheared off on each side. Their remnants left for your discovery.

Tie plates are another item you will see lying about. They are square steel plates with a groove in the middle and four holes on the sides. The base of the rail sat within the groove. Four spikes were driven into the holes and then into the wooden ties. There, four spike heads held the rail in place. And the plate prevented the spikes from wobbling about. The strange washers you will see, that look like the letter nine, are a special form of lock washers. I guarantee you'll come across a lot more remnants of railroads than I've described here. Some will leave you scratching your head. But we don't need all the answers, do we?

And, of course, there's the antique trash. Leave no trace was unobserved in the early days of rail travel. Littering, a national right. The desert an appropriate repository of trash. Lest smugness creeps in, a present traipse across any desert near a town shows we haven't come far.

But back to the Q. The practice on any train ride appears to have been, "Pop, I'm done with my soda. Well, wing the bottle, child." And so, they did.

Luckily trash, like graffiti, develops some charisma with age. (An example of the latter, the ceiling of the Abu Simbel temple in Aswan, Egypt is covered in the fascinating, homesick candle smoke messages of Napoleon's soldiers.) Thus, the sun-stained bottles, rusting Prince Albert tobacco cans, and dusty bric-a-brac make for great diversion as you put in your miles. To all the souvenirs you see on the trail that you are tempted to carry home, why not capture it with a photo instead? That way, the next person gets to have that same smile.

Chapter 14

Cell Phones

Verizon is king and queen of reception in all remote areas of the western United States that I am familiar with. The Death Q is no exception. But that is just my opinion and experience. Others will swear by their carriers. The truth of the matter, though, is this: For the majority of the time, you will be completely out of range, no matter who your telecom is. Which is arguably a worthy goal on a long hike.

If you are a habitual cell phone user or photo snapper, invest in a solar charger. If not, town charging should get you through.

Chapter 15

Gear

Basically, I took the gear I used on my PCT thru hike.

The big three were a Gossamer Gear Mariposa pack, a Z Pack Hexamid Solo shelter and a 20 degree Jacks R Better down sleeping quilt with a Thermarest Neolight sleeping pad.

I set up the shelter less than 10% of the nights. We had rain a few nights and snow twice. Rarely was I cold using the sleeping quilt.

I would guess my base weight to be around 12 pounds. Base weight being the weight of everything you're carrying, minus food, water and fuel. Speaking of water, I used the two-bottle AquaMira water treatment system to purify all the water I drank on the Q. The system has yet to fail me.

If you are unsure of what you need in general, peruse the abundant posted PCT gear lists to get an idea. Try to avoid over packing, which I would define as a base weight over 25 lbs. The objective is to go as light as possible. For 20 to 25 miles a day is the goal. Not a huge amount but still honest miles. The less pressure on your feet, the easier those miles will prove to be. Accompanying that ease is a corresponding decrease in the likelihood of injury. Speaking of feet, a newborn pair of shoes will be ready for the grave after 811 miles.

The other side of the equation is a backpack that is too light. Which can translate into insufficient gear to deal with conditions. Here are some backpacking categories to consider. Lightweight backpacking is considered to be a base weight of 10 to 20 lbs. This is the category I usually find myself in. More ambitious is ultralight backpacking, which is under a 10-lb. base weight. This is the category I aspire to. Most ambitious of all, is the under 5-lb. base weight, super ultralight backpacking category. An approach that requires the skill to discard all but the most essential gear. And perhaps an ability to suffer hardships that come from hiking on the edge of need versus necessary. But these are just categories. Each backpacker must arrive at their ideal relationship between comfort, pack weight and miles.

Experimenting with limits is all part of the fun. And expense, as ultralight gear can be expensive, if you lack the skill to make it yourself.

Worthy of mention is a third approach to backpacking. One not recommended, but admirable in its creativity. For a number of weeks on the PCT, I had been following very deep shoe prints with a distinctive tread pattern. To satisfy a goading curiosity, I picked up my pace. With time, a second set of shoe prints joined the first. They were shallower and less distinct, but still evident. With yet more time, the riddle was solved. It happened with the rounding of a bend one bright morning. There stood a twenty-something-year-old. On his back was an enormous pack.

His body language indicated the pack to be a significant burden. A subsequent conversation confirmed the pack was around sixty pounds and filled with every kind of gear imaginable. Sixty pounds is an incredible amount to carry through three states by anyone's definition.

Next to the young backpacker was the second set of shoe prints. They belonged to a grizzled veteran backpacker. His pack was firmly in the lower end of super ultra-light. A smile of contentment radiated from the older gentleman's face. The faint outlines of an umbilical cord between the two packs somewhat discernible. The image of a whale with attached parasitic remora fish came immediately to mind.

In the end, to each their own hike.

Chapter 16

Leave No Trace

Leave No Trace (LNT) a backpacking credo, has seven fundamental principles.

1. Plan ahead and prepare
2. Travel and camp on durable surfaces
3. Dispose of waste properly
4. Leave what you find
5. Minimize campfire impacts
6. Respect wildlife
7. Be considerate of other visitors

Summed up. Try to make the next hikers think you never preceded them. Your footprints they will see. Deserts scar permanently and easily. The wagon wheel ruts of pioneer settlers are still viewable throughout the west. But footprints should be about the extent of your scar. The Death Q is almost entirely on public lands. There are few organized campgrounds. The desert spreads in every direction from the railbed. When you're done for the day, simply turn your back on the trail and head out 200 feet. Find flatness. Settle in. Privacy ensured. Your camp obscured. Then in the morning, spend a couple of minutes erasing evidence of that camp. And please hump out all your trash. Remember, we're the good guys.

Toilets: Out of town, you're on your own. Dig that cat hole 6 to 8 inches deep. Not tough in the desert. Once again, 200 feet from the railbed, please. Cover and camouflage the hole. The toilet paper comes with you in a Ziploc bag. Bury it and it just gets dug up by some animal enamored with your intoxicating scent and salt. Liberated, it is free to become a windborne eyesore. Burn it and you're asking for a conflagration nightmare. Nope, you have to hump it out. Which is an unpleasant task. Interested in an alternative to toilet paper? Allow me to present the "azblaster," the solution to the toilet paper dilemma.

The azblaster is basically a portable bidet. It was developed for use by women after their pregnancy. Its technical term is a Lavette Bottle or Perineal Bottle. Basically, it is a small plastic bottle with a multi-holed spray cap at the end. The azblaster is 6 1/2 inches tall, and fits in the palm of your hand. It weighs less than one ounce and costs under two dollars. And can be purchased in any medical supply store or ordered online using its technical term for the search. Best of all, it eliminates the need for toilet paper. A planet-wide scourge that requires the deaths of 27,000 trees a day.

A COMPARISON	
Toilet Paper:	Azblaster:
Costs money	Free after initial purchase
Might run out	Never runs out
Have to carry out in Ziploc bags	No trace
Bad for environment	Good for environment
Not recyclable	Recyclable
TP flower bombs	Watering the flowers
Burnable/fire	Used to put out a fire
Not waterproof	Waterproof

The method. Fill the azblaster with 8 ounces of untreated water. Dig hole. Squat. Shit. Then blast clean by squeezing bottle in direction of exit point. Smile, it's refreshing. Assist cleaning with the other hand if so desired. Hey, that's the way much of the rest of the world does it. Then drip dry or dry with a 2" x 2" towel. Then hand sanitize. Finished.

Endorsed and test-driven by the following PCT thru hikers: Red Beard 2013, Orbit 2013, Slack 2013, Blast 2013

Medically approved and certified by: Doc 2013

For further testimonials, google "azblaster pacific crest trail."

Chapter 17

Costs

Costs are difficult to predict because they are personality based. Primarily, what is your personality when you reach a town after being in the bush for a while? Do you refrain or splurge? Hotel room, restaurant meals and beers at the bar? Or a quick resupply and back into the bush? Every reader knows their answer from experience or acquaintance with themselves. The latter style of hikers could easily do the entire Q for a few hundred dollars. The former can spend to the limits of their desire.

But the trail isn't free. There are no free hiker boxes full of goodies. Trail magic (the generosity of strangers) certainly exists, but it is spontaneous rather than organized. Resupplies, unless you're pre-shipping packages, tend to be more expensive than the national average. That is because most of the stores are smaller, falling into the convenience category. Remote locations, with minimum clientele, go hand-in-hand with higher prices. However, a couple of the major towns do have supermarkets. But once out in the bush, you couldn't spend a dime if you wanted to. There's just no one out there to take it from you.

Chapter 18

The Website

The website for the Death Q is located at www.storiesfromsteve.org. This is where I kindly ask you to send in updates, observations, suggestions and criticisms. Especially changes that affect the course of the actual trail. Hearing about your hike itself would be most appreciated. Simply go to the website and click on the "Death Q" link to get started.

Chapter 19

Getting to the Start of the Death Q

The best way to get to Ludlow is to be dropped off by someone and subsequently picked up. As Ludlow is not considered a destination by anyone, there is no direct public transportation service to it. If you drive yourself to Ludlow, consider that 35 days is a long time to leave your car in one place. Especially a place like Ludlow with so many comings and goings. If this is your only option, talk to the locals to see if you can arrange a car caretaker situation. There is certainly no shortage of parking spaces in Ludlow.

Barstow, on the other hand, does have a couple of public transportation options. (Informationally, it is 57 miles from Barstow to Ludlow on the highway.) If public transportation is your only possibility of arrival, then you might want to consider starting the hike in Barstow. Though it might not be an attractive starting point from a hiking perspective, it would be most attractive in terms of transportation.

Barstow's first option would be Amtrak's Southwest Chief, which runs daily between Chicago and Los Angeles. If you're flying into and out of Los Angeles, there is a shuttle from LAX airport to Union station. From there the Southwest Chief leaves daily at 6:15 p.m., arriving in Barstow at Casa Desierto at 9:56 p.m. Returning is inconvenient. The Southwest Chief leaves Barstow at 3:39 a.m., getting into Union station, Los Angeles, at 8:15 a.m. The cheapest fares each way are $25. By no means should my mention of Amtrak be considered an endorsement, as I personally find their treatment of customers to be abhorrent. I am simply listing a transportation option that I would never take again.

Another option is Greyhound. Which has a number of daily departures from   its downtown Los Angeles station to Barstow. The ride is shorter, at two hours and ten minutes. And the saver fare less, at $19 each way. The Greyhound station in downtown Los Angeles is a short taxi ride from Union station. The Greyhound station in Barstow is at Barstow station. (1611 E. Main Street, 760-256-8757.) This is where the large McDonalds is located. To get into town from the station, walk out to Main Street and turn right. Follow Main Street into downtown, toward Vons supermarket and various motels. If you keep walking on Main Street, you will come to First Street. Where, if you turn right, you end up at Casa Desierto and the Death Q.

Yet another option is Bolt Bus. Which leaves from Union station in LA twice a day. It takes a little longer than Greyhound but is cheaper yet again at $12 each way. The huge drawback of Bolt Bus is that it drops you some six miles from downtown Barstow. At a Carl's Jr., no less. That's a long road walk for a few bucks.

If you're coming from the east, as in Las Vegas, both Greyhound and Bolt service that route as well. Since Barstow is equidistant between LA and Las Vegas, the fares are roughly the same. Check out their websites for more information. Unfortunately, there are no train services between Las Vegas and Barstow. Flying is not an option, as there are no commercial services at Barstow airport. If you did start your hike in Barstow, simply begin at Day 34 and hike east toward Ludlow. At Ludlow, start your hike on Day 1. The added convenience is that you would finish at Barstow with its public transportation options.

Of course, if some other point on the Q is convenient for you, have at it and start there. Simply find your starting point in Part Two of the book.

Chapter 20
Weather on the Death Q

Baker, California	Oct	Nov	Dec	Jan	Feb	Mar	Apr
Average max temp (F)	87	72	62	63	68	76	84
Average min temp (F)	54	42	33	34	39	45	51
Average total precipitation (in.)	0.25	0.31	0.41	0.47	0.71	0.51	0.2
Average total snow fall (in.)	0	0	0	0	0	0	0
Barstow, California	**Oct**	**Nov**	**Dec**	**Jan**	**Feb**	**Mar**	**Apr**
Average max temp (F)	82	69	60	59	64	69	77
Average min temp (F)	47	37	31	31	35	39	45
Average total precipitation (in.)	0.21	0.36	0.55	0.75	0.61	0.62	0.22
Average total snow fall (in.)	0	0	0.4	0.7	0	0.1	0
Average total snow fall (in.)	0.1	0.1	0.5	1.8	0.5	0.3	0.5

Beatty, Nevada	Oct	Nov	Dec	Jan	Feb	Mar	Apr
Average max temp (F)	79	66	57	54	60	65	74
Average min temp (F)	45	34	29	27	30	33	41
Average total precipitation (in.)	0.16	0.49	0.44	0.53	0.61	0.32	0.44
Average total snow fall (in.)	0.1	0.1	0.5	1.8	0.5	0.3	0.5
Bishop, California	**Oct**	**Nov**	**Dec**	**Jan**	**Feb**	**Mar**	**Apr**
Average max temp (F)	76	63	54	53	57	64	71
Average min temp (F)	37	27	21	21	26	30	36
Average total precipitation (in.)	0.24	0.53	0.87	1.14	0.9	0.48	0.28
Average total snow fall (in.)	0	0.3	1.3	4	1.4	0.7	0.3
Tonopah, Nevada	**Oct**	**Nov**	**Dec**	**Jan**	**Feb**	**Mar**	**Apr**
Average max temp (F)	63	49	40	37	42	50	60
Average min temp (F)	41	31	25	22	25	29	37
Average total precipitation (in.)	0.55	0.34	0.44	0.36	0.39	0.6	0.62
Average total snow fall (in.)	0.4	2.4	2.5	2.3	2.2	2.4	1.8

Chapter 21
Death Q Map

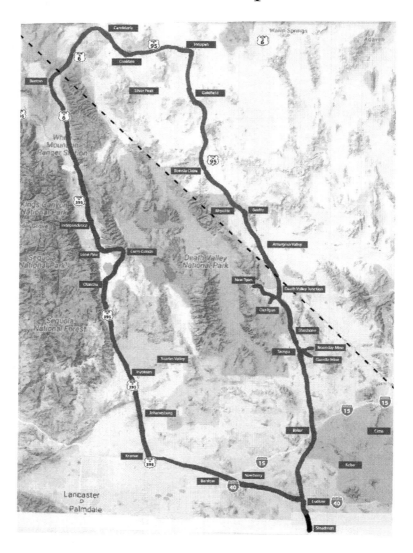

Chapter 22

Death Q Hiking Schedule

Towns in bold indicate a resupply point with population. Towns with an asterix indicate population but no resupply. Towns in regular print are devoid of both.

Total Mileage	Stations	Distance between stations
	Ludlow	8.00
8.00	Steadman	8.00
16.00	**Ludlow**	12.68
28.68	Broadwell	8.81
37.49	Mesquite	4.19
41.68	Crucero	3.70
45.38	Rasor	4.00
49.38	Soda	8.44
57.82	**Baker**	7.68
65.50	Silver Lake	9.50
75.00	Riggs	5.35
80.35	Valjean	9.25
89.60	Dumont	4.73
94.33	Sperry	4.16
98.49	**China Ranch**	4.65
103.14	**Tecopa**	13.00
116.14	Gunsite Mine, Noonday Mine	13.00
129.14	**Tecopa**	2.06
131.20	**Tecopa Hot Springs**	2.03

133.23	Zabriskie	5.21
138.44	**Shoshone**	12.67
151.11	Evelyn	12.30
163.41	**Death Valley Jct.**	7.00
170.41	Old Ryan	15.00
185.41	New Ryan*	20.00
205.41	**Death Valley Jct.**	7.00
212.41	Bradford / **Longstreet Casino**	4.60
217.01	Scranton	10.74
227.75	Leeland	10.46
238.21	Ashton	11.61
249.82	Gold Center*	2.41
252.23	**Beatty**	5.00
257.23	Rhyolite	4.00
261.23	Original Bullfrog Mine	5.00
266.23	Mud Spring	6.00
272.23	Petersgold	6.00
278.23	Midway	12.00
290.23	Bonnie Clare	7.00
297.23	San Carlos	6.00
303.23	Wagner	7.00
310.23	Stonewall	4.00
314.23	Ralston	13.00
327.23	Red Rock	4.00
331.23	**Goldfield**	13.00
344.23	Klondyke	18.00
362.23	**Tonopah**	13.00
375.23	Millers	12.00
387.23	Gilbert Jct.	8.00
395.23	Blair	7.00
402.23	Coaldale	13.00
415.23	Redlich	7.00

422.23	Candelaria	6.00
428.23	Candelaria Jct.	15.00
443.23	Basalt	8.00
451.23	Summit	8.00
459.23	Queen	10.00
469.23	**Benton**	11.00
480.23	Hammil*	10.15
490.38	Chalfant*	9.85
500.23	**Bishop/Laws**	15.90
516.13	Alvord/Zurich	2.80
518.93	Monola	1.57
520.50	Superfly Spur	9.83
530.33	Aberdeen	13.90
544.23	Independence/ Kearsarge	9.70
553.93	Owenyo	5.00
558.93	**Lone Pine**	13.00
571.93	Swansea* Via Cerro Gordo*	20.00
591.93	Keeler* via Owens Dry Lake	20.00
611.93	**Olancha**	4.80
616.73	Loco	4.40
621.13	Haiwee	4.20
625.33	Talus	4.30
629.63	Coso	4.10
633.73	Mabel	3.20
636.93	Little Lake	4.00
640.93	Narka	3.60
644.53	Linnie	4.40
648.93	Brown*	4.60
653.53	Rollie	4.50
658.03	**Magnolia/ Inyokern**	4.80
662.83	Terese	4.10
666.93	Code	5.50

672.43	Rademacher*	4.40
676.83	Searles Tunnel	14.00
690.83	**Johannesburg**	3.00
693.83	**Randsburg**	3.00
696.83	**Johannesburg**	1.80
698.63	Osdick/Red Mountain*	3.20
701.83	Atolia	9.10
710.93	Fremont	14.40
725.33	**Kramer Junction**	27.00
752.33	Hinkley*	7.00
759.33	**Barstow**	2.30
761.63	E. Barstow*	4.00
765.63	W. Daggett	2.30
767.93	**Daggett**	11.70
779.63	**Newberry Springs**	5.00
784.63	**Punjab, India**	7.80
792.43	Hector	6.20
798.63	Pisgah	13.20
811.83	**Ludlow**	All done!

Chapter 23

Introduction to the Start

The Death Q is a loop trail that ends at its beginning. When you jump on a loop, there has to be a starting point. The starting point chosen is Ludlow. Which just happens to be the nexus of the Q and of the Ludlow and Southern Railroad descender. The descender being the technical term for the semi-straight line on a Q. Write a book, learn something. In that vein, the letter Q has been in use since the Fourth Century.

From Ludlow, a hiker will head north and counterclockwise. The directions are not tech savvy. There are no GPS coordinates and exact compass headings. No, the directions are of the old-fashioned turn left, turn right variety. They should be reasonably straightforward to follow, only occasionally requiring a detective's perspective.

So, whether you're tuning up for a major thru hike, looking for a modern adventure, or just in need of a 35-day self-therapy session, it's time to sit up. Abandon that winter couch. Turn to the first page of your Death Q story. And begin a hike of strong memories. Unknown till now.

Photo 1 - Former rail water tank, Steadman, California.

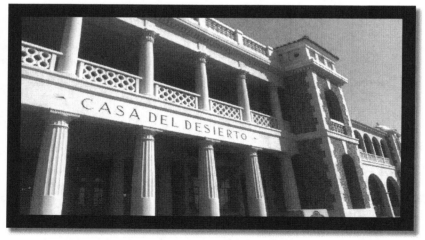

Photo 2 - Barstow rail depot and former Harvey House, Barstow, California.

Photo 3 - The snow remembers where the tracks were.

Photo 4 - A memory of Candelaria, Nevada.

Photo 5 - The Slim Princess. Gone but not forgotten.

Photo 6 - Carson and Colorado railbed. East Owens Valley with the High Sierras wearing their winter coat.

Photo 7 - A mine headframe.

Photo 8 - Historical mining park, Tonopah, Nevada.

Photo 9 - Millers, Nevada.

Photo 10 - Forgotten pumice mine.

Photo 11 - The swamps around the Tinemaha Reservoir.

105

Photo 12 - Salt tramway still hanging more than 100 years later.

Photo 13 - Salt tram tower, high above the Owens Valley.

Photo 14 - Collapsed salt tram tower.

Photo 15 - Home for the night.

Photo 16 - The road to the ghost town of Cerro Gordo.

Photo 17 - Leftover mill on the Jawbone Railroad.

Photo 18 - Spring wild flowers along the railbed.

Photo 19 - Searles Tunnel.

Photo 20 - Entering Armagosa Canyon on the Tonopah and Tidewater Railroad.

Photo 21 - Defunct laundromat at Tecopa Hot Springs.

Photo 22 - A section of the Tonopah and Tidewater Railroad.

Photo 23 - Another section of forgotten railroad.

Photo 24 - Oasis outside Zzyzx, California.

Photo 25 - The "Beach."

Photo 26 - A sit-down to contemplate Soda Dry Lake.

Photo 27 - Orbit tries to steal the past to explain the present on Silver Lake.

Photo 28 - Autumn in Armagosa Canyon.

Photo 29 - Dublin Gulch cliff homes near Shoshone, California.

Photo 30 - Goldwell Open Air Museum, Rhyolite, California.

Photo 31 - Rhyolite jail for canines and humans.

Photo 32 - Death Q cuts across a thirsty dry lake.

Photo 33 - Welcome to Death Valley National Park.

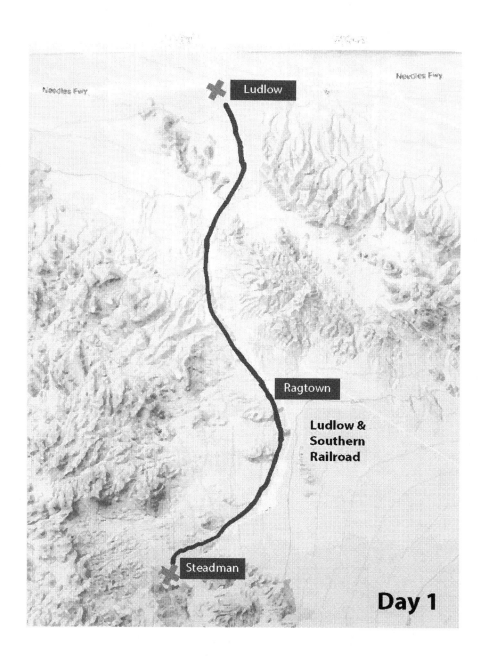

Part Two – The Hike
Day 1

Ludlow-Steadman-Ludlow

Welcome to Ludlow. A town founded in 1882 as a water stop for the Santa Fe Railroad. A minor stumbling issue was the lack of water at the water stop. Wells were dug, but the water located was unacceptable for various reasons. Not a significant problem when you own a railroad. It was arranged for water to be brought in by railroad tank cars. This was fine when Ludlow was a speck. Which it was assumed it would always be, until it sneakingly boomed. At the height of Ludlow's boom, the Santa Fe was delivering 170,000 gallons of water a day. As Ludlow, from the beginning, had plans of its own.

Why did Ludlow boom? Well, sometime in the 1890s, John Sutter, an employee of the Santa Fe railroad, was told to head south into the desert and find some water. Apparently, the Santa Fe was getting tired of the water delivery business. Mr. Sutter headed out. One eye was employed by the Santa Fe and was looking for water. Which it never found. The other eye had Mr. Sutter's best interest in mind. It was looking for gold. Which it did find, along with copper. The rest of that story is coming up.

Suffice it to say that a mine known as the Bagdad Chase got dug. In response, a railroad known as the Ludlow and Southern Railway got built in 1903. The railroad started in Ludlow and ended at that Bagdad Chase mine, some 8 miles away. Ludlow became the shipping point on the Santa Fe for the mine's bonanza. It also became the entertainment center for the miners, as the Bagdad Chase mine was ever so dry. Alcohol and women being banned.

In 1905, the good news continued its flood of Ludlow. Francis Borax Smith rolled into town and announced he was going to build a railroad north to Tonopah, Nevada. Its juncture would also be Ludlow. From a water stop, to a town with three railroads coming and going, the boom was launched. For the next 25 years, prosperity rained on Ludlow. There was a main street lined with general stores, saloons, cafés, bordellos, garages, hotels, pool halls and a dancehall. There was a bathhouse, tennis court, a church and a school. The population climbed to one thousand.

That population swelled on the weekends when people came from the surrounding area to raise hell. Whiskey barrels were occasionally looted from passing trains to lubricate dance parties. Main street paralleled the Santa Fe railroad. Which today is the still-functioning BNSF (Burlington Northern Santa Fe) line. A balloon track (a track shaped like a balloon that allows a train to do a 360° turn) circled the town like an inverted moat. Stand on the vacant Main Street now, next to the BNSF tracks, and try to summon up the action from the crumblings and the dust. It's a challenge.

In those glory days of Ludlow, there were two significant personalities. The Murphy brothers and Ma Preston. The Murphy brothers were the premier capitalists in town. Their real estate holdings included a restaurant, garage, warehouse, and the main general store. The two-story remains of which still stand. If you squint at the store's east wall, the "Murphy Brothers" lettering is still visible. But the Murphy brothers conducted their business in the shadows of Ludlow's dominant personality. A large French woman, born in 1850, who went by Ma Preston. A shrewd businesswoman who owned a saloon, hotel, café, pool hall, and a number of houses.

More than that, Ma had reputations. When she entered a room, conversations altered. To start with, there were rumors of bordello ownership in her past. Had she owned and run them in her day? The historians debate. Was she a shark at poker? Nobody debates that. Did she act as the bouncer in her own saloon? Tossing unruly miners ass over tea kettle onto Main Street? There is the testimony of miners who confirm it. Did she swear like a preacher's son? Worse, they say. Ma bought $20,000 worth of war bonds to finance World War I. Was it the largest donation in all of San Bernardino County? Records indicate it was. When a frog leg shipment to Goldfield missed its connection at Ludlow, it ended up being sold to Ludlowians before it went bad. Instantly, it created an addiction. Did Ma have a hand in the theft of future frog leg shipments? Nobody dared point fingers. On

119

payday, out at the Bagdad Chase mine, was the afternoon train christened, "The Whiskey Special," in her honor? It was.

When Ma got old enough, she developed a nostalgia for France. The Murphy brothers made her a fine offer in 1920 and she took it. Ma returned to France a wealthy woman. She lived on another six years, her dreams full of the dust and the heat. Today, there are but the shattered foundations of Ma Preston's empire. Kick around the sand and you will discover them just north of the BNSF tracks. Ozymandias comes to mind. Ma's laugh, distant.

For those of you who haven't had the pleasure, allow me to introduce Percy Bysshe Shelley and his 1817 poem Ozymandias. For it will come to you often on this hike. It is a poem so great that even the likes of me can appreciate it.

> I met a traveler from an antique land,
> Who said, "Two vast and trunkless legs of stone
> Stand in the desert...Near them, on the sand,
> Half sunk, a shattered visage lies, whose frown,
> And wrinkled lip, and sneer of cold command,
> Tell that its sculptor well those passions read
> Which yet survive, stamped on these lifeless things,
> The hand that mocked them, and the heart that fed;
> And on the pedestal these words appear:
> My name is Ozymandias, King of Kings;
> Look on my Works, ye Mighty, and despair!
> Nothing beside remains. Round the decay
> Of that colossal wreck, boundless and bare
> The lone and level sands stretch far away."

Booms must be accompanied by busts or else they are confusing. There was to be no confusion in Ludlow. The Bagdad Chase petered out, which caused the Ludlow and Southern Railway to do the same in 1916. The Depression of the 30s hit hard. Borax Smith's Tonopah and Tidewater Railroad limped through it but collapsed soon thereafter. The locomotives of the predecessors to the BNSF got stronger and faster, causing them to lose their urge to stop in Ludlow to catch their breath. The town edged toward the ghosts.

Then, a saving second wind. In 1926, Route 66 from Chicago to Los Angeles was completed. Though not fully paved until 1938. Route 66 tracked the BNSF railroad lines from Needles, California to Barstow, California. It passed just north of Ludlow. So, what was left of Ludlow picked up and migrated to Route 66. Cars replaced trains as the new life blood. Main Street was abandoned to the passing locomotives.

Route 66, or the "Mother Road," grabbed America's attention. At first, thanks to its promoters. Among many promotions was sponsorship of a 1928 footrace across the United States. The race course included the entire 2,448 miles of Route 66. Its finish line was Madison Square Garden in New York City. The prize $25,000. A few hundred thousand dollars in today's money. The race gripped the nation. It became known as the "Bunion Derby." The foot race was won by Andy Payne, a Cherokee Indian from Oklahoma. One hundred ninety-nine starters, fifty-five finishers, eighty-four days, 3,400 miles in total. But more importantly, Route 66 entered the American lexicon.

It became a trucking route as trucks began to offer an alternative to the railroads. It became an escape route in the 1930s for farming families fleeing the dust bowl. So much so, that at one point, Los Angeles sent police officers to the Ocean-to-Ocean Bridge at Yuma, Arizona. The Ocean-to-Ocean Bridge is where Route 66 crossed the Colorado River. The police officers were there to stop, or at least slow, this massive internal migration. Many of these farming families were from Oklahoma. Which is how the term "Okies" came to be applied to those California-bound farmers. The Okies that could not show sufficient funds or prove the certainty of a job in California were turned back. Many of those rejected settled in Yuma. Where their neighborhood is still referred to as Okietown.

Tourists also used Route 66 to take in the Southwest from its lanes. TV shows were based on it. Songs were sung. "Get your kicks on Route 66." Lesser known, the "dark desert highway" in the Eagles "Hotel California" is referencing Route 66. The list goes on. And Ludlow was there to service the traffic. If you walk east from town, on the now neglected

Route 66, you will pass a string of forgotten buildings that once catered to migrations.

In 1973, the I 40 freeway was completed. Yet again north of Ludlow. Fortunately, it was constructed using traditional methods, rather than 1963's Federally proposed "Operation Plowshare." Which was a plan to use 22 clean nuclear devices to detonate an I 40 path through the nearby Bristol mountains. The plan took three years of study and testing before the Feds finally gave up on it. A plaque in front of the Ludlow café commemorates this idiocy. Route 66 was decommissioned in 1985, but it really died, at least for Ludlow's purposes, when the I 40 opened its lanes.

What could Ludlow do? It got up and moved again. This time it clustered near the freeway's exits. And its age-old water problem? Solved in the 1960s by a water witcher. Who was commissioned to wander around Ludlow with his dowsing rod. When the tip swung downward, on a patch of desert sand, he declared drinkable water. A well was drilled, and sure enough, there it was. Though its temperature was warm and its taste a little less than memorable. With the discovery, water no longer needed to be hauled from Newberry Springs.

By the 1970s, the town of Ludlow had passed into private ownership. The new owners were of a religious bent and banned the sale of alcohol. A tradition that continues to this day. And to this day, Ludlow soldiers on. Population ten. Its residents operate the still existing businesses.

A Dairy Queen/gas station/minimart lies to the north of I 40 (760-733-4709, M-Th 11a.m. to 9 p.m., F/Sa 11 a.m. to 9:30 p.m., Su 11 a.m. to 9 p.m.).

A 24-hour Chevron gas station/minimart, small motel and the Ludlow Café exist just to the south of I 40. If you stay in the motel, you get free soft drinks at the Chevron minimart. As well, 10% off at the Ludlow café. Motel check-in is at the Chevron minimart (760-733-4338). The café has a fine breakfast (760-733-4501, 6 a.m. to 5:30 p.m., seven days a week).

LUDLOW	
1. Food Supply	Yes
2. Restaurant	Yes
3. Water	Yes
4. Hotel	Yes
5. Beer	No
6. Pool Table	No
7. ATM	Yes
8. Post Office	No
9. Casino	No

Be sure to check out the old photos of heyday Ludlow on the café walls. As well as the mining relics out front. Which include a wooden water pipe with coiled metal wire casing. If you have time, take it and wander around Ludlow. It is photogenic to the extreme. The cemetery on the southern side of the tracks, with its unnamed wooden crosses reaches hard for the heart. If interested in Patton's old camp, head directly north on the dirt road that passes the DQ. In less than a mile, you'll see lined rocks stretching out on both sides of the road.

Significant modern events in Ludlow include the aforementioned Big Barbecue of 2014. In 2008, a 5.1 earthquake centered in Ludlow further collapsed the remnants of the Murphy brothers and Ma Preston. But if I were a betting man, I would never wager against Ludlow. For it is a town that refuses steadfastly to arrive at its obituary. One wonders, what will cause the fourth boom? The only thing certain is, it will be to the north.

Let's take a look at the Bagdad Chase mine, which will be your Day One destination. As already mentioned, John Sutter found gold when he was looking for water in the 1890s. He collected some samples and hauled them to a mill. The results promised profit. Sutter must've smiled hard as he turned his eye toward horizon events. First, though, he had to dot his T's. He began staking claims to the surrounding area. (This is done by marking the four corners of the claim with wooden posts. Then filing your paperwork with the proper mining district. The established practice was to put a copy of the claim in a glass jar. The glass jar was then placed at the base of one of the posts. Usually concealed in the rocks supporting the post. As a hiker passes along the Q, they will still see these posts in remoter areas. Though most of the glass jars are long gone.) Once the claims were staked, Mr. Sutter hired some miners and got down to the mining business.

With time, a camp began to grow around the mine. At first it was named Bagdad. Which became Rochester. Then Copenhagen. And ended up with the name Steadman. Sutter's problem was getting the ore to a mill. There wasn't enough water on site to build a mill so Sutter was forced to transport it to Barstow for that milling. This was profit problematic. When Sutter tired of bumping into limits, he took the usual route. Which was selling out to the usual group of wealthy New York businessmen. The price? $100,000.

Fortune preferred the new owners. Not long after their purchase, a new rich gold vein was discovered. The assay reports indicated $17,000 per 1000 tons of ore. Those kinds of numbers made people rich. Jigs were danced in New York. Decisions were made to increase profits yet more. If the mill couldn't come to the gold, then transport to the mill must become more efficient. In 1901, construction of the Ludlow and Southern Railway began between Ludlow and Steadman. A distance of eight miles. By 1903, it was ready for operation. With the railroad, the mine flourished. At its height, 115 men worked there. Two hundred tons of ore a day were removed. Gold, silver and copper were produced. By 1910, $4.5 million in gold had been mined. The economic panic of 1907, which closed half the mines in California and Nevada, didn't even touch the Bagdad Chase.

There often seems to be a quirk in historical tales. The Bagdad Chase was no exception. Its quirk was no women of the soiled dove variety (which was the euphemism of the day for a prostitute), no booze and no gambling. Which to a miner might translate into low entertainment. To prevent smuggling, the mine manager made his brother first engineer on the Ludlow and Southern's locomotive. Eventually, the mine manager discovered that Scandinavians responded best to this enforced morality. A bonus was their advanced work ethic. He hired so many that Steadman became known as Copenhagen for a number of years. But even Scandinavians need a little fun now and then.

So, fun presented the miners with two options. The first was Ragtown. A tent encampment some three miles from the Bagdad Chase. Ragtown was a popular name of the era for a red-light district. It also indicated a portability. The rags of Ragtown referred to the tents. If a ragtown achieved a level of permanence and respectability it garnered a proper town name. The Bagdad Chase's Ragtown was a 40-minute walk from the mine. A party was always available. The miner was free to return to work when he could or had to. A supposed marker, and some rusted cans are all that remains of Ragtown today. Though we never found the marker. The second option was riding into Ludlow on the train. A 40-minute ride but a forced early return according to the train's schedule. Flat cars available for the unconscious. (A flat car is a rail car without the walls or roof. In other words, a floor with wheels.)

The early years were the glory years for the Bagdad Chase. Production slowly and steadily declined with the passage of time. Various owners gave it a shot, but the gold did not produce in sufficient quantities to encourage dedication. By 1916, the Ludlow and Southern had thrown in the towel because of a lack of demand. At its height, Steadman had over 40 buildings, including a post office and school. There were four vertical mineshafts of between 120 feet and 400 feet. One tunnel reached 450 feet into the mountain. In all, there were several thousand feet of connecting tunnels.

Over the succeeding years, the mine opened and closed multiple times. In World War II, it was one of only four gold mines in California allowed to stay open. (For the most part, gold was considered noncritical to the war effort.) From 1972 to 1975, open pit mining was tried. Nothing lasted. But over the years, money was made. Between 1880 and 1970, the Bagdad Chase accounted for half of all the gold mined in San Bernardino County. In 1993, the mine shut down for good. News of imminent reopening always on the tongues of optimists. Nowadays, vandals have destroyed all of the buildings in Steadman. Though there are plenty of mining artifacts and foundations about. Rumors persist that the vertical mineshafts were once used as launching silos for U.S. government rockets.

Now let's turn to the Ludlow and Southern Railroad itself. The Ludlow and Southern was built to haul ore. Nothing else. To make it beautiful was not a priority. Construction of the railbed commenced in 1901. By 1902, the railbed was complete. Keeping costs down was a particularly interesting subject to the New York capitalists. Which is why, when it came to buying rail, they bought used. When it came to buying the railcars and locomotives, used once again. When it came to wages, low by the day's standards, $4.50 a day for the engineer, $3.00 a day for the fireman. Three dollars a day to shovel coal into a furnace, when the outside temperature might exceed 115° and drinkable water was at a premium. Perhaps, the definition of an honest wage.

Of course, rent and purchases at the company store were removed from those wages. Rent ran between $8 and $12 a month. When it came time to maintain the railroad and its train, once again, costs were kept low. Any band-aid would suffice. The Ludlow and Southern developed a reputation as a second-rate railroad. But the ore moved and that is all that counted in New York.

By 1903, the railroad was open for business. Eight miles of track were put in service at a construction cost of $80,000. Gravity a friend. Steadman was 600 feet higher than Ludlow. So, when the load was heavy with ore, seven of the eight miles were downhill. Easing the strain on the locomotives and saving money. Ore one way north, supplies and water for Steadman on the return trip. Average speed 12 mph for the 40-minute trip each way. A telephone line tracked the rails. Unfortunately, the route to pursue gravity also tracked dry riverbeds and washes. Flooding was a constant threat. For a sudden cloudburst on sandy soil often translated into a flash flood and damaged railbeds. Maintenance was an ongoing battle.

The Ludlow and Southern Railroad saved a lot of money for its owners. Saved money is made money. For 10 years, the Ludlow and Southern did just that. But its fate was tied to the mine. Steadily declining revenue at the mine no longer justified the cost and maintenance of a railroad. In 1916, the decision was made to shut down operations. The locomotives and railcars were stored in Steadman. The track was kept functional so that the mine caretaker could move back-and-forth between Steadman and Ludlow on a rail tramcar. Its temporary theft for joyrides a constant issue.

126

This remained the state of affairs until 1932. In that year, an avenging rain came down. The resulting flood took out a mile of track. On an 8-mile line that is a significant loss. Neither the will, nor the finances existed to rebuild. Later, in the same year, a fire burned down the engine house and cooked the best remaining locomotive. Fate was explaining itself. The white flag was run up. The rails were pulled up in 1938 and sold to a sugar plantation in the Philippines. As were the remaining locomotive and rail-cars.

A footnote. In 1944–45, World War II was trying to wind down. General MacArthur was fulfilling his promise to return to the Philippines and recapture it from the Japanese. American forces overran a sugar plantation during their advance across the Philippines. There, they found the Ludlow and Southern still chugging along. Today, the railbed directly out of Ludlow is in poor to non-existent shape. That is because it crosses a broad floodplain. As the railbed nears Steadman, it markedly improves.

Now that your head is stuffed with history, it's time to loosen up the legs.

Day One is a 16-mile jaunt to the Bagdad Chase mine. Since it is an out-and-back, one's pack can be left in Ludlow. Take plenty of water as there is only one sketchy source along the entire route. Have a bulk up breakfast in the Ludlow café, then exit onto Route 66. A hiker is now standing on the nub of the Q descender. At the end of the day, the descender will be in the bag.

Exiting the cafe turn right (east on Route 66). Then take your first right, just past the old service station, onto the Bagdad Chase Road. This road will lead you back to the BNSF tracks away from the I 40. Shortly, you will come to an earthen looking dam. This was actually part of the Tonopah and Tidewater's balloon track. Next, on your right you will observe the old school. Dogs will indicate their displeasure at your passing from behind a fence. Followed by the two-story Murphy Brother's store, also on your right. The store much damaged by earthquakes.

Cross the tracks, with appropriate caution, when you come to them. Immediately turn right after the tracks and walk to the last sugar shack on your left. The shack is exhausted and leaning hard. It may be collapsed by the time you get there. Two dead cars are parked in front. Inside, the skeleton of a pool table is sheltered. When looking south, note two metal storage tanks to your right and an earthen berm to your left. The berm is the start of the Ludlow and Southern. Stand on it. Get the feel of its narrow, elevated walkway/railbed. For the next 811 miles, you will be looking for exactly this.

Unfortunately, this railbed does not go far. Floods have pretty much eradicated this initial section. You could follow it for some distance. Eventually, you would come to a washed-out bridge. Then all traces fade, and one ends up meandering here and there for way too long. Searching for railroad ties long washed away. Much easier, after investigating the sugar shack, to head back east along the tracks toward the other buildings. You will pass the Red Dog Mine buildings, then a row of 70s era derelict vehicles, before finally arriving at the cemetery. Pay your respects if inclined. Then follow the dirt road that heads south toward the two big towers on the hill. Stay with the dirt road as it veers right and climbs out of the valley. The power lines will remain on your left. Continue following the dirt road until you come to a pass. At some point, along this stretch, the Ludlow and Southern has joined.

At the high point of the pass, you will see a park road marker with number NS7823 on it. Within a few feet of that marker you will observe the berm of   a railbed curving to the right. Say hello once again to the Ludlow and Southern. Follow the railbed down the wash. Along the way, you will pass through an old fence. There are a lot of old cans here. Perhaps this was Ragtown. The railbed disappears and reappears repeatedly. Subjected to nature's flooding. Gradually the outline of the railbed becomes stronger.

After you have hiked about a mile from the pass, the Ludlow and Southern begins a turn to the right. The ground pipes you see on your far left are gas lines. At this point you'll be approaching a modern metal mine headframe on your right. As well as an older mine, on the side of the hill, to your left. The railbed takes a hard right turn up the wash toward the metal headframe. Though it is hard to follow at this point.

At the last minute, the Ludlow and Southern turns left away from the metal headframe and begins a swing toward the mountains. Now the railbed is easy to follow. Telegraph/telephone pole stumps and poles begin to appear along the railbed. Another mine appears on a hill to your left. Other vertical surface mines pop up near the tracks. Dug by independent miners hoping for a strike near the convenience of transport. Eventually, the Bagdad Chase Mine/Steadman comes into view center stage.

As you approach the mine, in the far distance to the left, you will see the 100,000-year-old Amboy Crater. An extinct cinder cone style volcano. The BNSF tracks that pass through Ludlow also swing by this crater. Nearby is the town of Amboy, population two. But, at one time, a bit of a boomtown itself due to Route 66 splitting the town. The I 40 replacement freeway, passing far to the north, murdered the town's aspirations. Many buildings remain from those Route 66 glory days including a very charismatic, very closed, 50s style motel. Two remotely and bizarrely placed Chinese stone dragons guard the eastern approach to the town. At various times, the entire town has been up for sale. It is now owned by a chicken restaurant entrepreneur.

A classic Amboy tale. One morning, at the height of Amboy's boom, a resident went out onto his front porch and saw black smoke billowing out of Amboy crater. Word spread quickly. "She's going to blow!" Panic ensued. Evacuations began. Word was sent to Ludlow, where evacuations were also commenced. Before things got too far out of hand, someone thought to go out and have a look. Peering down from the rim revealed a large pile of burning tires. The pranksters were eventually determined to be some seniors from a not-so-distant high school. Apparently, the sheriff was unable to keep a straight face during their dressing down.

As you close in on the Bagdad Chase, note a small railspur to the left. Follow it to its ending point on the side of the hill. You will pass foundations, metal shop shavings and a round wooden tank base. Retrace back to the Ludlow and Southern and turn left. The railbed carries you right into the heart of the Bagdad Chase mine. Lots of mine leftovers lay about. Keep your eyes peeled for a long, cylindrical metal tank. The tank has a top and there's water inside. Perhaps, if treated, drinkable in an emergency. Another water tank with spray-painted warnings has been routinely assaulted with gunfire. Two quasi-swimming pools are also on site. One has water. A good place to soak a hat for the return trip, should the sun warrant.

No evidence of rockets or their launching pads were come across. Some notable sights are an old truck, plenty of foundations and multiple mines across the face of the slopes. When explored out, retrace your steps back along the descender to Ludlow for a cold...Coke. And please do not disturb anything at the mine, nor take any souvenirs.

The Ludlow and Southern makes a good warm-up hike. It will also hone your railbed finding skills. For multiple reasons, the railbeds around Ludlow are hard to follow. So, if you master them, the rest of the Q should be child's play. And once you're heading north out of Ludlow, the Q becomes much easier to pursue.

Thanks to Henry Peacor who accompanied me on this section of frustrated railbed searching. Henry is a fearless hiker unfamiliar with his limits. He handled his dehydration very well.

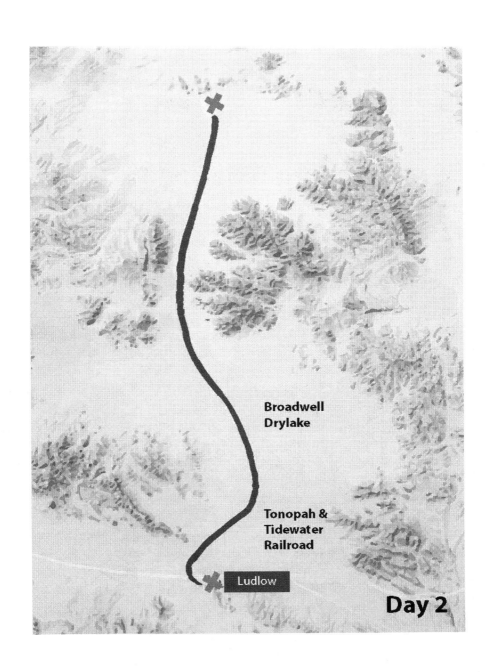

Broadwell
Drylake

Tonopah &
Tidewater
Railroad

Ludlow

Day 2

131

Day 2

Ludlow-Broadwell-Mesquite

Another Ludlow morning. Before setting off north on the Tonopah and Tidewater railroad (TTR) here's a little background to inform your steps. The railroad you're tackling was the TTR. The founding personality was Francis Marion "Borax" Smith. The two are inextricably intertwined. The man came first. Smith was born in Wisconsin in 1846. He grew up, went to college and then, like many of his generation, sought his fortune out west. He started as a woodcutter in Columbus, Nevada. A location you will ultimately hike by. While working there, he discovered a deposit of borax at Marietta, Nevada. Cleverly, he put together some financing and jumped into the business that would give him his nickname. And never looked back.

Soon, he controlled borax works throughout the Mojave Desert. His financing, always creative. Some would say questionable. At one point, he tried and failed to corner the U.S. borax market. In 1890, he consolidated all of his borax holdings into the Pacific Coast Borax company (PCB.) Later he would combine with a British borax company to become one of the world's first multinational corporations. Smith was ambitious and intelligent. Qualities that would take a man far in those days. And they did.

Transport of borax was always Borax Smith's biggest challenge. The strikes were remote and the ore heavy. In the late 1800s, Smith used 20-mule teams to haul the ore from the Death Valley region to the railhead at Mojave, California. (Go Mustangs!) A ten-day, one-way trip. The 20-mule teams eventually became the logo for the PCB. The teams were a fascinating slice of Americana. The wagons were, and are, the largest ever pulled by horse or mule. The wheels alone were over seven feet high and eight inches wide. There were two wagons in each team. Each wagon was capable of holding ten short tons of ore. Which was half the capacity of a typical railcar of the day. There was also a 1,200-gallon water tank wagon attached to the rear. Fully loaded with borax, the entire operation weighed 73,000 pounds or 36 ½ tons.

All of this was pulled by 18 mules and two horses. Which works out to be an incredible 3,650 lbs. per mule/horse. The horses were physically stronger and could handle the distraction of being next to the wagon. Which is why they were placed there. But the mules were smarter and mentally tougher. Motivation was provided by a driver with a whip. The whip had a six-foot-long handle and a 22-foot-long lash. Direction of travel was maintained by a 120-foot-long jerk line. A steady pull indicated a left turn. A series of sharp jerks suggested a right turn. Wherever the lead mules went, so followed the others. The other crew member, known as a swamper, rode in the second wagon. Their job was to apply the brakes when needed. Teams coming from Death Valley hauled ore. Those going toward the valley carried supplies that were stored along the way for the return trip. (The only remaining, original, 20-mule team wagon is on display near the Death Valley Visitor Center.)

Twenty million pounds of ore was shipped in this manner. And the hauling method was reliable. Never once, in all those years, did a wagon breakdown. In fact, in 1917, mules pulled an original wagon from Oakland, California to New York City for the World's Fair. Once again, without incident. But they were slow. Their top range was 17 miles a day. Which is a lot slower than you. So, Borax Smith tried out a series of steam tractors as mule substitutes. The steam tractors were faster but incredibly unreliable. And it was too much for Smith to take when he saw mules rescuing the tractors time after time. So, Smith decided to try his hand at building a short railroad to haul borax near Barstow, California. It worked. Which got him to thinking sometime later on. Why not a longer railroad to his Death Valley borax mines?

And so, Smith's TTR grew from a seed, or a botfly if you will. Its initial plan grandiose. A railroad from Tonopah, Nevada, with its great mining strikes, to Tidewater. Which is a colloquial term for the Pacific Ocean at San Diego. In the end, the railroad came up short in both directions. Once Smith had some financing in place, he settled on a plan to build a railroad out of Las Vegas, Nevada to Beatty, Nevada. He planned to connect to his borax mines along the way. Mr. Smith chose Las Vegas because he could tie into the new Los Angeles and Salt Lake Railroad that passed through Las Vegas. That way his borax could go east or west. To tie in at

Las Vegas, Borax Smith needed an OK from the all-powerful Senator William Clark. (Present day Las Vegas is in Clark County, which was named after the not-always-honest Senator.)

Senator Clark had widespread investments in Nevada and saw a railroad connecting with the mines around Tonopah to be to his benefit. He bestowed his blessing. Borax Smith went to work in 1905. After 12 miles of railbed were graded, Senator Clark changed his mind. He had arrived at the revelation that it might be better if he owned the railroad. His blessing withdrew. Smith was without recourse. You didn't challenge Senator Clark in Nevada. Greatly annoyed, Smith turned his back on Las Vegas and looked elsewhere.

After a search, Smith settled on Ludlow, California. It was 50 miles longer, but what's a railroad builder to do? At Ludlow, Smith could tie into the ATSF (Atchison Topeka Santa Fe railroad which later morphed into the BNSF railroad) lines that would give him access to the Los Angeles market and facilities. From Ludlow, his railroad could make its way north to his original target of Tonopah, Nevada. The race began. Senator Clark, with his Las Vegas and Tonopah Railroad out of Las Vegas and a 12-mile head start. And to the west, Borax Smith out of Ludlow with his TTR. Financed, in part, by the sale of those 12 graded miles to Senator Clark. Both planned standard gauge lines.

The TTR began construction in November 1905. The rails headed north, past Broadwell Dry Lake. Followed by the crossing of the Los Angeles and Salt Lake line at Crucero. The negotiations for permission to cross consumed four months. By March 1906, Silver Lake had been reached. And by May, 75 miles of line had been laid, which found the TTR construction advanced point just north of Dumont. But then it started getting hot. Unfortunately, this coincided with the most difficult phase of construction. The 12-mile climb through uninviting Armagosa Canyon. Fifteen trestles would need to be built, as well as three bridges. There would also be much dynamiting and infilling. All in an area prone to flash floods and extreme heat. At times, as high as 130 degrees. What to do but to get to work? It would turn out to be an easy decision to make in a pleasant office. On the ground, those 12 miles consumed a year and cost $55,000 a mile.

The problems were many, their solutions varied. Building uphill through a canyon is just one long battle with gravity. So, the builders took the old Arab adage "the enemy of my enemy is my friend" to heart. Instead of building uphill, they flipped and built downhill. Trains would bring the supplies as far as they could from the south. At the terminus point, crews would load supplies onto wagons. And haul them to the high point of Armagosa Canyon at Tecopa. From there the crews worked backwards and downhill. Gravity defeated.

Another problem was labor. Many Anglo workers didn't like the extreme heat. Others caught the mining bug going around. Which is understandable. Strike it rich or a dollar an hour? Logically, a collected paycheck became a ticket out of the canyon for many. Various alternative employment schemes were tried. Some with success, such as bringing in Mexican workers. Some, such as bringing in Japanese workers, without. Though, on paper, that decision appeared promising. As the Japanese had a reputation as hard workers. So, 100 were brought in during the bowels of summer. It was a rolling disaster. Only one of the hundred could speak English. Their rice-based diet a near impossibility in this remote location. On the first day, most reported sick. On the second day, the Japanese tied their mess tent off using the rails. Then went in to eat. When the train arrived, the ropes were severed with the predictable pandemonium. On the third day, only 17 men reported to work. Half swung a pick, while the other half mouth-sprayed water on their partner as they labored in the heat. The fourth day was July 4th. By noon, the entire Japanese workforce was patriotically hammered from smuggled sake. On the fifth day, the Japanese were fired en masse. Experiment over.

In the end, Armagosa Canyon was conquered, and on May 2, 1907, the TTR moved north. By now, there were 1000 workers advancing the line. In August, the line reached Death Valley Junction. It must've felt like working inside a stoked furnace. Finally, on October 30, 1907, the TTR reached Gold Center. Just a couple of miles south of Beatty, which was the preliminary goal. Unfortunately, by this time, the financial crisis of 1907 was roaring. To be on the safe side, Smith stopped at Gold Center. And rented continuation into Beatty and Rhyolite on the Bullfrog and Goldfield

Railroad. Reaching Tonopah was shelved altogether. Though access to Tonopah was achieved by renting space on other railroads.

In November, freight service commenced. And by December, passenger service was up and running. This included Pullman sleeping cars from Los Angeles to Tonopah. Total train time from Ludlow to Beatty was about eight hours to cover the 169 miles. For passengers coming from Los Angeles to Beatty, the TTR route was five hours faster than following the LVT route via Las Vegas. And the race? Senator Clark's Las Vegas and Tonopah Railroad won when it reached Beatty in October 1906. A full year ahead of Borax Smith's TTR. The LVT may have won the battle, but they lost the war. As, ultimately, the TTR outlasted the LVT and even took over some of their route.

In the early years of operation, the TTR made money. As well, it accomplished Borax Smith's goal of transporting his borax to mill at a much-reduced rate. But in 1928, there was a dramatic shift. Massive new and easily accessible deposits of borax were discovered at present day Boron. In 1929, the stock market crashed. Then the Depression began. Passengers on the TTR declined rapidly. The PCB closed its Death Valley mines. All of which were coffin nails for the TTR.

The TTR found itself running out of uses. The transport of tourists to Death Valley was tried, but the automobile and the Depression eventually quashed this possibility. In 1931, Borax Smith died. The corporate officers of the PCB weren't nearly as emotionally attached to the TTR as its creator had been. They began looking for ways to cut TTR expenses.

First, they reduced the frequency of trains. Then in 1933, they abandoned the section between Ludlow and Crucero. Thus, making Crucero the southernmost point on the TTR. There, freight and passengers, for the time being, could still make it to Los Angeles. Maintenance costs on the aging line continued to rise. While revenue did the opposite. In 1938, a six-day storm took out five miles of TTR track. The expensive repairs took several weeks and further sapped the will of the PCB to continue. The TTR was worn out. Locals nicknamed it the "Tired and Tardy." Debt piled up. In 1939, PCB had had enough. They applied for abandonment. And in 1940, it was granted. In 1942, the rails were torn up for the needs of World War II. The TTR was just 33 years old when she was laid to rest.

One of the finer troubadour documentarians of the old west, Ken Graydon, had this to say about the TTR in one of his songs: "Tonopah and Tidewater."

As railroads go, it wasn't very much. They called it the Nevada
   Short Line
Couple hundred miles of fifty-two-pound rail
They laid 'em out in nineteen nine
Haulin' ore from the mines and food for the miners And people
   where they wanted to go
It's the Tonopah and Tidewater blowin' for a curve Rollin' down
   the grade into Bullfrog
From Ludlow north to the Tonopah terminal
And back across the desert floor
Haulin' ice for the beer from the Gold Center brewery In between
   the loads of ore.
'Til the mines played out and the people moved on And there
   wasn't anyone to hear
When the Tonopah and Tidewater whistled for the curve Pullin' up
   the grade out of Bullfrog.
Now it's eighty years later. The rails are all gone They tore them
   up in World War Two
And most of the towns on the timetable schedule Have gone into
   memory too
But sometimes at night when the moon's ridin' full And the breeze
   plays gentle on the hill
You'll hear the echo of an engine with a full head of steam
   Blowin' down the wind out of Bullfrog
It's the Tonopah and Tidewater with a full head of steam Tryin' to
   raise the ghosts out of Bullfrog
'Cause when the ore gives out and the boom goes bust The people
   leave and they never come back
Now the depot up in Rhyolite's a solitary memory Of steam and
   smoke and long vanished track
          (*Printed with permission from Phee Sherline.*)

Now it is time for you to tackle the O of the Q. Your next reliable water is 33 miles away in Zzyzx. (The greatest hangman word ever created.)

137

Your next reliable food is 42 miles away in Baker. Head back to the BNSF tracks. Turn right, before the tracks on old Main Street, just after passing the Murphy Brothers store. Immediately, past the store, your eyes are greeted by a large pile of railroad ties on your right.

Behind them lies the remains of the TTR station and maintenance yard. Note the concrete pits that allowed access to the undercarriages of the railcars. A kiln with firebricks is also visible. Imagine the swirl of activity that once was. Find ties moving west. Follow the multiple lines until they coalesce into one. See the raised bed curving right and north? That's the TTR. Stop and look around. If you pull off the Q, in 811 miles, you'll be standing right here again. Regardless, good on you for taking a forgotten route in life. You're off!

Follow the curve toward the I 40. Pass a washed-out section. Rejoin the railbed. Get the hang of that. Continue along the curve past the old water tanks plopped directly on the TTR. Cross defunct Route 66. Dead end at the tractor-trailer advertisement. The I 40 slicing our fine railbed unceremoniously. Turn right and follow the freeway for about one hundred yards. To the right is Route 66 and a shattered bridge. Turn left at the wash and pass under the I 40 bridge. Immediately you come to a tarmac road. Turn left until opposite the tractor-trailer advertisement. Looking north you will spot the raised railbed and some ties. Follow the dirt track toward the railbed. Once on the railbed, keep an eye out for clue relics.

The railbed begins a big, sweeping curve to the east. Complete a religious cross with the north-south dirt road you come to. Once across the dirt road, the railbed bends north towards the large dry lake bed. This is Broadwell Dry Lake. You are going downhill towards it, as all dry lakes are located in the lowest possible point of any valley. Don't despair if the railbed comes and goes due to past flooding. This is one of the most difficult sections to follow on the whole Q. But Broadwell Dry Lake is your destination, so getting lost would be an extreme challenge. A north-south line halving the dry lake will begin to take shape, depending on the quality of your vision. That is the TTR and your destination. Shoot for it, and all will be fine.

Once on the lake, there is a reasonable chance of some small puddles. Wouldn't count on it though. Lunch at the north end of Broadwell is a worthy goal. For perspective purposes, Broadwell Dry Lake is 4.3 miles long. It was named for a local prospector. The Cody Mountains are to your left and the Bristol Mountains to your right. Can you imagine nuking those textured Bristol Mountains to build a freeway?

Past Broadwell Dry Lake the railbed gradually climbs to a small pass. To your left, in the hills, are the remnants of the Old Dominion mine. At the top of the small pass, you will find the slight remains of Broadwell. The first stop on the northbound TTR. A few foundations and the usual rusting cans honor the spot.

You have now walked 12.68 miles since leaving Ludlow. Continue north. Ties start to reappear. For a distance, the railbed parallels a dirt road. Then it passes some power lines. Eventually, a sign announces you have entered the Mojave Preserve. Fires are not permitted but backcountry camping without a permit is.

Pass a few old cars, dead without burial. At times, you're walking on the railbed, and at other times, next to it. Depends on your convenience. For whatever reason, there is an abundance of tarantulas in this area. Or at least there was. Harmless and cute. The ties become thicker and thicker. When the sun gets tired it is time to call the day. Pick your spot 200 feet off the railbed. Ours was in a field of scattered bones. The journey to sleep accompanied by the melancholy train sounds of the distant Union Pacific line.

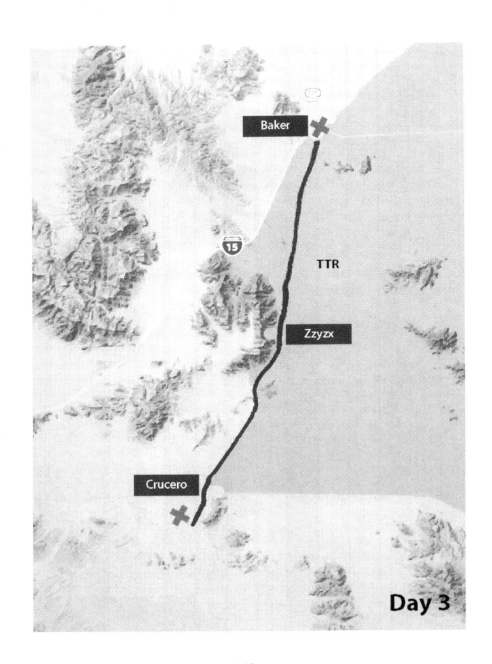

Baker

TTR

Zzyzx

Crucero

Day 3

Day 3

Crucero-Zzyzx-Baker

Arise to the deafening collision of the three main components of a desert morning: clarity, quiet and stillness. Welcome them and the introspection they bring. Try allowing this introspection to run amok as the days of the hike pass. Who knows, maybe by the Q's end, you will arrive at the end of yourself as well.

The railbed begins a turn to the east. Pass some makeshift stoves made with firebrick. Purpose unknown. The next landmark is a solitary cast-iron bathtub. Purpose known. It sits gracefully near some tamarisk trees. An unavoidable dry soak and photo. The TTR bears down on the east-west, still functioning, Union Pacific (UP) Railroad. The squash you see everywhere are called coyote melons. As discussed, much less than edible. The TTR crosses the Union Pacific at Crucero, some 26 miles from Ludlow. The Mesquite Hills are just to your right. Along the UP tracks to the east lies Las Vegas, to the west, Los Angeles.

Crucero, which is the Spanish word for crossing, was a busy place once. Now all that remains are some foundations and fallen cottonwoods. Crucero was where a crossing diamond was installed that allowed the north-south TTR to cross the east-west UP. The switching was accomplished using a series of control levers. A TTR flagman was in place in the early years. A green flag meant clear, a red flag meant the UP line was blocked. There were mistakes.

In 1915, a UP train derailed, allegedly after the TTR flagman failed his duty. Eventually, a two-story control tower and a station house were built. A post office operated here until 1943. Over time, a small village formed around the station. A school, operating out of an old railcar, began in 1931. An adorable photo, from another age, exists of a student wearing a dunce cap and sitting in front of the Crucero school. As said, in 1933, Crucero became the southern terminus of the TTR. After the TTR gave up, Crucero's sole reason for existence evaporated. The village was abandoned to its current state of vanishment.

Follow the railbed north. Immediately after Crucero, the impressive government fence marking the Mojave preserve makes an appearance on your right. This fence is your guide through this section, because you are entering, "The Beach." A combination of wind patterns and mountains sometimes puts the desert in a mood to pile up sand. Especially when the windborne sand runs into a mountain and somersaults backward. Enough grains and dunes appear. This is one of those spots. Accept the beach. Take off your shoes and go for a stroll of half steps. The fence is key. Keep it just to your right and all will be fine. This is because, at least for this stretch, the government used the TTR as its property line. The TTR will surface, then submerge, depending on the sand. Its ballast rocks and bridge foundations often visible. Generally speaking, the TTR will be just to your left. You will be hiking down a sand track that splits the fence and the TTR.

Keep sand-marching. Pass a blackened area, where an ATV burned to death. The fence always to the right. To your far right, the massive Kelso dunes appear. Third tallest in North America. Near their base is the little used town of Kelso. A water stop, prior to the Cima Grade climb, on the Santa Fe (now United Pacific) Railroad. The center of which is the once abandoned, Santa Fe mission style rail depot. At one time, for sale for one dollar and a commitment to restore. A gorgeous and charismatic building.

A building that was once the center of my plans to import camels and camel drivers from India to provide camel treks across the dunes. Tourists would stay in the depot/hotel and go for a multi-day camel trek across the dunes. Lawrence of Arabia fantasies for a price. The depot ownership mine for that one dollar and some minor restoration cost. With dreams of wealth in my eyes, I went to India. Where I located the necessary personalities and camels. Including one fascinating individual who could speak six languages but thought he could ride his camels overland to the U.S. Upon return to the States, I learned the Federal government had beat me to ownership.

The restored depot is now headquarters for the Mojave National Preserve. Which includes the Kelso Dunes. The restoration of the depot cost $8 million, which, perhaps, was out of my projected budget range. Kelso is well worth a future trip. The sand dune climb is monstrous. Running down its steep face, after attaining the peak, a joyous reconnection with childhood. On maps, the Kelso Sand Dunes are marked as the Devil's Playground. And alas, are minus camels.

Eventually, arrive at a genuine oasis. Massive cottonwoods shade perfectly. A couch and tree swing are in residence. There is a large fire pit. A TTR informational plaque is on the north side of the oasis. I defy you not to take a break. After which, continue north along the government fence. The TTR begins to curve northeast. In this area, you pass over the old Spanish wagon trail. The sand's stranglehold begins to weaken. Soon the railbed cuts through a mountain, then a hill. Followed by a long hug of the Springer Mountains to your left. With time, the palms of the Zzyzx Health Resort begin to pop up. In its day, the TTR cut right through the resort. In the middle of which was a TTR stop.

As you enter the outskirts of the resort, you will first come to some old corrals made from TTR ties. Then you pass some outbuildings. Eventually you arrive at the resort itself. Water is available here. At the heart of the resort, now a desert research station, is a palm-lined pond. This is where the TTR stopped. In the pond, resident ducks exude contentment. At the east end, a game of horseshoes beckons. Have a stroll around. The abandoned swimming pool and soak tubs on the edge of the dry lake are quite nostalgic. It has been 33 miles since Ludlow.

You're now standing in downtown Zzyzx. But it wasn't always Zzyzx. In the late 1800s it was Soda, named after the waterless Soda Lake to your east. A mill operated here. Prior to that, Camp Soda Springs was a military outpost to guard the Spanish Trail. And of course, before all of that, Native Americans used it as a drinking water source. You are part of a long tradition of passersby.

After the 1800s, things grew quiet for a while at Soda Springs, until the Springers showed up in 1944. Dr. and Mrs. Springer were what could comfortably be termed self-promoters. Others, less kind, might say fraudsters. Their M.O. was combining religion and health. Somehow, they landed in Soda Springs and saw Shangri-La. They filed a mining claim on over 12,000 acres and set to work building a religious center and health resort.

Dr. Springer named it the Zzyzx Mineral Springs and Health Resort. His radio show trumpeted the health and spiritual benefits of a stay at the resort. "Come to Zzyzx, the last word in health and English!" Dr. Springer had a flair for the catchy phrase. And people came in droves in the 60s and 70s. To soak in the healing waters of the natural hot springs and stroll along the natural palm lined oasis. To partake of Dr. Springer's bottled cures. And to hear the word of God. Which the good doctor provided.

The fly flapping around in the ointment? It was all bogus. Except the word of God part, which is beyond my pay grade to dispute. The rest, well... the palm trees were planted, the oasis was dug, the cures were snake oil and the natural hot springs were heated by a boiler. No different than a hot bath at home. Bogus or not, many came away feeling the better for the visit. The illusion of cure perhaps more beneficial than the cure itself.

Dr. Springer also sold his cures through the mail. The money sources competed to swell the Springer's bank account. But with money comes attention, specifically Federal attention. The mail order cures got him into trouble with the FDA. And a disinclination to pay his taxes brought the IRS to his door. It didn't end well. Dr. Springer saw some jail time and an end to the Zzyzx Health Resort. The "King of Quacks," as the American Medical Association dubbed Dr. Springer, practiced no more.

These days the oasis pond is full of chubb (tiny endangered fish). And Zzyzx functions as a desert research station. Scientists are occasionally around, having a look at the desert. Other than that, all is quiet. On a side note, a number of films have been made with Zzyzx as the backdrop. Including 'Zzyzx Road,' a film in which a number of people meet unfortunate ends. It is reportedly the lowest grossing film in movie history. The other film is titled 'Zzyzx.' In this film, a number of people also meet unfortunate ends. Ironically, both films were made in 2006.

The TTR leaves Zzyzx near the pond (Lake Tundee) and the Boulevard of Dreams. It heads north across Soda Dry Lake. At the departure point the railbed has been flattened into a dirt road. But it gradually narrows back into a railbed. Pass a couple of miniature weather stations. Old wooden drainage culverts begin to appear. Spikes you will see are in advanced states of disintegration due to the high alkaline content of the lake.

If it is a day of headwinds, as it was for us, the hike across Soda Dry Lake can be psychologically traumatizing. That is because Baker's skyline is quickly visible. Touchable in fact. Only it never gets closer. Never. My guess would have been one hour to Baker from Zzyzx based on my eyesight. Had I owned a TTR timetable at the time, I would have known one hour was optimistic for 8.44 miles. Have a look for yourself. Does it look like 8.44 miles?

Soda Dry Lake is the dead end of the normally dry Mojave river. Occasionally there is water in the lake, but it quickly evaporates to salt. Which is still mined from the lake. Around 10,000 years ago, Soda Lake was a much larger lake known as Lake Mojave. It was a greener time. Wooly mammoths, giant sloths and sabretooth cats roamed. But climates change. These days green is in short supply. Now all is white. Native Americans were there for thousands of years to witness the transition. Then missionaries, traders, dreamers and scientists. Now you. Soda Lake an always mute witness, whether dry or wet.

At 42 miles from Ludlow you butt into the I 15 Freeway, built unappreciatively across the TTR railbed. Baker is finally yours. Turn right and then turn left to go under the I 15 bridge. Immediately, you are on Main Street, Baker, California (population 730, elevation 930 feet). Baker was founded in 1908, as a water stop on the TTR. These days it tries to snare the tourists headed to, or returning from, Las Vegas. It sits at the base of the Baker grade. A long climb on I 15 up to a pass that is famous for overwhelming car air-conditioners. For Baker is hot. A high of 125° has been recorded here. The tall needle you've been tracking for eight miles is the world's tallest thermometer at 134 feet high. Logically it is capped at 134°, the world's hottest temperature ever recorded. That cooking occurred in near-by Death Valley. Once again, a validation of why we hike the Q in winter.

Turn right on Main Street and sit down at the mandatory Mad Greek Diner (open 24 hours). No idea what it is doing here but thankful its owners chose Baker. Great food and featured on multiple foodie shows. Definitely the only baklava shakes for 1,000,000 miles in any direction. Also in town, is the Alien Fresh Jerky store and several small markets for re-supplies. As is a close-up of that tall, functioning thermometer. Continuing east on Main Street, past the Mad Greek, is the Wills Fargo hotel (72252 Baker Blvd., 760-733-4477). The Wills Fargo is the only functioning hotel in town. Sixty dollars a night for two people. A rainy night quickly pushed us in its direction. The Baker Post Office is at 1 Lakeview Dr (760-733-4373, M - F 8 to 12, 1 to 4:30, closed Saturdays). To camp, simply head out of town in a northerly direction.

BAKER		
1.	Food Supply	Yes
2.	Restaurant	Yes
3.	Water	Yes
4.	Hotel	Yes
5.	Beer	Yes
6.	Pool Table	No
7.	ATM	Yes
8.	Post Office	Yes
9.	Casino	No

The next limited food selection is 46 miles away in Tecopa Hot Springs, California. Though there are snacks in 40 miles at the China Ranch. The next significant food market is in Shoshone, 56 miles down the tracks. The next water is the Armagosa River in about 36 miles. Keep in mind, "armagosa" means bitter in Spanish, and the water is not recommended for drinking. The next tap water is at the China Ranch.

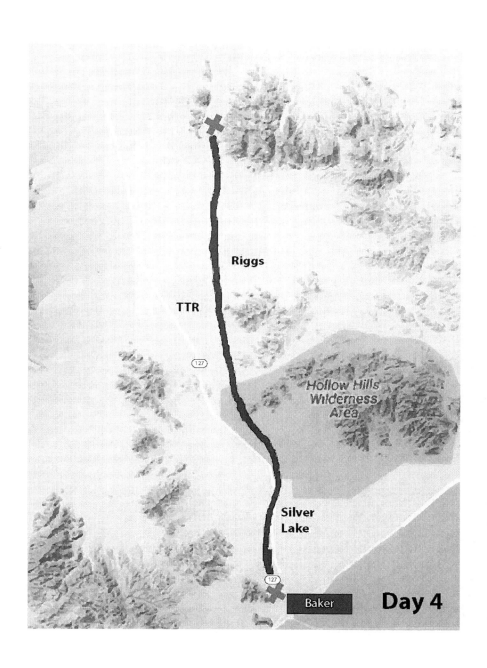

Riggs

TTR

127

Hollow Hills
Wilderness
Area

Silver
Lake

127

Baker

Day 4

147

Day 4

Baker-Silver Lake-Riggs

If you overnighted at the Wills Fargo hotel, head west on Main Street a couple of blocks to the Shell station. In front of the Shell station, you'll see the TTR emerge triumphantly from under the I 15. Like your dog when its thrilled to see you. Go to the rear of the Shell station and begin on the railbed. Follow the faint path as it wraps around the container yard to the left. Pass by a number of wrecked military vehicles. Head east toward the dry Mojave riverbed where the TTR crosses on a phantom bridge. Foundations still visible. Once across, the railbed drifts northeast. A number of buildings will be to your right. You will pass under some power lines and then approach the planeless airport.

The railbed passes to the right of the airport in a narrow corridor between the airport and the 127. The 127 is known as the Death Valley Highway. The TTR parallels the 127 until they both reach Silver (Dry) Lake. The 127 wisely veers east to skirt the shoreline. The TTR fears no dry lake and barrels straight ahead. The railbed across is impossible to miss, silhouetted as it is against the white backdrop. However, the locals deemed it a silver backdrop, hence the name.

Silver Lake was, at one time, part of the greater, 10,000-year-old, Lake Mojave. In periods of heavy rain, the Mojave River respects its name and starts flowing. Which can result in waves on Silver Lake. This last happened in 2005. In 1938 and 1939, sanctioned speedboat races were held on the lake. Put that one in your vision and see it. As you approach the northern end of Silver Lake, the railbed steers right to the ghosted ruins of what was once the town of Silver Lake.

Silver Lake used to reside directly on the lakebed. But a massive flood in 1915 convinced the town fathers that a beach location was preferable. So, they packed up and moved to the present location. Your morning efforts have brought you 7.68 miles from Baker. Silver Lake was created in 1906 as a water stop on the TTR. It lived for 34 years before peacefully passing away in 1940. A victim of the shutdown TTR. Its population peaked in 1907, at just over 100 souls. Though on weekends, the population would swell as miners and ranchers made their way to this entertainment center. Saloons competed for business. There was a bordello, telegraph office and rail depot. Another Ma, named Ma Palmer, held wild dances in her tented dancehall. The town newspaper was called, "The Miner."

Now, all that remains are adobe ruins, a few structures, the usual debris and a cemetery. And one more thing. Curious mounds of white powder. Pick up a pinch and rub it between your fingers. It's talc, which is used to manufacture tiles, pottery and paint. And of course, keeping baby butts rash free. It has also been known to be added to certain street drugs to artificially increase their value. The large talc mine was three miles away. But the scales, the remnants of which are still visible, were here in Silver Lake. As was the method to get the talc to market.

Living in Silver Lake must've been tough. I don't know when or if, electricity reached the town. But air-conditioning never did. The heat would have boiled. It certainly got to a few residents. In the October 8-11, 1932 edition, the LA Times ran a story about a Mr. Kruthaup. A Silver Lake station agent and assistant postmaster who was not fond of conditions at his workplace. His daily duties involved spending a couple of hours filling the water tank out in the oppressive heat. Then a train would come along and drain his work. Back out into the heat he would go. It quickly became too much. When the calendar reached his 13th day of employment, Mr. Kruthaup arrived at the end of his tolerance. He softened his exit by stealing $88,000 in money orders and $1,978 in cash. He then embarked on a first-class world tour. Presumably of locales that did not resemble Silver Lake. Upon return to the States, he was sentenced to three years in prison. Perhaps a fair-trade dollar value. His statement in court was, "I just had to get out of that hole."

Nowadays, Silver Lake is watched over solemnly by a 24-hour guard. Each guard working a 12-hour shift. The other 12 hours spent at the Wills Fargo hotel in Baker. This goes on 365 days a year. A Paul Auster novel in action. What are they guarding? Sitting at the junction of 127 and a side dirt road? I asked. Turns out, it's not the ruins of Silver Lake, but a massive back-up generator some three miles down the side road. The power company apparently didn't want their generator carted away. The guard we spoke to spent his hours listening to financial news and crafting his retirement. He was thrilled to learn he'd been sitting on top of a railroad staring at a ghost town all these years. We departed and left him to his job. His smile still visible from a long way off.

The railbed from Silver Lake parallels the west side of the under-travelled 127 for a while, before passing over to the east side. Take a side trip to the ghost boat on the dry lake. Irony in photography. Eventually, the 127 veers to the left, while the TTR does the same to the right. Lots of cellphone signal here, if inclined. The desert becomes progressively remote. Arrive at the water stop of Riggs, 17 miles from Baker. A large vertical pipe with water in it still exists here. Though it's drinkability is debatable, as we pulled a dead fox out of it.

This is a remote section of the TTR. Lots of 100-year-old debris lies about. Also, plenty of ties and washouts impede your way. Your bearing heading is the split in the mountains dead ahead. Your right view is peppered with mines. Also on your right, is Kingston Peak at 7,335 feet. Kingston Peak is forested and climbable. Known to be home to awe views, golden eagles and supposedly gila monsters. Gila monsters are very large, very rare, poisonous lizards. As previously mentioned, in all my years of desert hiking, I have never seen one in the wild.

Pass yet more talc loading docks as you begin a climb to the split. To your left are the Avawatz Mountains. There, a husband-and-wife team once operated a silver mine so rich that they only needed to work it six months a year. The other half they travelled the planet. Financed by their strike. They built a vault-like door inside their mine, to protect the silver vein while they were on the road.

When you reach the destination mountain, you will pass a mine on the left. Then you will see a second mine halfway up the slopes on your left. At its base is a dirt road. Leave the railbed and walk over to the road. Follow it to the left. It begins a short climb past some tailings and foundations. Continue to follow the road for 100 yards, as it transforms into a path. All the while tracking the curving base of the mountain.

Follow the path yet another 100 yards or so, until you stumble upon a sweet little mine. Lots of mining debris clogs the gulley in front of it. At the top of the gulley is an old fridge encased in rock. A semi-modern root cellar. The mine only goes back about 30 feet. Side trails radiate out in different directions.

This is a great example of a small exploratory mining operation. It is also a fine place to spend the night. Especially on a rainy night, with a mine acting as a protective roof. Note the talc mine high in the opposite Valjean Hills. Its loading dock down near the TTR. Please leave your sleeping mine the way you found it for the others to come.

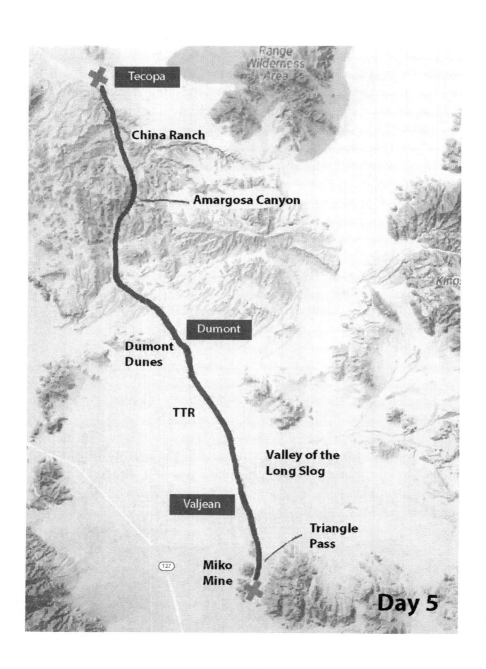

Tecopa

China Ranch

Amargosa Canyon

Dumont

Dumont
Dunes

TTR

Valley of the
Long Slog

Valjean

Triangle
Pass

127

Miko
Mine

Day 5

152

Day 5

Valjean-Dumont-China Ranch-Tecopa

Return to the TTR and head north. Climb to the rail cut at Triangle Pass. Named for the obvious rock. Just before the pass take a detour over to Miko Mine (pronounced Meeko) on your left. The mine is in excellent shape and well worth a look. An interesting fact about underground mines: they are the same temperature year-round. And that temperature is the average of one year's combined surface temperature above the mine. Which makes them warm in winter and cool in summer. But also unique to their area.

Once you clear Triangle Pass, a large valley opens up. As does a long straight descent. Otherwise known as the "Valley of the Long Slog." Pass Valjean, which is a settlement of cans 23 miles from Baker. The Dumont Dunes become part of the horizon on your left. These particular dunes are given over to off roaders. Keep hiking. Rest. Get up and hike. You know the routine.

Another cable fence appears on your right. This one is for the Armagosa Canyon Dumont Dunes natural area. Once again, the fence is your guide. The sands are back. The railbed drowns and revives often, struggling for future survival. Stick with the fence. Which the sands of Dumont are also trying to submerge. At one point, a railbed heads east. This is most probably the Dumont Siding. Ignore it. Stick with the fence. Eventually, you emerge from the sands and begin crossing increasingly broader and deeper canyons. With each canyon, your respect increases. All these filled-in dirt bridges were done with wagons and shovel work.

It was in this area, on January 14, 1921, that a work train and a regularly scheduled train collided. The work train was headed southbound and called in to central dispatch to confirm the location of the regular northbound train. The dispatcher said it was "ten minutes" late out of Silver Lake. The work train heard "one hour and ten minutes" late. Figuring they had plenty of time to get to the siding at Dumont, the work train proceeded.

153

The work train's locomotive was pushing three flat cars in front of it. Three workers were riding on one of the flatcars. Their time on this earth wasn't long. Meanwhile the northbound regular train was speeding north, probably trying to make up those lost ten minutes. Unrecognized suspense built. Smoke from the smokestacks was the first indication of the collision to come. Brakes were pulled, but it was too late. The northbound locomotive climbed over the flat cars on impact. The three workers never had a chance. When the two engineers met amongst the wreckage, the southbound engineer reportedly said, "What the hell are you doing on time?"

The trail at this point provides an excellent opportunity to practice your detour skills, as washouts are common. A series of rail cuts through the hills lead to a hard right. A sign announces a dead end. Not applicable to Q hikers. Some beauty coming up. After passing the sign, you emerge into the impressively wide Armagosa Canyon. To construct the TTR through this canyon took its builders over a year. At a cost of $55,000 per mile. The ribbon of water at centerpoint is the Armagosa River.

The Armagosa River is 200 miles long but only actually flows on the surface for 25 miles. Twenty of those miles are in Armagosa Canyon. The river starts in the plains above Beatty, Nevada and then follows a long U-shape before ending at Badwater, Death Valley. Badwater, at 266 feet below sea level is the lowest point in North America. Though it flows for 200 miles, the Armagosa actually ends about 50 miles from where it started, geographically speaking. But rivers are not crows. Sometimes it takes them a while to arrive at their destiny.

The Armagosa Canyon has been manufacturing history for a long time. A woolly mammoth skeleton was found in its cliffs. Native Americans started living on its banks 10,000 years ago. In the 1800s, the old Spanish Trail paralleled the Armagosa. The old Spanish Trail was the principal route from Santa Fe, New Mexico to Los Angeles for early travelers. Prior to that, explorers described the Armagosa Canyon in unflattering terms. "Meanest looking country I ever saw, fit for nothing but hobgoblins to live at." And, "Never during the whole of the route have I seen a place so sterile and the curse of God so visibly manifested as I did here. It seems as though God's strong displeasure has been exhibited." Perhaps the explorers were not strong admirers of the desert in general.

154

These days the canyon acts as a bird magnet. Though choked with tamarisk, it still attracts a wildly divergent bird population. Over 250 bird species have been spotted within its walls.

The railbed hugs the right side of the canyon. Gradually it lowers to the canyon floor. Where it passes the remnants of Sperry, yet another stop on the TTR. Sperry is 36 miles from Baker. Eventually the railbed crosses to the left side of the canyon. Views grow in pleasure. The foliage takes on a metallic orange hue, if the season is in the mood. A stone palisade cliff fortress presents to your right.

There is a lot of debris on the railbed, but it is easily navigable. Then a pause where the large rail bridge has been assisted downstream. No choice but to descend into the tamarisks and weave your way to the opposite bank. Wading through the river is not daunting. Anywhere else the Armagosa would be termed a stream. But the tamarisks will make you work for yardage.

Reconnect with the TTR by climbing out of the tamarisks to the opposite bridge foundation. This is the spot I had my, "It's a railroad!" epiphany. Follow the TTR along the cliff cuts and through fallen rocks. Rainbow colors abound. Arrive at the only functioning wooden rail bridge on the entire TTR. Its surface is covered in dirt so you have to pay attention to spot it. It's worth a close inspection. Note the mines on the other side of the canyon.

Right after the wooden bridge, you will see a man-made line of rocks cutting across the railbed. There is also a fine sitting rock. Look to the left and you will see a cairn. The cairn indicates a trail down to the riverbed. If you continue straight you will reach a washout cliff that is not passable. Instead, descend along the left trail to the river and turn right. Follow the trail along the right riverbank. Eventually, you dead end at a side wash. This is the wash that made the TTR not passable. Turn right and head up the wash for about 25 yards. There you will see some cairns that lead you to a climb-out point on the left. This is where you rejoin the TTR. Follow the railbed up the canyon, until it begins a swing to the left. You will come to another man-made line of rocks directing you right. Across the river valley you can see a white talc dump.

That talc dump is where you will be rejoining the TTR. The TTR originally curved to that white talc dump. But Willow Creek, the Armagosa tributary in front of you, obliterated the bridge. These days, getting through the thick tamarisks is a miserable endeavor. Much better to divert to China Ranch for a break of banana bread and date shakes.

To get to China Ranch follow the trail that leads to the right, at the man-made line of rocks. Follow the trail cairns up canyon. Eventually, the trail crosses Willow Creek through a tunnel of tamarisk and then joins another trail. Turn right at that juncture. Shortly, you will arrive at China Ranch, after passing some discarded vehicles from a bygone era.

China Ranch is just off the old Spanish Trail. As stated earlier, in the 1800s, this was the route between Santa Fe and Los Angeles. The route was unpopular because it was very indirect. It preferred to wander haphazardly from one waterhole to the next, rather than pursue a straight line. For its first 20 years, the trail was primarily used by horse thieves. They would steal horses from well-stocked California ranches and drive them to New Mexico. Where horse stock was in short supply and prices were high. By the time the rustlers reached the area around China Ranch, the pursuing posse had usually given up. One such raid, in 1840, netted over 3,000 horses. Half of whom were dead by the time the horse thieves arrived at China Ranch. Driven way too hard to escape a posse. But the raid still netted $100,000.

The legendary duo of John Fremont and Kit Carson passed through in 1843. Near here they ran into some Indians returning from a raid on Tecopa. Two Indians were killed in the resulting shootout.

In 1849, the California gold rush began. Many 49ers made their way west on the old Spanish Trail. Their days and nights filled with dreams of the wealth that was soon theirs to be.

China Ranch itself came into existence sometime in the late 1880s, as did the name. A Chinese or Tibetan gentleman, named either Quon Sing or Ah Foo, tired of the mining life. He decided to put down roots in the green area around Willow Creek. The gentleman planted crops and raised meat. Selling his excess to nearby mines. Things went well until 1900. That is when one Mr. Morrison, who perhaps was not a gentleman, showed up and ran the Asian gentleman farmer off at gunpoint. But as a courtesy he kept the name. As have all subsequent owners.

In the 1920s, date palms were planted. Half the palms are male and don't do much other than fertilize; a commonly heard human opinion. Each female palm produces between 100 and 300 pounds of dates annually. Which the owners turn into a variety of things that are lovely to put into your mouth after a long hike. Including that date shake. The date snack store and gift shop are open 9 to 5 every day but Christmas.

The 26-mile Tecopa Railroad side hike is coming up in five miles. If necessary, stock up on food supplies at China Ranch. For though there are limited food supplies   at Tecopa Hot Springs, there are no food supplies in Tecopa proper. The hot springs are two miles past Tecopa proper. And the side hike begins in Tecopa proper. To get food supplies at the hot springs for the side hike would necessitate a four-mile round-trip back-track. The bonus of those extra miles, though, is two nights of soaking in the hot springs. There is a small museum onsite at the China Ranch. Enjoy your date shake, as I did, which is how I found the TTR, which is how...

When you tire of your rest, make your way back down the trail to the TTR. You are walking on a wye track. (A triangle-shaped branch line leading off the main rail line. It allows a train to leave and rejoin the main line going in either direction. There is a switch at all three corners.) This particular wye track climbed steeply 1.3 miles to the Acme talc mine above China Ranch. At least once, a train coming down from Acme lost control and ended up in a heap.

The wye operated until 1919, when a cave-in killed the talc mine owner's two sons. In his grief, he closed the mine. As you descend, you will first pass a small cemetery for humans and then one for classic cars. Stay to the right side of Willow Creek as you descend. Pass the juncture where you joined the trail after crossing Willow Creek. Stay to the right. Shortly, you will pass a beautiful stone building with wood floors. The stones are hand carved tufa (a form of limestone) blocks. There is possibly a root cellar (a hole in the ground where produce was stored, prior to the arrival of refrigeration) out back. In literature, the stone building is variously described as a residence, assay office, saloon or stagecoach station.

After the multi-talented building, the trail climbs onto the ridge and ends just above the earlier spotted white talc mound.

Here was Morrison. A no-more village. Named after the guy who practiced personal eminent domain on the original Asian inhabitant of China Ranch. The only remaining relic is the talc loading chute for the TTR railcars below.

Walk down the slope and rejoin the TTR. Turn right toward Tecopa, which is 4.65 miles away. The railbed climbs steadily up the canyon. Eventually, you will run into dense vegetation that suffocates the TTR. Fortunately, a trail with trail signs has been built to detour around the section. Just veer to the right and you will encounter it. Stick with the trail. At times, it will be on the TTR. At times, not. Keep climbing. Suddenly you will hear water. This is caused by the strongly flowing spring at Red Cut. Coloration obvious.

It was here that a large landslide of spring-water-saturated earth once blocked both the cut and the TTR. Everything in the southbound train had to be hand carried across the slide. Then reloaded into a second train brought from Ludlow. Today, the Red Cut Spring has turned the cut into a swamp. Rationally, the trail climbs up around the swamp to the left. With time and perseverance, the railbed and trail climb out of Armagosa Canyon and flatten on a plain. From there, it is a straight shot into Tecopa. Right before entering Tecopa, note the remains of the Tecopa crushing mill. It is located on top a small hill on your left. Then enter Tecopa proper from the south, just as the TTR did.

The first Tecopa building on your right is the Tecopa jail. Check out the beds made in the same fashion as the cages. Even dreams were imprisoned. The building free of walls on your left is the old community center. Both of these buildings stand on former Main Street, which crossed the TTR vertically. Continue on the railbed/road toward a blocking fence. The old railcar on the right was the former TTR freight house at Silver Lake. Moved here after Silver Lake closed its doors.

Where the railbed dead ends at the fence, turn left. Where you will find an exit. Walk over to the front of the Tecopa Post Office (M to F, 8 to 12, 1:30 to 2:30, closed Sa/Su, 760-852-4314). You are now in Tecopa proper. Tecopa proper is owned by John Zellhoefer. You might bump into him at the craft beer place he owns near the post office. Ask about his plans for a shotgun golf course. If you desire a roof over your head in Tecopa proper, check out the Ranch House Inn and Hostel (760-852-4580, 2001 Old Spanish Trails Hwy).

In front of the post office, note two wood ties still in the parking lot, that are TTR leftovers. The railbed crosses the Spanish Trails Highway in front of you. All two of its lanes. It then passes through a very marshy area, before pushing across the semi dry lake bed. Its route marked by telephone poles. After the dry lake, the TTR crosses the road to Shoshone. This short section is a slog. Much better to take a short alternate. Turn right on Spanish Trails Highway for 100 yards. Then turn left on your old friend, the 127, at the clump of cottonwoods. Follow this road for just under two miles, until you reach body luxury at Tecopa Hot Springs.

But, I get ahead of myself. First the 26-mile side journey on the Tecopa Railroad.

So, find yourself a place to sleep around Tecopa.

The Tecopa Railroad hike starts from the center of Tecopa, in front of the post office. In the alternate, you can continue on to the hot springs and spend the night there. The next morning backtrack to the Tecopa Post Office to begin the Tecopa Railroad side hike.

Tecopa was the crossroads of the TTR and the Tecopa Railroad. The town moved here from another location when the TTR arrived in 1907. Its namesake was Chief Tecopa, a local Paiute Indian leader. Tecopa flourished for a while when the mines were active. But when the mines passed away, Tecopa faded.

These days some Tecopa buildings are inhabited and some aren't. There is a bar in the village center, but I've never had the good fortune to find its good doors open. The bar's website is deathvalleybrewing.com (open F-Su, 12 to 6 and holiday Mondays, 760-852-4273). The beers and homemade fries get very favorable reviews. Cash only. (Just as this book was going to print, a small, two-table restaurant opened its doors in Tecopa proper. My mother dined there and gave it multiple thumbs up. It is located next to the craft beer bar.)

As mentioned, the Tecopa Hot Springs are two miles down the road. They are little known in Southern Nevada. But for those who do know, there is much love. A small village of loyal adherents has built up around the springs. This has always pretty much been the case. For thousands of years, Native Americans used the same waters. These days the hot springs are owned by Inyo County. The County, in turn, grants a concession to a private business to operate the hot spring baths. The baths are sex segregated. Though a private bath for couples or families is available for rent. To maintain the purity of the water, bathers must first shower, then enter the water nude. The atmosphere is very relaxed.

Testaments to the healing powers of the naturally hot water are biblical in volume. I don't disagree. Admission is seven dollars per person for a 12-hour block of time. The baths are open 24 hours. Limited food supplies are available in the Tecopa Trading Post next to the hot springs. This is the only place to buy food in both Tecopas. The trading post is open 10 to 6, seven days a week (760-852-4329). And it must be mentioned, the ice cream selection is stunning. The next food market is in Shoshone, ten miles down the TTR. Surrounding the hot springs is that small village.

The county has issued a limited number of private hot spring permits. Thus, many of the houses in the area have their own hot spring baths. As do a couple of campgrounds, people with rooms to rent, and a small motel. The main campground is directly across the street from the county baths. It also has a cafeteria. Inquire as to the method of dining there. Directly south of the county baths is Pastels Bistro (760-852-4420). A fine dining experience in my non-refined opinion. A motel, camping area and hot springs are attached to the restaurant. Recent news is that a pizza restaurant is about to open just north of the county baths. The Second Wind Hot Water Retreat (27 Elias Way, 760-752-4115) has rooms and private tubs. The reviews are flattering.

Alternatively, there is Delights Hot Springs Resort (800-854-5007). Delights, just north of the public hot springs, has cabins with attached hot spring baths.

Delights was started in the 1950s by a man named Elias. Who was crippled by arthritis to the point that death was imminent. Convinced by a friend to try out Tecopa, he left Los Angeles with little to lose. The good ending found Elias cured by the Tecopa waters. Elias decided to stay on.

Bizarrely, he was able to purchase the future resort land from the Federals using Civil War script his grandfather received after the Civil War. An obscure federal law permitting this was still on the books in those days.

To round off the offerings of Tecopa Hot Springs, a masseuse is in residence.

If you are tight on funds, there is a small rustic spring just east of town. Admission free. Locally known as Hepatitis Springs. Your call. I certainly survived.

To get there, head north out of town. Until you come to the impossibly photogenic, sinking, Quonset-housed laundromat. The requisite sinking vintage truck positioned nearby. Turn right just after the laundromat and follow the dirt road east out of the valley, until you come to the bath in a clump of tamarisks.

TECOPA PROPER – TECOPA HOT SPRINGS		
1.	Food Supply	Yes in Tecopa Hot Springs
2.	Restaurant	Yes in both
3.	Water	Yes in both
4.	Hotel	Yes in both
5.	Beer	Yes in Tecopa proper
6.	Pool Table	No
7.	ATM	No
8.	Post Office	Yes in Tecopa proper
9.	Casino	No

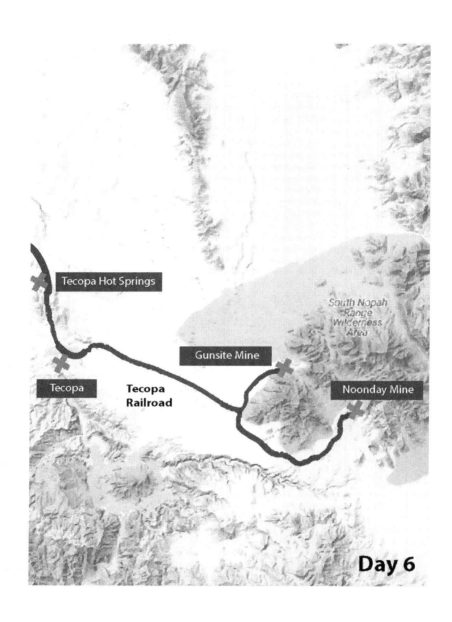

Tecopa Hot Springs

South Nopah Range Wilderness Area

Gunsite Mine

Tecopa

Tecopa Railroad

Noonday Mine

Day 6

Day 6

Tecopa-Noonday Mine-Gunsite Mine-Tecopa Hot Springs

Stand in front of the Tecopa Post Office. For something new and completely different, why not go for a hike? Your destination mines are great testimonials to past efforts. Keep in mind there is no food or water along this 26-mile roundtrip hike. Also keep in mind it is an out and back hike. Thus, ditching your main pack is an option.

Walk out to Spanish Trails Highway and turn right. Walk toward the triangle of trees. The Armagosa river is to your rear. For the first mile, the Tecopa Railroad is under asphalt. Follow the road out of town past the old motel, then the tiny school. Pass Cemetery Road. Not long after, the road begins a bend to the right. Look to your left. You will see a raised railbed moving east. Your clue is a telephone pole centered directly on the railbed. Bid adios to pavement and jump on the Tecopa railbed. Ties are thick along this section.

You are now hiking on the Tecopa Railroad. The railroad's sole purpose was to service the mines of the Nopah Range. Which is the string of mountains you are currently walking towards. Mining began in the Nopahs around 1875. The valuable ore found there was laden with silver and lead. The problem was processing the ore. There were two choices. Mill it onsite or haul it out. The original owners tried the onsite option, but the process expenses outweighed the profits. For a while, the mines operated in fits and starts. By 1906, $300,000 worth of ore had been extracted. All without profit.

The owner was fed up and only too happy to sell to a syndicate known as the Tecopa Consolidated Mining Company (TCM). The purchase price was $175,000. The TCM suspected a windfall potential in the group of mines they brought. So much so, that they decided to double down and build a railroad to connect with the TTR. Only, Borax Smith wouldn't let them. He wanted to build the railroad himself. Potential profit motivated both parties. For a year, there was a standoff. TCM held back shipping ore and threatened to build a large mill that would greatly reduce TTR shipping profits. Smith, for his part, asked the reasonable question. How long can you hold off shipping your ore? In the end, TCM won the poker hand.

In 1909, TCM began construction on the 13-mile spur. One hundred men, and even more mules, started grading. The construction went along smoothly, but there was friction between the two project managers. Matters came to a head when one of the managers announced he was quitting. The other manager got drunk in response and attempted to dissuade the quitter. By reasonably shooting him in the ear with a Derringer pistol. Construction proceeded despite the discord. By 1910, the railroad was ready to go.

Unfortunately, a contract was signed for ambitious ore delivery that could not be met. This resulted in the mines being shut down for two years. But in 1912, business affairs were straightened out, and the mines were back in business. As was the Tecopa Railroad.

The first serious wreck occurred on July 5, 1913 when the engineer lost control of the downhill train. It cost him his life. The brakeman and firemen jumped to survival. By 1928, the mines were played out and the Tecopa Railroad shut down for good. Much of its stock ended up as scrap metal for World War II. Though, it is believed the rails were pulled up prior to that.

Back to the hike. Eventually, the railbed re-crosses the Spanish Trails Highway. You're headed directly toward the black Nopah Range in front of you. The railbed is easy to follow. Close in on the mountains. Just as you arrive at the base of the mountains you reach a wye. One branch goes left, one right. The branches are triangle-capped at the top by a connector line, allowing trains to move in six possible directions. The left branch is for the Gunsight Mine. The right for the Noonday Mine. Take the right.

The right branch hugs the mountain before arriving at an expansive valley. A wide dirt road, with accompanying power lines, moves up the center of the valley. The railbed has ambitions to bring religion to the road by crossing it. But no missionary work today. About a half mile short of the dirt road, the Tecopa Railroad veers to the left. This is easy to miss. So, I've marked it with a cairn. (If you miss the railbed veering left, don't

164

worry. Just continue to the wide dirt road. There you will see a large paved area. Perhaps a runway at one time. Turn left on the wide dirt road and proceed up the valley. Rejoin the directions at "Turn left on the dirt road continuing uphill." Which is contained in the following paragraph.)

Turn left at the cairn. After about 200 yards, the railbed becomes distinctive again. Follow the railbed uphill toward the head of the valley. Note the 100-year-old tent rock outlines still visible. Eventually, the railbed rejoins the wide dirt road. This point is also marked by a cairn. Turn left on the dirt road continuing uphill. Note the cairn location for your return journey. The Tecopa railbed is under the dirt road at this point. Climb over the valley high point.

A side valley of massive headframes presents. In order, from the left, the Noonday, Columbia, and War Eagle mines. Mining for lead and silver took place here from the late 1800s until 1957. In all, four million dollars' worth was removed. As you approach the side valley, veer left on a narrow semi-paved road.

You're back on the railbed again. The desert radiates out from you. Follow the railbed up the left side of the valley. With time, the railbed begins a long right curve across the valley. Its path drawn toward the tailings of the Noonday mine. Once the tailings are reached, follow the dirt road left, up a sharp climb along the ridgeline. Note the tramline coming down from the Noonday mine.

Continue up the ridgeline on the dirt road, passing ruins in various states of surrender. The extent of foundations indicates a once busy mine. Most of the foundations are from the single men's camp. The married men's camp was elsewhere. These camps were lived in until 1957. Climb to the ruined car. Follow the dirt road as it veers right across the shallow valley. Stay on the path that climbs to the mines. Mineshafts are plentiful. Though the rock looks unstable, which explains the extensive wood cross bracing visible.

Also plentiful is the opportunity for exploration. But entering these mines looks unforgiving. Climb to the main Noonday Mine above the large wooden chute. The chute has a large pulley at its base that pulled carts up and down the tram. The tramway inner works are still evident and quite impressive. Note the massive tram shaft descending into the mountain behind the wooden chute.

Just past the wooden chute is an interesting horizontal mineshaft with curving baby-gauge rails. Its structure appears more stable. Tailings are dispersed widely in front of the mine entrance. In practice, these tailings were brought out in ore carts pushed by men. When the edge of the tailings was reached, the carts were dumped by releasing their gates. And that is how the tailings expanded, one cart at a time. In some mines, horses and mules were used to pull the ore and tailing carts. Some of these unfortunate creatures lived their entire lives underground, gradually becoming blind.

Once your explorations are over at the Noonday, follow the tramway down to its base. Then turn left and make your way to the tailings pile. Note the storage lockers built into the hillside. Continue along the track as it keeps its hill elevation. Arrive at a smaller mine with a wood dumping chute. Outstanding views can be had of the Columbia mine with its headframe in the foreground and the mighty War Eagle mine in the distance. The War Eagle's wooden chute appears massive from your angle.

Scout the terrain that leads to these two mines. Quickly lose your enthusiasm for hiking there. Check out the antique tire dump in the valley below. Rolling exhausted tires downhill apparently passed for entertainment in those distant days. Retrace your steps back to the railbed. Leave the three mines behind. Keep retracing all the way back to the original wye. The wye will be on your left. Mark the wye in your mind as you will be returning to it.

Once past the wye, you're on the railbed toward the Gunsight mine. Climb steadily along the base of the Nopah Mountains. Enjoy a sudden man-made rail elevation grab. This section was so challenging to locomotives that only a couple of railcars could be pulled up at a time. Then the railbed cuts through solid rock as it veers right. After the turn, a visual bonanza as the lead and silver producing Gunsight mine makes its appearance. A haunting air hangs heavy over the mine. Especially in the grayness of dusk.

The Gunsight mine was in operation from 1912 to 1928. The mine is equipped with another large upper chute and tram. Though much of the tram has collapsed. Its extensive stone foundational work testifies to the effort involved in building the tram. At the bottom of the tram is the collapsed lower cable tower. Now just confused wood. Climb up to the stonework, above the main wooden chute. Remnants of a house are visible from this vantage point. The tailings are extensive, indicating a deep mine. Explorations of this area were cut short by increasing rain and approaching darkness. As always stay out, stay alive.

Retreat to Tecopa by following your footsteps back to the wye and turning right. Toes to heels. When you arrive at the trees of Tecopa proper, turn right on the 127 and head for a deserved soak. Once again thanks to Henry Peacor, who accompanied me on this side leg. A fearless hiker unfamiliar with his limits. He handled his hypothermia well. As did the curative hot springs, which rescued him from that hypothermia.

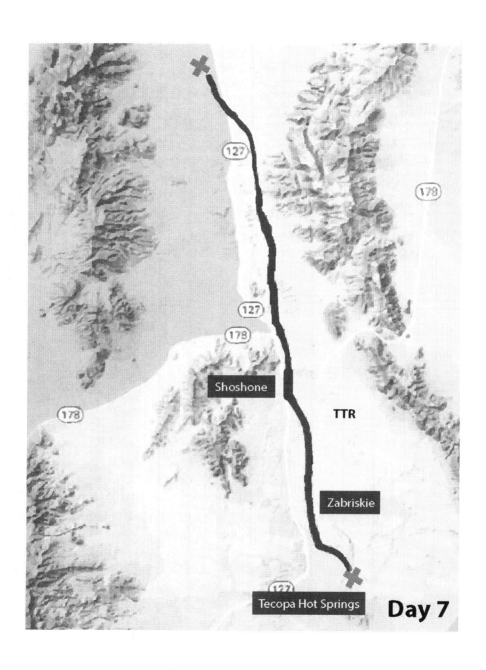

127

178

127

178

Shoshone

TTR

178

Zabriskie

127

Tecopa Hot Springs

Day 7

Day 7

Tecopa Hot Springs-Zabriskie-Shoshone-Near Eagle Mountain

Morning and time to move on. But maybe one last soak. Depart Tecopa Hot Springs by following the 127 north out of town. Pass the old laundromat on your right. Hike about a mile along the road, as it skirts the shore of the dry lake. In the process, pass reed beds and Grimshaw Lake. Where a mastodon skeleton was once discovered. At the top of the dry lake, you will see old telephone and telegraph poles crossing the road. This is where you turn right onto the TTR. Food and water are only nine miles away in Shoshone. The railbed is evident. Follow it north up the river valley.

A couple of miles out of Tecopa Hot Springs brings you to Zabriskie. Once a small town. Though you'll need imagination goggles. Here, in the earliest of days, twenty-mule teams hauled borax to the recently arrived rail depot. As well, it was a collection point for other types of ore from Death Valley. The wagons returning to their mining camps, laden with supplies that kept the mines functioning. There was a freight depot, post office, telegraph office and store here. Now history is reduced to cans and the ruins of a borax loading ramp. Not far to the west, lie the bleached remains of the Armagosa Borax Works.

Continue north along the TTR railbed. Note that it parallels the old telephone/telegraph poles. The poles are your compass and guide. All day long they will provide companionship. Glass wire insulators and downed telegraph wire are common sights. Sometimes the 127 sneaks near you, and sometimes it is far to the left horizon. To your right is the subterranean Armagosa River. Eventually, the letters DV clarify on the side of a mountain. At the mountain base, Metbury Spring makes its way to the surface. Around which lies Shoshone, population 31, five miles past Zabriskie.

The TTR aims straight for the heart of Shoshone (www.shoshonevillage.com). It stumbles onto the local airstrip while veering toward the 127.

169

Though it never actually joins the road, preferring to stay just east of Main Street. Cross over the Pahrump and Las Vegas bound 178, (a.k.a. Charles Brown Highway) and arrive in the center of the village. Where all your needs will be met.

The first stop will most likely be the Crowbar Café and Saloon (8 a.m. to 9:30 p.m., 7 days a week, 760-852-4123, Wi-Fi available). Once you've ordered, be certain to check out the TTR photos on the walls. Note the set of tracks in one photo that incorporate both narrow and broad gauge rail on the same line. An old TTR timetable is on the wall of the bar. Its handwritten notes captivating.

Next door, to the north, is the Shoshone Museum (9-3, closed Tuesdays, 760-852-4524). The museum building was originally located in Zabriskie. It bulges with information about the TTR and associated life. Pick up the walking tour if you want to expand your knowledge of Shoshone architecture and lore. Immediately south of the Crowbar is the Sheriff's office. Though it once was the chow house for the TTR. Its walls are constructed of adobe formed by TTR bridge building crews. The original chow house was made of wood.

In 1925, an aggressive fire started in the wooden version of the chow house. The flames grew quickly. Embers rained down over the rest of the town. The museum looked to be the first to join the inferno. The rest of the town soon to follow. As all the men were off at the mines, it was left to the women to save Shoshone. Which they calmly did by organizing bucket brigades, first to the roof of the museum, and then where else water was needed. The town rescued in the process.

Across the street from the Crowbar is the post office, as well as public restrooms. The post office will hold packages for you (M-F 8-12,12:30-2:30, Sa-Su closed, 760-852-4212). There, also, you will find the Charles Brown General Store (7 a.m.-8:30 p.m., 7 days a week, 760-852-4242). Not a huge selection, but enough to resupply. On certain days, when the California Powerball Lottery climbs into the hundreds of millions or even billions, floods of hopeful Nevadans might be found lined up outside the Charles Brown General Store. There, after a 30-minute drive from the Vegas area, to purchase a ticket scented with the promise of instant wealth. Ironically, Nevada has no lottery. Possibly based on the immorality of such

170

activities. The odds of instant lottery fortune hover around one in 292 million. For comparison purposes, those Nevadans are 246 times more likely to be struck by lightning waiting in that long, outdoor line.

Keep in mind when resupplying that Death Valley Junction, 25 miles away, has water but very limited food supplies. Seven miles past Death Valley Junction is the Longstreet Casino, which has a food market. But before you get to the casino, you will have two full hiking days out of Death Valley Junction on the Death Valley Railroad side trip. Which leaves from and returns to Death Valley Junction. So, plan on stocking up at the general store for 3.5 days of hiking in Shoshone. The wagon in front of the store was the original TTR freight wagon. Adjacent to the general store is the Shoshone Inn (760-852-4212) with 16 rooms.

SHOSHONE		
1.	Food Supply	Yes
2.	Restaurant	Yes
3.	Water	Yes
4.	Hotel	Yes
5.	Beer	Yes
6.	Pool Table	No
7.	ATM	No
8.	Post Office	Yes
9.	Casino	No

The Charles Brown General Store is named for the much beloved Charles "Charlie" Brown. Who predates the cartoon character. Mr. Brown was born in Georgia in 1883. A silver spoon was never placed in his mouth. His first job was working in a mine at age 11. With time, Mr. Brown found himself in the mining boomtowns around Death Valley. For a while, he worked at the Lila C Mine in Old Ryan. Then he married the daughter of Ralph "Dad" Fairbanks, the founder of the town of Shoshone. So nicknamed, because the local Indians heard his 11 children calling him "Dad" so often, they assumed it was his name. Eventually, Dad and his family moved on from Shoshone. Mr. Brown and his wife, Stella, covered the departure by moving back to Shoshone to take over the running of the family town.

During this time, politicians in the well-populated western part of Inyo County neglected the unpopulated eastern half where Shoshone is located. Mr. Brown decided to get into politics to do something about this neglect. Though the odds against an eastern candidate beating the well-entrenched western incumbent were of lottery-size proportions, Mr. Brown ran for County Supervisor. And, shockingly, won. Mainly by rousting local miners out of their mines and convincing them to vote. After 16 years in that position, Mr. Brown ran for the State Senate. Once again, Mr. Brown's humbleness, combined with a reputation for honesty, carried him to victory. For the next 20 years, Mr. Brown used his position to bring much needed development funds to this forgotten corner of the desert. His career in the State Senate only ended by his death in 1963. His grave, as well as Stella's, is in Shoshone. Tended to by their descendants. Who still run the town of Shoshone to this day.

But it is a tale from Mr. Brown's early life that needs telling. It seems that Mr. Brown was living in the copper mining boomtown of Greenwater, California. Not all that far from present day Shoshone. The year was 1907. And Mr. Brown found himself, at the age of 24, without employment.

The 2,000 residents of Greenwater also had a problem. In a word, lawlessness. And no way to combat it. The inevitable committee was formed to excessively discuss the problem. Followed by the equally inevitable petition to the authorities to fix the problem. That authority happened to be a sheriff in the far-off Owens Valley. On the other side of Death Valley. The sheriff sent back a badge with a note attached. Which read, "Pin it on some husky youngster who is unmarried and unafraid, and tell him to shoot first."

The committee promptly pinned the badge on young Charlie Brown. Which ended his joblessness. Charlie was known about town to be quiet and calm, but also undaunted by confrontation. He didn't have to wait long for that confrontation.

Death Valley Slim was a good guy. Until he went on a drinking binge. And then he wasn't. The first stop on this tale's particular binge was Death

172

Valley Junction. But word made it to Death Valley Junction prior to Death Valley Slim's arrival. Familiar with his tendencies, the town boarded up and the sheriff fled to Beatty.

The next logical stop for Slim was Greenwater. There, Slim arrived before the news of his arrival. He found the doors of the Greenwater saloons wide open. Slim went in the first door he came to. And began shooting and drinking in no particular order. This was followed by customers and staff launching themselves out of whatever exits were most convenient. Then, Slim moved on to the next establishment. And continued his activities. This time using the bottles behind the bar for target practice.

By now, Charlie had been summoned. But his cabin was a mile away. He holstered his pistol and began to walk towards town. Most likely unhurried, as was his nature. Surely considering the merits of his new occupation along the way.

Charlie found Slim in his third saloon. His mind now saturated by liquor. But not his pistol aim. Bullets were being equally distributed between the chandeliers, the prominent bosoms of the lady in the painting behind the bar, and the feet of patrons being forced to dance at gunpoint. Charlie walked in with the majority of the town's population peering over his shoulders to see what would happen next. Charlie politely explained to Slim that it was unacceptable to hog all the fun in Greenwater. And for that reason, it would be best for Slim to hand over his pistol. Slim, in turn, suggested that he would add Charlie's guts to his list of targets. Before Slim could accomplish that, Charlie jumped him.

The brawl lasted 30 minutes. And became legendary for its savagery. There were no rules. Sometimes the fighting was standing toe to toe. Other times on the ground, ranging across the entire saloon. Furniture was smashed. No one dared interfere. Finally, Charlie managed to get Slim in a simultaneous leg and arm lock. And from that, came enough of an advantage for Charlie to place iron manacles on Slim's wrists. Then Charlie stood Slim up against the bar and most likely explained to Slim that he could consider himself under arrest.

Slim wasn't quite ready for that. He reached for a bottle to bring into contact with Charlie's head. To which, Charlie quietly advised, "Slim, if

173

you lift that bottle, you'll never lift another." Apparently, Slim saw something in Charlie's eyes. For his hands let go of the bottle, and he accepted the state of affairs.

Which brings us to the next chapter in the tale. For the good committee had awarded the position of sheriff but had failed to build a jail. The nearest one being located some 150 miles away at the time. So, Charlie had to improvise. Which he did, by bringing Slim home with him. There, Charlie kept the manacles on but removed Slim's shoes. This strategy was based on a certainty. The gravel road back into town contained the remains of thousands of smashed liquor bottles. Nobody in their right, or wrong, mind would risk that journey barefoot.

Charlie went to sleep content. And suddenly woke up to the opposite feeling. For Slim had escaped. Wearing Charlie's size 12 boots. Charlie immediately had to accept the flaw in his incarceration strategy. He grabbed the only other pair of shoes in the house. Only to discover Slim's feet were considerably more petite than his own. What to do but stubbornly pursue justice. Along that same glass-littered road into town. Barefoot the entire way.

At two a.m., Charlie finally tracked Slim to a blacksmith's shop, where Slim was having the manacles removed. Charlie re-invited Slim to his humble abode. But not before repossessing his boots. Slim mixing his own blood, with the blood left earlier by Charlie, on the long walk back through the glass. Upon arrival, Slim was firmly hog-tied, so that he could properly await his fate. And that is how law and order came to Greenwater.

Fate proved kind to Death Valley Slim. As it also would to Charles Brown. Slim went on to ride with Pancho Villa in Mexico, before returning to the U.S. and maturing into an upstanding citizen. Eventually, Slim moved to the east coast and established a sanatorium. Whose clients tended to be wealthy. Which allowed Slim to retire a very rich man. Whether he dropped his moniker, "Death Valley Slim," is open to conjecture. If he did drop it, what name he returned to I could not find.

That same fate did not look kindly on Greenwater. Though the initial discovery of copper in Greenwater was spectacular, it was almost all on the surface. The strike had very little depth. But through hype, that initial discovery attracted over $140 million dollars in investments. Major copper speculators jumped on the bandwagons. As did many small-time investors. Money and miners poured into Greenwater. Upon arrival, they discovered shortages. Primarily, water and copper. To make up for the shortage, water was brought in on wagons. A barrel of water sold for $15. Which translates into $250 per barrel in today's money. Dehydration must have been rampant.

The lack of water was not fatal to Greenwater's prospects. But the lack of copper was. It took less than two years for the scarcity of copper to be confirmed. The town promptly collapsed and dispersed. Taking all those millions invested with it. Which left a bitter taste in the mouths of the fleeced public. And cooled area mine speculation and investment for many years to come.

Among the last of the Greenwater businesses to close shop was the town magazine, known as the "Death Valley Chuck-Walla." I'll let the Chuck-Walla's subtitle from December 31, 1907, serve as Greenwater's epitaph: "Published on the desert at the brink of Death Valley. Mixing the dope, cool from the mountains and hot from the desert, and withal putting out a concoction with which you can do as you damn please as soon as you have paid for it. PRICE, TEN CENTS." Today, all that remains in Greenwater are splinters and cans.

And with that, goodbye Greenwater, Charles Brown and Death Valley Slim.

A mandatory and very short side trip in Shoshone is Dublin Gulch. Go south, just past the post office, and turn right at the drilling contest rocks. Follow the wash uphill past the cemetery. After a couple hundred yards you arrive at Dublin Gulch. Which is basically a wash edged with clay cliffs. Miners in the 1920s carved homes out of the soft clay contained in those cliffs. The clay was topped with a hard tufa layer. This layer served well as a roof. Holes were drilled through the tufa and piped. Instant chimney. Outhouses were located in the wash.

Over the years, the rooms expanded. Some caves become two stories. One added a garage. The attraction was obvious. Warm in the winter, cool in the summer and free to a miner willing to follow their natural inclination to dig. One cave was home to English royalists. Guests were served formally using a proper silver tea set. Across the way was a contingent of

German Socialists. One wonders whether their debates were heated or calm. The last resident moved out in 1970, leaving emptied cans to celebrate their residence.

With needs satiated, it's time to resume northward. The TTR goes thru a nasty bit of swamp as it leaves Shoshone. Strong rumor has it that moonshine was produced within this protective swamp during Prohibition. Best to avoid swamp bog and old stills by sticking to the road for the first mile out of town. Hike past the Death Valley Academy (50 students, 7 to 12th grade, who commute up to 60 miles to attend). Then past the RV park and out of town. Once you clear the road cut, you will see a sign that says "Badwater turnoff in ¼ mile." At this point, the railbed is obvious to your right, and you can rejoin it.

The TTR then proceeds to pull away from the 127 and enter the Amargosa River Valley. Old mining claim posts dot the landscape. As mentioned, back in the day, the claim documents would be placed in a glass jar and buried at the base of one of these posts. You can still stumble upon these jars in remote areas. As you make your way up the river valley, stick with the telegraph posts or their stumps. They mark the railbed when it becomes difficult to follow. After a while, you will arrive at a large bridge washout. Once past the wash, the TTR turns toward the 127 and crosses it. And continues on the left side of the road.

At some point, the railbed returns to the 127. Where it stays under the 127 for a while. Occasional old telegraph poles or stumps confirm you're headed in the right direction. Just stay with the 127. Note the old washed out road paralleling the 127 on the right. Avoid being detoured by the manmade dams that mimic the TTR railbed. Don't be overly concerned if you lose the railbed for stretches. Both the 127 and the TTR share a common destination in Death Valley Junction.

When you can no longer tell a dog from a coyote it is time to call it a day. Where it pleases you, pick a spot for the night and settle down. Remember to avoid sleeping in washes. Flash floods prey on the slumbering. As well as trains, which the next story details.

Back in the day, in this neck of the woods, a TTR culvert was taken out by yet another flash flood. The rails were left suspended in the air. An unsuspecting train hurdled toward the trap. The momentum of the lead locomotive carried it cleanly over the rails. Not so for the following refrigerator car, which ripped apart when the suspended rails gave way. The impact sent meat and vegetables exploding across the countryside. The destruction was forever after known as the, "Big Salad Wreck."

And now a bedtime story, for your reading pleasure, that references a section of trail you will tackle tomorrow.

Plates

Shootz Dining Hall owned the culinary sensibilities of Tonopah, Nevada. This possession began in 1914 and ran pretty much uninterrupted for 18 years. That the "Hall," as it was known, could do so, was a bit of a curiosity. For you see, the Hall lacked flash. No "public draw," as advertisers of the day termed it. It was located in an old wooden building that complained often and leaned slightly.

The Hall had but four tables that ran long. Each could seat 20 diners. Communal dining was enforced, not encouraged. The menu, written on slate at the entrance, mimicked the set up. There were four options on any given day. The desired number called out by a diner as they sat. The food itself, at least by menu description, did not suffer from pretension. Prices were directed at the workingman. Though that didn't slow the Tonopah elite from squeezing in and calling out a number.

The Hall housed two personalities who controlled their respective sectors. The boundaries between them not broached. The kitchen was run by quiet Ken Shootz. There, he kept a firm hand on the rudder. Choreographing the preparation and cooking in such a way that each meal seemed a finale of years of planning. Molding one thru four, so that they were as he saw them in his mind.

In the dining area, the older Jimmy Beane held sway. From his stool by the front door, the gregarious Jimmy greeted the arrivals. Knowing them, or learning them, as they walked in. And seating them accordingly with reactive banter. The two men led very public lives for the simple reason that the Hall was open seven days a week. Outside the Hall, the two kept to themselves. Their lives prior to Tonopah unknown. They resided in adjoining homes on 6th street. As neither ever married, there were whispers. Which were generally too quiet to be heard. The food cornered focus.

So, what drew the hungry? Quite simply, the food itself. An article in the April 7, 1921 Tonopah Miner attempted to capture the Hall by interviewing departing diners. Some extracts:

"I ate beans and pork all my life. But Mr. Shootz made me think I hadn't. They tasted so different in a darn good way."

"I took the first bite of steak and just pulled back from the table. There I chewed and chewed enjoying myself. It was the slowest meal I ever ate."

"Shootz has a gift my wife don't."

"That meal was unexpected."

"Ken is explaining cooking to people!"

The article ran long with compliments. Diners loved the way Ken tweaked a meal to confuse tradition. With equal emotion, they welcomed Jimmy's welcome.

And so it went for 18 years. The Hall steady, as the mines that built Tonopah boomed and busted around it. Surviving even those early years of the Depression. Staleness a non-issue, as Ken kept exploring new taste. While Jimmy avoided exploring by being himself. The diners never tired of any of it. Every night, 8 p.m. would visit, and the men would lock up. The doors on 6th street waiting to be opened.

That rhythm uninterrupted until 1932 and a chilly night. Ken at a chopping block pondering the potato. Jimmy on his stool. Hearing his name called to the right, Jimmy turned in that direction. But, there was no one. With that, the rest of the vessel in his brain ruptured. A floor waited for Jimmy as a dead man.

The next day the Hall's door was closed to all. Black bunting framed the lack of entrance. Few would admit there was as much sadness about the Hall being closed as about death itself.

The funeral, as would be expected, was well attended. The pews sat full. The sides and back standing full. To avoid being asked about the Hall's future, Ken arrived late. Which cued the minister to begin. Admirably he kept to the requested 15 minutes. Then backed away from the pulpit giving no indication.

Eyes turned to Ken. The silence extended. Until it was slowly muted by the sounds people make when they're trying to be quiet. Finally, Ken's feet made the decision for him. He stood and walked toward the pulpit. True quiet made a return.

"If Jimmy were here he'd thank you for coming. Then he'd have you back to the Hall. Inviting you with sweeter words than I have." Smiles broke out. "But he's not here, he's gone." With that Ken looked around the upper parts of the church, almost as if to see where.

"I should say my name is Ken Shootz. Jimmy was my partner. And has been for 20 years." The audience very tuned. Whispers returning. "We came to Tonopah in 1914 and opened the Hall. Many of you have eaten there. We thank you for that. But before Tonopah, Jimmy saved my life by saving me from myself. It's a little story. The story of the plates. But if you have time I'd like to tell it. For to me, it's Jimmy." Questions answered make for an interesting funeral.

Ken started into the tale gently. "I came west from the east. Ready for the wilder west I had read so much about. I figured I'd make my name as a gunslinger. To earn it, I wore my Dad's sidearm on my hip. A parting gift he never gave. Chances though, for gunplay, were hard to come by. So, I advanced my cause by giving myself a name, "Kid Shootz." Laughter swept the church. The kind not expected at a funeral. The crowd trying to digest the incongruity of their mild cook roaming the west as a gunslinger.

When the interruption passed, Ken returned, seeming to warm to the volume of words. "The hate I carried in those days didn't allow laughter when it was called for. Anyway, a time came in those wanderings when my money was no more. To eat, I needed work. Word was, the Lila C mine in Ryan was hiring. I saw myself as mine security with a quick gun and that is what I went offering. They saw me differently."

"Which is how I ended up as cook's assistant, at the Lila C, to my Jimmy Beane." The outrageousness of Jimmy in a kitchen caused the listeners to exhale relieving laughter. It also allowed the misword "my" to flee the listener's attention. Ken continued.

"Jimmy was seated peeling onions when I walked in. He might as well have been on his Hall stool the way he sized me. I was upfront with him. Told him how the job was beneath me and I best not be crossed. He just smiled through the tears. And then that mouth opened and it all began."

The faces faded from the pews and Ken returned to that day in Ryan. Alone with Jimmy now, the congregation forgotten. The Lila C dining tent shading them. Jimmy's knife conducting his words like an orchestra.

His first notes. "You don't say. Well, I suppose I should know who I'm not crossing. Whom am I addressing?" "Kid Shootz."

"Heard talk of you."

"From who?"

"More reputation than conversation. But I'd say here in Ryan your reputation showed up a month or two ago. It bespoke of a man not to be trifled with."

"Sounds about right."

"Then I'll tiptoe around trifling. But a question would be all right, wouldn't it, Kid?"

"I suppose so."

"Is asking a man to sit down and reduce onions with me trifling with that man?"

That is how we met. So occupied was I with holding back tears from the onions that it wasn't until hitting the bunk that I realized his name was still unknown to me. The next morning Jimmy's smile was still in place.

"Kid, what can you do with an egg?"

"Who's asking?"

"Jimmy Beane to one and all."

"Cook 'em."

"Try some of mine." A plate was handed to me. "As you swallow them would you imagine there have been complaints?"

"Yeah. Your fire was too hot."

"How would you know?"

"They're dry."

"But how would you know?"

"About what?"

"About fire and its relationship with eggs?"

I gave him serious eyes. "Sorry kid, I'm trifling. I'll refrain. But do you mind being the boss when it comes to eggs and the morning shift?"

With that I found myself in a kitchen again. A place I'd sworn was only for the east.

Over the months that we cooked for the "Ghosts," our term for the miners coated in white borax, Jimmy eased my story out of me. Without ever asking a question. I won't share it all now. Nor ever again. It was more than enough for this life that he knew. About what my father had seen and whom he had seen me with. On a late fall afternoon when dry leaves crackled in warning but weren't heard. About how a father beat his son to

181

return him to being a man not perverse. Made it his daily habit. But only ended up handing his son surplus hate.

That son only finding refuge in a mother's kitchen. Where I learned to do a thing right, after so much wrong. Finally, when my gifted hate was too much, I picked the Wild West of the paperbacks to deliver it. Looking to spill blood in atonement, so a father would accept his wrong and go on to accept his half of a son. But leaving silently in the morning, so I didn't kill the man with his own gun. Stolen from his hiding place. My mother and her kitchen pushed to memory, for there can be no tenderness in a gun-slinger's life. And above all, above all, a desire for the past to be buried until it was dead.

I guess death comes in many more than a few forms. Jimmy knew that all along. He laid the groundwork for the long death of my hate in his own conversational way. For who does not resist death? Not I, who still saw value in my hate. My father in me, Jimmy let be. Instead he came at my mother's strength.

After a meal, where I had taken chances, the miners lined up to shake my hand. Jimmy waited it out. When I turned, his words were ready. "Food comes first for everybody, Kid. That terms it important. A gift making it, is a gift to all."

"Perhaps I'm not generous."

"OK, that's where it gets dangerous. For a gift left unexplored is a slap in the face to our God."

I gave it more thought than I let on. Would it be enough revenge on my father? Being this version of me? A man who cooked for others in a kitchen? A man my mother perhaps foresaw in a boy?

Jimmy pushed me that way as the months coaxed each other out of the way. My mother his favorite topic. Stories of her his barter for my most disliked tasks. Tricking me into saying love every time her name left me. Isolating my hate. All the while holding his end up, by washing those damn pots with sand. And smiling on.

Then a night of strangeness. Jimmy quiet after emptying a bottle. Then suddenly, a long monologue about one's public and private face. The value to be found in the maintenance of both. How each could be happy if circumstances proved right. But the cost of loneliness, should those circumstances turn wrong. It seemed pitying and I asked him what the hell he was trying to get out. His short answer, after a long time, was "Not yet, Kid." With that he went somewhere else without moving. Leaving me to wonder.

It was 1914, and things were winding down at the Lila C. The borax had gone into hiding. A new borax strike, miles deeper in the mountains, had us moving the kitchen from Ryan to Death Valley Junction. Our allotted boxcar we loaded full for the morning run. A second trip, for the rest of things, was self-evident. The sole remaining bar in town still welcomed. The end of a day seemed a fine time for a beer. And some news I had arrived at. "It's time for me to move on, Jimmy." For once there were no words from the golden mouth. He just finished his beer and walked away. A part of me enjoyed that, but more of me didn't. The more I drank, the more I didn't. My mood turned foul. When I went out to get rid of beer, I didn't see Fritz coming in. Nor him, me going out. Our collision required little.

Fritz was known. He was big. He was unlikable. He preferred apologies to resemble begging. It did not start well. "You're an ugly one, aren't you?" My father ever present. Curious about my inevitable acceptance of a beating.

Fritz continued, "Well, shit, you spilled my beer. I'll take another on you."

"I didn't notice that beer."

"Kitchen boy, you're running out of time."

It was the wrong night. I rested my hand on the pistol grip. My hate felt good to revisit after so much time. "This says I have all the time I need."

Fritz reconsidered. "So, you won't fight a man the proper way? Then it follows that that gun makes you a coward. And a little goddamn old-fashioned, I might add. Who the hell wears a pistol anymore? But fine, Boy, have it your way. I can find me a weapon by tomorrow night. I'll be seeing you here, then, about this same time." He turned to his others. "The Wild West is back, boys!" With that, I was no more to him.

The next morning was spent with my hangover in the shade, waiting for the train's decision. I tried to relax into my last sure alive day before telling a distant Jimmy the story about Fritz. It seemed to lack sense in the telling. But not to Jimmy. He rested his hand on my shoulder. It stayed there. I wanted it to. This I thought about. Finally, he asked, "Are you any good?"

"At what?"

"Using that pistol."

"I am."

"How certain are you of it?"

"Certain enough to end Fritz with the first shot."

"Well, we'll be back in Ryan this afternoon. I'm thinking a confirmation is in order. Have you heard of the caboose test?"

"Are we talking about the end of a train?"

"I am."

"I haven't."

"Well, Wild Bill was said to have hit nine out of ten. Billy the Kid eight out of ten. Though John Wesley Harding was good for only four out of ten."

"What are you talking about?"

"Why don't I just show you?" With that, he said no more. Just got up and walked off. As was becoming his habit.

Time in the shade was time well spent in that heated part of the world. I kept my eyes open for Fritz. So, the pleasure doubled when I saw Jimmy returning. His confidence enjoyable from a long way off. "Load 'em up, Kid. The wheels are about to turn."

From the back of the caboose we watched Ryan stay where it was. And Fritz too. His thought caused my gut to drop. Jimmy stepped into the thought. "You ready?"

"Hard to be for what I don't know is coming."

"It's simple. The caboose test measures the acumen of a gunslinger. A plate is thrown from the roof of the caboose. That would be my endeavor. The plate must always be white. The rulebook plainly states this. The gunslinger, you, stands at the back of the caboose. When I yell 'Pull,' I will throw. You draw and squeeze that trigger. One bullet, one plate. Ten plates in all. Your score indicates your level of competence and preparedness for a gunfight." With that, Jimmy climbed to the roof and asked for the crate of plates.

I tried to still myself, but the caboose seemed unfamiliar with the rails. My father's breath was hot. "Pull," sudden. My shot errant before even the plate's descent. I reloaded after six shots. Six unharmed plates lay about the trailing desert. My anger alive. This time I yelled "Pull." It didn't change a result.

The next plate I fired twice. After the tenth miss I called for an eleventh through the tears. Nothing. I took aim through the roof. Pausing long enough to redirect the last bullet at the wind. The realization that my father would never let go caused a snap. I flung that son of a bitch as far as I could down the tracks. The sound good when the gun hit rail. Then I lay down to myself. And wept it out.

The hand returned to my shoulder when Jimmy came down. With time, came a hug he never pulled away from. The hate seemed to retreat. It made me curious as to what was left. When I pulled away, Jimmy was looking at me. I looked back at him. And that was enough for a while. "What about Fritz?"

"He's back there. You and I, Ken Shootz, are headed in a quite new direction." It was but a small first kiss.

The collective gasp of the congregation brought me back to Tonopah and its church. My immediate guess being, that was a few too many words. A couple of people stayed, but most joined the flood of the departing outraged.

I finished that little speech with this. "I was never Kid Shootz again. Nor did I ever hear tale of any caboose test. Though, I listened for it from Jimmy or general talk. Good one, Mr. Beane. I miss you my love."

I left Jimmy in the Tonopah ground. Then spent what was left of a day wrapping up our lives. The Hall burned that night. A victim of confession, I guess. I left in the dark of morning, no longer interested in life's ashes. East was my direction. A choice. For a mother might yet still be alive. Traveling from love to love felt very right.

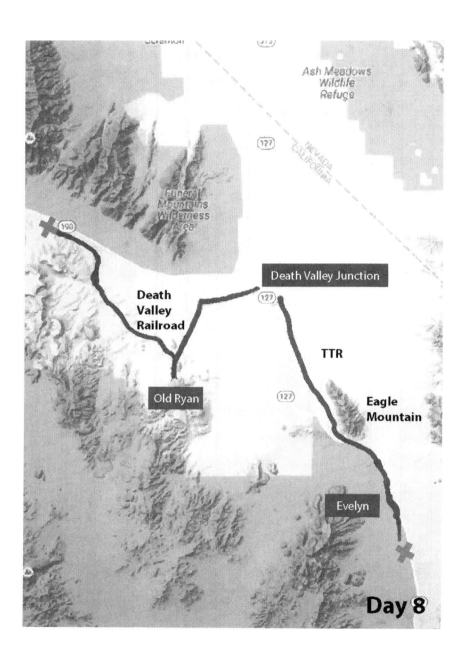

Day 8

Death Valley Junction-Old Ryan

Eventually, depending on where you laid your head, the TTR reappears on the left of the 127. Then it once again dives under the asphalt. So, there will be some road walking. But at about three cars an hour, it is not particularly onerous.

A fatal train wreck occurred in this area on August 9, 1908, when a flash flood poured down off Eagle Mountain. The water took out 70 feet of the railbed but left the rails. Which waited patiently in ambush for the next train. The rear Pullman sleeper car managed to stay on the tracks but the preceding cars did not. The two crew members and an unfortunate stowaway were killed.

Once again, the TTR comes up for air on your left, and yet again, back down right as you arrive at the centerpiece of your view. The monolith of Eagle Mountain. A stand-alone without neighbors. A little climb to 3,806 feet with very satisfying views, if you're so inclined. The route is located within the Internet.

Back to the TTR. For the length of Eagle Mountain, the TTR is under the 127. When you reach the far end of the mountain, you will observe the telegraph posts continuing straight and the 127 veering to the left. The TTR faithfully sticks with the posts. The posts, for their part, will always stay just to the right of the TTR. They never cross it. In effect, the TTR is a shortcut to Death Valley Junction (DVJ), as the 127 ranges far to the west. Stay on the TTR straight line bound for Death Valley Junction.

Soon, you will come to a telegraph stump with a rock on it. Under the rock is a jar with a 40-year-old mining claim in it. Check it out, and then put it back for the next hiker, please.

Past visions of the "never arriving Baker" will return to your psyche. Death Valley Junction is right up ahead but it stays right up there. The railbed is easy to follow. You can count poles to massage your sanity. Like all hikes, the goal becomes an arrival. As you come into town, piles of interesting leftovers celebrate your entrance. There are also some leftover TTR buildings and water towers. As well as a housed boiler that was part of the Death Valley Junction Mill. See the second photo section for a photo of the original mill.

To your right is a large tailings pile, then a failed hydroponic scheme. If you divert attention to your left, two Death Valley Railroad (DVRR) spur lines heading west will become apparent. They are your plan for tomorrow. Shortly, you will find yourself in Death Valley Junction (population between two and 20), where things are as they have always been. One hundred and twenty-one miles from Ludlow.

Death Valley Junction was built by Borax Smith's Pacific Coast Borax Company. Who, as you remember, was also responsible for building the TTR itself. Like many stops along the TTR, DVJ started out modestly under an alias. DVJ's was "Amargosa." Once again meaning bitter water. Amargosa consisted of two railcars that were put in place in 1907. The first female agent/operator in TTR history ran Amargosa from 1908 to 1912. Starting a female-in-charge trend that would reappear later in Amargosa/DVJ's history. Amargosa slumbered along for a number of years serving the local borax mine at Old Ryan. Tents began to spring up around the station. There to service miners. "Saloon," "Restaurant," or "Store," painted on their canvas to indicate their contents. "Brothel" was not painted, though there was one.

The borax mine at Old Ryan was called the Lila C. Though in those days Old Ryan hadn't yet been told it was old, because New Ryan had yet to be discovered. The Lila C was affectionately named for the original mine owner's daughter. As with all things related to borax, though, Borax Smith eventually came to own the mine. By 1906, its shafts extended 3,000 feet into the mountain. Borax was being produced at a satisfactory rate. The question was delivery.

The TTR was slow in arriving. So, Borax Smith ordered the 20-mule teams back into service. For a few months, they delivered borax to Zabriskie, where it, in turn, was loaded onto the TTR. Hard to imagine that much action, having stood yourself in downtown Zabriskie.

By 1907, the TTR had arrived in Amargosa. In that same year, Borax Smith completed a 6.68-mile spur line that linked Old Ryan and the Lila C mine with the TTR at Amargosa. This spur line was christened the Death Valley Railroad (DVRR). The TTR itself continued its northern construction march.

By 1914, the Lila C had come to the end of her shelf-life. But new, rich borax sites had been discovered far into the Greenwater Range, some 20 miles from Amargosa. It was decided that the best route to get there was to follow the DVRR's Lila C line to the 3.5-mile mark. Then to branch right and extend the DVRR 17 miles up a long valley. Followed by a turn along the high slopes of the Greenwater Range.

Construction on this new branch of the DVRR began in 1914 and was completed in 1915. The new borax mine town was christened New Ryan. The year 1915 also saw the abandonment of the Lila C and Old Ryan. As well as the remainder of the DVRR track after the 3.5 mile split. Most of Old Ryan's buildings were moved to New Ryan.

Meanwhile, back in Death Valley Junction, life was oppressive. A mill had been built to process the borax brought from the Lila C. It was the main employer in town. Dust generated by the mill choked the air. Extremes of heat and cold wore workers down. Yet, no safety net existed. If you couldn't work, you weren't paid. A line from "Amargosa," the 2000 documentary, captured well this chapter of Death Valley Junction history. "It was a time of hard men, and harder Gods." Most mill workers didn't make it past six months. The working environment was that brutal.

One day heavy on fate, Zane Grey stepped off the TTR and into the DVJ station. Zane Grey was a novelist whose specialty was westerns. His bestselling 'Riders of the Purple Sage' is still widely read 100 years later. Suffice it to say, in those days, if Zane Grey wrote something, it was eagerly consumed by the reading public. And Mr. Grey didn't like what he saw in DVJ. He was appalled by the working and living conditions. When he returned to New York, he wrote an article in "Harper's Bazaar" that informed the readers of his disgust. Strong public reaction followed. The PCB felt the sting of backlash. To cast the company in a more positive light, the directors decided to build a proper town.

With the construction of the DVRR, Amargosa changed its name to Death Valley Junction. It also began an expansion that resulted in its present size. At least in terms of buildings. The expansion and subsequent improvement in living conditions, arguably a reaction to Zane Grey's article and the power of the pen. The centerpiece of DVJ was built in 1923 by the PCB. It was a large U-shaped Spanish Colonial building constructed by Mexican masons brought in from Los Angeles. The cost of construction was $300,000, a significant sum in those days.

Originally, the building housed a hospital, hotel, PCB offices and a movie theater. A far cry from the original tent city. And a development that surely brought relief to long suffering mill workers. Around this time, tourism began to take an interest in Death Valley. The PCB, ever open to profit, rechristened the PCB hotel the "Amargosa Hotel" and opened its doors to tourists. It also began to organize rail tours to New Ryan on the DVRR. There, guests could stay at the PCB owned Death Valley View Hotel.

Unfortunately for DVJ, outside events were conspiring. In 1927, an enormous deposit of superior grade borax was discovered in Boron, California. Closer to LA and dependable rail, the PCB soon moved its offices there. Then the stock market crash of 1929 decimated tourism and everything else that distributed wealth. Also, in that year, the borax mines at New Ryan stopped producing in favor of Boron. The DVJ mill was then logically moved to Boron. By 1930, the heyday was over. The Death Valley View Hotel closed that year, and the DVRR was dismantled. Death Valley Junction limped on with the still functioning TTR. But when even the TTR gave out, Death Valley Junction's demise was certain. Until a flat tire changed everything.

In 1967, Marta Becket was passing by Death Valley Junction with her husband when a tire got tired of it all. From the perspective of Mrs. Becket's life, the flat tire would be termed an intervening circumstance. It stopped her where she would never have stopped and gave her time to see things she would never have seen. And what she saw that fateful day slammed the brakes on her life trajectory, though it was no longer much to look at. The Amargosa Hotel before her was crumbling after 44 years in the desert sun. Unloved and headed toward ruin. But Marta Becket peered past that and saw the old dance hall. And a plan formed around an impulse.

Marta Becket was born in 1924 and grew up in New York City. Drawn to the stage from an early age, she studied ballet intensively. This led to a career on Broadway. Which morphed into a traveling one-women dance show that crisscrossed the country, until that flat tire and plan arrival. The plan was simple. This dance hall will be my stage. Here I will perform. Marta knew this from the moment she peered through a tiny hole into the dance hall. Her words, "I had the distinct feeling that I was looking at the other half of myself."

She tracked down the owners and arranged rent of $45 a month. Then she started repairs with her husband. All the while performing three days a week. Often, there was no audience. She performed anyway. Thus solving the conundrum "Which matters most, the performer or the audience?" Still, dancing to no audience is irksome. The solution to it all arrived by way of brilliant insight and flash flood. While cleaning flood debris out of the dancehall it came to her. "Why not create permanent spectators?"

The audience chosen was from the Spanish Renaissance. Their portraits painted on the walls and ceiling of the dance hall. My favorites were the nuns next to the ladies of the night. The second group's faces based on actual ladies who worked at a nearby bordello and were regular attendees. Their Madame insisting on culture. For six years, Becket labored alone on the walls and ceiling. When it was done, Marta Becket never again performed to anything less than a full house.

Other highlights of the opera house walls are a portrait of a donor who reneged on a promise of donation. For that he received a Pinocchio nose. At the back are portraits of two cats. One of whom tripped Marta while she was practicing. A broken hip was the result. Also, note the spotlights made from coffee cans. A tour of the Amargosa Opera House will set you back five dollars. It's hard to imagine a better way to spend those five dollars.

In the early days, breathing, paying audiences were thin. It was a long way to nowhere from anywhere. One night in 1970, while Marta performed to no one that could clap, a National Geographic writer stumbled through the doors. He took it all in and then wrote about it. Fame spread, and audiences began to make the trek. They were entertained for sure. But perhaps, more so, they saw a solo woman living a self-created life without excuses. In that, there is charisma. The shows went on for decades. Along the way her husband drove away. But Marta Becket never left. A fine 2000 documentary about her life titled, "Amargosa," was nominated for an Academy Award. When she could no longer dance, Marta sat and told her story. But, time eventually grabs us all by the ankles. Marta Becket's last show was in 2012.

After retirement Marta continued to live in a house behind the Amargosa Hotel. Then, on January 30, 2017, she danced away from her found paradise at the age of 92. Her death appearing in obituaries across the country. Fortunately, the show in Death Valley Junction has not ended. A protégé of Ms. Becket has taken over and performs weekly. (For hotel and performance information, www.amargosaoperahouse.com).

The Amargosa Hotel (760-852-4441) also remains open. Rooms are available, as is ice cream, hot drinks, water and a very small store. Keep your senses open for the resident child ghost. Many thanks to manager Mike Perez and his kind hospitality.

Recent news is that the Amargosa café, in the old PCB complex, will reopen. An event worth wishing for. Stepping out of the Amargosa Hotel, you will see the small TTR museum on your right (Open Th-Sa, 9:30-4:30, 775-751-4608, tandtrr.org). There, John Slikker and a small group of volunteers are slowly re-creating a scale-model rail version of the TTR. Stop in for a chat, and let them know the silliness that you are up to. They are excellent people.

Across the street, behind the abandoned garage, lies the original 1909 TTR freight house. Still standing, waiting for the return of purpose. Next to it is the bizarre Peter Lik gallery. There, in the windows, one can view several large, stunning landscape photographs. The building itself is sealed and unmanned. The location curious. It reminds of the remote faux Prada store near Marfa, Texas.

The rest of Death Valley Junction lies abandoned. The smokestack you see behind the Amargosa Hotel is from the old hot water boiler, now deceased.

Once satiated with Death Valley Junction, it's time to head back into the desert. And to take a turn from the Q toward the heart of death. But first, make sure you have enough food and water for two days of hiking. As there is none to be had on this side leg. Return to the south side of the garage, next to the failed hydroponics scheme. Observe the branch railbed heading to the west. This is the upper branch of the Y that leaves the TTR. It is also the start of the narrow-gauge Death Valley Railroad. Which you will be following for the better part of the next day and a half. To Old Ryan and beyond.

As you stand looking west, imagine the train loaded with borax ore that one day, many decades ago, arrived from Old Ryan. It stopped where you stand. After coming to a halt, the locomotive promptly blew up, killing both members of the crew. But that is not your fate. Head west. The upper branch of the Y quickly joins the lower branch that left the TTR near the water towers. After the meeting point, continue west on the joined railbed. Immediately, you cross the 127 and begin a long, straight line toward the Greenwater Range. This range of mountains is often snow-capped.

Shortly after crossing the 127, there will be a briefly confusing section as you pass a fence. A possible railbed seems to move off to your right. This is actually a berm for the airfield. Just stay west and straight toward the mountains. The confusion will quickly dissipate. Continue for 3.5 miles. Note much evidence of wild horses. I heard often about the herd, but I never spotted them.

At about the 3.5-mile mark, the railbed begins a long bend to the right. A large pile of wood in the middle of the railbed warns of a washout. At this point, you have arrived at the main Death Valley Railroad split. The right branch heads off to New Ryan. The left leads to Old Ryan. Standing by the large pile of wood, look across the wide wash. There you'll see the continuation of the left branch to Old Ryan. Note the difference in railbed material. The left branch is rock and gravel. The right branch consists of yellow soft shale.

Cross the wide wash and follow the left branch for 3.5 more miles to Old Ryan and the Lila C mine. This section operated from 1907 until 1915. You are now on the trail of broken plates. The reason why so many old white dinner plates were smashed along this line is lost to history. Perhaps an overworked dishwasher. Or maybe they were used for target practice after all. Unexplained, also, are the mounds of piled stone that you pass. So many curiosities as we move through life.

The railbed continues its slow curve to the left. Eventually the tailings of the Lila C come into view. Upon arrival, you will see extensive tailings amongst impressive volcanic remains. To your right, it is possible to discern the outlines of the town grid based on the cleared areas. The remnants of the mill lie embraced with tailings. Alas, no structures remain at all. Though the two sealed tubes at the entrance to the mine would make Dante proud.

Leap back, though, a little over 100 years, and you're in downtown Ryan. Around you are some 50 buildings. There's a store, post office, blacksmith shop, boarding houses, even a reading room. A brass band entertains in the evenings. Two hundred and fifty people are your neighbors. The intense heat of the summer causes the mine to shut down and those same neighbors to seek cooler climates. But come September, it all starts up again. A total of $8 million worth of borax will be removed from under the lava. When the mine played out, the town literally moved on. After that, the tracks were pulled up, and now you are left to stand amongst history and mine junk. Time to leave Old Ryan to its memories.

Your next destination is New Ryan. Rather than wasted backtracking to the Y split, follow an attractive "deathcut." Maybe a better word than shortcut, don't you think? Reach it by retracing along the railbed for about a quarter mile out of Old Ryan. Until you come to a dirt road that crosses the railbed. Turn left on that dirt road as it charts its northwest direction.

Eventually, you will come to a proud volcanic mountain with a post on top. Keep following the dirt road northwest and to the left of the mountain. The rolling terrain is reminiscent of a lunar garden. Keep hiking. Simplicity, plus effort, equals bliss.

Then you arrive at a well-maintained, wide, dirt road. A cairn is in place here. Turn right on this dirt road and make a beeline north for Route 190 and the distant Funeral Mountains.

Do not convince yourself to continue up the northwest road past the cairn, into the oncoming canyon, as I did. Though beautiful and the correct crow-flying direction, it boxes after many miles. Forcing one to climb out of the canyon, cross various plateaus and then plunge into yet more canyons. With time, the plunges are happening in dark. And internal conversations tend to focus on levels of lostness and hours wasted. External solo conversations seem to involve the word "dumbass" a lot. So, do yourself a favor and turn right on the wide dirt road.

About 60 yards before the 190, you will arrive at the Death Valley Railroad. Your clue is the many piles of gravel about. Turn left and head up the valley toward the pass. The 190 will be to your right. You are now on your way to New Ryan.

If you want to stick with the railbed out of Old Ryan, and avoid setting out on a cross country shortcut, it is your right. Simply retrace the narrow gauge track 3.5 miles back to their original Y split. Turn left at the Y crux and head up the valley. From there it is a long straight climb to the pass. The pointed mountain, directly in front of you, is your destination. After a mile or so, you reach another Y. The right branch heads over to the 190 and large piles of tailings. The left branch continues toward the pass. Stay on the left branch. Along the way, you will pass a well-maintained dirt road heading south. Now both deathcut and retracing are one.

Once you crest the pass, begin a long downhill. Right after the pass, note the extensive slab city on your left. These were trailer foundations for a local mine until the 80s. Now renegade RVers use them rent free. I stopped and spoke with one who knew these hills well. A typical sunbaked, content nomad. We discussed local points of interest, and then suddenly the conversation shifted to Colonel Ataturk's secularist policies in 1920's Turkey. One never knows what's around the corner in the desert. Continue downhill. The DVRR stays high, while the 190 dips away. That should be enough for the day. Find yourself a camp and hunker down for the night show.

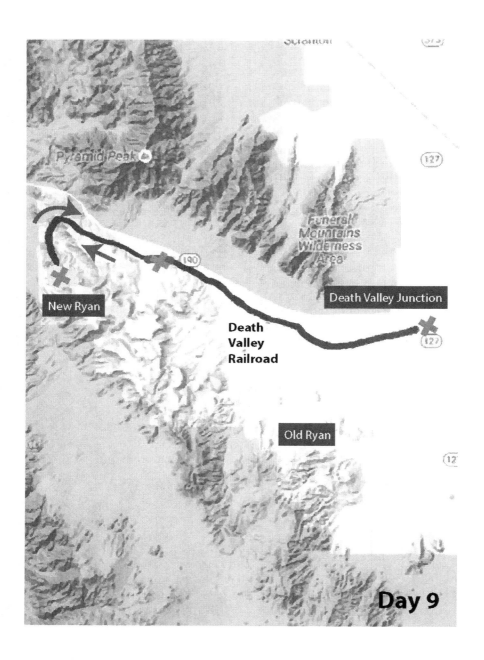

New Ryan

Death Valley Junction

Death
Valley
Railroad

Old Ryan

Day 9

196

Day 9

New Ryan-Death Valley Junction

Rise and shine. Be off like a herd of turtles, one of my father's favorite expressions. Coasting downhill, you will eventually arrive at the first of three rail trestle bridges. All long ago swept away by flooding. The first one is a dicey climb down and out. Note the cleared, old tent site just before that dicey climb. Also, check out the purposeless old toilet seat. Rather than mess with the dicey canyon, it is honorable to retreat about 50 feet to a cairn on your right. Then, follow the obvious series of cairns uphill to an old maintenance road that skirts the canyon. Stay on the old road to the other side of the canyon and rejoin the DVRR.

From here, the canyons become progressively deeper. Filling them in must have broken a few backs. Arrive at a massive washout of a bridge. This was probably the bridge, featured in the second photo section, with the Cadillac driving across it. Here the crumbly soil provides a good grip during submerge and emerge. The soil is incredibly porous. At one point, I slipped, and my hiking pole plunged through the soil all the way to its grip. Once you've cleared the third, easier canyon, the railbed begins to turn left.

Just as the views begin to open up, the forgotten rooms of a stone village appear on your right. The stonewalls look to be the foundations of a tent city. One larger structure was perhaps the mess hall. Possibly, railroad and bridge builders lived here during construction. Continuing on, the vistas achieve the dramatic. Now you are high above the floor of Death Valley. At times, 3,000 feet above it. As you skirt small previous avalanches, you begin to appreciate the lengths investors were willing to go to extract valuable minerals from the earth. A conclusion that no railroad belongs here is easy to reach.

Follow the railbed's curves. Note the little roads carved vertically by manic, merry little bulldozers. Pass some fantastic eroded cliffs. The views become stunning as the Panamint Range across Death Valley joins the show. Then you pass under impossibly vertical power lines and round a bend. And catch your first glimpse of New Ryan. You can see it. But an hour remains until you arrive. That is due to an extended U turn, around the head of the canyon that separates you from New Ryan. Lots of downed telegraph wires carpet your way. Then a forgotten ore cart on the railbed.

Next up is a crumbling mine with very soft tailings. This is possibly Colemite, a railroad stop and borax mine on the DVRR. Shortly thereafter, is a No. 4 marker; its significance unknown to me. The hiking here is gorgeous. Next, in the stumbling-upon department, is a forgotten miner's village. Replete with root cellars as well as collapsed dugouts and buildings. I've read there is a cemetery nearby, but I didn't come across it.

With steps, you continue to eat away at the U-turn. At the height of the U is a large, washed out bridge. Your alternatives are a long dirt road detour to the right or an easy trail to the left. Note the well-laid stonework. Shortly afterward is a man down. You'll know it when you see it. As you near New Ryan, keep an eye out for a strange, petite railcar wagon on your left. Its purpose confusing, though it is kind to the camera.

Then you are coming into the privately owned New Ryan, but a "No Trespassing" sign explains you are unwelcome. I wouldn't pass the sign. The caretakers here have a reputation for being extremely hostile to trespassers. In the west, that has implications. Console yourself that the views of New Ryan from the sign are pretty good. I believe you are in a similar position to the photographer who took the New Ryan photograph in the second photo section. The photo that shows the train departing New Ryan. There is talk of New Ryan becoming more accessible to the public in the future. As the Park Service is reportedly in talks to take it over. Let's root for that. For New Ryan would make a great water stop and exploration.

New Ryan was built in 1914 to house, feed and entertain borax miners. Originally, it was called Devar. A clever extraction from Death Valley Railroad. The main mine in the area was known as the Biddy McCarthy mine. But there were a number of mines that extended into the surrounding hills. Two of the more prosperous were the Widow and Played Out mines. Transport of borax, from these spread-out mines to the railhead, was accomplished by the construction of a baby gauge railroad. Which was serviced by a toy train. The tracks were two feet across. Elaborate trestles and tunnels allowed the baby gauge to reach four miles out to these more distant deposits.

The toy train could haul three tons of borax ore back to New Ryan. There it was dumped into large wooden chutes from above. Below, the larger cars of the DVRR waited. They would receive the borax ore when the valves on the chutes were opened. Then the DVRR would transport the ore to Death Valley Junction, where it would, yet again, be transferred to the still larger TTR. Baby gauge to narrow gauge to standard gauge. Oh, the joys of different gauged railroads. From DVJ, the borax ore was hauled to one of two processing plants in California or New Jersey. All this transferring was time-consuming and costly. No wonder the PCB was thrilled when borax was discovered in Boron, adjacent to a major standard gauge railroad.

Early life in New Ryan was tough. Most of the buildings were brought in from elsewhere. They tended to be vermin infested and inadequate for the desert extremes of hot and cold. Flies, attracted to the hogs and mules, made even the most mundane tasks bothersome. In fact, many miners preferred to live in mountain dugouts away from the town center. Holes in the ground, basically. When the breakfast whistle blew, their heads popping out of the ground reminded of prairie dogs.

Attempts to unionize the mine in order to improve the situation failed. But complaints about living conditions resulted in changes. The Catholic Church in Rhyolite (you're headed to Rhyolite) was hauled down to New Ryan. It became a recreation room. As well as an entertainment center, after a stage was added. Silent films, accompanied by piano and violin, were shown. Imagine the places a film could take your mind, after days of digging underground.

Around this time, a new mine superintendent was brought in from Australia. His name was Major Boyd, as he had been in the military. His accent was a source of endless amusement to the local miners. "Pay day" becoming "pie day" was a favorite. The superintendent of the TTR loved to introduce him as Major Bird. The major would always pitch in "No, not Boid, the name is Boyd." (Say it out loud, you'll get it if you've ever spent time around Australians.) Upon arrival at New Ryan, the major took a brief tour of the miner's cabins. At the end, as a commentary, he threw a lit match on a mattress. Thereafter, proper housing was built. Along with a sewage system and upgraded water delivery. Which lured the miners out of their dugouts and back into the town center.

Favorable economics kept the mines running until the late 20s. In all, about $30 million worth of borax ore was extracted. But, as stated earlier, a new borax strike closer to LA and the stock market crash double-slammed the mines of New Ryan. For a while, tourists kept New Ryan afloat. Railroad public relations campaigns that featured Hollywood starlets riding the baby gauge were conducted. (See the second photo section.) The miner's dormitory became the Death Valley View Hotel. The DVRR brought in proper railcars for the tourists. (One of which is completely restored and waiting for you at the Laws Museum near Bishop, CA. The Death Q will take you right to it.) The TTR did the same to bring the tourists from Ludlow to DVJ. The three-day package, from LA to New Ryan and back to LA, cost about $60.

But it was all swimming upstream. The stock market crash had everyone thinking about keeping their house, rather than the joys of Death Valley. By the end of 1931, New Ryan had shut down and the DVRR had been pulled up. Its stock and rails sent to Carlsbad, New Mexico.

New Ryan went to sleep. But in the early 40s, tourists started coming back. The baby gauge tour was reinstated and rooms once again made available. But an accident and subsequent lawsuit in the mid 1950s, once again closed the baby gauge to the public. The last private tour was in 1967. Two derailments added to that final experience. Needed expensive repairs sealed the baby's doom. New Ryan returned to slumber. Watched over by the corporate successors of the PCB. The current corporate incarnation of which is Rio Tinto. Off limits to vandals and everyone else. Preserved due to its inaccessibility.

Do an about-face and see the DVRR from a different prospective, all the way back to DVJ. Twenty miles in all. This time stay on the DVRR the entire way, until it is time to say goodbye to that fine railroad. Once back at DVJ, you have choices. Stay here or continue seven miles up the TTR to the Longstreet Casino. But that would be a big day. One option is to

200

spend the night at or around DVJ and then hike to Longstreet for break-fast/resupply. Option two, an evening trek straight to the casino for steak and bed. Regardless, the following seven miles in Day Ten are applicable.

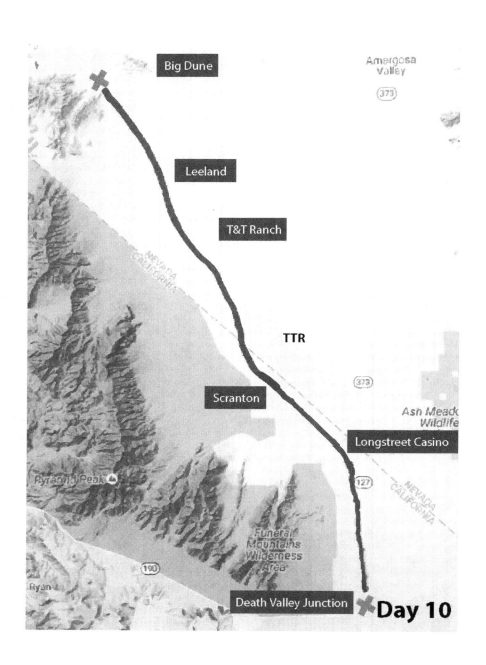

Big Dune

Amargosa Valley

(373)

Leeland

T&T Ranch

NEVADA
CALIFORNIA

TTR

(373)

Scranton

Ash Meadows Wildlife

Longstreet Casino

Pyramid Peak

(127)

NEVADA
CALIFORNIA

Funeral Mountains Wilderness Area

(190)

Ryan

Death Valley Junction

Day 10

Day 10

Death Valley Junction-Longstreet Casino-Leeland

Head north out of DVJ, past an interesting wood tie water dam. The TTR is on the right side of the 127. The railbed parallels the road for a while. You are on your way to Nevada. There aren't many cars. But chances are pretty good that an off road, silhouetted hiker is a conversation starter in the cars that do pass. Eventually, the TTR recrosses the 127 and veers to the left. Keep an eye out for random mason jars. North is your direction. The Funeral Mountains to the west stand witness to your efforts.

Fifteen miles to your east is the Ash Meadows National Wildlife Refuge. The largest oasis in the Mojave Desert. There, Crystal Spring flows at 2,800 gallons per minute. And mammoths once sipped from it. In all, there are 28,000 acres of wetlands in the refuge. Within its boundaries lies Devils Hole. A 6'x 8' geothermal pool. It is over 500 feet deep, which is a best guess because the bottom has never been found. Though divers have tried. The water temperature rarely varies from 92 degrees Fahrenheit. Scientists estimate the hole's age at 500,000 years old.

And who are the sole inhabitants of Devils Hole? The Devils Hole Pupfish who chooses, without choice, to swim nowhere else. They've been isolated in this hole for at least 10,000 years. Perhaps longer. Their only meal is wall algae. Which is fertilized by sun and the poop of barn owls. Devils Hole is extremely sensitive to earthquakes elsewhere. Major earthquakes in South America and Asia have caused mini tsunamis in the normally tranquil waters of Devils Hole. The largest waves exceeding six feet. The pupfish's reaction to this sudden chaos is undocumented.

There is a lot more to Ash Meadows. In all, 30 species of plants and animals live here and nowhere else. That is the largest concentration of endemic species in the U.S. At one time, there was a tough ranching community that survived in Ash Meadows. Jack Longstreet, the gunslinger, lived there. A TTR engineer, on a scouting trip through Ash Meadows, remembers seeing a very young boy laying on the ground suckling on the teats of a hound dog. The boy grew to 6' and later became a teamster on the TTR.

And the Ash Meadows kicker? All of the water making its way to the surface here melted during the last Ice Age.

At one point, Ash Meadows was slated to become a major housing development. Work was started on bulldozing those Ice Age springs to create suburban manicured lakes. That is when the Federal government stepped in and turned Ash Meadows into a National Wildlife Refuge.

Back to the TTR. Keep hiking, until you come to ruins on your right, and a bizarre mock set-up of a wild west town on your left. The left, I cannot answer. But the ruins on your right I believe to be Bradford. A small settlement that served as a shipping point for clay. The clay was brought to Bradford from mines to the east. A four mile narrow gauge spur line connected those clay mines to the TTR. Behind "possibly" Bradford, you can locate the old spur line railbed. Hop on board and make your way east to the Longstreet Casino. It is the large building on the horizon and in your future. In a little more than a mile, you will arrive.

The Longstreet Casino (775-372-1777) has double rooms for $75 a night. No bathtubs though. The food market in the Longstreet is equivalent to a well-stocked convenience store.

LONGSTREET CASINO		
1.	Food Supply	Yes
2.	Restaurant	Yes
3.	Water	Yes
4.	Hotel	Yes
5.	Beer	Yes
6.	Pool Table	No
7.	ATM	Yes
8.	Post Office	No
9.	Casino	Yes

The next food and water is 46 miles away in Beatty, so this is a good resupply point. The steakhouse closes at ten p.m. The restaurant opens for breakfast at seven. Oh, and welcome to Nevada. Make sure to have a read about the giant cow in the parking lot and the other giant cow who grew up in the casino. The Longstreet is owned by Nevada legend Jim Marsh, a car dealer in Las Vegas who has been around forever.

Growing up in southern Nevada, I fondly remember one of Mr. Marsh's ads where he called out the IRS. Its seems the IRS had audited Mr. Marsh. In response, Mr. Marsh aired an ad where he is wearing a barrel and nothing else. His pitch "I have to sell cars to pay the bills because the IRS has taken everything else."

Anyway, for his own reasons, Mr. Marsh took an interest in rural Nevada. Other than the Longstreet, he owns Goldfield's Santa Fe Saloon and the Tonopah Station in Tonopah. The Death Q will take you to the front door of both establishments. And both doors wouldn't be open if not for the hospitality and support of Mr. Marsh.

When asked why he built the Longstreet, Mr. Marsh responded, "Brain damage." One day I'll buy a car from that man.

The Longstreet Casino is named for Jack Longstreet (1834-1928). A character still talked about in these parts. So, why don't we?

Most days, back in those days, nothing happened. Then one day, out of the haze, Jack Longstreet rode into town. His arrival through the swinging doors turned heads and stopped saloon conversations, Hollywood style. Longstreet quickly displayed a lack of tolerance for nonsense and a willingness to use the multi-notched pistol he wore. (A notch indicated a death by way of that pistol.) As often with such men, his past became the subject of conjecture.

Here were the beliefs of that time. Longstreet was from Tennessee based on his drawl. He rode cavalry in the Civil War. At one point, he was a Pony Express rider. He had one ear chopped off by angry ranchers who caught him and his cohorts stealing cattle. Longstreet was only 14, and spared for his youth, but his friends were hung. But these were rumors, as few were willing to quiz Longstreet directly. At a minimum, Longstreet wore his hair long to cover a missing ear. All were sure Longstreet was a man who won gunfights. Certainly, he was a man whom the law was interested in.

Not conjecture, is the life he led after arriving in the area. Soon after showing up, Longstreet married a Paiute woman and learned the Paiute language, eventually being accepted into the tribe. One of his first jobs was as a hired gunman for the Tonopah Stage. There, he promptly killed his brother-in-law. Longstreet claimed self-defense. A jury acquitted him. Then he turned to public policy. He became known as an advocate for the local tribes. Writing letters on their behalf to the Bureau of Indian Affairs. The letters resulting in the local Indian superintendent losing his job. He also led an Indian worker revolt at a local mine. It seems the mine manager owed back wages to the Indian workers. So, Longstreet and the Indians dragged the manager out of his tent. They then proceeded to publicly spank his bare ass with a stick until he agreed to pay up.

During Prohibition, Longstreet operated a still in Ash Meadows where his cabin still stands. A still is a device to make your own alcohol/moonshine. Stills were illegal during Prohibition, when all alcohol was banned. At one point, he ran a saloon. His pistol served as a bouncer. The holes he shot in the tent roof provided a calming effect. At other times, he was a rancher and miner. Disputes with his neighbors resulted in some of them being shot in self-defense. Even into his 50s, Longstreet was still being hired for his gun during some claim wars. Oddly, a posse could never be raised to go after him. His end came at age 94, fittingly, when he accidentally shot himself. At first not fatally, the infection needed time to take old Longstreet down. Had he survived, he probably would have claimed self-defense.

When ready to leave the Longstreet, head out the back door of the casino and shoot a bearing straight for the Funeral Mountains. Don't get taken down by aggressive ducks from the casino pond. Cross the dry riverbed of the Amargosa River. Turn right when you make contact with the TTR. Follow the straight railbed through white mineral deposits. Eventually, the TTR re-crosses the Amargosa. Bushwhacking is the order of the day here. The thorny nasties that tear at you are known variously as "wait-a-minute" bushes or "vampire" bushes. In Sudan, their equivalents are known as "choke" bushes. There, the long thorns are capable of both deep wounds and yanking passengers off the back of trucks. With persistence, you will be able to fight free and return to daylight.

Pass a probable, former cement plant to your far right. Possibly this was the station of "Muck." But the lack of enthusiasm in the town's name spread to its inhabitants. And Muck did not last long. Next, arrive at the ghost town of Scranton. You are now 12 miles out from DVJ. All that is left is a fenced-off well. At one time, there was a 20-car siding here and some houses. It was named after investors from Scranton, PA. Keep your heading north toward civilization and its unloved twin, trash. On some former bridge abutments graffiti makes an appearance. Local sport appears to be shooting bottles on the elevated railbed. Then come to a geographical survey marker, raised high above a pile of rocks, on an iron bar. This indicates that in 1921 surveyors said, "Here is Nevada, there is California"

Welcome to Nevada, yet again. For at some point during the morning hike, you slipped back into California without border formalities. More hiking. Arrive at yet another survey marker. By the time of this marker, cement was being used. Thus, we have initials and a date in the overpour. Posterity enshrined. Pass a number of older trash dumps. The trash has nowhere to go but to your observation. Then the granddaddy of trash dumps. Much of it old. Some unique, like the dead cow or waterless boat. Hauled out from the Amargosa Valley and dumped in a dry riverbed. There to be washed back to the valley by the next hundred-year flash flood. Testament to the cyclical nature of trash.

After much desert hiking, you will start to see farmland to your right. The major farm in your view is the T and T Ranch. Yes, the same T's as the TTR. It was founded in 1915 to supply the railroad construction crews with food. These days the farm grows alfalfa, pistachio nuts, almonds, apricots, pomegranates, pecans, carob beans and figs. The emphasis is on organic. More northern advance brings you to a red container house and the Amargosa Farm Road.

Cross Amargosa Farm Road to Mojave Road. Continue straight on Mojave Road until Mesquite Road. Turn left on Mesquite Road. This allows you to bypass a small farm that smothered its particular section of the TTR. Walk on Mesquite Road until you see the TTR. Turn right on the TTR. Continue along the TTR until you come to another fenced-off portion. Turn right, then left, following the fence until you reach a road. Turn left on the road and, pretty much immediately, the TTR gifts itself. Turn right and walk away from habitation.

Soon, you will come to the slight remnants of Leeland. Here was a 25-car siding, post office, water tanks and various buildings. In 1931, a prospector lost his mind and decided the best course of action was to burn down most of the buildings in Leeland. Once his work was completed, he proceeded to take his own life. Remembered history tends toward the dramatic, for that is what sticks. Not much of the dramatic left in Leeland these days, though. Your target is the mountains ahead that peter out at the TTR.

Note the large sand dunes to your right. After much thought and even more debate, they were named Big Dune. At 3,526 feet, fair enough. To your left are still the Funeral Mountains, bookended by the northern Schwab Peak at 6,448 feet and the southern Pyramid Peak at 6,703 feet. The Funerals are riddled with past mines and fantasies of gold. The TTR redelivers you to the wilderness. Pick a bedroom for the night.

Photo 34 - 20 Mule Team making its way through Death Valley. (Wiki Commons/Public Domain)

Photo 35 - Consolidated stamp mill outside Goldfield, NV, the ruins of which the Death Q passes through. (Wiki Commons/Public Domain.

Photo 36 - Francis Marion "Borax" Smith, father of the Tonopah and Tidewater Railroad. (Wiki Commons/Public Domain)

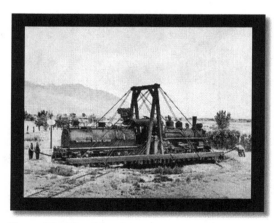

Photo 37 - The Slim Princess being turned around on a rail turntable. (Wiki Commons/Public Domain)

Photo 38 - The Death Valley Railroad train leaving New Ryan. (Wiki Commons/Public Domain)

Photo 39 - Death Valley Railroad trestle bridge. The car on the bridge was a 1912 Cadillac, specially adapted to fit on narrow gauge rails. It was used for maintenance. In the car is Major Boyd, the Australian manager of the New Ryan mines. (Wiki Commons/ National Park Service/Public Domain)

Photo 40 - Randsburg, California, under a rare blanket of snow. (Wiki Commons/Public Domain)

Photo 41 - Death Valley Junction Mill. The building farthest right is possibly still standing. (Wiki Commons/Public Domain)

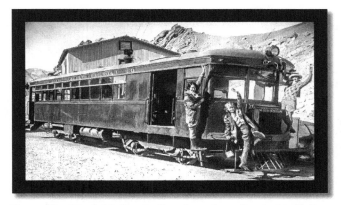

Photo 42 - Death Valley Railroad tourist railcar with Hollywood starlets. Part of the public relations campaign to increase tourism to Death Valley and keep the Death Valley Railroad alive. (Wiki Commons/Public Domain)

Photo 43 - Saline Valley Salt Tram. View from the control tower down into the Saline Valley, which is over seven thousand feet below. (Wiki Commons/National Park Service/Public Domain)

Photo 44 - Ludlow Cemetery.

214

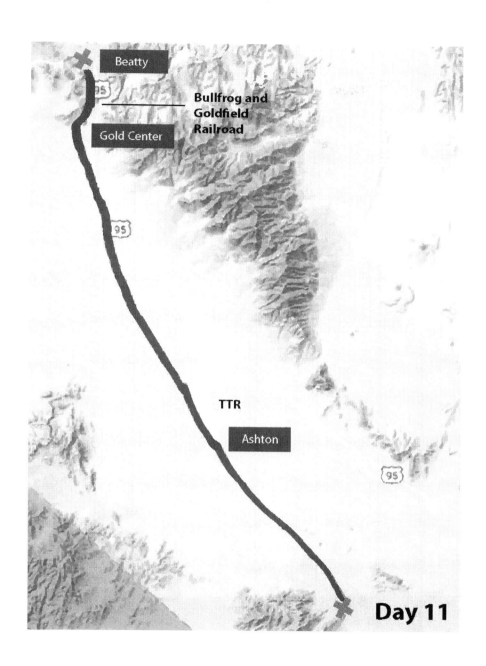

Beatty

Bullfrog and
Goldfield
Railroad

Gold Center

95

TTR

Ashton

95

Day 11

215

Day 11

Leeland-Gold Center-Beatty

A cold night makes for early starts. The full moon powerful enough to render headlamps useless. Competing with moonfall, the Las Vegas glow from beyond the mountains to the east. Continue straight up the valley tracing the Amargosa River dry bed. Try to sense the waters of the Armagosa River coursing somewhere in the sands beneath you. Pass the forgotten cans of Ashton. Once a five-car siding with associated buildings. Begin to close with the 95 road and another forgotten railroad. The Las Vegas and Tonopah Railroad. You will soon be acquainted.

The mountains on your right are the Bare Mountains. Named locally because they look naked. The highest point of nudity is Nugget Peak at 6,316 feet. To your left is the Amargosa range. Pass a strange, white building to your left. You will encounter more of these along the Death Q. Apparently, they are part of a ground-based radar tracking system for aircraft. Next up are old mine ruins to your far right. The ruins are tethered to the TTR by a long, straight line, which was formally a tram line. This is, or was, Carrera.

Carrera's name origin is Carrera, Italy. Home of marble deposits mined since Roman times. When marble was found here in 1911, it seemed an appropriate name. By 1913, a town had sprung up. Complete with a hotel, post office, store, swimming pool, restaurant and marble-lined town fountain. One hundred and fifty souls made their home here. Water was piped in from Gold Center and electrical power brought in from Rhyolite. The town newspaper, "The Carrera Obelisk," spouted the limitless possibilities of the future.

In furtherance of that future, a three-mile tramway was constructed from the quarries down to the Las Vegas and Tonopah Railroad. It gently carted the marble slabs down to the terminus using gravity. Basically, the loaded cars going down pulled the empty cars back up the hill. Alongside it ran Pompeii Avenue. Italy absolutely dominated the town's imagination.

After the Las Vegas and Tonopah went belly up in 1918, a spur line was built to connect with the TTR a half mile west. But there was a flaw in it all. The marble itself. Though of good color, texture and quality, it was much fractured. The big commercial pieces just weren't there. The town stumbled and fell. By 1924, the fountain was filling with sand. For the curious, it is still there.

The next ruin you see on your right, is the Elizalde concrete plant, built in 1936 by a company from the Philippines. The plan was to ship the cement back to the Philippines. This proved completely unfeasible at the time, and the plant was abandoned within a year. Plans to try the Philippines' scheme again a few years later were quashed by bombs falling at Pearl Harbor.

Soon after Elizalde, you will pull tight with the 95. Twice, you have to pass under the road fence to stay on the TTR railbed. With time, you pull away to the left. Quickly you are in Gold Center. Home of the former Bikini Brothel and not much else. This is Nye County, where prostitution is legal. The TTR passes within throwing distance of the brothel. The word shadows of "Cat House" can still be made out on the side of the building. Apparently "Cat House" is an illegal advertisement in Nevada, so the owner had to paint it over. The brothel closed in 2013, after that same owner passed away. Ironically, the deceased owner made his original fortune in the building and operating of short line railroads in the Midwest. He must have felt at home because, in its day, Gold Center had three separate railroad lines stopping in its downtown.

Gold Center was not aptly named. No gold was found here but it was convenient. The stage line from Rhyolite to Beatty ran through town. As eventually did the TTR, the LVT and the Bullfrog Goldfield Railroad (B&G). Moreover, it had water, which is gold in the desert. So, I reverse myself on the misnaming.

Gold Center became a town in 1905 with the arrival of the post office. Basically, the post office was the McDonalds of its day. When the post office arrived, the town was on the map.

The town grew to include a newspaper, hotel, restaurant, stores, corral and a number of saloons serving locally produced Gold Center beer.

Responsible for the beer and also ice, was the Gold Center Ice and Brewing Company. Whose production facilities were located underground. A large ore mill was also built here, the remains of which are still visible. Revenue was raised by selling water to local mining towns. Remnants of the Goldfield-Carrara water line can still be stumbled upon. By 1918, Gold Center was gone. Bypassed by the north/south railroads after the towns of Rhyolite and Bullfrog shut down.

The railroad history of Gold Center is convoluted by much overlap. This is caused by the three railroads' habit of assuming and relinquishing each other's lines throughout their brief history. Since this is not a complete railroad history, but more a hiking guide, I will attempt to simplify matters toward relevance. Picture an upside-down triangle. The bottom point is Gold Center. The right point is Beatty. The left point is Bullfrog and Rhyolite. To the far north of the triangle lies Goldfield and Tonopah.

Now, assume that at one time the B&G started in Goldfield and then passed south through right point Beatty and bottom point Gold Center. Then back up the triangle to left point Bullfrog and Rhyolite. Assume the LVT started in Las Vegas and went north to bottom point Gold Center then up to right point Beatty then over the top of the triangle to left point Rhyolite and Bullfrog. After which it swung west, before heading north to Goldfield. Finally, the TTR came from the south and arrived at Gold Center. At various times, it continued up both sides of the triangle, to left points Bullfrog and Rhyolite and to right point Beatty. The TTR never reached past Beatty to its stated goal of Tonopah. Though both the B&G and LVT did reach as far north as Goldfield from the Beatty area, they too never reached Tonopah. Eventually, though, the TTR took over both these lines. So, in a way, the TTR did at least reach Goldfield.

Okay, so my attempt to simplify failed miserably. How about this for purposes of the Death Q? The TTR ends at Gold Center. From Gold Center to Beatty you are on the B&G. At Beatty, you switch to the LVT for the hike to Goldfield. At Goldfield, yet another switch to the Tonopah and Goldfield Railroad (T&G) to Tonopah and beyond. Better?

As you leave Gold Center, you run straight into a mountain. Ignore the left branch headed toward Rhyolite, and, instead, follow the right branch up the river valley. There is no water for the thirsty in Rhyolite. And

Beatty, with its bountiful water, is but three miles away. Stay on the railbed as it moves up the riverbed. Pass multiple broken water pipes. Eventually, arrive at a reed-choked pond. This is Bombos Pond. Another enjoyable word.

It is a fine point to turn around and wave farewell to the original TTR. Note the abandoned old mining operation terraced into the hillside. Unfortunately, the 95 submerges the B&G for the last mile into town. You are forced under a fence onto the shoulder of the 95. Luckily, the road shoulder is quite wide. The trickle to your left is the mighty Amargosa headed for dead-end Bombos Pond. At least a dead-end on the surface. Shortly, the B&G reappears on your left, but it is covered by multiple fences. Easier to stick to the road for this short bit.

The B&G that you are on now, sort of, was built in 1906. It started in Goldfield, next to the Santa Fe Saloon. From there it ran south to Beatty, Gold Center, Bullfrog, and Rhyolite. The total length of the line was 84.7 miles long. It was built to take advantage of the Rhyolite mining boom. Unfortunately for investors, just as construction was completed, the mining boom deflated. In 1908, the B&G joined forces with the TTR out of economic necessity. There simply wasn't enough traffic to justify all these railroads. As Rhyolite's collapse drained the entire region of economic vitality. A few years later, the TTR sold the B&G to the LVT. But the president of the LVT had lost his enthusiasm for railroads. Many believe this coincided with a malaise that developed after his son drowned in the 1912 Titanic disaster. By 1918, the LVT had closed its doors and the B&G returned to the TTR fold.

Eventually, one rail line was formed from remnants of the TTR, B&G and LVT. This line reached from Ludlow, CA to Goldfield, NV. All excess portions were abandoned. By 1927, the decline in value of Goldfield mining led to the Goldfield/Beatty section of the railroad being abandoned. Since this was the section that the B&G was responsible for, its role ceased to exist. And so, the B&G was laid to rest. A stage line immediately took over their duties.

Continue on in to Beatty. Population 800-1,000. Where your hiking day ends. There are many hotels in town, as well as a campground. If you want to camp for free, head out of town to BLM land by beginning Day

219

12. Keep an eye out for wild burros, as you and they make their way through town. Continue up 95, past the TTR mural, until you come to Main Street. Just before Main Street, on your left, is one of two small food stores in town (Beatty Mercantile, 201 W. Watson St., 775-553-2255, M-Sa, 8 a.m.- 6:30 p.m., Su. 9 a.m.- 6 p.m.).

BEATTY		
1.	Food Supply	Yes
2.	Restaurant	Yes
3.	Water	Yes
4.	Hotel	Yes
5.	Beer	Yes
6.	Pool Table	Yes
7.	ATM	Yes
8.	Post Office	Yes
9.	Casino	Yes

Beatty is very compact and centered around the Main St/95 intersection. Turning left on Main Street brings one to Mel's Diner (600 S. U.S. 95, 776-553-9003, open every day, 6 a.m. – 3 p.m.) for breakfast. Also left is the excellent Betty Museum (417 Main Street, admission free, open daily 10 a.m. – 3 p.m., 775-553-2303). Where you should let them know what you are up to.

To the right, on Main Street, is the Beatty Post Office (600 E. Hwy 95, 775-553-2495, M-F 8 a.m. - 1, 2 - 4:30 p.m., closed Sa/Su). Before the post office is the Space Station RV Park, which has the second food store in town (775-553-2378, open 24/7).

Just after the post office is the Stagecoach Hotel and Casino (775-553-2419, stagecoachhotelcasino.com).

Next in line, is a large Rebel gas station (775-553-2378, 24/7) that carries an amazing array of bulk food. A Family Dollar Store is located at 401 South 2nd Street (775-382-1022, M-Sa, 8 a.m. to 9 p.m., Su, 9 a.m. to 9 p.m.).

220

Across the street, at the Main Street/95 intersection, is the Sourdough Saloon. There, great pizza, beer, pool tables, and road trip ambiance are to be had. If you are keen for a soft bed, The Atomic Inn (775-553-2250) gave us a hiker/local discount that reduced the room rate significantly. They have a pretty good DVD selection if you want to chill. The Atomic Inn can be reached by turning right at the main intersection and then taking your next right at First Street. Then proceed one block down.

Your next food and water is at Goldfield, some 79 miles of hiking to the north. Figure three solid days of hiking. I didn't bring enough water, as I relied on the road map distance, rather than the actual rail distance. A miscalculation. But on the third day, I crossed a road with traffic. Within ten minutes of standing by the road, waving an empty water bottle, a kind soul stopped and refurbished my supply.

Beatty is the only leftover town from the Rhyolite boom that is still populated. Though the Shoshone and Paiute Tribes have been calling the area home for at least 11,000 years. The actual town got its start around 1905. It was founded by Walter Beatty and his Indian wife (whose name I was unable to discover), when they settled near some local springs. Mr. Beatty served as the first postmaster, until government officials figured out he could neither read nor write. But Beatty really took off in response to the Rhyolite mining boom, four miles to the west.

At first, Beatty was a freight center for Rhyolite and all the other area mining camps. Wagons hauling supplies from Las Vegas arrived in Beatty needing water. Which Beatty had plenty of. Fifteen hundred horses were involved in hauling the freight between Las Vegas and Beatty and back to Las Vegas. From Beatty, these supplies were distributed to the various mining camps. Then the railroads took over. Arriving, in order, the LVT in 1906, the B&G in 1907, and the TTR in latter 1907. A rail depot was built to handle all this traffic, but it burned down when the station agent's wife decided to clean her skirt with gasoline. The replacement depot functioned until 1940, when the last railroad shut down.

Early on, Beatty's future appeared bright. Supplying the boom brought in heaps of revenue. But one's future is often fickle when it relies on others. By 1911, Rhyolite was all but abandoned. Beatty limped on as an infrequent transport center. But through the twenties, new mining strikes would lift hopes.

The story is told of a tailor who traded two suits for $150 worth of stock in a non-promising mine. Shortly thereafter, a rich vein was struck at that same mine. Those two suits brought in $10,000. But mining was mostly in decline. Still, Beatty remained the economic hub of the area.

During prohibition, Beatty served as the region's moonshine producer. In 1931, gambling was legalized. And 1933 saw the opening of Death Valley National Monument. Automobiles began to frequently pass through town, creating an avenue of income. In 1940, the U.S. government opened the 3,000,000 acre Nellis Air Force Range just to the east. There, Air Force pilots practiced for WWII. The area remains off limits to this day. With the arrival of WWII, all the local gold mines were shut down. The War Department deeming them unessential to the war effort. Only mines that produced war material were allowed to stay open. Many miners working in such mines were not drafted into the armed forces, as their work was considered too valuable.

In 1951, the Nevada Nuclear Test Site opened up within the Nellis Air Force Range. Residents were told they had nothing to fear from the nearby atomic tests. Though the government did announce that it was best not to be underground, in mines, when nuclear devices were detonated. In the early years, most of the detonations were above ground.

The detonations were also pre-announced. So, Beatty locals would make their way south of town to a viewing point out over Yucca Flats. There to watch the day brightened by detonation. Closer, were the soldiers who were often ordered to have front row seats. In all, there were 928 nuclear explosions at the test site. The above ground tests sent up mushroom clouds that were observable 100 miles away. Which made them discernible in Las Vegas. The shock waves a brief interruption to card players trying to clean out casinos.

One 1962 crater, created by a nuclear detonation testing the viability of peaceful nuclear explosions, is still visible. This test was made for the infamous Operation Plowshare. Memorialized on the plaque in front of the Ludlow café. Over the years, the test site has provided many jobs in the area and is not a universally unpopular neighbor.

In my early years, I worked for a man who had built fake towns at the test site that were subsequently nuked. He reminisced, "A nuke would go off and the crews would rush right back in to begin construction of the next town. The workers were given radiation badges that would change colors if overexposed to radiation. Luckily, they never changed colors." I'll say no more.

Fortunately for Beatty, it is generally upwind of the testing area. Thus, although the explosions were sometimes heard and felt in Beatty, there was not a related increase in cancers. Not the case in St. George, Utah, which was often downwind. And suffered an extraordinarily high rate of cancer in the years following above-ground testing.

The nuclear tests began in 1951 and ended in 1992. Of the 928 nuclear explosions at the test site, 828 were under ground. The last above ground test was in 1962. Since then, Beatty continues to survive, but jobs are always an issue. Employment rates subject to outside whims beyond Beatty's control. Which explains the fluctuating population estimate. Though tourism seems to keep things reasonably afloat.

In 1987, a large Federal project in nearby Yucca Mountain looked to bring major employment to the area. This was the positive angle. The flip side was the nature of the project. The Yucca Mountain Nuclear Waste Repository proposed to store up to 7,700 tons of nuclear waste under Yucca Mountain for up to 1,000,000 years. This waste would be transported from across the USA.

Battle lines quickly formed. Many locals, the Feds, the military and the rest of the states thought Yucca Mountain would make a fine repository. Nevada politicians and environmentalists, not politely, disagreed. The battle has raged ever since. To date, no nuclear waste has been stored at Yucca Mountain. A conversation on the topic is perhaps best avoided in Beatty.

Another hope for Beatty's future lays in new mining techniques that are able to extract gold from old tailings. Or locate new gold sources underground, that the old-school miners missed. At various times in recent Beatty history, successes in this area have brought population influxes. But the gold always peters out and Beatty returns to its quiet ways. There to await your arrival.

223

A not-to-be-missed side trip from Beatty is the Bailey Hot Springs (775-553-2395). You've earned them, I believe. There is also a campground and Wi-Fi on site. The springs are five miles north of town, on the 95. And once were a stop on the B&G Railroad. There are three housed springs. Warm, hot, and hotter. The exhaled sigh alone, at first immersion, is worth the trip. Hours are 8-8, seven days a week. Entry to the springs will set you back $8. There are even buffalo about. As well as a teepee.

On the way out to the hot springs from Beatty, you will pass a crashed airplane on the left. The plane has two tales for you. It seems a local brothel was inspired to promote its business through contest. A mattress with a target was laid out. The first skydiver to nail the bull's-eye got a free night with the companion of their choice. On the given day, the ladies lined up by the mattress in all their finery. Perhaps it was engine failure or crosswinds or a very distracted pilot, but the contest never came off. Instead, the plane carrying the skydivers crashed in front of the brothel. Luckily no one was injured. The party went on. And the plane stayed where it died. Or a drunken pilot clipped a power line and crash landed in front of the brothel. Both stories compete for listeners. Take your pick.

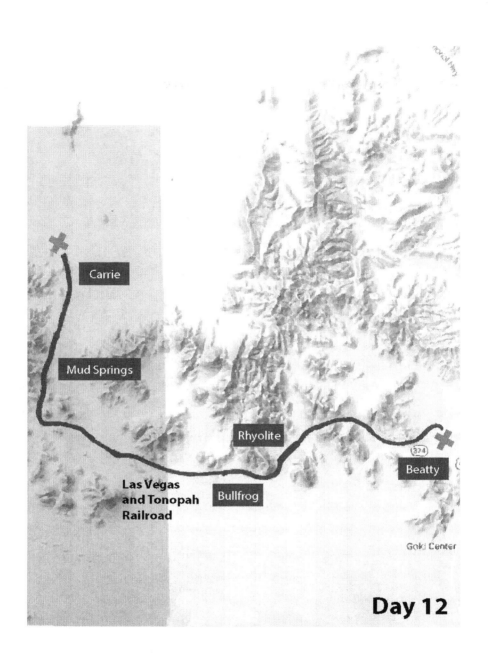

Carrie

Mud Springs

Rhyolite

Las Vegas
and Tonopah
Railroad

Bullfrog

Beatty

Gold Center

Day 12

225

Day 12

Beatty-Rhyolite-Bullfrog-Mud Spring

After a fortifying breakfast, leave Beatty and your short relationship with the B&G. Head west on Main Street in the direction of Death Valley. Pass the museum on your left. Just past the El Portal Hotel, turn right on Irving Street, then left on Cave Street. Followed by a quick right on Center Avenue. Follow Center Avenue uphill to its terminus. Immediately, you will see the Las Vegas and Tonopah railbed to your left. Welcome to a new railroad. Hop it and follow the railbed through the cuts. At one point coming close to the 374 road, before curving away.

Eventually, you will pass the massed tailings of a 1980s strip mine. There are lots of older mines scattered about. Consider the risks to your longevity if curiosity draws you underground. After a couple of miles, you will emerge into a widening valley. There may be lots of wild burros about. If so, they will snort their disapproval at your existence. The ghost town of Rhyolite will begin to appear. The first significant building you spot will be the LVT station house. The railbed becomes a dirt road that heads directly to the station house, which is your short-term goal.

Before that, pass a rail spur that leads off to your right. Now you are an expert at spotting railbeds in the terrain. A side trip up this spur follows the canyon, past the Steinway mine, to the Montgomery Shoshone (MS) mine. The MS was the largest producing mine in the area. And arguably the biggest contributor to both the rise and fall of Rhyolite. At one time, it was owned by the steel magnate Charles M. Schwab. This rail spur once led directly to the MS mine. These days, though, the railbed dead ends directly into a tailings mountain. Deposited there by the more modern strip mining approach. Summit the tailings and stare down into the gaping quarry hole, if so interested. Multiple older, single hole mines stretch in every direction of your gaze. Return to the LVT and continue to the station house, past some small ruins. The remnants of Rhyolite begin their presentation. Hoping their old death gains traction with the present.

Rhyolite is more than a stunning ghost town. It is a monument to the cruelty of mass optimism. In 1904, "Shorty" Harris started all the optimism by locating gold on the side of an area hill. Shorty's life refuses to be imprisoned in a sentence. For he lived expansively. Sometimes on a public stage. More often alone. Where expansiveness is somehow more impressive. The facts of his life are muddled, for Shorty was a gentle fabricator. He often claimed he could smell gold. But was even that an exaggeration? For time and time again, Shorty discovered gold when it was trying to hide.

In many ways, he was the classic prospector. Wandering the hills, burro behind and pick in hand. Chasing what he smelled. His front teeth encased in the same metal. At five feet four inches, not much taller than his burro. But Shorty differed from many prospectors, in that his desire was not to strike it rich and retire. The former, Shorty found quite acceptable. The latter, not at all. And when he did strike that rich vein, a great smile of anticipation would begin its spread. For Shorty Harris loved two things in this life. The hunt for gold and a party that lasted for calendar pages.

The process of his love was well observed. Shorty would corner a rich ledge of gold bearing rock exposed to the sun. Usually in some unnoticed canyon. Quickly, he would collect some samples and stake out a claim. Then a beeline to the nearest town. Where a grinning Shorty would open his mouth and spew tales of gold. The words passing the glint of their substance. The stories nonstop, as a person long isolated and without conversation can best provide. Few could resist, despite Shorty's reputation as one who kept a distance from the truth. The inevitable stampede would follow. Day jobs be damned. A mining camp would soon arise around Shorty's claim. The search for wealth from the ground going on in every direction. But Shorty wanted none of it. For he was a prospector, not a lowly miner. And anyway, it was time for his second love.

Shorty found that second love in whiskey and women. The order not critical. As the hysteria around the mining strike built, Shorty would begin acquiring the two W's on credit. While others dug. When Shorty was far enough gone in drink, someone would make him a lowball offer on his claim. The offer seemingly over generous after several bottles of Oh Be Joyful whiskey. His beverage of choice. At the rare return of sobriety, Shorty would be confronted with his witnessed signature of offer acceptance. The new claim owner would chuckle at the stupidity of his fellow man. Shorty would do the same. And both would turn to the business at hand.

Which is exactly the scenario that played out at Bullfrog/Rhyolite. Shorty was prospecting with his friend Ernest Cross. They found an outcropping of promising quartz. The rock they picked out was thick with shiny yellow. It was also green. Bullfrogs came to Shorty's mind because of the color. And so, the area was christened Bullfrog. The pair headed north to Goldfield with their samples, after staking out claims. Goldfield being the nearest significant town at the time.

There, Shorty emptied his mouth. The words flooded the town. Packing became a race, which turned into a stampede. Some men walked the entire 80 miles to Bullfrog pushing wheelbarrows stacked with supplies. Shorty leaned back on his barstool and awaited offers. He was 47 years old. (Which was the average U.S. life expectancy at the time.) And his smile was at the maximum width.

A week later, Shorty and Ernest left their party at Goldfield and made their way back to Bullfrog. By now, over 1000 dreaming and digging souls neighbored their claims. Saloons were already up and running. Shorty entered through one of their tent flaps and didn't leave. At the same time, a sober Ernest started negotiating. For he was that different kind of prospector, who saw mining as a means to an end. In that end, Ernest sold his half of the claim for $125,000. At a time when the average U.S. worker earned $200 a year. With funds in hand, he escaped all temptation and fled to Lone Pine. There he succumbed to the alternative temptations of marriage and ranch ownership. A man set up for all his years.

Back in Bullfrog, Shorty was having nothing to do with rationality. For six days, Oh Be Joyful and women competed for his embrace. Somewhere in those days, Shorty signed a document. On the seventh day, he came to. And learned that he was $25,000 richer but claimless. Shorty also

228

became aware of the $100,000 differential between a drunk and sober negotiation. What could a man do? A return to the party was the only option Shorty could make out. The W's stretching out as far as he could see.

And that is how Shorty Harris lived his life. If you visit the outdoor sculpture museum in Rhyolite, you will come across the metal silhouette of Shorty Harris. He is followed by a penguin. His most common hallucination brought on by Oh Be Joyful. Shorty died in 1934. Broke and pleased at the end of a well-lived life. He was 74. In recognition of his impacts, Shorty was honored with a burial in Death Valley. It was reportedly the first proper Christian burial in the valley. Three hundred paid their respects. His tombstone inscribed in his own words. "Here lies Shorty Harris, a single blanket jackass prospector."

Returning to Bullfrog. The hills surrounding Shorty's original strike also proved to be full of promising ore. More miners were drawn to the flame. Yet more strikes were made. The tent towns, easily movable should new strikes appear, sprung up in rapid fashion in Bullfrog, Amargosa, Gold Center and Rhyolite. Lots were laid out. Streets gridded. Free water was offered. Wild claims boasted. All in order to win the competition for residents. Quite quickly, Rhyolite (named for the mineral Rhyolite, a volcanic, glassy rock quite common in the area) came out on top. Much of this was due to the proximity and promise of the nearby MS mine. Also attractive was the town promoter's ability to actually supply water. Rather than just talk about it. By 1905, three water companies were piping in water. Water and gold, what else does a town need?

A bold prediction was made. "Rhyolite will be the largest city in Nevada." This prediction was logical. Around the same time period, the Tonopah boom resulted in $109 million being taken from the ground. Forty miles south of Tonopah, lies Goldfield. During the Goldfield boom, $80 million was extracted. Rhyolite was 70 miles south of Goldfield. Rhyolite's residents believed similar results were certain, if for no other reason than proximity. Lots of folks started counting chickens.

And the way you counted chickens in those days was by building. It was a solid demonstration of one's optimism. Permanent property advertised longevity to new arrivals. By the end of 1905, 1,500 people were living in tents in Rhyolite. Then the wood began to arrive and more solid structures went up. Dynamite explosions, in the surrounding 2,000 mining claims, were constant. Three million dollars was offered for the MS mine, the offer immediately refused. In 1906, the LVT arrived. In 1907, the LVT began building the depot you are now standing in front of. The next year, the B&G made it to town from the south and built a wooden depot next to the jail. By 1906, 3,000 people called Rhyolite home. Stone buildings started going up, which absolutely demonstrated unquestionable permanence.

By 1907, Rhyolite was steam rolling. It had three swimming pools, concrete sidewalks, a stock exchange, three churches, newspapers and magazines. Electric lights lit the streets. Telegraph and telephone services were available. There were both police and fire departments. Sixteen restaurants fed the hungry. The Alaska Glacier Ice Cream Parlor took care of post meal sweet teeth. It was owned and operated by the Countess Morajeski. A hospital provided care for the horrific injuries from the mines. A (still standing) concrete jail housed the wayward. Ownerless dogs were also held there or in the Bullfrog jail. Until their howling led a Judge to order them chloroformed. The steel doors to the jail still appear formidable. There were ten lawyers and seventeen brokerage firms trading in mining stocks.

The jewel was the John Cook Bank, whose three-story ruins still cast shadows. Stained glass windows, marble stairs and indoor plumbing garnished the concrete building. Construction costs were over $90,000. More than a million in today's dollars. Other significant buildings, in various levels of decay, still populate the main drag. Fading informational plagues give a taste of what once was. For salvation, there were a number of churches. For the cultured, there was an opera house and symphony.

For the rest, there were more than 50 saloons. Within their walls, gunplay was not uncommon. One of the most remembered gunfights was between John Sullivan and James Clayton. The shootout occurred in the Monaco Saloon. Both men moving towards each other blasting away. By the end, their guns were almost touching and eight shots had been fired. The two men collapsing to the ground, one still trying to choke the other. Both dead within 30 minutes.

With 50 saloons in action, bottle houses were soon built. One remains. Known as the Kelly House, it was built by a mining engineer of the same name. Fifty thousand bottles made up the walls. Upon completion, he sold 400 tickets at $5 each and then raffled it off. Hopefully earning a tidy profit for his recycling efforts. Paramount Pictures restored the bottle house in 1925. Presumably to use in a film. In recent times, the bottle house walls were destabilized by nearby modern mining blasting. But since all is quiet now, the bottle house stands on.

The two-story school is another standing relic. One that continued to haunt nearby Beatty for decades. In 1905, students were but a trickle in Rhyolite. One teacher, and a small school funded by donations sufficed. But the boom brought droves of new scholars. By 1907, there were 270 school age children in Rhyolite. Which quickly overwhelmed Rhyolite's modest schoolhouse. In 1907, a vote was taken, and the decision to build a new schoolhouse passed overwhelmingly. A bond for $20,000 was issued.

In 1907, construction started on a large, two story, concrete school-house. In 1909, it was ready for students. But by then, the lights were being turned off all around Rhyolite. The students joined the flowing exodus. In its first year of operation there were only enough students to fill one class-room. Not long after, all the students were gone and the unused school began to ruin. The bond debt left to the surviving town of Beatty to pay off. Which it took until 1978 to do.

The red-light district lay in the southeast corner of town. Near the still standing concrete jail. And not far from where the TTR/B&G wooden station house once stood. The joint railroad's railbed that led to Gold Center is still visible as it hugs the base of the mountain in a southeasterly direction. That is until it vanishes under some massive modern tailings. (This is not the direction you will be leaving town.) Back in the red-light district, one wooden brothel remains. Or at least it is labeled as such. The perimeter of the red-light district was strictly controlled. That way, the respectability of the rest of the town was left unpolluted.

Economics was a different matter than respectability. At one point, the property value of a single bordello was higher than the MS mine. The general value of the bordellos charted Rhyolite's rise and fall. An example. In 1905, one of the first prostitutes to arrive in town, Mabel Vaugn, bought

231

herself a lot for $150. And got down to business. She did this by paying a licensing fee of $5. By 1907, the estimated value of her property was $7,400. In 1908, a fire burnt down the bordello she had constructed. In 1914, she let the delinquent lot go for the grand total of $4.96 in back taxes. At its 1908 pinnacle, Rhyolite had hundreds of prostitutes. By 1910, there were less than 20.

One of Rhyolite's most famous prostitutes is still in residence. Isabella Haskins was born in 1887. Her life path brought her to Rhyolite in 1907. There she worked as a prostitute who went by the name of Mona Belle. Until 1908 that is. Her sunny personality made her a popular resident of the red-light district. For reasons lost to the years, Ms. Haskins decided, at the age of 21, to leave her profession. Her pimp, Fred Skinner, who did not share her sunny personality, was having none of it. To prevent her career change, Skinner shot Ms. Haskins four times in the back.

After her funeral, Ms. Haskins' friends and supporters began a procession to the Rhyolite Cemetery. Along the way, their path was blocked by the good women of the town. Who strongly objected to a nonrespectable being interred with the respectable in hallowed ground. Passions ran high, but eventually the blockade carried the day. The procession did a U-turn and buried Ms. Haskins on the edge of the red-light district, not far from the jail.

Over the years, her grave has become a shrine of pilgrimage. Her resting place littered with trinkets and mementos left by visitors. I was unable to locate Fred Skinner's fate. But if you would like to pay your respects to Ms. Haskins, make your way over to the jail and continue in the general direction of Beatty. Quite quickly, you will see Ms. Haskins' white cross and grave fence. Some historians propose a counter theory. That Ms. Haskins is buried elsewhere. And that this grave is not legitimate. But that belief is not nearly as much fun.

So why Rhyolite's stunning decline? Most agree that at one point in its brief history, Rhyolite was the third largest city in Nevada. Unfortunately, its entire boom and bust took place between the 1900 and 1910 census. Some put the population peak at 5,000 in 1907-1908. Others go as high as 10,000. The 1910 census found 611. The 1920 census, 14. In 1922, a passing LA Times journalist found a 92-year-old man, sole resident and acting mayor. Try to imagine that kind of population decline in your hometown.

Once again, what happened? At first, the world outside could be blamed. The San Francisco earthquake of 1906 rerouted capital and supplies toward the rebuilding of San Francisco. This negatively impacted Rhyolite's growth. More damaging was the Financial Panic of 1907, which was caused by a failed attempt on Wall Street to corner the copper market. As the panic spread across the country, banks failed and investment capital dried up. Suddenly, the money to open new mines and expand existing mines wasn't to be had. Mines began to close. Miners went on to greener pastures. Businesses without customers closed doors. And so, the dominos fell.

The final nail came in 1908. And this time. responsibility was local. The giant crushing mill at the MS mine, built in 1907 to handle 300 tons of ore a day, seemed to be underused. Stockholders in the MS mine became concerned that the mine was overvalued. They demanded an independent review. Samuel Clemen's (a.k.a. Mark Twain) quote, "A mine is a hole in the ground owned by a liar," is instructional. The review came back blackly pessimistic on the MS's future. As the MS went, so went Rhyolite. By 1910, the MS was closed. Remember Tonopah and Goldfield's respective production of $109 and $80 million? Well, good old Rhyolite's total production of the MS and surrounding mines was a paltry $1.8 million. In retrospect, all was illusory. With the MS shuttered, Rhyolite's back was broken. The electric lights were turned off near the end of 1910. It was time to live somewhere else and leave all that permanence behind.

Rhyolite, in modern times, sees a steady trickle of visitors. In all, 21 films have been made in, and around, its ruins. But the most charismatic modern addition has to be the Goldwell Open Air Museum. There you are free, which is also the admission, to roam amongst various outdoor sculptures. Most of the sculptures were created, quite predictably, by a string of Belgian artists. The ghost figures are especially powerful. Their creation accomplished by draping live, local models with wet plaster. The museum is just downhill from the Bottle House. It never closes. Further yet downhill, lies both the Rhyolite cemetery and its inhabitants. A hike there leads past wash after wash cluttered with goods the citizens of Rhyolite once considered necessary.

When your tour of Rhyolite is complete, return to the LVT station house and depot. This depot was built in 1907 and opened in 1908, at a cost of $130,000. In 1907, that was very serious money. Its completion just in time for the population exodus. The depot held on until 1916, when it was finally closed. Since then, it has been a residence, a gift shop, and most significantly, a bar and casino in the 30s and 40s. As the "Ghost Casino" sign testifies to.

These days the Bureau of Land Management (BLM) owns the depot, as it does almost all the land you are hiking on. Because of structural insecurity, the BLM has fenced in the depot. Though, if the caretaker is around and you ask nicely, he or she will open the fence and let you have a look in the windows. Also at the depot is an old Southern Pacific Caboose. At one time, it was a gas station operated by a Native American woman. She and the pumps are long gone. The caboose has stuck around for your photography needs.

Time to leave Rhyolite on the LVT. If you are looking at the front of the depot, turn your head to the right. You will notice a parking lot with bathrooms. Walk toward the parking lot. On the left side of the parking lot, behind some yellow rocks, you will see a flat road leading toward the mountains. That is the continuation of the LVT to Goldfield. Follow it, until you reach the mountain pockmarked with multiple mines.

The railbed continues left along the side of the mountain. At some point, during this section, stop and take in all that was Rhyolite. Soak in the mines that litter the hillsides. Now would be a good time to quote Ozymandias if you can. Hike onward. You will come to a mine entrance dug directly into the railbed. The very height of historical disrespect. Its entrance welded shut. Higher on the mountain lie the Denver and Gilbrater mines. Pass under them as the LVT bends around the bend.

Now that you're on it, it seems appropriate to talk about it. The LVT reached 197 miles from Las Vegas, Nevada to Goldfield, Nevada. You joined it at Beatty, which is 118 miles in from Las Vegas. From Beatty to Goldfield is yet another 79 miles. The LVT and the TTR arose out of the business animosity between two men. Borax Smith, the "Borax King" who built the TTR. And William A. Clark, the Montana/Nevada banker, politician and mining magnate, who built the LVT. Clark is infamous in history as the man who bribed the entire Montana legislature to elect him U.S. Senator. Caught and exposed, his response was, "I never bought a man who wasn't for sale." A refreshingly honest take on realpolitik, somewhat lacking in modern U.S. politics.

But Clark was about more than just politics. Amassing wealth also pleased him greatly. His copper mine in Jerome, Arizona, produced $400,000 a month in personal profit. That's $10 million a month in today's money. This production went on for years. In contrast, a miner working in that same mine earned just two dollars a day. Which would be about $50 a day in today's money. Injustices like these laid the foundation for the insult, "Robber Barons." Clark comfortably ignored the insult. He lived and built lavishly. His 121-room mansion in New York City for his family of four cost $7 million to build in 1905. A comparison. In 1915, Yankee Stadium was built for $2.4 million.

When Clark died in 1925, his net worth was $200 million. Which would be a cool $2.2 billion today. Not bad for a kid born in a log cabin in backwoods Pennsylvania.

Mark Twain had this to say about Senator Clark, "He is as rotten a human being as can be found anywhere under the flag." I'll give Senator Clark the parting shot. When confronted about the extensive environmental degradation caused by his mines, Clark retorted, "Those who succeed us can well take care of themselves."

For fascinating reading, check out the story of Huguette Clark. Senator Clark's youngest daughter. Who died in 2011, at the age of 104. A recluse with $300 million in the bank and multiple mansions dotted across the United States. Most of which were fully staffed but not lived in for decades.

Back to the LVT and a refresher on the LVT/TTR conflict. So, it seems that Clark and Smith had a handshake deal. The shake allowed Smith to build a rail line from Las Vegas to Smith's mine, the Lila C, at DVJ. Unfortunately for Smith, Senator Clark assigned little value to handshakes. At Las Vegas, the line would join with Clark's rail line that passed through

Las Vegas connecting Salt Lake City and Los Angeles. The year was 1905. In that same year, Las Vegas was founded. Its population, roughly 50.

Borax Smith got to work. After 12 miles of graded rail was complete, Smith got a nice message from Clark, which in essence said, "I've changed my mind, you can't connect." This probably had a lot to do with news of repeated gold strikes starting to come out of Rhyolite and environs. What could Smith do but pack up? Which he did. Then Smith discovered Ludlow. And that is how Mr. Smith ended up building the TTR from Ludlow to Beatty. In the meantime, Mr. Clark took over the 12 miles of graded railroad and started building the LVT. Which reached Goldfield in 1907.

The LVT didn't last long. The portion that you are hiking, between Beatty and Goldfield, was in use between 1908 and 1914. The tracks torn up for scrap during World War I. The southern portion, between Beatty and Las Vegas, survived until 1918. Now, for the most part, the southern section is under the 95 highway, as its rights were purchased by the road builders. The 197-mile journey between Las Vegas and Goldfield took roughly eight hours by train. The northern section you are hiking, took 3.5 of the eight hours for the 79 miles to be traversed. You, perhaps, not so speedy.

Returning to the trail at hand. As you round the corner, you will spot a big red barn on the plains below. This is the artist's center for the sculpture garden. Next up is an old tram line. Then you arrive at a barbed wire fence blocking the LVT. This is to keep people out of an abandoned strip mine ahead, which eradicated this LVT section. You must reroute. Do this by making your way downhill, along the barbed wire fence, to the mine with the picturesque gallows. Note the trailer supporting the gallows. Have a look in the mine. Just inside the welded gate, you can see the old time-keeping stand. As you leave the mine entrance, turn right. Follow the mine road downhill, until it reaches a long tailings push. Cross the push and head for the fence that tracks the wooden power poles. Turn right at the fence and stay with it, as it skirts the bottom of the tailings mountain.

Eventually, the fence will lead you back to the LVT, as it emerges from under the strip mine tailings. When you reach the LVT, turn left. The railbed spends a while cutting through terrain, before beginning to veer right and climb. At this point, the railbed is also a dirt road, as off-roaders sometimes use it. But you know it's a railroad, because all the canyons are infilled.

With time, you pass the original Bullfrog mine and town site. Before Bullfrog picked up and moved closer to Rhyolite. The mountain to your right is, of course, Bullfrog Mountain. All 4,959 feet of it. The mountain's shame at not reaching 5,000 feet is not obvious. Right after Bullfrog, you enter Death Valley National Park. A sign eaten by wind and peeled by sun is your only hint. There are no tourist crowds in this part of the park. In fact, there is no one. You are the sole representative of your species. All rhythm and poetry. Soon, the dirt road you are walking on turns right toward Goldfield. Ignore it and stay to the left with the LVT.

Here the LVT begins a wide swing to the west, to build momentum and reduce grade in its climb to the pass. The railbed turns west, then swings back east, before a final turn north to the pass summit. This is a particularly beautiful and colorful part of the trail. At the summit, a spur track leads off to the east, where it dead ends at a mine. Mud Springs is just past the summit, though I saw neither hide, nor hair, nor water. On the LVT schedule, Mud Springs is listed as a station, some 14 miles from Beatty. Begin a downhill trek following the railbed as it veers left. Pass an old concrete tank on the right, which is possibly Carrie Well. A former water stop for trains climbing to the pass from the north. At some point, if you spent a lot of time exploring Rhyolite, darkness pulls the curtain. Claim a bed by the LVT and initiate a chat with the coyotes

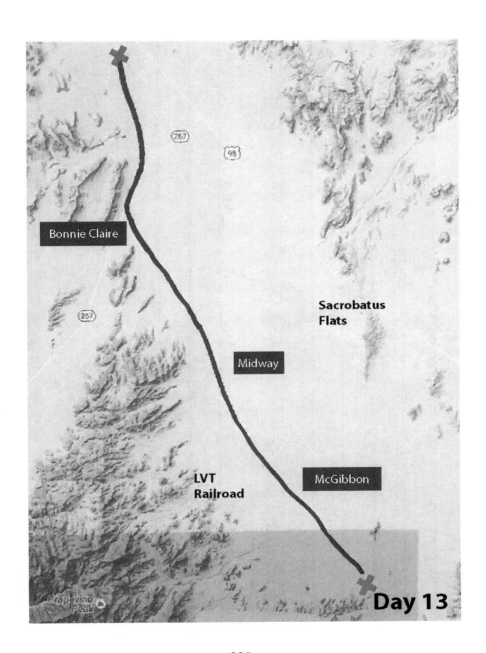

Bonnie Claire

267

267

95

Sacrobatus
Flats

Midway

LVT
Railroad

McGibbon

Grapevine
Peak

Day 13

Day 13

Midway-Bonnie Claire-San Carlos

A sun greets. Up and on the move. Check out hill innards, as you make your way through a series of cuts. You're moving in a northwesterly direction. The railbed becomes overgrown at points. Note multiple wooden culverts. Your exit from Death Valley National Park is marked by a fence. Joshua trees make an appearance. Were the early Mormons right about the resemblance to Joshua beseeching his God?

The LVT continues straight down the length of the valley. The B&G is far to the east, though both railroads share the same destination. Later they will come within kissing distance. Pass several ex-settlements marked by cans and 100-year-old trash. The first was McGibbon. The next, Midway, was a water stop for the LVT from 1907 until 1914. It is located 26 miles from Beatty.

The mountains to your left are the Grapevine Mountains. Highpoint is Grapevine Peak, at 8,738 feet. Climbable, if you have a hankering to see juniper trees. To your right, the stretched expanse of the wonderfully named Sacrobatus Flat. The white you see is salt. The green bushes that populate the dry shoreline are greasewood. Their scientific name of Sacrobatus Vermiculatus providing the flat's moniker. From the Greek, sacro means "flesh," and batos means "bramble or thorn." The greasewood is characterized by a love of salt and a deep tap root, often more than 50 feet deep. Known to the Native Americans as excellent sources for arrows, spears, planting sticks, and medicine. Later shown by modern medicine to be full of antioxidants.

Keep plugging along. Note the mountain on the left with a white scar on the top. Walk for what seems like a week. Then note the white scarred mountain in the exact same position vis-à-vis you. A confusion understandable as to who is actually not moving. Come to a fence. It is an anti-ATV fence. Pass it and continue skirting the flats. Inevitably, a hostile head wind will spring up to coat you in flat dust.

Slowly, the flats take over the railbed, turning it white. The salt swells the ground, turning it softly crunchy. A unique hiking sensation. Tumbleweeds make an appearance. You are now genuinely a desert rambler. Pass a lone, large, stone marker. The railbed aims for the mountain in front of you. Crest a rise and cross the front and center valley. Your target is the mine on the far side.

Eventually, an abandoned cabin and mine come into view. The LVT passes right by them. It is an interesting site with dumped refuse from the ages. It's also a great retrospect on a solo miner trying to make it on their own. Note the cemetery 100 yards to the right. Two lonely graves lie saturated with grief from another time. This area is known as Bonnie Claire. At one time, 100 folks were in residence. Stores, saloons and a post office offered services. All of the materials to build Death Valley Scotty's Castle were off-loaded from the B&G/LVT here. But when the railroad went, so did the town. Though the post office held on until 1931. The large mine to your left was built to rework the tailings of earlier mines. You are 38 miles from Beatty and 41 miles from Goldfield.

Just past the abandoned cabin, the railbed gets lost for a bit. Continue straight on the dirt road until you reach the 267 road. Turn right on the road. Turning left would lead you to Scotty's Castle, just over the California border. Scotty's Castle is named after Death Valley Scotty. A member of a class of characters that views sunsets as destinations.

Scotty was born in 1872. But Kentucky didn't suit him, and he soon found himself out west. For a while he rode with Buffalo Bill and his traveling show. Then he drifted towards mining, or some would say, the con of mining. His specialty was convincing wealthy backers to finance his search for gold in Death Valley. In reality, they were underwriting Scotty's lifestyle.

Over the years, he perfected the rhetoric, and his personality expanded to meet the rhetorical image. He spent time in jail. But to balance that, he set the Transamerica rail speed record in just under 45 hours. His ability to self-promote pushing him forward through life. Eventually, one of his marks called Scotty out on his gold mine con and came out to have a look for himself. The mark's name was Albert Johnson. When Scotty's fraudulence was exposed, Johnson was initially highly annoyed. But over time, he forgave Scotty and a friendship formed.

Ladies and gentlemen, the talented Ken Graydon once more. This time with his take on Death Valley Scotty's successful attempt at setting the Transamerica rail record.

Coyote Special

On the ninth day of July in nineteen-hundred-five
A locomotive whistle split the day.
And the Death Valley Coyote left Los Angeles behind And headed
    for Chicago along the Santa Fe.
They made San Bernardino ten minutes to the good, Doubled up to
    pull the pass they call Cajon, Smoked it into Barstow nearly
    half an hour ahead,
Changed engines in three minutes and once again had flown.
Doubled headed into Trinidad eleven hours later, Arizona and New
    Mexico behind.
The Coyote found her stride and hit a lope for Kansas City And let
    the lonesome prairie miles unwind.
Then ninety miles an hour in a streak across Missouri To Illinois in
    four hours' steady roll,
She clocked one-hundred-six a few miles west of Galesburg While
    the hogger pulled the throttle and Scotty shoveled coal.
At the Dearborn Station platform, the Coyote stood at last,
Six minutes short of forty-five hours out
And Scotty in his glory was the hero of the hour As he spoke of
    what the run was all about.
But it took nineteen engineers and nineteen locomotives And the
    working force of half the Santa Fe
And a hundred tons of pride in doing things the way they should be
    To put Scotty in Chicago on that day.
Scotty's got the highball to Chicago. The Coyote Special's got the
    right of way, And if steam and steel will only hold together
They're out to set the record come what may.

(Printed with permission from Phee Sherline.)

Mr. Johnson's health was fragile. His visits to the desert reduced this fragility, so he decided to build a vacation home in the Grapevine Mountains, on the edge of Death Valley. He also built separate accommodations on the same property for Scotty. The scale of the 1922 mansion was staggering for the area/era. Total construction costs ran to $2 million. A 270-foot swimming pool was started, but the stock market crash prevented its completion.

The delivery of materials necessary for construction kept Bonnie Claire and the B&G, which had succeeded the LVT, afloat for years. Scotty, who by now was going by Death Valley Scotty, expanded his tales to match the extravagance of the construction. Soon he had the public convinced the castle was his. Financing accomplished by his gold mine hidden under the castle. And that is how Scotty's Castle was born. Mr. Johnson, the real owner, just kept smiling in the audience.

Today, a visit to the grandeur of Scotty's Castle, which is run by the National Park Service, is possible. Though flooding, in 2015, has closed the castle until at least 2019. A short hike to nearby Tie Canyon, reveals the stacked remains of 70 miles of B&G railroad ties. Which were purchased by Mr. Johnson after the railroad's demise. His plan was to use them as fuel for the castle's 14 fireplaces.

As mentioned, when you meet the 267, turn right. The LVT is either under the road or just to the right of it. Mostly, it is under it. In a few miles, the LVT emerges from under the road. Your choice is to walk the road, with its nonexistent traffic or hike the rainbow shaped flood control arches to your left. Preferable, if you are in a rhythmical mood. However you do it, continue along the 267 for those few miles.

Pass a sugar shack with a white bus parked in front. In the distance, you'll see the LVT tracks veering to the left. While the 267 heads off to the right. The departure of the LVT, from the 267, is marked by cairns. Follow the railbed, as it climbs upward to the pass. The 95 traffic is obvious to your far right. Eventually, the LVT will cross the 95. Somewhat prior to that, I suggest calling it a night.

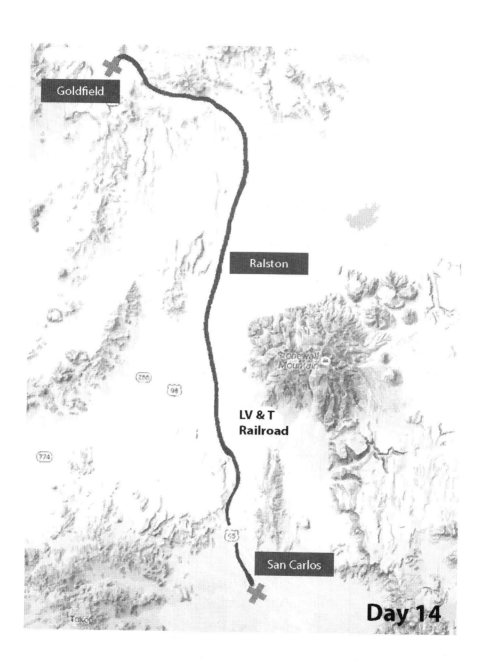

Goldfield

Ralston

Stonewall
Mountain

LV & T
Railroad

San Carlos

Day 14

Day 14

Stonewall-Ralston-Goldfield

Roughly speaking, if you are following the schedule, the dawn will find you around San Carlos. A former water stop for the railroad, just west of the 95. San Carlos is some 34 miles from Goldfield. This would be a fine day for a very early start. For the day is long. Once your rituals are complete, continue your climb toward the pass east of Stonewall Mountain. But you do no more than threaten the pass, as the LVT crosses the 95 and continues up a side wash. To cross the 95, go under the fence and then through the gate on the other side. Note the neat handle that tensions the fence gate. Be sure to close the gate.

Before you go through the gate, there is a decision to be made. You are still some 30 plus miles from Goldfield. There is no water between you and Main Street. Though, on my particular day, there were snow flurries. Staying with that particular day, I found myself short of water. Unsure of the onward terrain and actual distance to Goldfield, I needed to develop a remedy. The only thing I could come with was water hitching. This involves holding my empty water bottle upside down and shaking it by the side of the 95. An uphill pull-off point is conveniently located. The fourth car stopped and replenished my supply. My thanks for that kindness. Thus, water hitching is an option, should you find yourself short.

In the end, water hitching was a fine decision for me. The LVT arrives in Goldfield through an extended backland of mines. My arrival there was after dark. Quickly turned around and confused by various lights, I wandered those backlands for hours. Trying not to fall into mines. Until finally stumbling on to Main Street. Without water, my mood would have been darker than the surrounding night. I'll try to provide a smoother arrival for the reader.

Follow the railbed up wash as it skirts the hills to the left. You pass Wagner, Nevada. Population zero since 1918 when the water tower was removed. Soon the B&G railbed appears on your left. The two lines seek the other's company. At one point, coming within 50 feet of each other. Only capitalistic insanity could foster the kind of greed that would lead to the same-time construction of two parallel railroads with matching destinations. Did the competing engineers wave or give each other the bird? Surely, they raced. The two lines curve to the left. Where they crest the pass. And begin a subsequent downhill. When you come to a point where the lines embrace, then break away, take the right branch. This is the LVT, which is always to the right of the B&G, from this point on.

Head out across the valley. Carriage bolts and spikes lay drowning in decades of sand, trying to stay evident. In this remote section, the railbed is much eroded. Probably due to the material used. Note the large number of severed carriage bolt heads. They remind of fossilized mushrooms. These once connected the rails to each other. When the rails were recycled, the bolts were sheared off with a chisel, rather than the nuts removed. My guess is that this area had fairly high humidity. Which caused the nuts to rust on. As WD-40 wasn't invented until 1953, shearing was the most convenient option. Arrive at Forks Station. A beam on a hill its only reminder.

The 95 is to your left. The B&G veers off toward it, while the LVT heads toward the mined hill in front of you. The building you can see on the far 95 is the Cottontail Ranch. Yet another house of desire that has been closed and for sale for over a decade.

Howard Hughes, the tycoon and aviation pioneer, was an occasional guest during its heyday. A record compilation of Cottonwood Ranch tales, artfully titled, "Coming My Way," was published in the 70s. When the LVT reaches the intended hill, it turns right. Tracking Stonewall Flats to your right.

The flats, as well as the mountain behind them and the ghost town at its base, are named for "Stonewall" Jackson. The Confederate General in the Civil War whose troops held their position against repeated Union assaults during the First Battle of Bull Run. Hence the nickname, "Stonewall." The town of Stonewall came about in 1904, when silver was discovered in Stonewall Mountain. Quickly, there were 150 people in town. The silver just as quickly ran out. By 1905, there was no one left to say hello to.

Reading about the west of those days, it is difficult not to imagine nomadic populations incessantly roaming from gold rush town to gold rush town. Chasing rumors and witnessing the boom and bust cycle over and over again. These days Stonewall and everything else to your right, is part of the Nellis Air Force and Gunnery Range. It is very much off limits. The occasional explosive thuds you hear reinforce this.

The black speck on your horizon is Ralston. It's a fine goal. These days Ralston consists of an old railcar that was converted into a house, as well as a very large steel tank. Lots of mines dot the hillside behind the downtown. Apparently, silica was extracted from the mines. Enough to support a store and saloon at one time. The LVT maintained a 48-car siding here. A siding is basically a side track that allowed trains to move off the main line. Either for unloading and loading or allowing another train to pass. By 1928, all in Ralston was part of the past.

The Ralston stop is 17 miles from Goldfield. Keep going straight. Until you veer left into the Chispa Hills. Continue up a long wash. With time, Blacktop Mountain at 6,396 feet becomes visible. Keep your eyes peeled for animals during this section. I saw four wild burros, two jackrabbits, two pronghorn antelopes, a red-tailed hawk and eight wild horses that raced across the LVT. All in a fairly brief period of time.

The railbed comes to a wash. Its continuation, on the other side, is marked by cairns. Soon the railbed turns into a well graded dirt road. Follow this road into Goldfield. Note the original wood culverts still in place that confirm you're on the LVT. Goldfield is ahead, it just takes a while. Visually, the railroad seems to pass Goldfield on your left but eventually it curves back around. Mine tailings of all possible hues are everywhere. As are multiple headframes. Mine buildings in various states of collapse complete the picture.

Slowly you lose altitude. After a number of rock cuts, you arrive at a big dirt road that cuts in front of you. There is a gate on the opposite side of the road. Behind it, a prominent headframe with containers spaced around it. Though the containers might have been moved by the time you arrive. Turn right on the dirt road, keeping the tower to your left. Walk 400 yards and rejoin the railway cut to your right. The cut is marked by a cairn.

Follow the railbed through a Technicolor minescape. Soon you come to large piles of green and yellow tailings. Right after them, encounter that same old dirt road. Turn right on the dirt road and head up hill. The railbed would have continued straight at this point, but it is obliterated by more recent mine tailings for the remainder of its length into Goldfield. Continue up the dirt road, seemingly away from Goldfield, until you come to a T intersection. The intersection is marked by a sign saying, "Diamond Field." Turn left at the T and walk toward the slashed mountain with the antenna on top. Hereafter, known as Columbia Mountain.

Continue along the dirt road, as it curves in front of Columbia Mountain. Be aware of an unpleasant dog in the area. The road then makes its way into town. Note the horizontal scar that runs along the base of Columbia Mountain. Yet another abandoned railroad. This was once the very short Consolidated Railroad. It was in place to haul ore from Goldfield's mines out to the Consolidated 100 Stamp Mill. This mill was located on the northern side of Columbia Mountain. Eyeball the scar, as you will be returning to it for your Goldfield departure route.

As the dirt road enters town, it evolves into North Main Street. Pass the small Dew Drop Inn on your left. (In name only, not for lodging.) Continue to the first major road turning left. This is Aluminum Street. It is not signposted, but does have a stop sign on it for North Main Street. The stop sign is your clue/cue. Turn left. Walk 50 feet and take your first left. This is Pine Street, also not marked. Walk down to the next corner. Note the concrete safe at the center of the former and extensive T&G maintenance yards to your right. The Tonopah and Goldfield Railroad (T&G) will be your companion railroad for some time to come.

Exploring the maintenance yard is fascinating. At one time, there was an eight-stall garage for locomotives and railcars that needed maintenance. The garage ringed a train rotation turntable. Where a locomotive, for example, would be driven on to the turntable. Then rotated so it could be backed into the chosen maintenance stall. After repairs, the locomotive was then driven back on to the turntable and pointed in the necessary direction. The foundation of the turntable is still in evidence amongst the bushes. As are collapsed, massive, wooden doors, an oil sump pit, various foundations, and the aforementioned safe. Up close, the stenciled letters

"T&G Railroad" are still visible over the safe door. The small wooden building, on the other side of the street, was once the T&G ice house.

Many thanks to Jim and Joann Price for taking the time out of their day to explain to us the workings of the Tonopah and Goldfield railroad yard. Their knowledge on the topic was impressive. As is their work to preserve various aspects of Goldfield history. Also in need of mention is their generous offer to store Orbit's truck while we completed our hike of the Death Q. It turned out to be that ill-fated truck's last rest, before its personal decision to leap off a cliff. But that is another story.

After explorations, return back up Pine Street to Aluminum Street. Turn left and follow Aluminum Street to its end. Along the way, it morphs into Pearl Street. At the terminus is the Santa Fe Club, built in 1904. Reportedly the oldest continuously-operated bar in Nevada. Which also happens to be run by the meanest bartender in Nevada. Or so she and the sign say. My guess was a softness behind the façade.

This is yet another Jim Marsh owned establishment. Inside is warmth, a pool table, pizza, and much of interest on the walls. Especially the photos in the back room near the pool table. Make sure to pick up a free Goldfield walking tour and map near the door. Also, eight rooms and a laundromat are available, if a hot shower, bed, and clean clothes are of interest. They were to me. If not, there is plenty of vacant space out of town to camp with the dirt. You have now hiked five abandoned railroads for a total of 331 miles. Good on you!

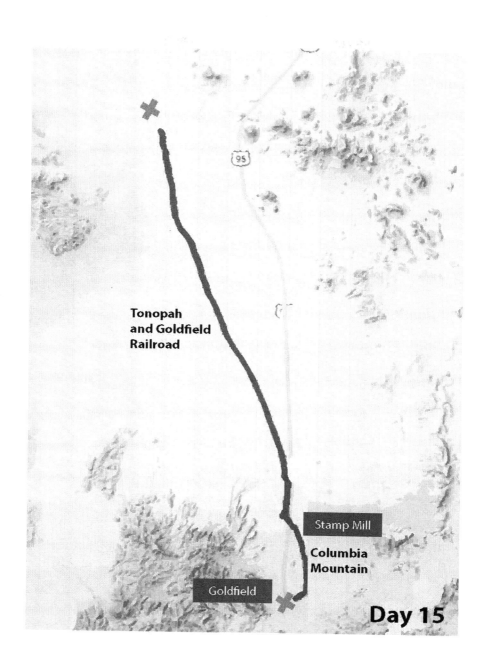

Tonopah
and Goldfield
Railroad

Stamp Mill

Columbia
Mountain

Goldfield

Day 15

249

Day 15

Goldfield-Klondyke-Area Southwest of Tonopah

Time for a tour of Goldfield's offerings. Directly across the street from the Santa Fe is the original B&G depot. This is where the railbed you were paralleling yesterday ended up. The owner of the depot is a collector. Their collection spreads about and is fascinating. Photos and discovery inevitable. Once done, leave the B&G Depot and turn left. You are now on Fifth Avenue. Head into town and breakfast. When you reach the 95, which runs straight through town, turn left. Walk two blocks to Dinky's Diner (775-485- 3231, Open 8-4 M-S, 8-2 Sunday) on your left. The only restaurant in town. And a fine breakfast.

Taking care of business, the amenities of Goldfield:

GOLDFIELD		
1.	Food Supply	Yes
2.	Restaurant	Yes
3.	Water	Yes
4.	Hotel	Yes
5.	Beer	Yes
6.	Pool Table	Yes
7.	ATM	Yes
8.	Post Office	Yes
9.	Casino	No

The next food and water is 31 miles away in Tonopah, NV. The General Store is located at 777 Crook Avenue and faces the 95 (775-485-3477, 8 a.m. – 8 p.m., 7 days a week). There is an ATM on site. The Post Office is open 1-5 M-F (400 S. 4th St., 775-485-6374). Interestingly, for such a small town, Goldfield has a radio station, KGFN 89.1 FM. Its very public broadcasting studio is on the 95, across from the Goldfield Hotel.

Goldfield is yet another Nevada wild ride. In 1901, gold was discovered. The nearby newspapers of Tonopah spouted the potential. Word spread. The rush was on. Only this time, the hype was justified. The deeper the shafts reached, the thicker the gold became. In 1903, there were 175 residents. By 1907, there were 20,000 residents. Some say 30,000. All deathly ill with gold fever. Without a doubt, the largest town in Nevada at the time.

The mines kept producing. In the first 40 years of the century, almost $90,000,000 in gold and silver was removed from Goldfield's mines. That's approaching $2 billion in today's dollars. In one mine, that measured 373' x 700', almost $9 million worth of ore was extracted. It was a place to make your future.

But not for all. Miners, working for mine owners, were paid $4 for an eight-hour shift. The millions made, funneled their way upward to the mine owners and their backers. A downward spread was not in the cards. Resentment festered. The miners unionized. Their dues built a 64-bed hospital. Necessary for the horrific mining injuries common to early miners.

In 1907, the unions wanted to raise the wage to $5 a day. The mine owners were not receptive. They had their own complaints. Shootouts between union and non-union miners had taken place. Hi grading, which involved sneaking out small pieces of gold heavy ore at the end of a shift, was commonplace. To combat the practice, mine owners instituted a rule that miners change their clothes on company premises after every shift.

Outright robberies of mine properties were on the upswing. The accumulation of wealth was hampered, and the mine owners didn't like it. They approached the sympathetic Governor of Nevada for help. He, in turn, convinced President Theodore Roosevelt that anarchy in Goldfield was imminent. Though no one else in Goldfield seemed to see it that way. Teddy sent in the troops. The miners put down their tools and walked out. But they kept their strike non-violent.

The mine owners responded by immediately and predictably, lowering miners' wages across the board. They also banned unionized miners from working in their mines. With no alternative, the miners went to work as cheap construction laborers. This fueled a building boom way out of proportion to Goldfield's future prospects. Soon, Teddy figured out he'd been hoodwinked and recalled the troops. But it was too late for the unions. They were broken. The strike was over. And unionized miners had no choice but to renounce their membership in order to return to mining work, at the new, lower wage instituted by the mine owners during the strike.

In 1904, Wyatt and Virgil Earp arrived in town. Their fame, from the infamous shootout at the OK Corral, some 23 years earlier in Tombstone, Arizona, draped over them like an aura. Wyatt stuck with mining, but Virgil was sworn in as Deputy Sheriff, despite having lost the use of his left arm in a retaliatory ambush following the OK Corral shootout. Virgil contracted pneumonia while carrying out his duties and died in 1904, at the age of 62, after a six-month battle with the illness. Wyatt, the sole surviving participant of the shootout at the OK Corral, returned to California shortly after his brother died. Where he lived until his death, at age 80, in 1929.

In the heady boom times, Goldfield was full of man-made drama. Banks were robbed. Horses ran into cars and vice versa. Shootouts were fairly common. The first suicide occurred when a bartender drowned himself in the town's water tank. The body wasn't discovered for an unfortunate period of time. Squatters claimed land and mines, and were driven off with shotguns or court orders. Whichever was more convenient. Dog fights and anything else of interest, were gambled on. Scams and con-men were rife. As was scandal.

An example: In 1906, a Russian Count named Podhorsky seduced the wife of one Mr. Hines. It took Mr. Hines until 1907 to track down the Count at a Goldfield restaurant. Where he promptly shot the Count four times. Killing him immediately. It took a Goldfield jury ninety minutes to decide that it was a reasonable reaction to a seduction. And Mr. Hines was set free to go about his business.

As the boom tapered off, home invasions increased. Telephone poles were stolen for firewood. The dramatic headlines tend to go on and on.

Not all was dark. Goldfield was also a party. There were over fifty saloons. One bar extended so far that it required eighty bartenders to serve its customers. Or so it was claimed. The Goldfield Brewery cranked out fifty barrels of beer a day. Which kept the red-light district lively day and night. Twenty-seven restaurants quieted the hungry. Incredibly, fourteen cigar stores were in residence. There was a Vaudeville theatre. Multiple baseball teams. And in 1907, a cinema screened the first silent film. A band of gypsies was in residence to explain your fate. A feeling of great possibility existed. In the back room of the Santa Fe, there is a photograph that somehow captures the essence of that time. It depicts a circus parade of elephants and assorted animals sauntering down Main Street. The crowds agog, yet comfortable, at the strangeness of it all.

But perhaps the most remembered event in Goldfield's history is the September 3, 1906 lightweight boxing championship between the African American Joe Gans and Oscar "Battling" Nelson, who was White. Gans, thirty-two, was known as "The Old Master" for his 187-fight career and sportsman-like boxing style. Nelson, twenty-four, was famed for his incredible durability but dirty fighting tactics. This fight was to be his seventy-first. Nelson was born in Copenhagen, Denmark, and was known as "The Durable Dane." Measurements of Nelson's skull determined that its thickness was comparable to a Neanderthal. And his heartbeat of forty-seven beats per minute was well under the average human's heart rate of seventy-two beats a minute. In other words, Nelson was custom-designed to take a beating and survive.

The fight was brilliantly promoted. It was the first fight in history to be termed, "The Fight of the Century," ahead of time. The entire $30,000 purse was displayed in $20 gold coins in the window of a Goldfield bank. Both fighters agreed that it would be a fight to the finish. Though this decision clearly favored Nelson. But Gans desperately needed the money, and was willing to agree to any condition. For that reason, Gans accepted a guaranteed purse of $10,000. Nelson secured the remaining $20,000 for himself.

Fifteen thousand spectators showed up to witness the fight. Many sleeping in their train cars or on the ground due to the lack of available hotel rooms. The writer, Jack London ("Call of the Wild," "White Fang") was there to document it, as were a number of celebrities and politicians.

The tension in the town prior to the fight must've been phenomenal. Three hundred armed deputies were organized to control the crowd. As both fighters put on their gloves, the temperature in the outdoor arena climbed to over one hundred degrees. Prior to the fight, a number of telegrams were read to the crowd. Including one from Gans' mother which encouraged him to, "Bring home the bacon." And that is how that term entered the American lexicon. For the phrase had been unknown to the American public up to that point.

Both fighters instructed the referee to ignore any towel thrown in from their corner. Shortly after three p.m., the fight began.

In the early rounds, the crowd was solidly behind Nelson. But round after round went to Gans as he out-boxed his opponent. Twice, Nelson was knocked down. But it mattered not to Nelson. He was designed for this and kept coming. As the rounds wore on, a frustrated Nelson's boxing style became dirtier with multiple low blows and head butts. Crowd favor swung to the older, more gentlemanly, Gans. The fight was relentless. The sun acted as a neutral opponent by beating both men down equally. Each corner fanned their fighters with large towels between rounds in an attempt to bring down core body temperatures. Ten rounds went by, then twenty. In round thirty-three, Gans suffered a broken hand but fought on. Round forty found both fighters predictably delirious. The crowd wild with it all. By round 42, the referee was so annoyed with Nelson's cheap shots that he awarded the fight to Gans. The exhausted crowd mustered what pandemonium they had left.

The fight is believed to be the longest boxing match in history. And is commemorated on a plaque next to the courthouse. For the curious, there is silent video of the fight still circulating on the internet.

Such a battle could not but impact both fighters' lives. Gans, weakened by the fight, still managed to go on and fight Nelson two more times. But he was a sick man, as he was suffering from tuberculosis. Nelson won both rematches. Gans died prematurely of complications from the tuberculosis at the age of 35. Many would argue, as the greatest boxer of all time. Nelson also did not fare well. The constant beatings took their toll and he reportedly spent his last days living in an insane asylum. Where he died at the age of seventy-two. Both men are members of the International Boxing Hall of Fame.

Goldfield had three major railroads and one minor one. Now it has none. As discussed, the B&G depot was across from the Santa Fe Saloon. The LVT depot was on Fifth Street at Point 129 of the walking tour. While the T&G depot is on the 95, at Point 133. Nothing really remains at either of the latter two for your viewing pleasure.

What is a pleasure are the remaining buildings. Memorable is the 154-room, four story, Goldfield Hotel overbuilt in 1907, at a cost of $300,000. Each room possessed electric lights, heated steam and telephones. President Theodore Roosevelt once gave a speech from one of its balconies. The hotel hung on until the end of World War II. Peering through its ground floor windows at a different age is a treat. Rumors of its renovation are endless in Goldfield. The fear is that the renovation would disturb the incredibly crowded array of ghosts that are in residence at the Goldfield Hotel. Acknowledgement of their presence resulted in the hotel being featured on TV's, "World's Scariest Places."

Also of interest, is the three-story, 1907 high school currently under renovation. At its height, 400 students attended class there. Their echoes no longer even whispers.

The 1907 County Courthouse is still in use. It remains the county seat for Esmeralda County (population 790, size 3,589 square miles). At 240 residents, Goldfield has to be one of the smallest county seats in the USA. The Nixon Bank building, on Main and Ramsey, also provides great window voyeurism. But really, the whole of Goldfield makes for splendid wandering. At a minimum, make sure to walk the length of the 95 through town. You won't regret your discoveries. While strolling, stop on the sidewalk and close your eyes. Imagine a day, 111 years ago, when the Fourth of July crowd was so thick you couldn't cross the street. Open your eyes. All gone. And please frequent local businesses when possible. They survive on people passing through.

There would even be more to see, if not for fire. Reading through the history of Goldfield, one finds fire to be a most common thread. Again and again, parts of the town were engulfed in flames. The problem was often water pressure. Specifically, the lack of it. Gravity-fed water hoses don't shoot water very far when they are poorly designed. A spectacular fire in 1905 provides an example. As the fire spread through the business district, firefighters tried to fight it with water. But local residents had drained the lines in order to prepare the defense of their homes. When all seemed lost, local bartenders swung into action by saturating blankets with beer from kegs. The blankets were used to douse flames and protect unburned buildings. Beer also coated the throats of those battling the flames. With effort, beer and buzzed firefighters beat back the flames. Be sure to peek in the windows of the 1907 Firehouse, next to the general store. There a neat treat awaits you.

So, what happened to Goldfield? By now you are familiar with the familiar story. Mine production started dropping off and people migrated. By 1910, the population was under 5,000. In 1913, a massive flood took out a large section of the city. Fewer and fewer folks moved about, amongst empty buildings from a different chapter. Many of those empty buildings were lost in the Great Fire of 1923. Which started when a liquor still caught fire in a house. The fire spread rapidly, consuming 25 blocks of Main Street and killing two people. The bartenders no longer around to roll out the kegs. Goldfield never really recovered. By World War II, the population had settled down to about a thousand people. But during the war the Federal Government banned all gold mining as unessential to the war effort. Goldfield slimmed down to around 200 residents. And there it has pretty much remained.

It's time to leave Goldfield. Head back to the Santa Fe. Just after the bar, turn left on Pearl Street and follow it back to North Main Street. Turn right on North Main Street and leave town the way you came in. Aim straight for the base of Columbia Mountain. You will reach a Y. Veer right for about 30 yards. In front of you is an ATV track leading up the hillside for about 100 yards. Until it reaches the Consolidated Railroad. Follow that track up to the Consolidated. Turn left on the old railbed and follow it straight out to the abandoned 100 stamp mill. At the major bridge washout, the detour is to your right. The mill not much further on. For perspective, go to the second photo section and check out the photograph of the Consolidated Stamp Mill when it was still functioning.

The mill ruins will capture your imagination on many levels. The mill was positioned here so its noise and pollution were distant from town. The mill operated from 1908-1919. Over half the ore produced in Goldfield was milled here. By which I mean, the gold and silver was removed from the rock it was found in. The waste produced is staggering. Its leftover canyons fill the valley below you.

Have a good mill exploration, before descending to the valley floor. Check out the massive wooden beams and wooden wheels that pockmark the ruins. Be sure to locate the geometric water tank base, on top of the hill, for the view alone. After you are through, follow the white rocky road downhill past the wooden trestles. When you reach the bottom of the hill, veer right into the waste canyon. Continue along the dirt road, through the eerie canyon, until you reach the opposite side. Proceed north as far as the old power lines. Turn left on the power line dirt road, following it until you're almost to the 95.

Just short of the 95, you will come to the T&G railbed. There is a cairn marking the railbed. Add a rock, if the gesture seizes you. Turn right and continue along the railbed north. This railbed originated in Goldfield, at the T&G turntable but is difficult to follow out of town because of recent sewage pond construction. Which made a diversion to the Consolidated Railroad very desirable. Follow the railbed, as it moves toward the 95. Eventually, you must pass under the 95's road fence. There, the T&G meets the 95 and gets drowned for a bit. For your purposes, cross the 95 and go under the opposite fence. There you will find telephone poles and a dirt road paralleling the 95 road fence.

Follow the dirt road north for about half a mile. Eventually, you will see the raised railbed start up again and head off left. A telephone pole sits directly on the separation point. Follow the T&G railbed as it slowly parts with the 95. Begin a straight shot up the valley. The desert here has adopted a distinct personality. You can judge it for yourself. Pass a washed-out bridge, then a black water tank. Climb out of the valley. At mile 13 out of Goldfield, you pass Klondyke. Most likely named for the Great 1898 Klondike Gold Stampede to Yukon, Canada. Where 100,000 set off for Dawson City, Yukon, under all the wrong conditions. And only 30,000 actually arrived. The rest dying, disappearing, or turning back. But we saw no evidence of the Klondyke that was.

If you spent a significant amount of time exploring Goldfield, your world is dialing dark. We made it to a big water tank and cow watering trough. These were visible, as only the desert can offer, from a hell of a long way off. Upon arrival, the trough proved to be full of desperation water. By this point, someone had road graded the railbed. We spent the night near here and awoke to the only measurable snow of the trip.

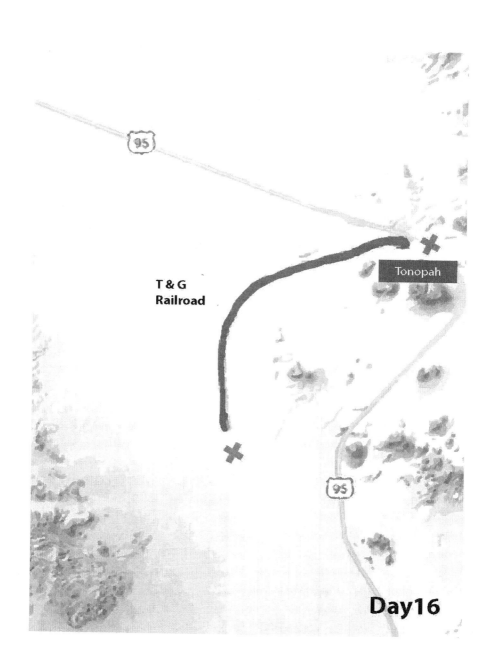

95

T & G
Railroad

Tonopah

95

Day16

Day 16

Area Southwest of Tonopah-Tonopah

Comes the morning. Today is a day that will find you with your feet up early. Nearby Tonopah is your destination. It should also be mentioned that you are now on the Tonopah and Goldfield Railroad (T&G). The railroad was built in 1905 and managed to hang on until 1947. Its total length was 100 miles from Goldfield to Mina, Nevada. Though you will only be hiking 84 miles of it. At Mina, the T&G connected with another line, which in turn connected with the major east-west lines of the Southern Pacific Railroad. It began its life as a narrow gauge railroad but quite quickly converted to standard gauge. Originally, the T&G was built for servicing mines, but after that industry declined, the railroad turned to passengers for survival. Which kept it afloat for some time. As did freight. But not very afloat. The automobile was winning its battle against rail for the heart of the American consumer.

World War II temporarily returned the upper hand to the T&G, as gasoline rationing was in effect. Cars were left in the driveway and it was back to the rail for everyone. Also, an Army airfield was built in Tonopah, which further boosted the T&G's prospects. Times were good for a while. But if you had T&G stock, now was the time to sell it. The war ended, as they all must, and the base closed. The economic recovery was robust. Passengers fled back to their cars, and the T&G convulsed for a couple of years before flatlining in 1947. Its rails torn up shortly thereafter. The locomotives and railcars sold to a Los Angeles salvage firm. Victim to a trend going on nationwide.

Back to north finds you moving up the Montezuma Valley. The Weepah Hills to your left. The word "pah" means water in the Shoshone language. It is commonly used in place names in the area. The San Antonio Mountains are to your right. Tonopah is up ahead. The word Tonopah is usually assumed to mean "greasewood water" in the Shoshone language. Greasewood being the plant that was spoken of back at Sacrobatus Flat.

260

Pass a murdered van on your left. It never really had a chance. Come to a massive Y. Here, the T&G splits into a northwest and northeast branch. A connector line way up top seals the wye triangle. Take the right branch. Come to a concrete railroad bridge covered in graffiti. Apparently, the van and environs is a remote party spot.

Hike toward two rows of power lines. The second row tracks Route 6. Right before that road is a second Y. Once again, take the right branch and head into Tonopah. Pass an old mill site on the way. For a while the railbed parallels Route 6, until you come to a gate. The gates sign asks that you, "Please close the gate." Follow the dirt road that leads to Route 6. Which is now smothering the T&G. Road walk the wide shoulder into Tonopah. It is one mile to a Burger King/Subway/convenience store. Two miles to downtown, the Mizpah Hotel and the outstanding mining park.

Tonopah has everything that you will need.

TONOPAH		
1.	Food Supply	Yes
2.	Restaurant	Yes
3.	Water	Yes
4.	Hotel	Yes
5.	Beer	Yes
6.	Pool Table	Yes
7.	ATM	Yes
8.	Post Office	Yes
9.	Casino	Yes

The next food and reliable water is in Benton, CA, which is 107 miles away. This is the longest stretch without resupply on the Q. There are three unreliable water sources along the way. But definitely not something to count on. Plan accordingly. Of course, there is always possible water hitching at a number of spots.

For eating, the friendly Tonopah Brewing Company (775-482-2000, 315 Main St., open 11 a.m.–9 p.m.) has good BBQ and beer. The Scolaris supermarket (775-482-6791, open 7 a.m.–9 p.m., 7 days a week) is, unfortunately, at the far end of Main Street/95 where Air Force Road crosses. It's a bit of a hike, but the market is fully and widely stocked. It is right next to the Tonopah Station Casino. The Tonopah Post Office is at 201 Erie Main (775-482-3359, open 9 a.m.–5 p.m. M-F, 12–2 p.m. Saturday).

For sleeping, the Mizpah Hotel at 100 Main Street is very hospitable (775-482-3030). The Pitman Café, located within the Mizpah, serves a filling breakfast (6 a.m.-10 p.m., seven days a week). A cheaper night can be had at the Clown Motel (521 Main Street, 775-482-5920) that you passed on the way into downtown. The Clown Motel is next to the town graveyard. I don't make this entertainment up. Cheapest of all, is a return to the desert.

But if you decide to stay at the Mizpah, you should be forewarned of its history. The five-story Mizpah Hotel opened in 1907. Until 1929, it was the tallest building in the state of Nevada. A genuine skyscraper for its time. The hotel paralleled Tonopah's boom and bust. For many years, it was the social center of a town with full pockets. Jack Dempsey, the former heavyweight champion of the world, was said to have been a bouncer there. Some say Wyatt Earp tended bar at the Mizpah. When Tonopah fell on hard times, the Mizpah joined the decline. At the turn of this millennium, the Mizpah closed its doors altogether. But in 2011, investors with emotional ties to the area reopened those doors. It is a treat to stay there.

Oh, and yes, the warning. The Mizpah is overpopulated with ghosts. The hotel website itself claims three child ghosts, as well as two miners who haunt the basement. The two miners were murdered while attempting to dig a burglary tunnel from the Mizpah basement into an adjoining bank. But the queen of the apparitions is the Lady in Red. Otherwise known as Evelyn Johnston. Back in 1914, Ms. Johnston was making a living as a prostitute at the Mizpah. Her room was 512. Outside of which, she was murdered by an ex-boyfriend who discovered her with a paying customer. Multiple credible sightings are made of the Lady in Red every year. A left token of her passage is a pearl on a pillow or nightstand. A not so unusual occurrence. Room 512 is now the Lady in Red Suite, available for those so inclined. Ghosts or clowns?

In Goldfield, the mineral of choice was in the name. In Tonopah, silver was the heavyweight. Though gold was also found. The story of discovery goes something like this. Around 1900, Mr. Butler had lost his mules. Eventually, he found them. Undoubtedly in a foul humor, he picked up a rock to throw at the mules. The rock was strangely heavy. So heavy that Mr. Butler forgot the mule beaning and took a closer look at the rock. Which appeared to be full of silver. And was. Mr. Butler went around shouting about his good luck. Mrs. Butler had the good sense to actually claim the discovered rock's surroundings. Word spread and the boom boomed.

In 1905, Tonopah was a town. By 1907, a city. Fortunes were quickly made. George Wingfield is a standout example. In 1896, at the age of 20, he was working as a cowboy. By 1902, Mr. Wingfield had transitioned to professional gambler/dealer at the card tables of Tonopah. He invested his slight winnings with the right people, in the right mining endeavors. As of 1904, he was worth $2 million. He kept investing. By 1906, his interests in Tonopah and Goldfield were worth $30 million. Including a major ownership in the Goldfield Hotel. Thirty million is $750,000,000 in today's money. Not a bad ten-year run for young Mr. Wingfield.

Then Mr. Wingfield did a most unusual thing. He observed the writing on the wall. Figuring, correctly, that the mines would begin to decline, he pulled his investments. Then moved to Reno. Where he bought real estate and casinos and stayed wealthy. By 1932, Mr. Wingfield owned 13 of the 32 banks in Nevada. He also loomed large in political life. At one time being simultaneously considered the boss of both the Nevada Republican and Democratic parties. An amazing feat that guaranteed victory. Then the Great Depression descended on Nevada and, without hesitation, cleaned him out. In 1935, George Wingfield declared bankruptcy. But you can't win them all, especially not in Nevada, where winning always comes to an end.

Pressures build in a boom. In 1900, there were 50 people living in town. By 1903, there were more than 3,000. The peak of 10,000 would be reached around 1907. Massive and rapid influxes of people brought competition for land, business and resources. A byproduct of this competition was to have international ramifications. A number of people arriving to take part in the boom were Chinese. They set up their own Chinatown and began providing services, primarily in the laundry and culinary fields.

Apparently, their competition was stiff, because Anglos soon began complaining about their presence. Specifically, Anglos who belonged to unions and who provided similar services. Sympathetic newspapers echoed their complaints, urging a removal of the Chinese cancer. Union members demanded local businesses not hire Chinese workers. A hostile atmosphere developed against the Chinese. The atmosphere was nothing new. Since the first Chinese landed in the western U.S., discrimination had been the main component of their welcome.

In the legal arena, the discrimination was particularly harsh. Chinese couldn't serve on juries because citizenship was impossible for them to obtain. Nor could they testify for, or against, U.S. citizens in a trial because they weren't Christians. And were thus unable to swear to tell the truth with their hand on a bible. Suffice it to say, in the early years of the west, the average Chinese stood little chance of prevailing in a court of law.

By 1903, laws had somewhat improved for the Chinese. At least on paper. Now a Chinese person could testify in a court of law. The Nevada law simply stated, "That it was up to the jury to decide how much weight to give each witness' testimony." Still, in 1903 Tonopah at least, there were harsh feelings against the Chinese. For example, Chinese were banned from working in the mines altogether.

On September 15, 1903, these hostile feelings came to a head. A gang of 30-50 men marched into Chinatown. Most of the men were believed to be union members. Many were armed. Some of the marchers demanded the Chinese leave Tonopah immediately. Others gave the Chinese 24 hours to depart, before they would be hung. Many Chinese were beaten. More were robbed. One was murdered.

To the credit of Tonopah, public condemnation of the attacks was swift. Newspapers now changed sides and derided the savagery of the violence against law-abiding residents of Tonopah. Seventeen men were arrested, mostly union members. Six were eventually charged with assault and murder. Many Chinese testified. Some were sworn in by using the ancient Chinese method of breaking the comb of a rooster. In the end, all six charged were found not guilty.

264

But that was not the end of it. The Chinese affected appealed to their embassy for help. The Chinese Government requested reparations from the U.S. Government, but the request was rejected. News of the Tonopah attacks eventually reached China, where a boycott of U.S. goods was organized in response. Perhaps the only positive to come out of the riot was a shift in attitude toward the Chinese in Tonopah. Chinese living in Tonopah, at the time, commented that the atmosphere became more accepting after the riots.

Not so in Goldfield. In 1905, a law was passed in Goldfield that Chinese couldn't get off the T&G when it arrived in town. Back in Tonopah, the Chinese chapter slowly closed. Ten years after the riot, there were still Chinese living in town. But as the mining declined, the Chinese left one by one. In the most recent census, there were no Chinese Americans living in Tonopah.

As in most cases, the Tonopah area was inhabited by Western Shoshone first. By the time Mr. Butler (who spoke Shoshone) arrived, the Shoshone were greatly weakened as a people by disease and attack. The beginning of mining in 1900 pushed them further out of the area. Though some Shoshone took part and contributed to the silver boom.

Tonopah grew steadily between 1900 and 1910. Though the financial panic of 1907 slowed things down for a couple of years. Tonopah had all the earmarks of a boomtown. Enthusiasm, rumors, excessive buildings, a red-light district, overnight millionaires, population surges and eventual decline. It provided a blueprint for the two rushes, Goldfield and Rhyolite, soon to follow. But really, these three were the last big mining boomtowns in the west. And, in a way, closed the last chapter of the Wild West. Never again would there be a mass influx of the wild-eyed seeking their fortunes from the ground.

As said, 1907 slowed things down. Construction even stopped on the Mizpah Hotel for a while. But progress reappeared and the hotel was completed. Five thousand of the town's 10,000 residents attended the grand opening. In 1908, a fire did $150,000 in damage to Tonopah's downtown. The flames visible in far off Goldfield. From 1910 to 1930 the town motored along nicely.

In 1915, Jack Dempsey, the boxing great, fought Johnny Sudenbary to a draw in Goldfield. Nobody liked the outcome, so a rematch was scheduled in Tonopah. The fighters trained in the Casino monitored by large crowds. Eleven hundred showed up for the fight. Dempsey took the early rounds, Sudenbary the latter. Once again a draw, for which both fighters were paid $100. Most felt Dempsey had won but it mattered not to the two fighters. After the fight, the two headed off together for sportsmanship beers at the Cobweb Saloon. There the bartender refused their money, saying drinks were on the house. All was going well till things got quietly still. Dempsey and Sudenbary swiveled around to see guns in their face. The west apparently still had a little wild in it. The bandits relieved them of their prize money and vamoosed.

The Depression of the early 30s dried up capital and closed mines. Hard times knocked on most doors in Tonopah. World War II saw the arrival of the Tonopah Airbase in 1942. This alleviated much of the Depression's downturn by providing local employment. B-24 bomber crews arrived in Tonopah via the T&G. Once there, they set about bombing, from various altitudes, four percent of Nevada. Which Congress had set aside for the base. But in 1945, the war ended and the base closed. The T&G gave up in 1947. And mining never really got started up again after the war. The red-light district shut down in the 1950s, when the Army complained about a soldier who had died in a brothel fire.

Today, Tonopah (population 2,478) is mostly a transportation hub servicing travelers on their way to brighter lights down south. Which makes sense, as Tonopah   is rated the best place in the United States to stargaze due to its lack of ambient light and pollution.

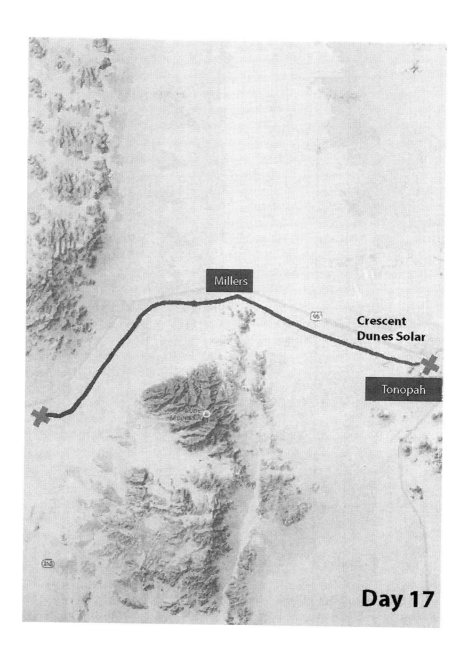

Millers

Crescent
Dunes Solar

Tonopah

Day 17

Day 17

Tonopah-Millers-Gilbert Junction

Awake to a Tonopah morning. Before departing town, be sure to visit the excellent Historic Mining Park. The park is located on Burro Street, behind the Mizpah Hotel (Open T-Su, 8 a.m. - 4 p.m., visitor center free, walking tour $5). The park is spread over 100 acres. It is here that Mr. Butler once contemplated beaning a mule with a heavy rock. And it is here that most of the $150,000,000 in precious ore taken out of Tonopah was extracted.

Wandering around the park is absolutely fascinating. Much of what you have seen on the Death Q so far is clarified in the park. And much new will be learned about mining techniques and the precarious mining life. It is estimated that 7,500 miners died during the early years of mining in the west. It is also estimated that a miner of that era had a 50/50 chance of surviving until retirement. You'll learn the biggest killer of miners in Tonopah was Silicosis. A respiratory disease caused by inhaling silica dust in underground mines.

All the details of the 1911 Belmont Mine fire that killed 17 men are explained. Including the poor decisions that were made and the heroics that took place. Firmly in the heroics category was Big Bill Murphy. As the fire spread, some miners were able to escape to the surface. No one volunteered to go back down and help others. Except for Big Bill. Twice, he went down alone and returned with unconscious miners on the lift. Yet a third time he descended, but from that he did not return. It is thought he personally cut the death toll in half. His name is known in Tonopah to this day.

You'll also come away with knowledge about high grading. Techniques included miners putting valuable ore in a glass bottle and concealing it in their rectum. The mine owners fought it but realized it was an inevitable cost of doing business. Also on display is an original T&G railroad trestle bridge. The walking tour takes one through how a mine actually operated, as well as the spectacle of a glory hole. The list goes on. The park worth hours.

Now that you're stocked and ready to leave Tonopah, exit the way you came. Walk past the Clown Motel, cemetery, and the pentagram house on your left. Return to the original gate. Pass through the gate and follow the railbed west. Pass two southern branches of the T&G. Ignore them and continue marching west. Note all the shining on the right. This is the Crescent Dunes Solar Energy Project. The exact science of which is beyond me. But here is my best understanding of the undertaking. The U.S. Government was interested in green, renewable energy alternatives. This led them to back a $737 million loan to a private company called Solar Reserve. Which provided the impetus for Solar Reserve to move forward with construction of the solar plant you are staring at.

How does it work? Basically the 17,500 solar mirrors that circle the central tower direct the sun's rays toward the tower. These mirrors adjust to track the path of the sun. The central tower itself is full of molten salt. The rays cook the salt to over 1,000 degrees Fahrenheit. The super-cooked salt is then stored in tanks, where it heats water into steam. The steam turns turbines which create energy. Enough to power 75,000 homes. In appreciation, Nevada has agreed to buy all the plant's output for the next 25 years.

Crescent Dunes began full operations in September 2015 and an immediate problem presented. "Streamers," or birds catching on fire when they flew through the directed beams of the mirrors. Some say hundreds of birds have died this way. Solution, yet unknown. But a definite clash of environmentalist polices and ideals. Solar or birds, which is best chosen?

Get used to the central solar tower. It clings to your miles like a needy child. Seemingly impossible to completely pass. Gradually, the railbed moves away from Route 6. Straight hiking brings you to an electrical switching station, some 13 miles from Tonopah. This is Millers. A stop on the T&G. Extensive ruins stretch out over a wide area. In the early days, there was a 100 stamp mill and a 60 stamp mill here. The mills ran 24/7 crushing Tonopah's ore. The noise was numbing. In fact, residents spoke of waking up at night, if ever both mills shut down simultaneously. The sudden silence deafening. The mills closed in the 1930s, and with them, Millers.

All that is left is what you see. Foundations, some pools and a number of structures. Note the flattened oil-can building that cows obviously find appealing. Millers is very picturesque, set among dunes as it is. Unless the wind begins to howl, which it did. Then there is haste in departure from the sand's pitting capabilities.

Leaving Millers finds the railbed buried by sand drifts. Simply continue west following the double pole power lines. When you get to the second-to-last power pole, turn left and walk about 50 feet to reconnect to the T&G railbed. There is a surplus of railroad ties at this point. Westward onward. Eventually, you arrive at a fine abandoned cabin surrounded by cottonwoods. An empty water tank and two dog graves are on site. I'm sure the dogs appreciate a friendly hello. Look back. That damn tower is still visible. More west. You enter a zone of salt marshes. Small ponds of varying clarity line the railbed. My guess would be high salinity, if you're tempted to imbibe.

With miles, your vision is served. As the Sierra Nevadas summit the curvature of the earth to dominate the skyline. The sky grows large. The desert opens up. You move down on the scale chart. Welcome to, as John Muir so aptly named them, "The Range of Light." The railbed drifts toward Route 6, then shies away again. Ties remain thick on the railbed. Note a large, replacement ceramic drainage pipe. Probably installed during the Second World War when there was a shortage of steel. Pick a bed. Your possible selection as varied as an American supermarket.

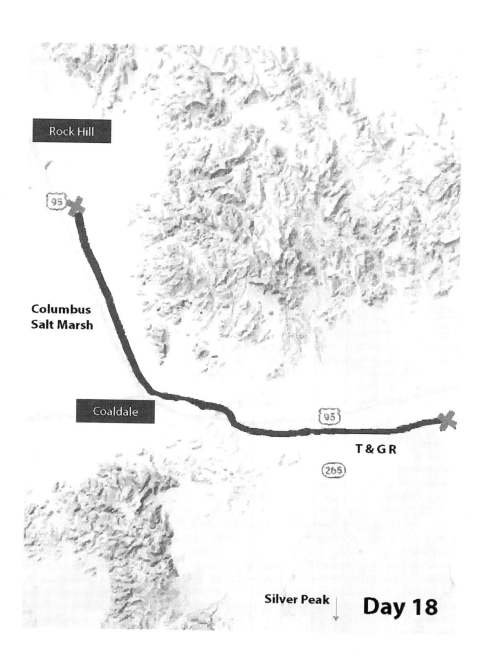

Rock Hill

Columbus
Salt Marsh

Coaldale

T & G R

Silver Peak

Day 18

Day 18

Blair-Coaldale-Near Rock Hill

You are waking up in the Big Smokey Valley. The Monte Cristo Range is to the north. The Silver Peak Range to the southwest. And the Weepah Hills are to your south. Weepah translates as "Rainwater" in the Shoshone language. Depending on how far you left Tonopah behind, you are probably opening your eyes somewhere in the vicinity of McCleans. Also known as Gilbert Junction. Here a road veered north to Gilbert, whose trajectory went: 1924 population zero, 1927 population 400, 1931 population zero. Gold will do that to you.

Follow the railbed to Blair Junction, 33 miles out of Tonopah. The 265 road branches south across the T&G and you will, in turn, cross it. A large dry lake is to your left. Rumor has it that there is petrified wood in the area. Keep your eyes groundward for it. Just before the 265 is Blair Junction. There are some remnants of what once was. Including a root cellar and a quite dangerous well that would ambush the unsuspecting.

And just prior to Blair Junction, keep your eyes open for the railbed of the Silver Peak Shortline. It passes just behind the FAA Ground Radar building that you can't miss. The hum of electricity indicates that the radar is still functioning. The 17.5-mile Silver Peak railroad connected the T&G to the mining boomtowns of Silver Peak, Blair and Weepah. It was built in 1906 and struggled until 1918. It never made a profit.

Silver Peak was one of the first mining towns in Nevada, having been established in 1864. The main mine produced well but sporadically. At one time, 900 called Silver Peak and the surrounding towns of Blair and Weepah, home. In 1907, a 100 stamp mill was built in Blair. This, combined with the coming of the railroad, initially bode well for the area's prospects. But the ore played out and most left in the 20s. Though some hardy folks stayed on in Silver Peak. Even after the town burned down in

1948. Today, mining is ongoing. The only lithium mine in the U.S. is located in Silver Peak on a dry lake bed. Lithium is what juices all those batteries. Around 100 people still reside in SilverPeak.

Silver Peak's most recent fame came in 1999 and had nothing to do with the town itself. Unscrupulous energy traders, at the infamous energy company, Enron, purposefully redirected electricity meant for California through Silver Peak. The problem was, the huge amount redirected couldn't pass through the tiny Silver Peak line. The energy traders were well aware of this, because it was part of their plan. The tiny line acted as a bottleneck, slowing the transmission of electricity tremendously. Until the line failed altogether. The failure completely cut the connection.

Suddenly, California was very short of electricity and had to scramble to buy electricity on the expensive open market. Where Enron had electricity to sell. Rolling blackouts ensued. Energy prices went up 71% that day in California. Enron made $7 million dollars on that very same day. And was later fined $25,000 for their deceit. Ah, the beauty of wheeling and dealing.

Cross the 265 and pass a ruptured metal tank. Continue until you intersect with the 95. Head to the other side and find the T&G paralleling the 95. Along this section, a sheriff stopped and walked over just because he had to know what the hell we were doing out here.

Eventually, the T&G gives up its hand-holding of the 95 and heads down a canyon. While the 95 climbs into the hills. The canyon slowly opens up, and you have the choice of following the flood-ravaged, intermittent railbed or an old graded road. Both lead you close to Coaldale, which you will see on your left. A short diversionary walk over to Coaldale makes a nice break.

Welcome to a modern ghost town. Originally, Coaldale was a mining town where coal mining was attempted. Unfortunately, the coal was of such inferior quality that profit was never an issue. And the town never flourished. With the passage of years, Coaldale morphed into a small service center for passing motorists. Leaking gas tanks in the early 90s shut down the gas station. The closure dragged the restaurant and motel down into the same economic hole. Arsonists contributed to the decline by torching the restaurant.

273

Then Hollywood checked in. Filming a forgotten biker flick called, "The Stranger," here in 1994. Now, all that is left are some abandoned buildings devoid of residents. Decorated by talented and not so talented, graffiti artists. Regardless, the free semi-art makes a nice apocalyptic backdrop for lunch. If you fall in love with Coaldale, the asking price, as of 2006, was $70,000. Coaldale is 40 miles out from Tonopah.

After Coaldale, stay to the right of the 95. From the immediate green highway mileage sign, the T&G railbed is obvious. Unfortunately, the T&G sticks with the 95 for the next 9 miles. Basically, until you reach the camel hump mound in front of you. The mound is Rock Hill at 4,825 feet. There are great views of the snow-clad High Sierras along this section. At least in the good years, there is snow. The long, dry Columbus Salt Marsh is to your left. There are possible lithium deposits there.

But back in 1871, it was borax that brought people to the area. The borax boomtown of Columbus was located on the northwest shore of the marsh. By 1875, over 1,000 people were living there. A stage line cut across the marsh from Coaldale to Columbus. A young Francis Smith, before he was "Borax," was employed as a woodcutter at one of the borax plants. Until he found his own borax deposit and began his fortune. Which would one day lead him to build the TTR and get this whole book started. Possibly not one of his motivations. By the early 1890s, the borax was gone, and so were the residents, businesses, newspaper, and post office. Now, all that remain are crumbling adobe walls and some permanent residents in the cemetery.

Keep the pace toward Rock Hill. Note the abandoned sugar shacks with grandiose views on your left. At some point, on the way to Rock Hill, you will be coming up on 25 miles for the day. Wander to the right until you find a king size. There will be more miles, eagerly awaiting your return, in the morning.

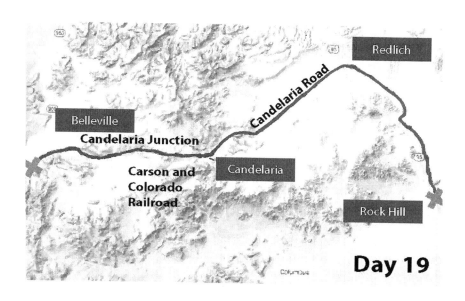

Day 19

Day 19

Redlich-Candelaria-Candelaria Junction

Back to your chase of Rock Hill. When you arrive, have a sit down in the shade or sun. When recuperated, begin an uphill climb toward Redlich Summit at 5,053 feet. After passing multiple mines on your left, the T&G turns lazy. Preferring to veer right, around the hills, rather than climb to the summit with the cars. Pass under the road fence, as you abandon the 95. Follow the T&G until you come to a large gravel pit that has unkindly obliterated the T&G. Skirt the pit on its right side and rejoin the T&G on the other end. Quickly, the T&G rejoins the 95. Just as quickly, you are in nothing-remains Redlich. The northern-most point on the Death Q and 53 miles from Tonopah.

It is possible to continue north on the T&G to Tonopah Junction. There, you would turn left on the Carson and Colorado Railroad (C&C). And rejoin the Death Q at Candelaria Junction. This route would keep you on railbeds the entire way for a distance of 17 miles. But this route is not as interesting, nor remote, as hiking the 13 miles through Candelaria. There is also a fair amount of vehicular traffic on the 17-mile leg. That is why we routed the Death Q through the ghost town of Candelaria and its gorgeous six-mile C&C branch line.

Redlich was a stop on the T&G railroad. Now, its ghost is pointing you to the west. Turn left, off the 95, on Candelaria Road and head into the Candelaria Hills. The turn is marked by a green sign almost immediately after the T&G meets the 95. Don't miss it. Before you get too far, a farewell to the T&G is in order. You shan't see it again. It is a seven-mile road walk to what remains of Candelaria. Traffic is nonexistent on the paved road.

The road walk will bring you to Candelaria proper. The first indication of Candelaria is the cemetery on your left, as well as a modern mining warehouse. The cemetery is worth the effort to pay your respects. Only four or five of the many graves are marked. The asphalt comes to an end here.

Over the ridge to your left, is a large, modern, strip mine where the suburb of Metallica City used to be. Metallica City, a.k.a. Pickhandle Gulch, had a population of three hundred in 1880. There were five saloons, a store, barbershop, drugstore, and of course, the mandatory post office. Now Metallica City is erased. Even the ground it stood on is no more. Continue along the dirt road to the remnants of Candelaria. Which was named for a Catholic Mass day.

Candelaria (5,000 ft.) began its life early. Midway through the Civil War, around 1863, Mexican prospectors were searching for gold here. Instead, they found silver. Though word was slow to get out. In 1879, a group of Anglo prospectors got in on the act. The area of their diggings became known as the Northern Belle. With effort, $15 million in silver was extracted from her tunnels. Now the word did get out. By 1880, Candelaria had doctors, lawyers, stores, newspapers, brothels, and the requisite 27 saloons. To counterbalance, there were no churches. In 1885, the Carson and Colorado Railroad built a six-mile branch line from the west to Candelaria. Which you will soon be hiking.

Candelaria had two significant negatives. One negative inviting the other. It was gifted with silver but devoid of water. The initial solution to this first negative was to haul water in by mule. Which raised its price to an outrageous $1.00 a gallon. The cheaper hydrating option became whiskey. Bathing a luxurious non-option.

Without water the mill could only operate dry. Which created choking clouds of dust and the second negative. This dust settled over and in everything. Including lungs. Which often resulted in miners consumption, a disease of the lungs, now known as pneumoconiosis, and a full cemetery. (Silicosis, from back in Tonopah, is one form of pneumoconiosis).

A water pipe from a distant spring finally brought the price of water down to five cents a gallon. For a while, Candelaria hummed. A $21,000 aerial tramway to deliver ore to the mill was built to the height of the mountains that hover over Candelaria. But production in the mines plateaued, then dived. By the late 1890s, the good times were over. Though the town held on until 1939, when the post office finally locked its doors. The crumbling buildings that witness you are all that remain of bigger times.

Of course, mining techniques improve as the decades pass. Reinterested mining companies returned to Candelaria in the 1980s. Open-pit mining was quite successful, as the massive sculpted tailings around town testify to. Over the years, $33 million worth of silver was dug out of the Candelaria hillsides. In addition to silver, Candelaria produced Horace Albright, who grew up here. After Mr. Albright left Candelaria, he went on to cofound the National Park Service, becoming its second director in 1929. Prior to that, he ran Yellowstone National Park from 1912 to 1929. Mr. Albright also helped create Zion National Park and Grand Teton National Park. A round of applause for Candelaria's contributions. Nowadays, Mr. Albright and his descendants, as well as the modern mining companies, have all moved on. Most likely, Candelaria is all yours.

After exploring the ruins of Candelaria, continue uphill along the dirt road. Pass the large ruined mill on your left. Its stonework impressively solid. This mill was the cause of so much lung grief in the town. Further on, is the Carson and Colorado Railroad's Candelaria Station, but we found no evidence of it. The C&C ducks under the dirt road for a while. Climb past mines on your left, both modern and modestly old-fashioned. With time, the road reaches a pass and a fork. Stay to the right at the fork. Almost immediately, you will see the C&C railbed veering high to the right. Jump on it. Do not descend into the wide valley.

The C&C begins a long, beautiful swing along the mountain's contours. The valley scooped out below you. Gently you lose altitude. The view doesn't have to grow on you. Keep your eyes open for wild horses. Their single file trails are everywhere. Come to the first of two large bridge washouts. The maximum train speed approaching these two trestle bridges was six mph according to C&C regulations. Not too much faster than you. Pick your way across the small canyon. A short hike, then a second bigger canyon. No worries to cross it. Now all is downward and home free.

You are now on a spur line of the Carson and Colorado Railroad. Laying tracks on the C&C began in 1880. The construction was financed by the mighty Virginia and Truckee Railroad (V&T), which was made staggeringly rich by the silver strikes of the Comstock Lode. Three hundred and twenty million dollars in silver was removed from the Virginia Range in Nevada between 1859 and 1892. That is billions in today's money. And why Nevada is called the "Silver State" to this day. The V&T hauled that wealth and grew comfortable. But they also realized the end of the Comstock Lode would one day present itself. Which caused them to look around.

One of the directions they looked at from the Comstock Lode was south toward Candelaria. Correctly figuring there would be other strikes in the area. Prodded by optimism, they began to build a railroad south to tap into the wealth to come. But they tempered their enthusiasm by building the C&C cheap. Thus, the railroad that left the V&T at Mound House, Nevada was a narrow gauge railroad. Cheaper to build and operate. Also cheap, was the labor to build it. Or at least that was the plan. But when the unions found out that Chinese labor would be building the railroad, the fan began to spread the "Ship High In Transport." In response, the backers backed off and hired out-of-work miners from the Comstock Lode. Though, eventually, Chinese did work on some sections.

In 1882, the C&C reached Candelaria, some 152 miles from Mound House. The plan was to continue to other Nevada mining centers as they developed. But a visit to the Cerro Gordo Mine in California's Owens Valley by a C&C investor altered that plan. The visit convinced the investor that mining's future lay in the long length of the Owens Valley. So, the C&C was diverted into California. Standing in opposition to the change in plans was the 7,150 feet Montgomery Pass. Undeterred, the engineers engineered the insurmountable. By building a railroad over the pass. The route included a 247-foot tunnel. The only one on the C&C. The 41 miles between Candelaria Junction, Nevada and Benton, California took a year to build. When you hike it, that year will seem rushed.

From Benton, the C&C continued down the eastern side of the Owens Valley. To the backers of the C&C this made sense, as that was where all the mines were located. To the residents of the Owens Valley, who all lived on the western half, the route was illogical and offensive. The grand plans for the C&C to reach its namesake Colorado River petered out at Keeler, on the western shores of Owens Lake. Some 293 miles from Mound

279

House. Here in 1883, at the base of Cerro Gordo, was far enough. The Colorado River still distant over the horizon. After a lot of hiking, you too will arrive in Keeler.

For a while, there was profit for the narrow gauge "Slim Princess," as the C&C came to be known. Then, as almost always, the mines began to die. Tied to their fate was the Slim Princess. In 1905, her prospects were bleak. The anemic profit couldn't even cover the interest on the C&C's debt. And then, into the picture stepped a buyer. The powerful Southern Pacific Railroad (SP) offered $2,750,000 for the Princess. The C&C owners considered neither long, nor hard, before accepting. They should have. Shortly after the purchase, the Tonopah boom began. Followed by Goldfield's windfall. All that wealth was hauled along the T&G to Tonopah Junction, where it was transferred to the C&C and transported north.

The SP made a long killing. To increase efficiency, the SP brought in Japanese workers to switch the northern 140 miles of C&C from narrow to standard gauge. This time the Japanese worked out fine. The switch was completed in 1905. The southern 153 miles of the C&C, from Tonopah Junction to Keeler, stayed narrow. And thus, kept her "Slim Princess" moniker.

A journey that occurred in 1883 proved quite prophetic. It seems that two of the major investors in the C&C decided to give their new railroad a tryout. The men were high end capitalists and accustomed to proper luxuries. Their 293-mile ride, from start to finish, took two days. The overnight stay was in Candelaria. Apparently, Candelaria's night life was a bit rough and rowdy for the refined pair. In no way honoring the Catholic Mass day. When the gentlemen reached the terminal at Keeler, one turned to the other and asked what he thought? His answer defined the Princess. "Well, sir, it seems to me that either we have built this railroad 300 miles too long or 300 years too soon."

The decline of area mining and the Depression were fatal twins for the C&C. By 1938, the C&C's northern section had been abandoned as far south as Benton. In 1943, the section from Benton to Laws was shut down. Incredibly, the last 70 miles of southern narrow gauge from Laws to Keeler held on. A railroad without a single significant town on it. The last remaining narrow gauge railroad, in the lower 48, operating west of the Rockies.

Diesel replaced steam in 1954. The Slim Princess rocked on until just short of her 80th birthday. Her tombstone reads April 29, 1960. The rails torn up the following year. Waiting all these decades for you to come and pay tribute to her.

Back to your journey descending from Candelaria. Note the dry lake on your left. Apparently, there is sometimes water in it. The wild horses we saw rolling around in it seemingly dreaming of a swim. Also obvious on the valley floor, is a large, water tank rail car mounted on rail ties. It raises water hopes. The hopes were unfounded on that day. However, there is an open trough at its base. Where we found a couple of liters of rain water. As you near the valley floor, you will come to two distinct horse trails that cut across the C&C railbed. Follow the first one over to the water tank, if you are in need and optimistic.

But don't count on water being here. When it comes to the Tonopah-Benton section and water, there are choices. Cache it, carry it, beg it or get lucky finding it. We chose the latter three. Which worked for us. Your choices are yours. If you went over to the water tank, simply retrace your steps back to the C&C and continue west. We saw five wild horses on this short section. Hike along the railbed until it comes to a dirt road. Just before the dirt road, turn right down the canyon with the railbed. After a canyon stroll, regain the dirt road and turn right on it.

Follow the dirt road toward Route 360. Come to a water tank (empty on that day) on your right, as well as a dirt road going north. The road is signposted as heading toward Belleville. To walk there is a side trip which translates into an eight-mile roundtrip. Your call. Belleville began life in 1872. There were two large silver mills there. The ruins and retaining walls of both still exist. Some of the retaining walls curve attractively.

The historical marker, near the old town site, explains life in Belleville, "The first bullion bar shipment of $9,200 was made in 1875." Ore was brought from Candelaria by wagon and processed here. The reason was water. It was here but not in Candelaria. Efficient milling required on-site water, as Candelaria quickly learned. The marker explains on. The town was well known for the following: "Wild West atmosphere, murders, drunken brawls, and sporting practical jokes were commonplace." I could find no examples of any of it, but it sounds like we missed a good party.

In 1882, the C&C arrived in Belleville. Five hundred people were in residence. There was a school, telegraph office, two hotels and proportionately seven saloons. Belleville was killed off when piped-in water finally reached Candelaria. This allowed the Candelaria mill to operate wet and not choke its citizens to death. Today, in Belleville, there is a lonely cemetery and interesting scattered ruins.

If you choose to hike down to Belleville, return to this same spot and continue down the dirt road toward Route 360. And its rare traffic. If you choose not to hike to Belleville, do the same continuing along the dirt road. About a mile before the 360, you should see a cairn. You are now in the vicinity of Candelaria Junction. The spur you just hiked on was built in 1882. At Candelaria Junction, the spur connected with the main line of the C&C. The junction is 13 miles from Redlich. In 1943, a 6.0 earthquake struck here, but nobody was around to notice.

Turn left at the cairn. Cross the big wash. Look for a second cairn marking the railbed of the C&C. If you miss the cairn or it is knocked down, your goal is the base of the hills to your left. Just make your way over there, and the C&C will place itself under your feet. Follow the C&C tracks along the Candelaria Hills, as it slowly curves back to the 360. As you near the head of the valley, it might be a decent time to call it a night. A clear night-time sky in this area, finds its black to be incredibly perforated.

And here for your evening's entertainment is a story of Belleville.

The Laugh

Charlie had long ago let the bottle take over. His drinking didn't cause him to turn mean or sad, nor even smile. No, Charlie's drink was about forgetting. It buried a past that would drown if it caught him. So, he ran. Every day after work. And hard through Sunday. Shots lined up. Followed by a tapering to darkness. It wasn't sustainable. Which was kind of the idea.

But the drink at Mr. McNabb's establishment wasn't free. To pay, Charlie worked his 12-hour shift, six days a week. Loading ore from Candelaria into crushing bins. From there, the ore funneled into steel stamps. That came down on the rock like the footfalls of rampaging gods. The noise and the haze kept a man from thinking at all. Which, once again, was the idea.

So, in the year of 1881, in the town of Belleville, Nevada, Charlie had things in order. Work, drink and sleep allowed one day to meet the next. Beyond that, Charlie wasn't interested. But events, it would turn out, were interested in Charlie.

Sunday morning was payday. Charlie was early to the bar and well into his religion. Mr. McNabb filled his empty. Words between them long ago ceased being wasted. Charlie gave himself half the shot. In the bar mirror he could see the edges were gone. Nothing left to erase but the center of the reflection. Later, from somewhere, he heard his name. But how could she call him?

Bill, Duck and Nate had finished the noonday meal at the Mill's canteen. The Sunday plan ahead not evolved much in the year and a half they had been working together. Money in the pocket. Into town to see if hell could be stirred. Which was their right as working men. Their version of hell didn't involve killing, nor even brawling. They were pranksters. Part of the practical joke craze that had swept through the town in the last year. And for that they were unpopular among the more steady townspeople, who had long ago tired of being victims. On this night, there were seven saloons to choose from. McNabbs won out.

There they found Charlie, the mystery. Already head to bar. Unresponsive to even his name. What to make of the man? He worked next to them. Then went to drink. None could remember a conversation with him. They all had drank next to him but never with him. Charlie just seemed unaware of the value of their companionship. Long ago, they had decided to rectify that particular oversight. He was an easy target. But the escalating pranks on Charlie failed to achieve the necessary result. Any version of a reaction. The failures eventually moved the three on to other victims. Though Nate wanted to keep at it. Duck, their natural leader, had cut it off with a simple observation. "The dead can't laugh." And since Duck's observations were also Bill's, that was democratically that.

The men set to drinking. Soon the saloon was full. Optimism settled over the place. As the drink caught them, men began to sense that tonight might be different. That maybe the outcome would be generous. But with late night came a flattening. Monday's lurking thunder began with a 6 a.m. whistle. Duck spoke the inevitable return to camp. The night's expectations forgotten, as they moved toward an exit to darkness. Their drunk turning bitter.

Mr. McNabb held them up. "You men mind taking your friend with you?"

Nate slurred, "No friend of ours."

McNabb revised, "You mind taking Charlie with you?"

It was Duck's turn. "What's in it for us?" The words attached to each other.

"Three beers on the house."

Duck again. "Why not?"

But Nate needed to know. "Hey McNabb, how come you let the drunk waste your stool all night?"

McNabb's southern drawl leisurely doled out the answer. "Just drink up, and take the man home."

Nate narrowed his eyes and leaned close to his two. "Next Sunday, we drink better and elsewhere."

The going was slow. Charlie's toes carved little trenches behind him. Rotations among the two supporting Charlie became frequent. As did the complaining. It was turning out to be a poor bargain. Nate was the first to suggest leaving Charlie wherever. Duck was of the same mind but did not want to darken his bar negotiation. Instead, he called a sit down. In the right place, as it turned out. "Hold on boys, I have a thought." With that he pulled himself up and crossed the street.

"Where you going, Duck?" Bill called out. But Bill had long ago waived his right to answers from Duck.

Duck was back soon enough. "I got a good one, boys. One that will stay around in our memory."

Duck's shine led Nate and Bill to get Charlie back up without complaint. They followed across the wagon ruts and past the undertaker's office. Behind the office was a large shed. Here coffins were put together. The pine brought from the hills. Duck swung the door open. "Easy boys. Lay him in that one." Which they did. The coffin smelled newly cut and was still sap sticky.

"Why, Duck?" asked Bill. But the broad question was ignored. Nate picked up on the shine. "Duck, this will be good."

Duck folded Charlie's arms across his chest. "Grab the lid Nate. Maybe we can teach the dead to laugh."

Once the lid was on, Duck pointed out a jar of nails and a hammer by match light. "Nate, you keep an eye. Bill, nail him in."

"How will he breath Duck?" Bill began to sober.

"Hell, good point. Light another match and find a hand drill. Give him a hole."

Nate came back in. "Let's take his money. He's dead anyway. You said so yourself."

"It's a practical joke Nate. We're not burying him. And we're not taking what he earned. Now get back outside."

Nate swallowed what he needed to and went back out. "Now get to it, Bill."

Bill brought the hammer down hard. Duck exploded. "Blazes Bill, there's a town out there and Charlie in here. Tap them in. There's plenty of moonlight."

When they were done, the men made their way back to camp. The night a success after all. By way of goodnight Duck said, "That'll get him talking."

Charlie came to at some hour. Right away he didn't know much. Just a little. It was dark, hot and he couldn't move much. He also had to piss. His head felt like all the mornings of his life. It wasn't much. Where was he, and what was going on, were yet to be decided. The process of answering those two taken away by a panic that grabbed him hard.

His hands beat upward into a wall. His boots did the same. His screams bounced around the darkness. When he was spent, nothing had changed. His tears surprised him.

For a while Charlie rested. Then again. This time lashing out by decision, not panic. The results not changed. The third time calmed him physically. After, he began a slow search with his hands. That is when he found a rough hole big enough for his finger. The temperature different on the other side of the hole. He was in a wooden box of some kind. No closer to big answers. What to do but wait by going back to sleep and hope this was dreaming. But sleep was no longer interested. Charlie was left alone with his thoughts. Quickly the panic returned. His body thrashed wildly. The piss left him. Before passing out, Charlie knew the darkness had him.

When he came back, Charlie had to accept Hell. To lay in your piss for eternity. So that was how people of his ilk ended up. Was he really in Hell? Did I die at McNabbs tonight? For that was the closest memory he could arrive at. His mind wandered more. And Hell clarified. Here, there was no work, nor drink. No movement at all. Just your mind. Charlie dammed thought for a long time. But since there was no time, how long was that? A point was reached where his thinking ran out of escapes and he had to accept the onslaught of a specific memory. His mind met it. Sober, he whimpered.

The war with the North was over and lost. Charlie came home from endless battlefields to a son he had never met and a wife he hadn't seen in two years. The small pleasure of his unexpected arrival became his surprise alone at the bedroom door. He fell back without a sound. The man on top his wife not recognized by the back of his head. Charlie's retreat brought him to a tavern. The owner was a patriot and let the soldier drink away the South's defeat at cost. Charlie returned to the house, blind with all the losses. He shot his wife as she slept. The candle he lit after showed the bullet had killed two, as their son was sleeping on her chest. From there he had run and run and run.

Now he couldn't. His past was his present. He began to sob. Until he couldn't anymore. Then, for the first time in 16 years, laying still in his piss, Charlie began to think about things to come. Which is where he stayed for a time not measured. Finally brought back by muffled noises that Charlie did not know what to make of. He lay and waited more, releasing the chain on the last of his thoughts.

The sound of tired hinges intruded on Charlie's thoughts. Vague light entered through the hole. He passed his hand through it. None of it made sense. Charlie shouted, "Hello, you!" to the void.

The void's answer was, "What the hell?" Followed by, "Hold on."

The pry bar took long to get the lid off. Charlie blinked through the widening light trying to make religious sense of what was happening.

"What the hell are you doing in there?"

"In where?"

"A coffin."

"I don't know."

"Well tell me what do you know and at the same time get out of there."

"I'm much obliged," came out as Charlie slowly climbed out. His story up to McNabbs was short.

The undertaker's ear sympathetic. "My guess is some asses thought it sporting to nail you in there."

"I have a pretty good idea who."

"Well you need to give some thought about how you're going to take your revenge."

"No, no I don't." Charlie felt a strange calmness. Almost a euphoria struggling through his hangover. The euphoria or whatever it was, brought an idea along with it. Charlie was quick with the words. "I have a proposition for you and some cash to help it along."

"I'm listening, but first, we need to get you cleaned up. Mother of God, you smell."

Duck, Bill and Nate came off their shift in high spirits. Sure that their punchline awaited in Charlie's bunk. Its emptiness a spoiler. Duck was first to words. "Hell, what game is he up to? Bill, go in and take a look behind the undertakers. If he's still in there let him out. But strike a deal with him before you do."

"Why me?"

"Because I asked you."

It was darkening when Bill got back. "He's not there."

Duck bit his lip and closed his eyes. "What do you mean he's not there."

287

"The coffin and Charlie are gone."

"Where?"

"I didn't ask."

Nate spoke up. "Let's go find out."

Duck pondered on it. "No, it could be a trap. We'll wait a day."

It was not a good night, nor a good day. Charlie in any part of it would've improved matters. Duck even gave thought to an apology. But only Charlie's things were evidence of Charlie at the end of their shift. The walk to town was not quiet. Theories created during their shift were given hearing. By arrival, the only thing decided was that Duck would do the talking. The first stop was the undertakers.

"Sir, a friend of ours is missing. We know him as Charlie."

"Yes, most unfortunate."

"What is, sir?"

"His death."

"You're joking, sir."

"I assure you, I'm not. He was buried Monday. I'm sorry for your loss gentleman. If you would like to pay your respects, his is the freshest grave in the cemetery. Good day." And with that he began to shut the door on the matter.

"Hold on a minute." Duck searched for questions. "How do you know he was dead?"

"Oh, he was quite dead I assure you. When I found a sealed coffin Monday morning, properly boxed, I was perplexed. So, I pried the lid off and found Charlie. Dead from the drink, I assume. Everyone knows he wrestled with it. Though there was a curious blueness to his face. Almost as if he lacked oxygen. (The undertaker at this point was ad-libbing and quite enjoying himself. As well, he was surprised the asses had bothered to show themselves.) It is something I, of course, will report to the sheriff during next week's visit."

Nate jumped in. "So, you buried him for free?"

"No, that would never happen. Whoever boxed him, was also kind enough to leave money in his pocket for expenses. And now gentleman, I have business to attend to." The looks on their faces would warm the man's heart for all the years he had left.

The cemetery wasn't far. Charlie's new grave was marked by stones. The two-plank cross said simply "Charlie - May 23, 1881 - RIP."

When Bill saw it, he simpered, "Jesus." The others stayed quiet. Duck and Bill removed their hats. Nate had to be told to do so.

Duck was first to speak. "Damn, Bill, I thought you drilled a hole."

"I did."

"Was it big enough for him to breath?"

"How big is that?" It was Duck's turn not to have an answer.

Nate filled the silence. "We keep our mouths closed and nothing will come of this." Then he looked to Duck. "I told you we should've taken his money. If we did, none of this would've happened."

"He suffocated Nate."

Bill headed in a different direction. "I don't want to live with this. It's poison to kill a man."

Duck took over. "Head on back. I want to think on this." Nate stepped over the grave, while Bill walked around it. Duck stared at the cross as the sky greyed. "I'm sorry Charlie, it wasn't meant to turn out like this," was the sum total of prayer offered.

On the lone walk back to camp, an unsettling began for Duck. Later in the night, it formally arrived. Duck sat up and woke the other two. One from sleep the other from dreams. "Come on, we need to talk." Once outside, Duck laid it out in a word. "McNabb."

Nate grasped the problem right away. "He'll finger us. We'll hang."

"And the undertaker will back him up," Duck added. "But Charlie being buried gives us a head start."

Bill was lost. "I don't get it."

Duck slowed things down. "You ass. McNabb will tell the sheriff we took Charlie out of the saloon. Then the undertaker will say he found Charlie closed in the coffin, and we were the first to show up asking about him."

Nate presented the solution. "We could kill McNabb and the undertaker."

"Three men in a week? You need to get in a right mind." Duck looked to the stars. "We need to run. And run now. It's our best chance. To make it even better, we need to run in three different directions. I'll head north. Nate, you take east. Bill go south. Never speak of this and keep on the

move. Put it out of your mind for your own good. And consider our association over."

With that Bill turned and retched. Then he turned back and let out,
"But if we run, they'll know we did it."

Nate was beginning to enjoy strategy. "They'll know soon enough.
At least this way we'll have a head start away from the rope."

"Damn right. Now, get packing." With that Duck stood up.

"What about our pay?" Nate asked.

"You can't spend when you're swinging." Bill let the words out slow.
Duck looked at Bill and felt an unfamiliar loss. Their remaining version of
friendship measured in minutes.

Charlie had waited until dark to leave the undertaker's office, Belleville and all he owned. He figured 25 miles now lay between him and that
place. A clean start pulling the whole way. The sun was in his eyes and it
seemed time to lie down and wait for the shakes. But first, he turned back
to the east and past. And reflected. "Some things have not changed. I'm still
a low murderer and beyond forgiveness. And I'm still running. But maybe
this time I'm running toward something. Toward another, better way of
paying for these sins. My death births another chance to do something right
before the reaper gets a second crack at me. For I am a man already boxed
and buried, aren't I?"

With this, the strangeness of a smile visited Charlie's face. He even
allowed himself a chuckle. "Not a bad joke at all. Wonder if them boys will
bite," he thought, before turning back to what lay ahead.

The cross ever lengthening between the four men.

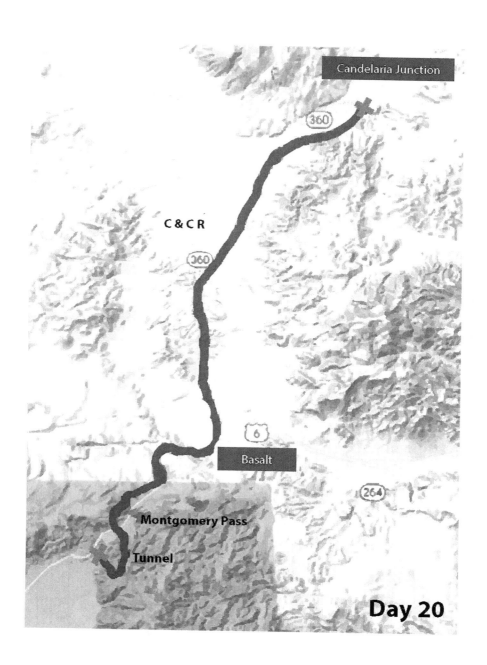

Day 20

291

Day 20

Basalt-Summit

Arrive at the 360, a road appearing on maps since 1919. Stay on the left side of the road in the drainage. All paths that lead uphill and to the left, away from the 360, are dead ends. Trust me on this. At one point, you can see a rail cut through a hill. It is the C&C, but it quickly returns to the road. Go over Little Summit Pass at 5,826 feet A large valley stretches before you. The 360 heads straight down into the valley, but the C&C disdains the depths. Instead it heads to the left. The jumping-off point is obvious. As well as its continuation. Stay with your railbed.

To your right, the dry salt plains of Teels Marsh come into view. Sand dunes edge the plains. It was there that Francis Marion Borax Smith jump-started his borax fortune. Specifically, in the town of Marietta, on the extinct shores of Teels Marsh.

Teels Marsh was a source for salt in the mid 1800s. It is thought that camels were used to transport the salt from Teels Marsh in a similar fashion to the caravans of Timbuktu, on the edge of the Sahara Desert. Where salt has been transported by camel trains across the desert since the 12th Century. Sometimes those Saharan salt caravans reached 10,000 camels long, such was the demand for salt. Even today, the camel caravans continue across the Sahara. Though trucks are slowly replacing the camels. Unfortunately, camels for transport never caught on in the States. Nor did the escapees, from various camel schemes that were tried, manage to breed and prosper in the western U.S. As the escaped camels of Australia have successfully pulled off. There, it is estimated 750,000 camels roam wild in the outback.

In 1867, Francis Smith showed up and claimed the area for borax production. Many of his borax miners were Chinese immigrants.

By 1877, Marietta was a town of 13 saloons and a few hundred thirsty people. Crime was rampant. Often quoted is the year 1880, when the stage was robbed 30 times. In one week of condensed criminality in that lawless year, stagecoach passengers were relieved of their valuables on four separate occasions by armed bandits.

Regardless, there was money to be made and Mr. Smith did just that. Until he found more extensive deposits in Death Valley. And headed in that direction, taking his new nickname of "Borax" with him. After Mr. Smith and his capital pulled up stakes, the town soon faded into obscurity. By the early 1890s, there was only wind. These days Marietta is noisy again. But only with the braying of burros that live on the 68,000-acre U.S. Government Wild Burro Range that Marietta is now part of.

Slowly, you cross the valley. As we ambled down the C&C, an SUV drove up with one Mr. Kelly and son inside. They were searching for a missing turquoise mine. And were tickled pink to learn they were driving on an old railbed. Proof of which was a railroad spike by their car door. Then we told them they were the first people we had seen in 400 miles on a railbed of the Death Q. They must have been thrilled because they started loading us down with trail magic. First, it was Krispy Kreme donuts. Anyone who has ever hiked long distances understands the tearful beauty of a trail donut. The generosity continued with cans of beans and sardines, bottles of water and finally samples of turquoise. Cheers to you Mr. Kelly, I hope that mine, when you find it, is full of riches.

As you move to the other side of the valley, note the UFO landing sites at one o'clock. You're welcome to alternative explanations. There is plenty of time to concoct one. Eventually, you rejoin the 360. On your left is a neat little drainage canal. Hop on! It's a nice roller coaster ride, before it dumps you into a big wash. There it's time to give up and join the road. The C&C is directly under the road for the next two miles of narrow canyon. It is a time of suffering. After you emerge from the canyon, there is yet another two miles of road walking, but at least there is now room to maneuver.

It was along this section that the day was warm and our water low. A bit of water hitching did the trick. It wasn't a completely uneven exchange. For there was curiosity to be satisfied on the driver's part. A nod to the goodness of others. And a note. Don't bother water hitching with 18-wheelers. Braking those heavy loads is too much to ask. Just before the one-mile marker, on the 360, the C&C veers off to the left. Follow the C&C.

It is now one mile to the intersection of the 360 and the 6. The C&C will arrive there, along with the road. The intersection obvious, even as the railbed becomes progressively harder to follow. Walk over to the intersection.

The ghost town to the south of the intersection is Basalt, elevation 6,339 feet. It was a stop on the C&C, some 15 miles from Candelaria Junction. Standing at the intersection of the 360 and 6, take the southern option. Which would be the continuation of the 360 had it any state authority to do so. Instead, there is a deteriorating roadway covered in a variety of painted traffic lines. Most likely created when a four-year-old took control of the line painting machine. Follow this roadway south through the squiggly traffic lines for a few hundred yards. Until you come to an intersection of sorts.

Pause here. Look to your right or west. Note the C&C railbed moving along the hillside, back toward the 6. This is your destination. At the intersection you are standing in, you will observe a stout 6 x 6 wooden post, that was painted white some decades ago. But now finds itself extensively sandblasted. Its faded lettering, roughly deciphered, is PAS662. Behind the wood post is a dirt road that leads to the railbed on the side of the hill. Follow the dirt road to the railbed and turn right at the railbed.

In this general area was Basalt. Though we saw no evidence of its existence. Once on the railbed, make your way back to the 6. When you reach the railbed/6 juncture, cross over to the other side of the 6. The crossing is marked by cairns. Look north up the canyon/wash. There you will see a large cairn. (Courtesy of Orbit, who backtracked miles from Montgomery Pass to create it.) To the right of the large cairn, are some smaller cairns. The smaller cairns mark a wild horse path that moves up the canyon. Believe it or not, but the C&C heads up this canyon. Don't stay on the 6 and miss this turn off the 6. It will deliver many forms of grief and backtracking, as it did us.

At first the railbed is washed out. Just follow the horse path up the narrow canyon. On your right is a large amount of volcanic lava debris. The horse path meanders at times. At confusing junctures, we've placed cairns. Ignore the road cut on the left side of the canyon, that looks like it could be a railroad but is not. After a half a mile, the horse path runs into a crossing dirt road. Do not turn on this dirt road. Continue straight across the dirt road. This intersection is marked by a cairn. Immediately after crossing, it becomes obvious you're back on the C&C. There are even some rail ties lying about for confirmation. Follow the railbed, as it hugs the right side of the hill to your north.

Once you get around the hill, a small valley presents. Look across the small valley and see the continuing C&C railbed on the other side of the valley. It is climbing upward to your right. Follow the railbed, as it slowly gains altitude across the small valley. The yellow water tank on your left was empty when we passed. Cross the valley. Keep an eye out for wild horses. Their evidence is everywhere. Cross a washout. An asphalt road climbs to the left to join the 6. Ignore it. Keep veering gently right, toward the hills in front of you.

You are in for a treat, as this is a spectacular section of the Death Q. Stay on the rail grade, as it climbs steadily into the pines. The climb is accomplished by strategic, sweeping turns that hug wide plateaus of the White Mountains. Incredibly, the Slim Princess used these turns to climb to Montgomery Pass at 7,150 feet.

As you climb, you might encounter snow. We did, and, accordingly, further replenished our water stocks. Geographically, you are now hiking in the 294-square mile Inyo National Forest. After a few miles of big climbs and panoramic views, you will find yourself looking down on the 6. Originally, we believed the C&C was under the 6 all the way from Basalt. We road walked to the point below. Looking up to where you are now, we spotted what was obviously a railbed. Our mood was, "rain on a picnic" as we climbed up the hillside and discovered our mistake. Followed by a backtrack, along the C&C, all the way to Basalt. And then a retrace back up. Still, beauty is always a gift to one's spirits. Though that day was long.

Continue your climb to Montgomery Pass. Just as you threaten the pass, there is a dirt road off the C&C. Turn right on it and follow it over the actual pass. Then join the 6 for a 60-yard road walk into Mt. Montgomery. Now a most forlorn, modern ghost town 23 miles from Candelaria Junction. At one time, in recent history, there were three hotels, restaurants and a gas station. As well as the Stateline Casino. Not anymore.

The Casino shut down in the 90s and burned in 2010. That was enough incentive for everyone else to give up also. Now all is abandoned, except for a Department of Transportation building cluster back off the road. (We didn't try to get water there, as there was enough snow on the trail.) Have a wander around the Mt. Montgomery display of orphaned buildings. But don't trespass where warned.

On the northern side of the 6 is the guestless Boundary Peaks Motel. In front of it is an equally unused paved road. The road starts just in front of the motel and continues along the pass. Follow it for a bit. Just as it begins a descent into the Owens/Benton Valley, you will notice a large pullout area on the other side of the 6. Leave your forgotten road and cross the 6. You will see two dirt roads leaving the pull-out area in the direction of the valley. The two roads are split by power poles. Take the dirt road on your right.

Soon, it becomes apparent you are back on the C&C railbed. The curving railbed quickly brings you to a presentation of Sugarloaf Mountain, all 9,182 feet of it. Also for your pleasure, is the gorgeous view out over the Benton Valley. The C&C crawls downhill by swinging wider and wider thru pine-stacked hillsides. Slowly searching for the kinder-to-locomotives valley below. Note the sugar shack looking down on the C&C. What a spot. You've been walking on their driveway.

Come around a turn to the Montgomery Tunnel. One of two tunnels on the Death Q. Once 247 feet long. Now partially collapsed. The wooden ceiling unable to support the relentless weight of years. Just like our bodies. Backtrack a few feet and follow the path that swings to the right of the tunnel. Arrive at the back of the tunnel. Here you can enter, if you want, and walk back to the cave-in. There are lots of bats and rock debris. The latter an indicator that the ceiling is not stable. Entering the tunnel is not recommended. The decision yours.

Continue downhill over tremendous infill bridges. Sweep back across the face of the mountain. Note the amount of effort required to lose ten feet of altitude. Slice through a pink rock cut. (As a side note, this is an area of strong cell signal.) After the cut, you will arrive at the base of the 6. Though far below it. Cross a dirt road that drops into the Benton Valley and follow the flat rail cut that hugs the hillside. You should be above the descending secondary dirt road. Follow the rail cut along the mountain until it dead-ends into infill from the 6. It is here that we called it a night.

As it was a day spent lost and backtracking. You are about 26 miles from Candelaria Junction. With another 15 to go to Benton and its plentiful cold water and hot springs.

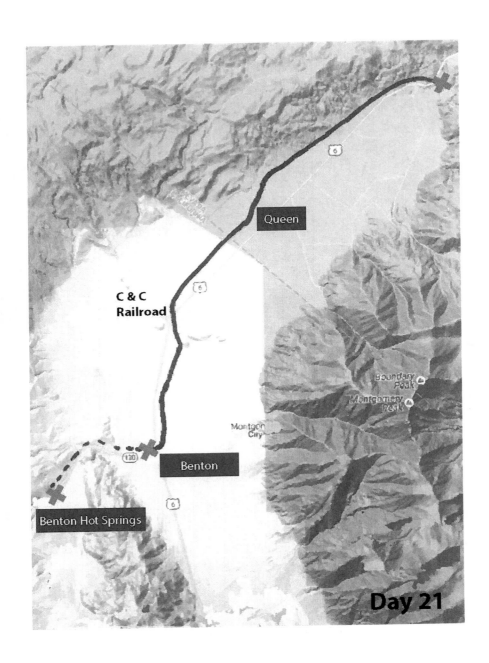

C & C
Railroad

Queen

Boundary
Peak

Montgomery
Peak

Montgomery
City

Benton

Benton Hot Springs

Day 21

298

Day 21

Queen-Benton-Benton Hot Springs

Pop up and continue along the C&C. Immediately and rudely, the 6 butchers the C&C. Climb up and over the 6 and back down to the railbed again. Follow it as it curves to the left, mimicking the paralleling abandoned highway. Come to a large debris pile. This blocks the railbed. Walk around it by following the 6 for 100 yards. Then look up to the right. You'll see the old highway. Look higher still. There she is. Climb up to the C&C and turn left. Follow it, as the railroad gradually loses altitude while maintaining its mountain grasp.

The valley continues to spread out below. Keep your eyes open for deer and wild horses. Note a canyon forming to your left. Eventually, the C&C drops down into the canyon and attempts to cross it. But fails. The bridge long since taken by floods. Cross the canyon pre-C&C style and follow the railbed as it veers to the right. Arrive at the remains of Queens Station. A water stop on the C&C, as well as the location of the Indian Queen Mine. Some small ruins hang on for your enjoyment.

The building to your far left was once a brothel, but closed some 20 years ago. My impression is that Route 6 is not conducive to Nevada businesses. Since not a one has survived between here and Tonopah. Keep moving down the valley. Pass by a white water tower that is roughly the Nevada/California border. On the side of the tower is written "We miss you already!" Whether this was connected to the brothel or is a farewell from Nevada, remains open to conjecture. Welcome back to California. The Nevada leg of your sojourn is complete. Cross a National Forest fence. Continue to close with the 6, but contact isn't made until the hill in the distance. A classic horizon event to contemplate.

The railbed tracks the right side of the 6, until finally turning across it just before the above-mentioned hill. Once across the 6, you will see the C&C railbed leading away from the road. Once again, toward the next hill on the horizon and yet more contemplation. The railbed begins a veer right,

299

just clipping the base of the contemplated hill. The C&C then turns right, a smidge before the telephone poles. From there it continues down the valley paralleling the 6. Your new hobby is creating mobile sand dunes in your shoes.

Move toward a large building that grows in size as you hike. It turns out to be a California State Inspection Station. Cross a number of dirt roads as you move past the inspection station. The C&C pulls closer to the 6. Then curves left as you arrive at Benton, population 280, elevation 5,387 feet. You stand forty-one miles from Candelaria Junction. Back in the highflying days of the late 1800s, five thousand called Benton home. Gold and later silver, the big draws. The C&C stopped in downtown. There, ore was loaded, as well as livestock and wool, for city markets.

But, once again, the mineral wealth proved finite. And the thousands moved on. Leaving the hundreds to stay on. The small Benton Paiute Reservation is out past the hot springs. The dominating mountains to your east are Boundary Peak at 13,141 feet (Nevada's tallest) and Montgomery Peak at 13,441 feet, which resides in California. Boundary Peak is climbable, if you are so inclined. The mountains are all part of the White Mountain range.

As you move through Benton proper on the C&C, you will come to a fence across the railbed that is signed "Private property." Simply turn right and walk out onto Route 6. Turn left and arrive in downtown. This is actually Benton. Benton Hot Springs and its lovely downtown, are four miles to the west along Route 120. Route 120 meets the 6 right next to the Benton Station Café.

BENTON / BENTON HOT SPRINGS		
1.	Food Supply	Yes
2.	Restaurant	Yes
3.	Water	Yes
4.	Hotel	Yes
5.	Beer	Yes
6.	Pool Table	No

7.	ATM	No
8.	Post Office	Yes
9.	Casino	No

The Benton Station Café is your one and only stop for a meal and food resupply. There is not a wide selection for resupply, but certainly enough to get you to Bishop and its Vons supermarket. Which is some 31 miles down the railbed. Water is available, after 21 miles of hiking, in Chalfant. The Benton Station Café (760-933-2231) is open 7 a.m.- 8 p.m., seven days a week. Kitchen closes at 7 p.m. The food was lovely, its excellence amplified by the long walk there. It is a time to indulge. Chocolate shakes, root beers, and burgers are available for just that. The post office is open M-F, 8:30 a.m. - 2:30 p.m., Sa, 8:30 a.m. - 12 noon and is located on Route 6. If you're planning on heading out to the hot springs, get needed food supplies at the Café.

The hot springs are located at the Old House and Inn (866-466-2824, 760-933-2287, www.bentonhotsprings.com). There are seven rooms in the 1940s-era ranch house. The hosts delightful. Breakfast is included with the room. And the floors are heated. Wi-Fi is also floating about. Three outdoor tubs are available for continual 24-hour soaking. The tubs are filled with natural mineral water that emerges from the ground at the rate of 800 to 1,000 gallons a minute. Its average temperature at emergence, an enticing 140 degrees. There are also ten other outdoor tubs available for day use and overnight camping at the attached campground.

If you can swing it, reward yourself. I actually made the reservation, walking past Basalt, when a cell phone signal suddenly descended upon me. The next day's hike was brisk and motivated. Strolling around the old town of Benton Hot Springs is memorable. Hitching out the four miles to the springs was not challenging, nor was the return hitch the next morning. Can one say enough about boiling under the stars, after hiking 450 miles in 20 days? And yes, I know it is an early day at 15 miles. But every once in a while, a kindness to oneself is in order.

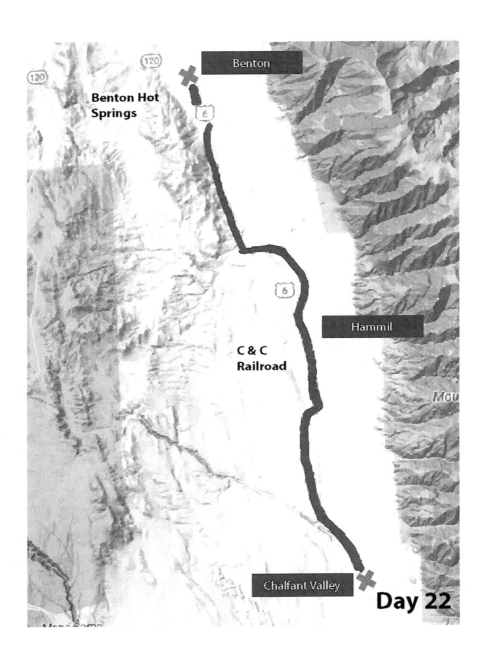

Benton

Benton Hot
Springs

Hammil

C & C
Railroad

Chalfant Valley

Day 22

302

Day 22

Benton-Hammil-Chalfant

When you get back to the Benton Café, continue south along Route 6. Get used to south. It will be your direction for many days to come. Leave town along the road, as residential private property has chopped up the C&C. Walk three or four miles along the road. Pass an elephant parade of trailers and some mine ruins. Both on your right. Go over a rise at the edge of town. Look to the right and spot green-tinged mine tailings at the base of a mountain. When you are even with the southern end of the tailings, leave the road and make your way over to the tailings.

You should immediately stumble upon a ground cabin with a pole beam sticking out of it. Once a home to a hard rock miner. Cross the wash in front of the cabin. When you arrive at the tailings, you also happen to be standing on the C&C. Turn left and follow the C&C down the wash. Just when you are wondering, "What were those guys thinking?" you'll see a rail cut develop along the side of the canyon. Follow it. Even when it crosses the road fence twice in a very short distance. A silly fence that is blindly obeying some obscure state regulation.

Continue with the cut as it gains strength. Go for a while before beginning a turn back towards the road. Soon, you will pass the first stream since the Amargosa River. A nice cold surprise. At the same time, note the monk meditation caves in the cliffs. Ok, maybe not. But at a minimum, a fitting location to place some Buddha statues. Remembering, of course, the admonition frequently heard across Asia, "Da bigga, da Buddha, da betta!" (Chant it fast and repeatedly. Now add a beat. Instant trail entertainment.) When you reach the road, cross over and return to the C&C. You are now looking down on Hammil and the Hammil Valley. The White Mountains are to your left, the High Sierras to your right. And the Owens Valley is coming up directly in front of you.

The C&C begins a long movement to the eastern part of the Hammil Valley. Eventually, you arrive at a private property fence. Turn to the left and follow it for 50 yards. Then turn, with the fence's turn, to the right and go another 50 yards to rejoin the C&C. Follow the railbed, until you reach two large, black water tanks. Turn right at the water tanks and follow the fence line uphill. It is no longer possible to go straight on the C&C due to extensive private ranches and farms in this area. Continue following the fence until the hill is topped. Take note of Route 6. Cut across about a half mile of desert to reach it.

Turn left on Route 6. Begin a long road walk through the stretched out ranching community of Hammil, some 11 miles from Benton. Hammil was named for the three Hammil brothers who homesteaded the area in the 1870s. It was a stop on the C&C. Up until 1913, there was a rail turn-table here. Hike at least three miles along Route 6. Past all the alfalfa farms sitting on top of the C&C. Until you reach Chidago Canyon Road at the end of the fields. Much of the walking can be done on a dirt road that parallels the right side of the 6. Turn right on Chidago Canyon Road. Before you turn on to Chidago Canyon Road, look back up at the White Mountains and observe White Mountain Peak. All 14,252 feet of it. Which makes it the third highest mountain in California.

Walk down Chidago Canyon Road until you reach the dirt power line road. Turn left and follow the power lines about a mile. Suddenly, the C&C emerges from the left. Where did it come from? That's a fine question. For a few hundred yards, the C&C merges with the dirt power line road. Then it breaks away to the left. Follow it as always. With miles through the Chalfant Valley, which you are now walking across, the C&C slowly makes its way back to the 6. Cross the road, but don't bother going under the road fence, as, immediately, there is a large private property fence. This fence blocks the entire valley. Much easier to just stay with the 6 for the final two miles into the small town of Chalfant. Pass the well named "Slim Princess Ranch" on the way into town. Benton is now roughly 25 miles behind you.

Chalfant has 651 residents. Critically, it also has a small store and café known as the Chalfant Mercantile (Open M-F, 7:30 a.m. - 7 p.m., Sa-Su, 9 a.m. - 7 p.m., 760-873-4645, 4750, Hwy 6). It is a worthy goal, as the staff is very friendly and the menu is stocked with burgers. (Unfortunately, just as this book was going to print, I learned the Chalfant Merchantile was closed and up for sale. Whether this closure is temporary or permanent remains to be seen. Best to check ahead on the Internet before relying on Chalfant.) Chalfant was also a stop on the C&C, originally named Paiute. On July 21, 1986, there was a 6.2 earthquake in the area which caused almost $3 million in damage.

After burgers, dark was upon us so we slept in the town park. Which is a block south of the Mercantile. For more privacy, head out into the desert.

During our hike on this particular day, we met a BLM range manager. He was pleased to tell us that all the BLM land is the property of the taxpayer. So, technically, we had been hiking and sleeping on our own land all this time. Further, he said, the BLM is happy that we were using the people's resources. We were equally happy to hear it. And to do it.

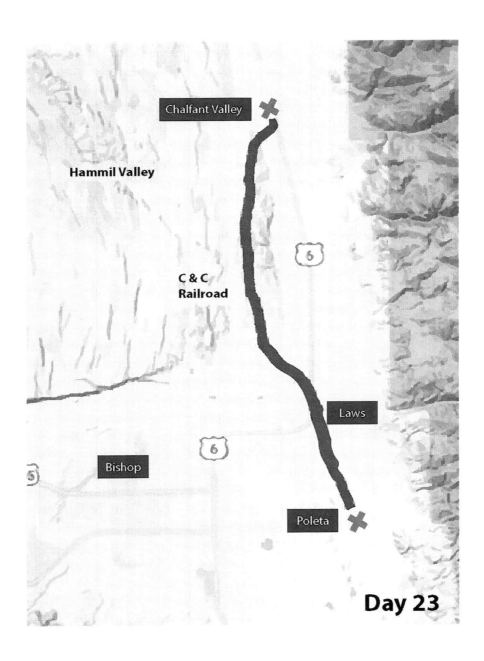

Chalfant Valley

Hammil Valley

C & C
Railroad

6

Laws

6

Bishop

5

Poleta

Day 23

Day 23

Chalfant-Laws-Bishop-Laws

After, hopefully, breakfast at the mercantile, head south on Route 6 for 50 yards. Take a right on Chalfant Road and walk down to the telephone poles. Take a left on the dirt telephone pole road. Follow the dirt road, as the C&C in this particular area is less than apparent. The telephone pole road slowly turns left towards the 6. Then changes its mind and veers to the right. Enjoy the fresh powdered earth. Which is, I believe, leftover volcanic powder. The poof poof clouds of dust remind an observer of Pig Pen making his way through the world. (I keep forgetting that the world is no longer universal. Pig Pen was a character in the Charlie Brown cartoon series, who refused to bathe. Dust clouds followed him everywhere.)

Continue along the pole road, until it reaches the first in a series of stunted hills. At the top of the first hill, look to your right. You will see some wooden mining construction set against the cliffs. Walk another 100 feet along the road and come to a wide, well-kept dirt road. Turn right and follow the road to a gate with a sign that politely says, "Please close gate." Just before the gate, look left and right. You have recaptured the C&C after its escape.

Turn left on the railbed and follow it toward the mine on your right. It seems pumice was mined here. Pumice is a very lightweight volcanic rock. Lightweight because it is full of air bubbles. So lightweight, that sometimes you come across it floating in the ocean. The bubbles occur when molten rock is shot out of a volcano at high speed. Two things happen simultaneously to the flying rock. The rock rapidly cools and it depressurizes. The same process occurs when an underwater volcano shoots molten rock into the surrounding water. This depressurization causes bubbles to become trapped in the rock. Rendering the rock full of air. And allowing you to easily toss around a very light rock.

The pumice mine is one of those serendipitous discoveries you're bound to make, if you explore enough desert. The mine tower itself is in wonderful condition. The photogenic qualities of the place are undeniable. It feels like the workers just picked up and left in the middle of a shift, never to return. The Par Ex packaging, still lying about, indicates the pumice mined was used as a garden soil treatment. The style of packaging suggests the cessation of mine operations somewhere around the 1950s or 1960s. But that is just a guess. What do you think?

For beauty of intimate details, check out the pile of bones outside the window of the small onsite shed. Perhaps leftovers from years of watchmen's lunches. Also charismatic, are the gigantic metal cones. Or the buried classic car in the wash. The list tends to go on.

Rejoin the C&C. Move past a still operating mine to your right. Continue past a BLM fence. The railbed becomes solid. The C&C now on a beeline for Laws. Pass through a gate. Be sure to close. Eventually, the railbed hits the 6 about a mile out from Laws. The tracks cross the 6 but are immediately swallowed by a large farm. Road walk the mile into Laws. As you walk into Laws you are also entering the Owens Valley.

The Owens Valley is named for a guide who helped the explorer, John Fremont, poke around the west in the mid 1800s. The valley itself is thought to be a couple of million years old. Having been formed by faults which line both the White Mountains and the Sierra Nevada Mountains. The true floor of the valley is thought to be thousands of feet below where you stand. But sediment from both mountain ranges has relentlessly filled in the valley. Raising the floor to its present elevation of roughly 4,000 feet. And providing plenty of cushion for your hike. Owens Valley is 75 miles long. A few hundred thousand years ago, the valley was volcanically active. Which explains the lava you will often cross paths with.

Glaciers also played a part in Owens Valley's formation. They dominated the valley until some 10,000 years ago. When they retreated with the rest of the Ice Age. The glaciers' leftover boulders are still strewn about.

Interestingly, the Sierra Nevadas act as a rain shadow for the valley. Snatching rain arriving from the Pacific Ocean to the west, before it can make it to the Owens Valley. Which explains why the Sierra Nevadas are often snow-blanketed and the White Mountains snowless. This rain shadow has led to the Owens Valley being labeled, "The land of little rain."

Still, the Sierra Nevadas are not complete rain bandits. For they do eventually deliver that snatched rain to the Owens Valley in the form of streams and creeks. Fed by both halted rainfall and snowmelt. So, with that briefest of introductions in mind, step into the Owens Valley.

As you arrive in Laws, you will see a "Laws Museum" sign. Turn left on Silver Canyon Road and walk to the Laws Museum. Here you will see what the C&C originally looked like. Laws is thirty-one miles from Benton and about ten miles from Chalfant.

Laws came into existence in 1883, as a station stop on the C&C. It was initially called Bishop Station, as this is where the residents of Bishop had to grumblingly travel to catch the train. The name was later changed to honor the surname of a railroad official. As rail activity increased, a town grew up around the station. There were stores, a hotel, restaurants and a school. The post office opened in 1887.

In 1910, the Southern Pacific Jawbone branch railroad connected Mojave and Los Angeles with the C&C. This happened at Owenyo, fifty-four miles south of here. Rail traffic increased. The prospects of Laws seemed worth celebrating. Until railroad history and the Depression explained to Laws that they weren't. In 1938, the C&C above Laws was abandoned. But, as stated earlier, the southern branch of the C&C held on until 1960. Then the trains stopped and the station closed. Without the station, Laws faded. The final surrender took place when the post office packed up shop in 1963. Laws became a memory.

Until Hollywood swooped to the rescue in 1966. When Steve McQueen decided to film his western, "Nevada Smith," in Laws. The set construction crews restored some of the old buildings. As well, they built some new "old" buildings. Around the same time, the town of Bishop decided a railroad museum in Laws wouldn't be a bad thing. A few handshakes and all the "Nevada Smith" buildings were donated to form the Laws Railroad Museum. Which opened in the same 1966.

The eleven-acre museum is worth a long look (760-873-5950, www.lawsmuseum.org open 10 a.m. - 4 p.m. year-round, $5 donation admission). A 1909 Slim Princess train is on site. As is the Death Valley Railroad diesel train car No.5, that ran from Death Valley Junction to New Ryan from 1927-1930. The same train car in the second photo section that is draped with Hollywood starlets. The talented and dedicated crew of museum volunteers keeps No.5 running. You are welcome to go in its maintenance shed and make No 5's acquaintance. Some other highlights are a still-functioning rail turntable, the original Laws depot, and the station master's house. (Now, you can imagine what the round pit rail turntable at Goldfield looked like.) Also fascinating, are the 30 out-buildings, each containing a slice of early Laws life. Take your time. The Laws museum generously fills in the imagination blanks of the 70 miles of C&C to come.

When your visual appetite is satiated, it is time to head into Bishop and resupply. Bishop is 4.5 miles away. You can walk it, hitch it by returning to the 6, or call Dial a Ride at 1-800-922-1930. A city-sponsored public transportation scheme. The ride into Bishop's Vons supermarket costs about $5 each way. Regardless of how you arrive in Bishop, you will find yourself at the terminus of U.S. Route 6. If you turned around and headed east, it would be a few sunrises before your hiking feet reached the opposite terminus in Provincetown, MA. After some 3,198 miles of road walking. From the 1930s until the 1960s, U.S. 6 actually reached Long Beach, CA, which made it the longest highway in the United States at the time.

Bishop has been around since the late 1800s and has a population just short of 4,000. It is located at the northern end of the Owens Valley at an altitude of 4,150 feet. For your purposes, Bishop has everything and "more."

BISHOP		
1.	Food Supply	Yes
2.	Restaurant	Yes
3.	Water	Yes
4.	Hotel	Yes
5.	Beer	Yes
6.	Pool Table	Yes
7.	ATM	Yes
8.	Post Office	Yes
9.	Casino	Yes

The Vons supermarket addresses resupply well (1190 N. Main St., open daily 5 - 1 a.m., 760-872-9811). The next resupply is in Lone Pine, 57 miles south. Though you will arrive at the water of the Owens River in about 17 miles. Walking down Main Street will bring you into contact with a wide variety of restaurants and hotels. There to service the tourists, who flock to the area for its outdoor pleasures, including great rock climbing. Tourism is the main source of income for Bishop. This has been so since ranching and farming dried up when the water of Owens Valley was diverted to Los Angeles. More on that later.

Also on Main Street are a number of gear stores, should replacement or need be an issue. The "more" part is the mandatory Schat's Bakery (Friday, 6 a.m. - 8 p.m., every other day 6 a.m. - 7 p.m., 760-873-7156, 763 N. Main St.). Saying the name out loud is an ongoing source of pleasure. Here Sheepherders Bread is baked. As it has been since 1907, recipe unchanged. Along with everything else that can possibly be baked. Including the gods-to-hikers gift of the dense Energy Loaf bread. Step in, fill up. The Bishop Post Office is at 585 W. Line Street (760-873-3526, M-F, 9 a.m. - 4 p.m., Sa, 9 a.m. – 1 p.m.).

Bishop is very accustomed to PCT thru hikers being in town to resupply. Don't be surprised by curious stares and questions. They are just trying to figure out what a thru hiker is doing in town during winter. Be hospitable and answer away. As a little hiker PR never hurts. When ready, return to Laws Museum.

Time to reconnect with the C&C. Head south along the tracks out of the Laws Museum. At first, it is hard going because of thick brush. But the miles thin the brush. Go past some old corrals and a couple of Los Angeles Department of Water and Power (LADWP) fences. Close all gates and be respectful, as you are now in a watershed. Practice strict LNT practices and no fires. Follow the railbed through former ranch land, as it moves along the unpopulated eastern side of the Owens Valley. The abandoned ranches are now owned by the LADWP. To understand all this, some history needs to be captured. So, as the sun collapses, settle down and have a read about the Owens Valley Water War.

The Water War was rooted in an expanding urban population and their insatiable need for water. But the start gets going even before that. In the early 1860s, ranchers started showing up in the Owens Valley with their cattle. The local Paiute were not impressed with the ranchers' cattle forcing out their game supply. A rough winter pushed the Paiutes to start hunting cattle. Now the ranchers weren't impressed. The U.S. Army was called in. The Owens Valley Indian War began in 1863 and continued sporadically until 1867. The inevitable Paiute defeat, fighting against overwhelming resources, resulted in the remnants of the tribe being marched to the Fort Tejon Reservation. Which is some 200 miles away. The forced march took place under armed escort.

With the new vacancy, farming and ranching began in earnest throughout the Owens Valley. Water was everywhere. The Owens River was 62 miles long. It was fed by snow runoff, which flowed from the Sierra Nevadas' innumerable tributaries. Early settlers speak of the Owens River reaching a mile wide when flooded. At the end of the river, in the southern bottom of the valley, lay impressive Owens Lake. All 108 square miles of it. Which is where all that run-off gathered.

By 1872, there was a steamer plying Owens Lake. Mining in the Owens Valley also ramped up. Mostly in the eastern half. Irrigation schemes spread the water to the far corners of the valley. Expanding agriculture to where it was never foreseen. "Switzerland" was a term that was often used to describe the valley in those days.

Meanwhile, in another part of California, Los Angeles grew and grew. Reaching 9,000 residents by 1905. But its water resources did not keep pace with the population expansion. The powers that be decided that, if growth were to continue, more water would have to be found. For even then, those powers recognized that water would ultimately be the currency of a dry Southern California. And without sufficient currency, their visions of a grand Los Angeles would dissipate. It didn't take them long to settle on the Owens Valley and a plan.

Los Angeles was 250 miles away but lower in elevation than the Owens Valley. The Owens Valley had a surplus of water. If Los Angeles built an aqueduct to the Owens Valley, gravity would kindly bring the surplus water to Los Angeles.

312

The fly in the plan's salsa was the law of water rights. Which, in a nutshell, stated that the person who owns property touching the water has first right to it. This meant the ranchers and the farmers of the Owens Valley owned the valley's water. The Mayor of Los Angeles, Frederick Eaton, knew this. So did his ambitious head of the Department of Water and Power, William Mulholland. (Mulholland Drive in Los Angeles, that Tom Petty likes to, "glide down over," in one of his more famous songs, is named after William Mulholland.) These two were basically the aforementioned, "powers that be." A solution to get around this problem was arrived at by the two.

That solution was two-pronged. First, convince the residents of Los Angeles that there was an immediate water crisis. Which Eaton and Mulholland did through a marketing campaign plump with scare tactics. The campaign succeeded, and the city of Los Angeles passed a bond that financed construction of a water aqueduct to the Owens Valley.

Mulholland himself supervised the construction of the 233-mile-long aqueduct, which took from 1907-1913 to construct. The demand for materials was so great that a railroad was built to carry them. This was the Southern Pacific "Jawbone" branch that you will join at Olancha, just south of Owens Lake.

The second prong of the solution involved acquiring the rights to the water of the Owens Valley. The only way to do that was to buy up Owens Valley property. Los Angeles set about doing this using city money. The Los Angeles land buyers had to hurry. As there was a Federal plan to greatly expand Owens Valley irrigation that was soon to be implemented. Such a plan would bring Los Angeles directly into conflict with the Federals. A conflict no city is optimistic about winning.

At the same time, the Los Angeles land buyers had to tread cautiously. A publicized land purchasing campaign would encounter local hostility and escalating prices. So, the buyers pursued a strategy that most agree involved trickery, bribery, secrecy, and lying. In the end, the land buyers were largely successful in securing the land rights they needed. And the Federal irrigation scheme was permanently postponed. But their tactics caused much bitterness in the Owens Valley.

In 1913, the aqueduct began draining water from the Owens Valley. At the opening ceremony, Mr. Mulholland infamously spoke these words about the Owens Valley water. "There it is. Take it." And so LADWP did, in ever increasing quantities.

Most of the initial water, upon arrival, was dumped back into the ground to replenish LA's San Fernando Aquifer. The water demand to accomplish this was enormous. Switzerland began a transformation to Sahara. (LA's need for imported water has not diminished. It is currently estimated that 85% of LA's water needs are met by water brought in from elsewhere.)

By 1924, Owens Lake was dry. The locals had had enough. Vandalism of LADWP property and sabotage of the aqueduct began. At one point, water gates were dynamited. Which allowed aqueduct water to return to its original Owens River course. Demonstrations were held, and armed protesters took over parts of the aqueduct. In all, there were ten instances of aqueduct dynamiting during protests.

In response, Los Angeles hired armed security guards to patrol the aqueduct. They were ordered to "shoot to kill" anyone attempting to sabotage the aqueduct. Tensions predictably rose.

Public opinion was generally with the protesters. Even the LA Times sympathized, "LA was an octopus about to strangle out their (Owens Valley residents) lives."

In 1927, fate turned on the protesters. The main bank of the Owens Valley failed. The bank was owned by the Watterson Brothers, who were leaders of the aqueduct opposition movement. The brothers were subsequently convicted of embezzlement. And the collapse of their bank caused a ripple effect that devastated the local economy and sapped the will of the protesters.

By 1928, the protests had ended, and Los Angeles owned 90% of the water rights in the Owens Valley. All that water wealth had the desired effect. By 1930, the population of Los Angeles had swollen to 1,238,048 people from that 1905 population of 9,000. Ranching and farming on a large scale was no longer possible in the Owens Valley. Mulholland, an engineering genius but perhaps not a sympathetic man, had this to say about the protests, "I half regretted the demise of so many of the valley's orchard trees, because now there was no longer enough trees to hang the troublemakers who live there." Not long after that comment, history ambushed Mr. Mulholland.

The St. Francis Dam had been built northeast of Los Angeles in 1924. (Near present day Santa Clarita.) The dam was roughly 200 feet high and 700 feet long. Making it the largest arch-supported dam in the world at the time. It held back 12,000,000,000 gallons of Owens Valley water. Which represented two years of water supply for the city of Los Angeles.

Mr. Mulholland had supervised the construction of the dam. Which was built quickly and under budget. The caretaker at the dam believed the St. Francis had issues and seemed to be leaking. He repeatedly relayed his concerns to Mr. Mulholland. Which Mr. Mulholland repeatedly dismissed. On March 12, 1928, the caretaker reported a new and alarming leak. Mr. Mulholland went out and inspected the dam. He saw no issues that overly concerned him and signed off on the safety of the dam.

Hours later, at 11:57 p.m., the St. Francis Dam failed spectacularly, when both the right and left sides collapsed. Six hundred acres of Owens Valley water was suddenly free to go where it wanted. That water translated into a 140-foot wall of water weighing 52 million tons. Immediate downslope towns were buried in a sea of mud and debris. The caretaker and his family were among the first killed. His vindication worthless. Their bodies never found.

The flood wave initially rushed for the Pacific Ocean at 18 mph. Sweeping all in its dark path. Electricity was cut immediately, as the power grid evaporated. Only sirens going off alerted down-canyon folks to flee their homes for the hills. The oncoming rumble most mistook for an earthquake. The confusion was understandable. Why would an earthquake come from a direction? Eventually, the wave lost momentum. It took the flood until 5:30 a.m. to travel the 54 miles to the Pacific Ocean. An estimated 450 to 600 people lost their lives in the biggest engineering disaster in U.S. history. Many of the bodies never recovered from that same Pacific Ocean.

At first, saboteurs from Owens Valley were suspected. But the suspicion was quickly dismissed. Mr. Mulholland, to his credit, took full responsibility. And in turn, lost his job and reputation. His comment on the disaster, "The only ones I envy about this whole thing are the ones who are dead."

Soon thereafter, he went into seclusion. Where he had time to contemplate his life. A life that began in Ireland under a father's continuous beatings. An escape to sea at 15 bringing a lifelong love of water. Eventually arriving in California. Where he took a job as a ditch digger with the LADWP. At night, reading every book he could find on geology, engineering and the nature of water. His self-teachings a point of pride. Perhaps hubris, as he rose through the ranks to eventually become head of the LADWP. There to await acquaintance with his destiny at the hands of Owens Valley and the St. Francis Dam. Mr. Mulholland had seven years to dwell on it all before passing away in 1935.

The Owens Valley Water War continues on, but now mostly in court. And sometimes in film. "Chinatown," made in 1974, derived its plot from the water war. It starred Faye Dunaway and Jack Nicholson and was directed by Roman Polanski. The film set the water wars in the 1930s and changed around the location and names, but not too much. It is generally regarded as one of the best films ever to come out of Hollywood. And was awarded an Oscar for Best Original Screenplay.

A second aqueduct was built in 1970, but LA did not completely live up to the terms of the agreement. Specifically, Los Angeles came up short on reducing the chronic toxic dust that blows off Owens Dry Lake, as well as revegetating the Owens River corridor. Litigation continues. And LADWP continues its efforts to repair and mitigate damage they've caused. Their success debatable. Take a look around and judge for yourself. Overall, there is still lingering bitterness in the Owens Valley. More than 100 years after completion of the aqueduct. A joke we heard more than once went, "Flush your toilet often, LA needs the water."

Regardless, you are moving across LADWP land. Which currently totals about 312,000 acres within the Owens Valley. Please treat that land with respect.

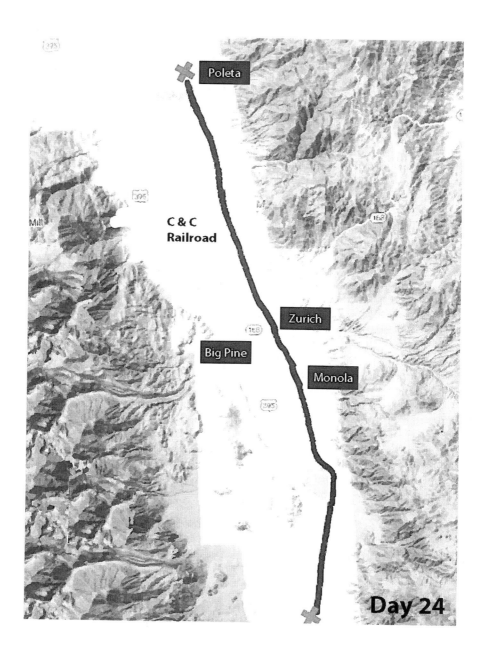

Poleta

C & C
Railroad

Zurich

Big Pine

Monola

Day 24

317

Day 24

Zurich-Monola-Aberdeen

Good morning, Owens Valley. Back to the C&C and south. Parallel a paved road for a while, before it takes a 90-degree turn across the C&C. Cross the road. Note the Department of Water and Power sign. There is no camping or campfires in this area. A nice dirt road begins to track the C&C and sometimes moves on top of it. Pass a skeleton umbrella garden.

Arrive at Cal Tech's Radio Observatory, home of multiple radar dishes. Come to a sign that says, "Only authorized Cal Tech employees." The sign riddled with bullet-hole commentary. Honor the sign by turning left on the alternative dirt road. This road passes closely by one of the massive dishes. Occasional rotations cautiously track the meanderings of aliens.

The Radio Observatory was begun by Cal Tech in 1958. Originally, Cal Tech used the dish antenna radio telescopes to search for radio waves in the galaxy. Since then, the telescopes have studied a number of things that I can't comprehend. And one star formation that, perhaps, I vaguely recognize. My apologies for being unable to pass on useful information. The dirt road you are on bends back to the right to meet an asphalt road on the south side of the observatory. When you get to the asphalt road, continue west another 50 feet and rejoin the C&C.

Follow the railbed south, traveling between the road and a fence. Eventually, you arrive at Zurich, some 15 miles from Laws. Zurich was a stop on the C&C and the site of a small town. It was so named because a local resident thought the mountains east and west looked like her native Switzerland. Zurich was the station for the town of Big Pine on the western side of the Owens Valley. (A side note. High above Big Pine, in the Sierra Nevadas, lives the Palisade Glacier. The glacier has been in residence for thousands of years. It has the honor of being the southernmost glacier in the United States. As well as the largest in the Sierra Nevada Mountains. The glacier is reachable if you like to hike.) There is a historical marker in downtown Zurich. And some few ruins.

Continue south. Quite quickly you come to Route 168. A lonely road headed over to the Saline Valley and an ancient Bristlecone Pine Forest located at 10,000 feet. Where two of the wind-stunted trees have been dated to just under and just over 5,000 years old. Which hands them the title of oldest, living trees on the planet, not cloned from an original colony. The younger of the pair is christened "Methuselah." Named after the longest-lived biblical personality, who reached a mere 969 years. The older of the pair prefers to remain anonymous. Try to wrap your mind around what the pair have seen in 50 centuries. Starting when they were saplings and the pyramids were under construction. The exact locations of the two elders are kept from the public to avoid our species' harmful tendencies.

Rejoin the C&C on the other side of 168. Pass the horseless corrals and reenter LADWP land. After about one mile, you pass a small dam. This is your first sighting of the Owens River from the C&C. You can refill water here if needed. Be sure to treat it.

Continue south on a dirt road that parallels the railbed. Pass a fence made from old C&C rail ties. About four or five miles out from Zurich you will come to a three-way split. One well-maintained road with crushed stone heads left toward a mine at the base of the mountains. The center branch continues dead south. This is the C&C. Give yourself a treat and take the right.

The spur rail veering right is known as the "Superfly" spur. Selfishly named for my daughter. A stroll down the spur leads to an enchanting riverside spot perfect for a break. There is plenty of water for a refill. But more so, it's the ideal spot to throw your feet up, or in, for a while. And listen to the birds chat about stream flow and bug density. Or tune into the gods seeking conversation with you through the cottonwood leaves. When rested, return back up the Superfly spur and rejoin the C&C by turning right.

As has become habit, keep moving south. Where you ease into a drained, desolate looking landscape. Tall, spare bushes begin to dominate, which ironically indicate groundwater. After a while the C&C fades. The answer as to why appears as you continue south. The Tinemaha Reservoir shortly stops you in your tracks. This is a large body of water, created by the Owens River being blocked by an earthen dam. The reservoir serves as an intake point for the aqueduct and is owned by the LADWP. It also drowns the C&C.

On the positive side, the Tinemaha area is an excellent birding location where loons, peregrine falcons and sometimes bald eagles are spotted. The waters hold a large number of catfish. Also, tule elk are known to winter here.

Tule elk are a subspecies of elk which were once widespread in California. Estimates put the population at 500,000 around the time Europeans started migrating to North America. By the 1860s, that population had been reduced to extinction through overhunting. The primary culprits were the gold rush miners, who began arriving in 1849 and were thus called, "49ers." These men needed cheap protein and clothing. The tule elk provided both. But the extinction assumption had one tiny flaw.

In 1874, two surviving tule elk were found living together in central California. Remarkably, they were a male and female. More remarkably, they were both of breeding age. And most remarkably of all, some conservation minded individuals succeeded in protecting the future of the subspecies through laws and setting aside habitat. Still, it was a rocky path to that protection. Against a variety of people hell bent on the tule's total demise. It wasn't until 1933, when a local Owens Valley rancher named Walter Dow released some tule elk onto his extensive ranch, that the tule elk began to thrive again. Today, there are over 4,000 tule elk roaming about California. Keep your eyes peeled for some local ancestors of the two survivors.

The C&C starts up again on the other side of the reservoir. To get there, you need to skirt the Tinemaha to the left. Do not go down to the shoreline and try to follow it to the left. As we did. If you do and the water levels are high, you will be mired in progressively worsening swamps. As we were. And you will disturb herds of large catfish, that thrash about the shallows in an alarming manner. Which will instantly convince your reptilian brain that crocodiles are coming for lunch. After an hour of swamping along a drowned road and yelping in response to numerous catfish ambushes, you will be turned back by deepening water. And spend another hour, re-alarming crocs, retreating to where you are standing now. As we once again did. Who would have thought, a swamp full of catfish on the Death Q? So, do yourself a favor, and turn left well before the reservoir.

Make that early left and keep the swamps to your right. Until you reach a line of sand dunes on the left side of the reservoir. At the base of the dunes is a dirt road. Follow it south to the dam. Stay off the dam itself. Follow the road that goes through the left bypass of the dam. The road comes out at the bottom of the dam by an old wooden walkway. Continue south, past a forgotten LORP canoe, until you arrive at a secondary earthen dam. Walk along it to the right, for about 100 feet, until you spot the C&C railbed emerging from under the dam. Charging along in a damp and contented manner. Jump back on.

All of the above brings to mind the only jokes I know. Your tolerance please.

Q. What did the fish say when it swam into a wall?
A. Dam!
Q. What did the fish say when it swam over the waterfall?
A. Dam it!
Q. What did the fish say when it saw another fish swim into a dam?
A. Dumb bass!

My apologies.

The bush thickens on the railbed to the point of aggravation. To avoid the emotion, follow the parallel dirt road. Note the lava flows on your left. They are part of a very large volcanic expanse that is, unfortunately, not visible from your sheltered position. The right-of-way narrows, as it is squeezed by old lava and an abandoned irrigation ditch on the left. And an equally abandoned ditch on the right. Remnants of farming days gone by. The C&C continues to be very overgrown at this point, so stay on the dirt road. Cows appear to salute your efforts. Their ancestor's bleached bones, as well as their fate, ignored with Zen detachment.

You are now in LORP (Lower Owens River Project) territory. LORP was initiated by the LADWP. The project's goal is to restore a 62-mile stretch of the Owens Valley to its original state, prior to LA's water diversion. It is the largest river restoration ever attempted in the US. The theory is, put the water back, and everything that was there before will come back. Local critics, however, contend that LORP is just another maneuver by LA to actually increase the amount of water they remove from the Owens Valley. In the end, the courts will most likely have the final say.

A bridge appears on your right. Here you can get water from the Owens River. Boil it or treat it, as the local cows are random and voracious defecators. Read the LORP signboard. According to it, you are free to walk about. Return to the railbed about 200 yards east from the bridge. Turn right, and keep going south. Pass what is left of Aberdeen Station, some 30 miles from Laws. Aberdeen was a C&C stop. It was mysteriously named after Aberdeen, Scotland. At one time, there was a post office here, as well as a store, gas station and school. The postmistress was only 17, the youngest in the U.S. at the time. Her post office closed in 1934. Try to summon up Aberdeen's former skyline. Continue on the railbed, which is easy to follow. Large power lines are to your right. At some point, surrender to the end of a day.

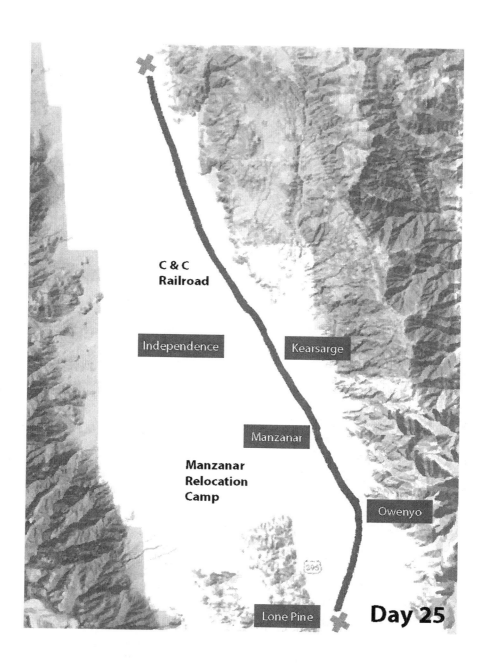

C & C
Railroad

Independence

Kearsarge

Manzanar

Manzanar
Relocation
Camp

Owenyo

Lone Pine

Day 25

323

Day 25

Kearsarge-Owenyo-Lone Pine

Moving south through the early hours. Crunching salt about the sum total of sound. Mountains beating back the sun's efforts to reach you. The valley your own. Another day of hiking the sole agenda. And so goes the life of a Q hiker.

The Owens River brushes the railbed multiple times during this section. Though it is choked with tule reeds. Which Native Americans used to make everything imaginable, including canoes and homes. And amazingly, at least once, the reeds were used as a snorkel device. When a six-year-old girl, who was a member of the Pomo Tribe, used a tule reed to evade detection by massacring U.S. Calvary troopers. She did this staying underwater in a lake and breathing through a reed tube. While the massacre took place on the shores around her.

The C&C gradually drifts closer to the east-based Inyo Mountains. Eventually, arrive at a rail cattle guard with a neat rail sample. It stirs the railroad's past. This is the last remaining cattle guard on the C&C. The rail sample is the fine work of the volunteers at the Laws Museum.

Continue south. There are a lot of rail relics in this section. As always, the ground holds memories longer than people can. Next up is a black water tank near the rail line. It was full of water, pumped up by a nifty solar pump. We treated it, but I suspect the water is fine. This is the last water for 15 miles.

Another mile on and you arrive at Kearsarge Station, 44 miles from Laws. Find yourself standing at 3,770 feet, which means you have lost 3,380 feet since Montgomery Pass. A diet that actually works. The folks from the Museum have been at work again. Cheers to them. There is an original railroad crossing sign in place. It says, "Stop, Look, Listen," which strikes me as an excellent parenting model, a summation of Buddhist philosophy and perhaps one of the better life approaches out there. A plaque is in place, as is another section of rail. An old picket fence echoes a long-ago attempt to bring order to the desert. Some foundation ruins and an informal pet cemetery complete the picture.

Some background. Kearsarge was the train stop for the town of Independence to the west. It began life as a stage stop in 1866. But in 1883, the C&C arrived and it became a rail stop. (The origin of Kearsage's name is coming up in a few pages.) Kearsarge never amounted to more than just a few houses for railroad staff. Though a post office did operate sporadically. The depot building itself was built in 1884, closed in 1932, and torn down in 1955. You can easily take a sweet side hike to the ore chute, just to your left. From this point, there are good views of Kearsarge Pass high in the Sierras. After which, rejoin the C&C railbed and more south.

Leaving Kearsarge, a rumble began in the lower Owens Valley. It was a progressing rumble. Increasing intensity as it neared. Before we could get to the ground and cover our ears, the blast was over us. The fighter jets were so low I could see the pilot's helmet. And then they were gone, chased by their roar. It took a long while to get back to 100 years ago. The fighter jets were not a one-off. We were practice dive-bombed five more times that day. Luckily, we weren't hostile, as there was no place to hide.

Just short of ten hiking miles, south of Kearsarge, is Owenyo station. Owenyo's name is derived from the combination of Owens and Inyo (the name of the county). This combining of two words is technically known as a portmanteau. It seems to have been quit the rage in this area and that time period. Owenyo was the train station for Lone Pine to the southwest. Here you will find extensive foundation ruins and large trash dumps full of discarded antiques. Explore away amongst the tamarisk trees. And keep in mind, Owenyo was once a very busy place.

It began its life in 1900 as a colony for Quakers. Which is a branch of Christianity that has been around since the 17th Century. Called Quakers because they are meant to tremble at the word of God. The group of Quakers who created the colony were known as the William Penn Colonial Association. (William Penn was a member of the Quakers, and the founder of Pennsylvannia. Which was the center of Quakerism in the U.S. at the time.) The association purchased 13,000 acres in this (then) remote section of the Owens Valley. Their plan was to establish an ideal farming community based on their tenants and beliefs. A taste of those tenants: liquor,

325

gambling and houses of ill repute were all banned from the colony. The association advertised heavily in an attempt to recruit like-minded people of a farming persuasion.

Why they chose here could be viewed as a mystery. Though the area was perhaps much greener in the days prior to the arrival of Los Angeles. And for that reason, the farming seemed promising. This belief was bolstered by the fact that there were already 40 miles of irrigation canals in the general area. A handful of Quaker-leaning families moved to the colony and gave farming a try. But the soil proved unresponsive to their agricultural efforts. In 1905, the association decided to abandon their remote life.

But there must have been Quaker joy later that same year. When the C&C came out of nowhere and offered to buy some of their unwanted land. Which was needed for the railroad right of way and planned Owenyo Depot. The remainder of the association's 13,000 acres, with its corresponding water rights, were snapped up by the ever-thirsty Los Angeles.

The C&C got straight to work at Owenyo. A rail depot was constructed. Slowly, a small group, of mostly railroad employees, took up residence around the train depot. But the big event in Owenyo's history, was the decision by Southern Pacific to connect their Jawbone branch line to the C&C at Owenyo. The Jawbone was already built as far as Lone Pine for purposes of aqueduct construction. It made business sense to continue another 4.2 miles to Owenyo and connect with the C&C. Which it did in 1910.

The problems with this connection were two-fold. First, the C&C was narrow gauge, while the Jawbone was standard gauge. This caused much talk about switching the C&C to standard but it never happened. Though at one point, the rooflines of the C&C stations were trimmed back to accommodate the anticipated wider trains. Thus, the Princess stayed slim, as was her nature. So, transfer docks were built, as well as a transfer trestle, at Owenyo. Here all freight was transferred laboriously by hand from the Jawbone to the Slim Princess and vice versa. This consumed a lot of time.

Which caused a wait. A long wait. The passengers who had paid $19.50 to get from LA to Laws were unimpressed. Especially after a dusty eight-hour ride from Mojave. Sometimes the transfer of freight took 12 hours, forcing the passengers to overnight. In response, the Owenyo Hotel was built to accommodate travelers. It was constructed by placing four boxcars together, with a common roof built overhead. Here, a primitive bed and meal was possible. The high aspiration breakfast was advertised as, "Such ham and eggs as were never seen on land and sea." It wasn't long before "auto stages" (a much better term than taxi, don't you think?) were running passengers into the comparative sophistication of Lone Pine.

The second problem was turning the trains back around. This was solved by building a wye track for the Jawbone. The remains of which are still visible, as you come into Owenyo. The Slim Princess, on the other hand, was turned around using a rail turntable similar to the one you saw in Laws. The base is still evident, east of the railbed, as you're leaving Owenyo.

Living in Owenyo was, at times, challenging. The heat could be punishing. As well as the dust, caused by piles of white soda ash. Which was collected from the (newly) Owens Dry Lake. A passing priest, in 1939, described Owenyo as such, "There are in this wide world, few spots half so desolate as the east side of Owens Valley near Owenyo." And, "Were it not for the green fields, and the stores, and the movies at Lone Pine eight miles away, the exiles of Owenyo men, women, and children would go stark raving mad." It is perhaps safe to assume the priest enthusiastically continued his passing.

A photo from 1948 shows the residents had taken steps to alleviate the heat. In the photo, a swamp cooler is attached to the side of the Owenyo depot. A swamp cooler works differently than an air conditioner, which blows cold air into a building. A swamp cooler blows hot, dry air across water. The water evaporates into the air, making it cooler. The moistened, cooler air is then blown into the building. Swamp coolers are still fairly common throughout the southwestern U.S. They have been around since Egyptian times. Their earliest form involved hanging wet blankets across open windows. I actually use a portable swamp cooler for my 1951 pickup truck.

Owenyo began to tire in the 1940s. In 1941, the post office closed. But it wasn't until 1960 that the funeral was held. In that year, the C&C was buried. The Jawbone followed suit by removing their tracks between

Lone Pine and Owenyo. In 1961, the buildings of Owenyo were dismantled. And taken to places where people lived. What you see is what was ignored in the move.

Back on the railbed. Walk south out of "town." Quickly, you come to sunken concrete footings. These were the transfer trestles where boxcars loaded with ore from the C&C were placed above empty boxcars from the Jawbone. The ore was then released into the waiting, empty boxcars with the aid of gravity. Note the branching that takes place here. The left line heading straight south is the continuation of the C&C. While the right branch is the Jawbone railbed reaching for Lone Pine.

Lone Pine is where you resupply for the next stage, so take the right branch. In the distance is another black water tank on the C&C. I don't know if it has water because we bypassed it. Hike the five miles into Lone Pine along the Jawbone branch. At times, it is a sand trap. Along the way, I saw three horned toad lizards groggy from their hibernation. It was March 12, and they were the first lizards of the new year. Your target beacon is the communication tower waiting on your horizon.

Just as you are arriving at the still-standing Lone Pine Station House, the Owens River makes an interfering appearance. Your progress stopped by a freefall from massive concrete pilings. The original bridge recycled by SP for other purposes.

Descend you must, to the river itself. A waist-deep ford your welcome to Lone Pine. Climb up the other side and continue on to the Lone Pine Station House of the Jawbone Railroad. Unfortunately, for exploration purposes, the station house is a private residence. This is reinforced by a fence across the Jawbone railbed. Respect it and turn left at the fence.

But before you do, note the loading platform and the extensive asphalt storage area. Indicators that Lone Pine Station continued after the C&C closed. Which it did. The station became the end of the line for the Jawbone from 1960-1982. A wye track was built so the trains could easily turn around. But in 1982, the Jawbone decision makers decided to shut down the northern part of the Jawbone after a tunnel fire at Searles. Which caused the Lone Pine Station House for the Jawbone Railroad to close its doors after 70 years of service.

As suggested, turn left at the fence and follow it around to the Lone Pine Narrow Gauge Road (LPNG). Enjoy the views of the Lone Pine Station House to your right, still waiting and ready for the trains to return. Turn right at the road and follow it into Lone Pine. Enjoy the residence to the left, built directly on the Jawbone right of way. The tracks, in their day, would have passed directly through the front gate. It is 1.5 miles into town along the LPNG Road.

Your walk is entertained with fine views of Mt Whitney. At 14,505 feet, the highest mountain in the U.S. lower 48. Whitney is not the prominent, deceptively large mountain in the foreground. That is Lone Pine Peak at 12,944 feet. Whitney is the recessed monolith to the right. With the two jagged teeth to its left. Worthy of mention is the view of the Death Q from the summit of Whitney. Which is sublime.

After a while, look left at the Jawbone heading out of town into the desert. Passing an abandoned house along the way. You will reacquaint yourself with the Jawbone, south of Owens Dry Lake, at Olancha. Continue into Lone Pine, past a still-functioning windmill on the right. The mechanism worth checking out. When you reach the 395, get ready to turn left into Lone Pine.

Lone Pine has a lot to offer. Perhaps most of all, a rest. You've hiked 559 miles in 25 days. That's 22.36 miles a day, on average. Taking a day off in Lone Pine, seemed like a fine idea to us. An idea that grew finer the closer we got. But I'm just presenting an idea. It's your call. As mentioned, when you reach the 395, you will be turning left. But, just to your right, on the western side of 395, is a mass grave of earthquake victims. Sixteen of whom are buried there.

At 2:35 a.m. on March 26, 1872, a quake estimated at between 7.6 and 8.0 struck. Its immensity caused by the fact that the two fault lines in the Owens Valley shifted simultaneously. The epicenter was Lone Pine. In scale, the quake was comparable to the San Francisco Earthquake of 1906. Most buildings in Lone Pine were flattened. Including 52 of the town's 59 houses. Which were unfortunately built with adobe blocks. A building technique that does not fare well in earthquakes. The shockwaves were felt in far off San Diego, where clocks stopped. The same thing happened in

Sacramento, 300 miles to the north. In all, 27 people were killed in Lone Pine.

John Muir the naturalist, who was sleeping in Yosemite at the time, ran from his tent as landslides crashed around him. He's alleged to have shouted, "A noble earthquake!" People were simply more poetic back then. These days a "WTF?" would be a more likely response. A plaque explaining the rectangular mass grave is on-site. The long dead probably most appreciative of your visit. After visiting, return to the 395 and walk south into town.

As you backtrack toward town, you immediately pass a small bit of Robin Hood on your right. For there exists a large oak tree that 100 years ago was but a small sapling in Sherwood Forest in merry olde England. How it came to live in the Owens Valley is explained on a sign.

Continue south into Lone Pine along the 395. A road whose modern incarnation stretches 557 miles, from southern California to the Oregon state line. Though, at one time, the 395 did a decent PCT impersonation by connecting San Diego with Canada. Originally, the 395 was known as the El Camino Sierra. Which was the name of an earlier pioneer trail from Los Angeles to Lake Tahoe that the 395 roughly parallels. Onward to Lone Pine.

Lone Pine has about 2,000 people. It became a town around 1870, when the post office was established. Which is still in operation, 145 years later. The town was named for a lone pine tree long deceased. Lone Pine now has a lone stoplight as a stand in. (Which, when you think about it, "Lone Stoplight" would be a great name for a small town.)

In the early years, Lone Pine mainly operated as a supply center for nearby mines. Until the 1920s, when Hollywood discovered Lone Pine and the nearby Alabama Hills. The hills and their rounded-rock formations proved irresistible to the makers of Westerns. And many other movies with a desert backdrop. In all, over 400 films have been shot in and around Lone Pine. One of the more recent being, "Gladiator."

How the Alabama Hills came to their name is an entertaining story. During the Civil War, there was a Confederate warship named the CSS Alabama. The Alabama raised continuous global hell with Union shipping for a solid two years. It is estimated the Alabama sunk 65 ships valued at

$6 million. Her exploits were famous/infamous worldwide, depending on your allegiance. But her days were finite. The end came when the Alabama was sunk off the coast of France. The Union warship Kearsarge did the sinking, following a one-hour battle.

News of the battle eventually reached Lone Pine. Pro-southern miners named the Alabama Hills in honor of the southern ship. In retaliation, Kearsarge Station and Pass were named after the Union ship by the pro-northern element. This naming battle is how the proxy Civil War played out in the Owens Valley. A quite civilized form of warfare deserving of imitation.

These days, tourism is the main moneymaker in town. Piles of backpackers pass through. Either coming off the PCT or out of the Sierras in general. Or pulling permits from the Ranger Station to head up Whitney or elsewhere. In other words, they are used to people with packs that smell like farm animals. For your purposes, everything needed is located on Main Street/395. Which cuts straight through town. Your next resupply point is at Olancha, 53 miles to the south. Some of the miles are physically challenging. Water is possible along the way, but not guaranteed. Certainly, it is available in Keeler at the 33-mile mark.

LONE PINE		
1.	Food Supply	Yes
2.	Restaurant	Yes
3.	Water	Yes
4.	Hotel	Yes
5.	Beer	Yes
6.	Pool Table	Yes
7.	ATM	Yes
8.	Post Office	Yes
9.	Casino	No

Joseph's Bi-Rite Market is at 119 Main Street (760-876-4378, open 8 a.m. -8 p.m., 7 days a week) and will provide the food you need for the onward journey. There are plenty of restaurants. For the exotically in-clined, the Mt. Whitney Restaurant advertises ostrich, elk and buffalo burgers (760 876 5751, open 6:30 a.m. - 9 p.m., 7 days a week, 227 Main St.). For a roof, there are a number of hotels. Our favorite was the Dow Villa (760-876-5521, 310 S. Main Street). Which charged $55 for two peo-ple to stay in the old wing of the hotel.

The Dow was built in the 1920s and exudes the histories of thousands of guests. Most walls are covered with portraits of the famous who have stayed there. Including every Hollywood cowboy that ever jumped on a horse. The Dow is a very relaxed and friendly place. And an excellent place to recharge. The Jacuzzi ensured it. As did the attractive karma of the Dow. For you see, the hotel was built by, named for, and run by the same Walter Dow who worked so hard to save the tule elk from extinction.

The Whitney Portal Store and Hostel (760-876-0030, 238 S. Main Street) is another fine place to unwind. There are a number of other places to stay in town, if neither of these suits your fancy. The post office is at 121 E. Bush Street (760-876-5681, open M-F 9:30 a.m. - 12:30 p.m. and 1:30 p.m. - 4:30 p.m.). There is also a gear store, called Elevation Sierra Adventure, at 150 South Main Street (760-876-4560). Elevation is open 9 to 6:30 Sunday through Thursday and 9 to 7 Friday and Saturday.

If you decide to layover for the day in Lone Pine and actually want to get out of bed, Manzanar ("apple orchard" in Spanish) makes a sobering side trip. It is located 11 miles north on the 395. The Paiute were the first to call Manzanar home, but they were evicted by the ranchers. Subse-quently, the ranchers had to leave because LA bought up all their water. Then in 1942, as World War II raged, the U.S. Government reached a de-cision that would have far reaching implications for Manzanar. They de-cided that U.S. citizens of Japanese descent, as well as Japanese citizens living in the States, were a threat to the nation's security.

The course of action the government chose, based on this decision, was to evict 120,000 Japan-connected men, women, and children from their homes. And order them to report to remote camps for internment. Roughly 80,000 of the 120,000 were U.S. citizens. One of these camps was built at Manzanar. Where 10,000 were held. There they were incarcerated, under armed guard, for the remainder of the war. Their living conditions unpleasant at best. Sometimes families were split up between the ten camps that were eventually built throughout the United States. This was all done without due process, trial, or compensation. Some called them relocation camps. Others, concentration camps. Regardless, few would argue that it was not a low point in American history. (A note of hindsight. During the course of WWII, ten Americans were convicted of spying for Japan. All of them were White.)

The U.S. Army, however, was not above allowing Japanese-American males of fighting age to volunteer their way out of camps and join the war effort in Europe. Though only rarely in the Pacific War, where their language talents would have been extremely valuable, but their race and sympathies suspect. The Japanese-Americans formed the 442nd regimental combat team. A 4,000-man strong regiment in the U.S. Army. The regiment's enlisted members were exclusively Japanese American. The officers, all White.

The regiment fought with incredible valor. The chip on their shoulder enormous. Though, at first, the regiment was disdained by its White officers. It came to be one of the most respected and relied upon combat units in the European Theater. By one and all. Certainly, the German Army lived in fear of the 442ND. The 4,000 men of the unit had to be replaced 2.5 times. In all, 14,000 men served in the unit. A total of 9,486 Purple Hearts were awarded. (A Purple Heart is a medal received when one is wounded in battle.) All the while, many of the soldiers' families back in the States were incarcerated in camps. The 442nd was the most decorated regiment in the history of U.S. warfare. And a fine vindication for men spurned by their own country.

For the full story, a trip to Manzanar is a day well spent. There you can wander through former (though reconstructed) barracks and spend hours in the camp's original auditorium. Which is now a museum detailing the injustice of it all. As a footnote, some of the internees were brought to Owens Valley on the C&C and Jawbone. In the winter, Manzanar is open 10 a.m. - 4:30 p.m. daily. Admission is free (760-878-2194).

Of course, a day-hike up Mount Whitney, for the punishment gluttons, is also a possibility. But in winter, it could be technically challenging

333

or impossible, depending on conditions. For information on permits, feasibility, and transport, call the Mount Whitney Ranger Station at 760-876-4444.

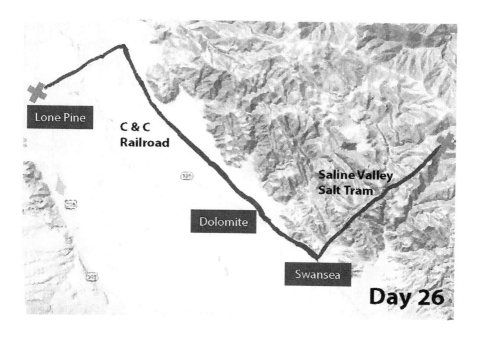

Lone Pine

C & C
Railroad

Dolomite

Saline Valley
Salt Tram

Swansea

Day 26

335

Day 26

Lone Pine-Dolomite-Swansea-Saline Valley Salt Tram

Whether you rest a day or not, retrace your steps north on the 395, until the LPNG Road. Turn right. Follow the road past the dirt-loading ramp that was built to service the Jawbone. Then past the old Lone Pine Station House. Stay on the road. Cross the Owens River, only this time, on a bridge. Then walk past the power lines toward a row of tamarisk trees. There, rediscover the C&C and turn right. You will pass a continuous series of mines. Each a separate explanation why the C&C was built on the eastern side of the Owens Valley. Ignore an empty black water tank due to an absent pump. Then pass a neat mine on the left, victim of a self-destructive cave-in.

Eventually, the railbed comes to mimic the asphalted Dolomite Loop Road. A number of buildings present on your left, including a rare, actually-lived-in house. Just in front of the house, an X is painted on the road. No treasures, just a former railroad crossing warning. Sure enough, rails remain embedded in the road. This spur led over to the Dolomite mine located at the base of the Inyo Mountains. There, dolomite is mined by the Inyo Marble Company, starting in 1885 and sporadically ever since. Dolomite is a mineral with multiple uses and properties that intellectually elude me.

Continue on until the C&C encounters Route 136. At the juncture, there is a plaque describing the Dolomite Quarry. Cross the 136 and rejoin the railbed. Owens Dry Lake and its remedial measures are now on full display. The railbed is swallowed by aggressive sand dunes in this area. So, straying from the C&C to the road is understandable. Soon, the base of the Saline Valley Salt Tram appears on the left side of the 136. Go over and have a look. Only the footings remain. But if you look up the hillside, you will see the foundation of a tramway support tower. Around you once rested the motorworks that powered a salt tram up and over the Inyo Mountains.

So, take a break in the strange concrete room to your right, and read up on the salt tram. Because, soon enough, you will be pursuing its lost cables.

Saline Valley is on the other side of the Inyo Mountains. Which are the mountains you currently find yourself staring at. Most of the valley rests within Death Valley National Park. To get there and get out takes effort. This has always been the case. In the late 1800s, borax mining began on the salt dry lake located in the basin of Saline Valley. Unbelievably, Borax Smith appears to have never owned this particular borax mine. The borax was transported to Lone Pine by wagon. Which proved to be a miserable 65-mile journey over a rough track. In the end, the costs outweighed the returns and the mining stopped. But not before one of the wagon drivers noticed how much salt there was lying about. On his own, he decided to start hauling the salt into Big Pine. Once again, the cost of transport broke the venture. But the driver, whose name was White Smith (no relation to Borax Smith), wasn't ready to give up on the twin ideas of salt and profit.

Mr. Smith formed a company and tried again in 1903, with the same result. Always, transport was the obstacle. Stubbornness encouraged a wild solution to bypass the rough track. Build a cable tramway from the Saline Valley floor at 1,058 feet, up through rough and tortured Daisy Canyon, to the top of the Inyo Mountains at 8,720 feet. Then down to Swansea (where you are more or less resting) at 3,620 feet. The total distance 13.5 miles. Elevation gain and loss, 12,762 feet. At the same time, run a short spur railroad line from the tram base over to the C&C. Then sit back and enjoy the mounting profits from the sale of salt. The project proved irresistible to Mr. Smith. Construction on the tramway began in 1911 and was completed in 1913. The accomplishment was stunning.

This is how the system worked. Fresh water from a spring was pumped out onto the Saline salt flats. When the water evaporated, salt was the leftover. The salt was then raked into piles. After drying for a while, the salt was loaded onto a two-foot-wide mini railway built out onto the salt flats. Such labor must have been brutal work in the glaring, white heat. Keep in mind the invention of modern sunglasses in Atlantic City would not occur until 1929.

Once the 16 wooden cars on the mini railroad were loaded with salt, they were hauled back to the tramway base by a winch. There, the salt was loaded onto gondola buckets which could each handle about 800 pounds of salt. In total, there were 286 gondola buckets along the 27 miles of cable. Each bucket had a hole in the bottom to allow the excess moisture to drain. Westinghouse electrical motors were located at each end of the tramline and four points in between to power the operation.

The loaded buckets then rode up to the summit in exactly the same manner as a ski lift. At the summit, there was a control station and operator's cabin. The control station allowed full and empty buckets to pass each other without hindrance. When the salt reached Swansea, after a long downhill, it was loaded into railcars and sent on its way. When food and supplies were needed in the Saline Valley, they were sent over in returning salt gondola buckets. When men were needed, same plan, two men to a bucket. Often sleeping off a hangover from partying in Lone Pine. The brand name of the salt was, of course, "Tramway."

The engineering was marvelous. And the system worked as planned. It was the steepest tram ever constructed in the U.S. and the largest of its kind in the world at the time. But it didn't solve the original dilemma. Once again, costs of transport outweighed the profits. Mr. Smith's hair pulling must've been a sight to observe. Through the years, the tramway operated sporadically. Watched over by a succession of frustrated owners. Not one of whom encountered a sustained profit. Then the Depression came along and depressed everything, including the desire for salt. Salt prices dropped significantly. Which doomed the tramway. It shut down for good in 1936. In all, 30,000 tons of salt were carried over the Inyo Mountains during the tramway's 23 years of operation.

So now you are in the know. The base of operations, once around you, was supposedly moved to Candelaria after the tramline closed. It's time for you to move on also. Continue to Swansea, which is indicated by the tree gathering to your south. Do this by returning to the 136 and walking along it, as the C&C is covered in sand dunes to your west. Shortly, you arrive in downtown Swansea.

Swansea, 13 miles from Lone Pine, started life in 1870 as a residential center for nearby smelting furnaces. It was named after Swansea, Wales, where many local Owens Valley miners originally hailed from. The furnaces received ore from Cerro Gordo and reduced it to silver. The output for the furnaces was remarkable for a brief period of years. One hundred fifty bars of silver, every 24 hours. Each bar an impressive 83 pounds.

From the smelter, the bars were carried down to a dock on Owens Lake. There, they were loaded onto a steamer and shipped across the lake to Cartago. From that port, the bars made their way to Los Angeles by wagon. It takes a strong imagination to picture this, when standing on the dunes of Swansea today, looking out over the wasted expanse of Owens Dry Lake.

The Swansea smelters were in business from 1869 to 1874. But Mother Nature appeared hostile to Swansea's continued existence. The 1872 Lone Pine Earthquake damaged the smelters and lifted the shoreline of Owens Lake. So much so, that the steamers could no longer reach Swansea's pier. Then, in 1874, a flash flood buried Swansea under a mass of debris. Swansea was too exhausted to rebuild. On site now is a plaque and a variety of photogenic buildings.

Keeler is three miles south, down the C&C. But it's time for a lovely little 20-mile detour up the Salt Valley Tramline. Followed by a packed-with-views ridge walk over to the Cerro Gordo ghost town. And finally, a descent down the Yellow Grade Road, under the Cerro Gordo Tram, to Keeler. Before you begin, take a look at conditions. If the weather appears ominous or the snow pack seems severe, consider heading straight to Keeler. For us, in mid-March, there was snow at the top of the mountains, but it was easily traversable. And it tasted lovely.

Ready? Across the 136 is a fenced-in home. Take the dirt road just to its left (north side of the house) and follow it up the wash. Have lots of water for this section, as it can get hot even in winter. And the climb is tough, 5,100 feet in all. Eventually the dirt road comes to a fork. Bear right and stay out of the left veering canyon. Climb slowly. Pass under nonexistent salt tram cables, which no longer hang at this point. Though tower remains are still visible. You are now even with the concrete room you took a break in.

Follow the dirt road as it climbs through a narrow canyon and curves back to the tramway. At this juncture, you'll see the tram supports laddering up the mountain to your left. The road itself drops away into a deep valley, before climbing again. Don't descend into that valley. For the Death Q is ready to perform some serious altitude acquisition.

As you stand at the road high point, face uphill. Walk forward to the ridge in front of you. Follow it uphill and to the right, along a forming ridge. As you move up, you will pass fallen tram cables on the ground. Then you will see some cairns. Follow them to the old construction trail. That trail will lead you back to the first big tram tower. Which is quite obvious. Then it will lead you up to the crest, past a number of support towers. No two of which are the same, due to their differing height requirements. Break and enjoy all that is the Owens Valley. Imagine Mr. White Smith sitting in the same spot, a little over 100 years ago, witnessing his dream slowly come to fruition.

Then go over the crest and down into the subsequent valley. Follow the tramway up the opposite slope to bisect the jeep road. Keep following the tramway and ignore the jeep road, as the road is a long detour. And not near as much fun. The tramway ahead seems to ascend sharply. As sometimes is, the climb is easier than it looks. Go straight, tracking the obvious tramway.

When you reach the distinct rock line, you will spot a tram construction trail veering right. Follow it as it zig zags up to yet another crest, passing a number of support platforms along the way. At the crest look down upon a subsequent, shallow valley. Don't embrace euphoria yet. There is a ways to go. Use the tramway as a bearing across the valley, until it climbs into rocks. Just below these rocks is a path that is somewhat overgrown. Follow this path to the opposite side of the mountain, where it joins a better trail. Follow this trail downhill as it transforms into an easy wash. Eventually, you will end up in the bottom of a canyon. The tramway above your constant guide.

Follow the tramway across the canyon and continue up the wash. Then turn up another wash to your right, as directed by the tramlines. Follow this wash toward the support tower. When the wash steepens, leave it and make your way up the right hillside to the ridge. Busting through contour line after contour line as you go. Follow the cable you encounter, on the ridge, up to the next tower. Continue up the ridge to the next support tower at yet another crest. Fun defined. Here note the low hanging gondola bucket, still suspended from the cable by its pulley arm. The lid with a safety mechanism still operable. Also check out the water drain in the bottom of the bucket. Few get to see this because of its remoteness.

And guess what? Another canyon. Accept the inevitable and climb down, then straight up the other side to yet another platform, on yet another crest. Have homicidal thoughts about White Smith. Note the massive stacks of stone that anchored the tower in place. Our start was late out of Lone Pine and this was as far as we got when nightfall draped. It was a fine spot to savor the Owens Valley and its former lake. This tower is roughly 0.8 miles from the summit.

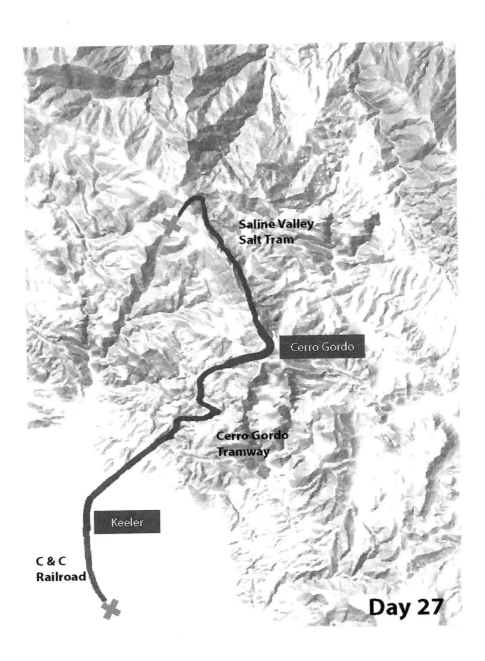

Saline Valley
Salt Tram

Cerro Gordo

Cerro Gordo
Tramway

Keeler

C & C
Railroad

Day 27

342

Day 27

Cerro Gordo-Keeler-Owens Dry Lake

When the sun pecks you good morning, look to the other side of the canyon along the tramway. A direct approach appears steep. Instead, leave your support tower and hike to the left, staying high on your canyon slope. You'll spot another platform on the other side of the canyon. Work your way along the canyon slope, gradually moving downward to meet the rising canyon floor. Eventually, you will naturally connect. Right about where you connect, note the footings of an old cabin. Move up the canyon looking for a right turn. Pass an old steel I-beam, leftover from tramway construction and now part of the canyon floor.

Soon thereafter, turn right up a tapered canyon. This is really your first opportunity to turn right since reaching the canyon floor, so it is hard to miss. Follow the tapered canyon upward, until you spot tram cables hanging about 12 feet above the canyon floor. They are left-turn indicators. Do so, following the cables out of the small canyon. Continue along the cables to the summit. There you will find yourself on top of the local world at 8,720 feet. Climbing well done.

At this highest point is the well-restored control tower, which allowed buckets going in opposite directions to pass each other. At one time, the walls were sheathed in corrugated steel, but no more. The former caretaker's house is also there and open. It has six rooms, some artifacts, and an information panel about life at the top of the tram. The views down into the Saline Valley, some 7,600 feet below, are deeply majestic.

When done exploring, turn right or southeast, along the crest dirt road. There might be snow. From here, into Cerro Gordo, you also happen to be hiking on a short section of the Lowest to Highest Route (L2H). A challenging route from Badwater Basin in Death Valley to the top of Mt Whitney. A total distance of 130 honest miles.

Follow the dirt road for a couple of miles. The views down into both valleys cause tennis neck. Take a moment to savor a life that allows you to escape capitalism and take hikes like this. For, doesn't it seem like we're often so busy chasing money that time becomes more valuable than dollars? As there is never enough of that time in a day. Yet wealth is only measured by the money we have and earn. Perhaps an alternative is to measure wealth by the time we have to devote to the important things in life. And if you have 35 days to hike the Death Q, you are a different kind of millionaire. For you see, 35 days breaks down into more than three million seconds. Which makes you wealthy indeed. And verifies the old saying, "Time is money," from a completely different perspective.

Continue on until the point where the dirt road drops rapidly into a deep valley. From your vantage, you can see the dirt road climb back up to a southern ridgeline. This is your destination, but, fortunately, you don't have to descend into the valley itself. An old water line trail, cut into the valley wall, is your savior. To find the trail begin a descent into the valley, but keep your eyes open on the left for a cairn.

When you encounter the cairn, the vague outlines of the trail are also discernable. Turn left and hike along the trail. The borders become stronger as you move along it. Remember, it has not been maintained for 70 years. Though it is in surprisingly good shape. Keep your eyes peeled for old, two-inch water pipes. Follow the level trail as it makes its way to that far southern ridgeline. Halfway, you start running into bonuses. First, a well-dug mine with piped in water and a drinking water cistern. Though not advised for that. Then, a collapsing pump house. And finally, a well-preserved miner's cabin, vacant for probably many decades. As you hike, note the waterline's T-handled valve turners and pressure relief pipes with wooden plugs. I believe this water pipeline was built in 1873, at a cost of $74,000.

Arrive at that southern ridgeline. Rejoin the dirt road that follows the water pipeline south. Eventually, you find yourself above the ghost town of Cerro Gordo (8,500 feet). Which is remarkably well preserved. That is because some very caring volunteers work hard to keep it that way. Hike down into the town. Meet those kind people. Take the ($10 donation) tour of the town. The tour is excellent value. Get them to tell you the "Levis in the mine" story and about the "Post office murder." The story of the

344

Hi/Low Dance Hall is also worth a listen. If you're nice, you can ask for water in Cerro Gordo with probable success.

Silver was discovered here in the late 1860s by Mexican prospectors. They named the area Cerro Gordo. Which translates pleasantly into English as "Fat Hill." Mining was slow at first, because Indians were resentful of miners exploring their territory. A shootout between five Mexican prospectors and a group of Indians resulted in death for three of the five prospectors. The two captured Mexicans were very open to negotiation. Which they did, promising never to return in order to secure their release. But, eventually, the Indians were deported and the miners returned en masse. News of yet more Cerro Gordo silver strikes reached Lone Pine.

There, the news found storeowner Victor Beaudry. He decided that it would be good business to mine the miners. So, Mr. Beaudry loaded up his wagons and headed for Cerro Gordo. Once there, he opened a supply store that provided goods on credit to the miners. Beaudry was generous with that credit. Then he sat back and watched the debt grow. When a miner could not pay a debt grown large, Beaudry would accept their claim as payment. Soon, his defaulted claims were producing enough to finance the construction of two steam-powered smelters.

The next historically significant persona to arrive in town was Mortimer Belshaw. He was a mining engineer by training and business visionary by nature. After establishing a partnership with Beaudry, Belshaw began looking around for ways to improve his financial prospects. One project involved building the Yellow Grade Road, which climbed 5,000 feet from the Owens Valley floor. He operated the Yellow Grade Road as a toll road (One dollar per wagon, 25 cents for a horse and rider). Then he began transporting silver by wagon down his toll road. The silver bound for Los Angeles. With the funds earned, he built a state of the art smelter. The silver he sent to Los Angeles helped finance the expansion of that city. Which returned the favor by building an aqueduct to remove the water from Owens Valley.

Beaudry and Belshaw's partnership proved powerful. The cost of smelting was high and the small mines were soon indebted to the smelters. One by one, the miners sold out to the partnership. Going from owners to employees in the process. The consolidation brought yet more profit to

345

Messers. Beaudry and Belshaw. With these profits, the men went after control of the town itself, through purchase of its assets. Sector monopoly naturally followed.

And so, the two men flourished, as did Cerro Gordo. Another smelter was built in Swansea. As mentioned, from there the silver was shipped by steamer across Owens Lake to Cartago. Then it was taken by wagon to Los Angeles. Soon 1,000 people were living in Cerro Gordo. With growth, the town grew wild. A newspaper editorial described the town as such, "Pistols continue to crack and good men go down before them."

In comparison, there were only 2,800 people in Los Angeles at the time. Fifty thousand dollars' worth of silver a day was being delivered to Los Angeles and its San Pedro port. On February 2, 1872, the Los Angeles News had this to say about the relationship between Los Angeles and Cerro Gordo. "To this city, Cerro Gordo trade is invaluable. What Los Angeles now is, is mainly due to it. It is the silver cord that binds our present existence. Should it be unfortunately severed, we would inevitably collapse."

This nearly happened in 1873. Torrential rains, and a spreading horse disease caused complete transport failure. A backlog of silver bars began to accumulate on the docks of Cartago and back in Cerro Gordo. In all, 30,000 silver bars were awaiting delivery. Imagine the security headaches. The bars were said to have been used to construct walls for shelters, while the wait drew out. With time, though, rains stop and horses recover. The boom continued for a number of years. But with that same passage of time, mining must slow down, then come to an end.

By 1876, Cerro Gordo was running out of steam, the ore harder and harder to find. A fire in the most productive mine, in 1877, crippled optimism. Then silver prices fell. The smelters shut down. Beaudry and Belshaw looked to the horizon. As did the saloons, brothels (including Lola's Palace of Pleasure), and other town businesses. By 1879, Cerro Gordo was a ghost town.

History retreats, then repeats. In 1906, new discoveries of ore were made in Cerro Gordo. Various companies tried their luck and failed. But every failure brought a replacing newcomer willing to take a shot. In 1908, a smelter was built in Keeler. As well, yet another tramway was built. This time from Cerro Gordo to Keeler. The tramway hauled ore down to the smelter at Keeler. Its tortuous path will be apparent to you, as you hike down the Yellow Grade Road.

In 1910, massive deposits of zinc were discovered in Cerro Gordo. The second boom went on for a while, but act three fizzled during the Depression. The last mining activity in Cerro Gordo took place in 1949. All but a caretaker moved on after that. Most of the left-over mining equipment was sent to Candelaria. In all, more than $17,000,000 was extracted from "Fat Hill." One of the highest producing silver mines in the history of California.

And so, Cerro Gordo slumbered until the 1970s. That is when Jody Stewart, who was working in the television industry in Hollywood, heard about Cerro Gordo from her uncle. Who also happened to be the town caretaker. She decided to have a look and drove up the Yellow Grade in her Porsche. In a fur coat and heels, she took a tour of the town. During the tour, she fell in love with what had been. Eventually, she bought the town with her accumulated savings. Then set about restoring what she could and organizing the tours you can take today. Her legacy and vision is all around you.

So, give yourself the time to wander around. Keep an eye out for the resident ghost. An often-sighted lumber cutter, who was prematurely murdered and thus prefers to linger. Accommodations are available in town by reservation only (760-876-5030, smpatterson1978@gmail.com). For a small contribution, you can join the organization that works to preserve Cerro Gordo.

When you're ready to leave town, start heading down the Yellow Grade Road. Don't go far at all. A couple hundred feet at most. Immediately, take the dirt road running horizontally along the hillside to your left. Believe it or not, this is the former Main Street. Follow it south around the point. After the point, immediately veer down to a fenced-off mine. Follow the dirt road that curves downhill around the mine. Continue downhill, along that dirt road, past various mines. The road enters a canyon that eventually rejoins the Yellow Grade Road. When you reach the Yellow Grade, turn left and continue downhill. Really downhill.

Bringing heavy wagons of ore down this grade was treacherous. The method finally settled on was chaining the wagon wheels together, so they couldn't roll. Then iron shoes were placed under the wooden wheels, so the wood didn't wear excessively. Runaway wagons crushing mules was a concern, so the teams of mules were hitched to the back of the wagon. There, the uphill mules were able to act as a dragging anchor for downhill wagons. The mules combined with the double-wheel brakes acted to create a controlled slide. Failure meant a tangled death. An image that surely ran through the minds of both man and mule.

An interesting rule of the road applied, when two wagons coming from opposite directions met on a narrow stretch of Yellow Grade Road. Backing up was out of the question. So, the smaller of the two wagons was disassembled and moved to the side. Enabling the larger wagon to pass. The yellow tinge of the road material answers the road name question.

As your thighs pound downhill, mule empathy develops. Note the tower platforms of the Cerro Gordo tram as you descend. A number of mining structures distract from your thighs. In all, it is 8.5 miles from Cerro Gordo to Keeler. Don't try to take that appealing major canyon to your right, as a possible shortcut to Keeler. On a map, it looked viable. In reality, it ends at a dramatic but impassable, waterless dryfall. Within a stone's throw of the destination Yellow Grade Road. Which results in a mentally unhealthy, uphill backtrack.

Continue down the Yellow Grade. When you pass a canyon with telephone poles, look up and to your left at a gondola bucket suspended high above the valley floor. A drone was sent up and found the bucket still full of ore.

One step in front of the other will inevitably lead you to Keeler. Note the old Keeler Smelter ruins, to your left, as you emerge from the canyon and approach town. This smelter, as well as the other smelters in the area from the same time period, used charcoal to reduce the ore into gold and silver. Why charcoal instead of wood? For a couple of reasons.

Both wood and its byproduct, charcoal, come from high in the Sierra Nevadas, on the other side of Owens Lake. Where the trees were. First, the trees were cut. Then slid down hand-built log flumes. Which stretched down thousands of feet from high in the mountains to the Owens Valley

348

floor. Upon arrival, many of the logs were brought to two hive-shaped charcoal kilns built on the western side of Owens Lake. The ruins of which still exist today. There, the logs were reduced to charcoal, which made transport a great deal easier. This easing of transport was critical, because the charcoal had to be carried to the eastern side of Owens Lake, where all the ore smelters were located.

The second reason that charcoal was preferred to wood was its much higher burning temperature. Which was necessary to superheat the ore in order to melt the precious metal desired. This melting allowed the necessary separation of ore and precious metal. An example, pure gold melts at 1,943 degrees Fahrenheit. Charcoal can provide those temperatures. Wood cannot.

The problem with charcoal is twofold. It is labor intensive and it is wasteful. For example, to make two pounds of charcoal requires 22 pounds of hardwood. But, these are modern problems that didn't particularly burden the late 1800s.

Close in on Keeler. Just before Keeler, the Yellow Grade bends to the left. Much easier to head overland straight into town. When you reach Route 136, cross over it and turn right. Make a beeline to the old petroleum station with the American flag flying. Two ancient pumps still sit in place. There, you can usually buy cold drinks from Suzanne. Have a sit in the shade and sign her Rockpile guest book. Make sure to let her know what you're up to. It's a nice place for a break. There are no other facilities in Keeler, save for a post office (148 Railroad Ave., M-F 8 to 2, Sa 8 to 12, 760-876-5635.

When rested, it's time to explore Keeler. Keeler has a current population of 66. Though in the 1870s, 5,000 residents crowded its streets. In 1872, a dock was built here to replace the earthquake-uplifted one at Swansea. In 1880, a new mill was built for ore from Cerro Gordo. Around these two, a town sprouted. The new dock was 300 feet long. From there, the steamship, "Bessie Brady," could carry 60,000 lbs. of silver across the lake in three hours. The same trip, by wagon around the lake, took three days. But in 1882, Bessie burned. "Launched in fire, not water," as her captain put it. Over the years, persistent tales that the Bessie Brady was loaded with silver when she sank have wormed their way into the public imagination. To date, none have claimed discovery of the treasure. How's that for a botfly? In 1883, the C&C arrived, eliminating the need for steamships.

Keeler's fortune tracked the mining industry's ups and downs for most of her life. But generally, things were good in the early years on the shores of Owens Lake. Until the aqueduct arrived. Then the lake began to dry up faster than anyone thought it would. And mining declined, until it stopped altogether in the 50s. In 1957, Keeler station closed, and soon after, the C&C folded. Blowing toxic dust off Owens (now) Dry Lake pushed the town toward uninhabitable. And most folks moved on. Though recent remedial efforts by the LADWP have somewhat reduced the blowing dust problem. Which has allowed 66 to still call Keeler home. Sobering is the fact that Owens Dry Lake is still considered one of the largest, single sources of dust pollution in the country.

For a Keeler tour, leave the ex-gas-station and turn right down Malone Street for two blocks. Walk until you reach Railroad Avenue. The C&C tracks came right through here, as the information plaque will tell you. The two-story building in front of you was the C&C Rail Depot. The depot was built in 1883. The second story was added in 1917 and is where the station agent resided. Nearby is the post office.

Continue on Malone Street to Old State Highway. Then turn left. Pass the old railroad loading docks and Keeler Fire Department. The fire department building was once the Owenyo Rail Depot, until it migrated here. At the old schoolhouse, turn right on Cerro Gordo Road and walk down to the former shoreline. Note the small dirt road running south on your left. Along this road is how you will leave Keeler. At the shoreline, check out the surfboard with faded lettering about campsites. As well as the community swimming pool, now unswimmable. The images of better times are easily perceived.

Backtrack to the dirt road and turn right to exit Keeler. Follow the dirt road south to the large loading platform. Just before the platform, turn left and walk a bit. Your railbed is somewhere in this general area, between the former shoreline and Route 136. But, blowing sand has covered much. Technically, the C&C ended in Keeler, but in reality, it continued a few miles south to the soda works on your horizon. Orient yourself by aiming your line of hike toward the white soda ash mounds to the south. Start hiking, and soon you will stumble upon the railbed. Follow the railbed and its ties toward the soda ash mounds. Or, at least, I believe they are soda ash mounds. If I'm right, here is a primer on the matter.

Soda ash (a.k.a. sodium carbonate), is a chemical compound. It is derived mainly from a white powdery mineral that is called Trona. Trona is found layered on top of, and within, dry lakes. From which it is scraped and collected into piles. As, I believe, you see in front of you. From the piles, Trona is refined into soda ash/sodium carbonate. More than half of all the soda ash, that is mined in the world, is used to make glass. The remainder ends up finding use in manufacturing, water softening, detergents, cosmetics, chemicals, taxidermy and, predictably, making German pretzels.

Soda ash was first used by the Egyptians some 5,000 years ago. Right around the time Methuselah was born. Today, soda ash is one of the most widely used commodities in the United States. So much so that the Federal Reserve Board uses monthly soda ash production data as an economic indicator of the overall health of the U.S. economy. Owens Dry Lake has the third highest concentration of Trona in the U.S. Searles Dry Lake, which you are coming up on, has the second highest concentration. Back to your hike.

Be on the lookout for Steve. A local ham radio operator, encyclopedia about the area, and avid hiker. The path you are on is his daily route. He was the first and last hiker we met on the Death Q, some 592 miles in. Pass the wreckage of a very old soda ash plant and glass factory. Then the railbed runs out and you hike away from your C&C companion. Keep the large soda ash piles just to your right. Walk through the surplus supply yard of the modern plant to your left.

When you emerge on the other side, find the old, abandoned National Highway roadbed to your left. Follow it south, past the dust suppression schemes ongoing to your right. Your goal is Olancha, about 18 miles away on the southern tip of Owens Dry Lake. Though it certainly doesn't look that far. There, you will rejoin the Jawbone line of the Southern Pacific, which you first saw in Owenyo/Lone Pine. Getting there involves hugging

the Owens Dry Lake shoreline into Olancha. For us, the day halted here.
A campsite in every direction. A lost lake, our neighbor for the night.

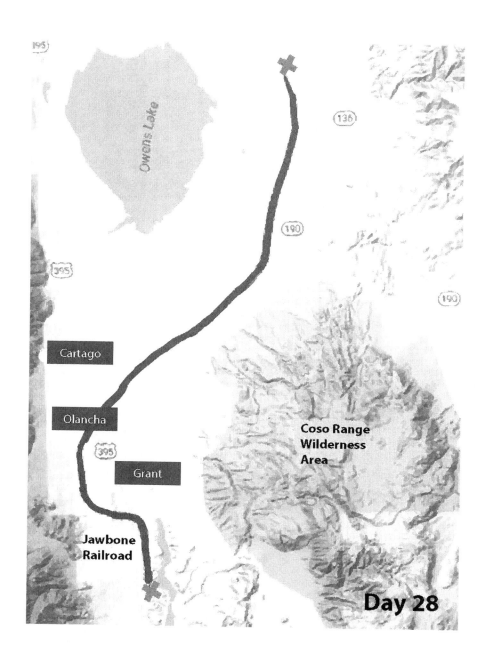

Owens Lake

Cartago

Olancha

Grant

Jawbone
Railroad

Coso Range
Wilderness
Area

Day 28

353

Day 28

Olancha-Loco-Haiwee

Awake and bid good morning to Malpais (Bad Country) Mesa Wilderness to your east. As well as the sun rushing to you after its time over the Atlantic. To your west, the Whitney Portal Road is visible climbing into the Sierras. Further southwest, are the Zorro zig zags of Horseshoe Meadow Road, which is also making its way up into the Sierras. The Horseshoe Meadow Road is an impressive feat of engineering. It climbs 6,000 feet before topping out at 10,000 feet above sea level. Which makes it the second highest paved road in California.

Ready to get hiking? Please rejoin your abandoned, crumbling road. Observe the desert's ability to consume the previous efforts of engineers. Continue south. Walk past an abandoned corral. Soon after, arrive at multiple cairns where the abandoned road takes a turn left toward the 136. At the cairns, a faint dirt road leads off to your right. Within a short distance, the dirt road gathers strength. Leave the asphalt road and follow the dirt road. If the cairns are washed away, simply walk 50 yards down the abandoned highway, past its big turn toward the 136. Then stop and turn right toward the lake. Before arriving at the lake, you will encounter the dirt road I am talking about.

Follow the dirt road as it tracks the curvature of the shoreline. Slowly, it makes its way to Route 190, which is the road in front of you. When you reach the 190, turn right (west). From here, it is 12 miles of road walking into Olancha. Luckily the traffic is light. About a car every 15 minutes. At least five cars stopped to offer water or a ride to the deranged. The Coso Range is to your left. This is an optically demented section of the hike. Which means your destination flees from you as you hike toward it.

About five miles out of Olancha, just before the first group of buildings you've seen today, there is a paved road leading to the right. Turn right and follow it down to the "Dirty Socks Hot Spring." The only inaccuracy in the name is "Hot." Still, the cemented ring of water makes a nice rest and warm foot soak. With views out over the flat, white expanse. Swimming in it would be a bravery.

Dirty Socks Hot Spring was discovered in 1917 by a drilling crew looking for fresh water. At 1,200 feet down, the drill tapped into highly pressurized water. Which promptly shot to the surface. Unfortunately, the water was far from fresh, because it was packed with minerals. Rendering it of no use to the drillers. The drillers tried to cap their unwanted well without success. The water has been making its way to the surface ever since. Celebrating its 100-year anniversary in 2017 with zero fanfare. Over the years, various attempts to commercialize the springs have fallen flat. This is perhaps attributable to the water's odor closely resembling the spring's namesake. The concrete ring around the spring is a remnant of one of those commercialization attempts.

Back to the road for the final push into Olancha. Sand dunes appear to your left. Plead with the weather decision-makers for a nonwindy day. As the blowing sands cut. Enter Olancha, population 192. In 1860, silver was discovered in the nearby Coso Range. A mill was built in Olancha and a small town grew around it. But in 1867, an Indian raid burned the mill down. Agriculture was left to take over. In the late 1800s, Olancha was a green, verdant place. It served as a stage and transport center for Cerro Gordo. And the docks of Cartago were just to the north. In 1910, the Jaw-bone reached Olancha. Followed shortly by the aqueduct. Soon after, the water and green flowed away.

The aqueduct is not the only party interested in Olancha's water. Crystal Geyser has a large water bottling plant here for its LA market. As well, Anheuser-Busch pumps water here for its Los Angeles breweries. The pure snow melt too much for such corporations to pass up. Which leaves Olancha residents watching their well levels. Films are occasionally made here. "Bug," "Ironman," and "Tremors," are some examples. In the late 1960s, Olancha briefly made the news as two fleeing Manson Family members temporarily took up residence here. Including the man who killed Sharon Tate. Though that was unknown at the time of his residence. Today, Olancha primarily caters to the tourist trade on Route 395. The Jawbone ceased operations in 1982.

When you T the 395, turn right and walk a quarter mile. There you will discover fine burgers and smooth chocolate shakes at the Ranch House Café (50 Fall Road, 760-764-2363, 7 a.m. - 8 p.m., seven days a week). If not in the mood for such fare, turn left on the 395 and walk south to the Mobil station for resupply. Stay on the left (east) side of the road. Walk past the post office (760-764-2329, M-F 11 a.m. - 3 p.m., 100 S. Highway 395). Immediately, come to a long row of tamarisk trees paralleling the 395. To avoid traffic, cut in behind the tamarisks and walk in relative peace. Judging from the sand footprints, this is how the locals do it. When you emerge, you are at the Mobil Station.

OLANCHA		
1.	Food Supply	Yes
2.	Restaurant	Yes
3.	Water	Yes
4.	Hotel	Yes
5.	Beer	Yes
6.	Pool Table	No
7.	ATM	Yes
8.	Post Office	Yes
9.	Casino	No

The Olancha Mobil station is open 6 a.m.-midnight, seven days a week. There is an ATM. There is also a sub shop inside (601 S. Highway 395, 760-764-2289). The convenience store onsite is sufficient to resupply until Inyokern, which is 46 miles away. There, a more extensive food market exists. Along this upcoming section, there are a number of water sources. Had a glimpse of the modern apocalypse in the Olancha Mobil, when the credit card machine shut down for an hour. It was not pretty at all.

Across the street is the charismatic Gus's Beef Jerky Store. There are three motels spread around Olancha. The Rustic Oasis, where parts of "Bug" were filmed (760-764-2209, 2055 S. Highway 395), the Olancha

RV Park and Motel (760-764-0023, 1075 S. Highway 395) and the Ranch Motel (760-764-2387, 1995 S. Highway 395).

When weighted down and ready to head out, briefly backtrack north from the Mobil Station. Do this by walking along the left side of 395 for about 200 yards until you reach Fall Road. Turn left (west) and hike towards the Sierras and the Jawbone. Follow Fall Road to its end. Cross the LA aqueduct river. And find yourself standing on the Jawbone railroad. After formal introductions, turn left and head south through the foothills. Encounter the old loading docks. Then pass a fascinating, abandoned mill locked in a time warp. Its warehouses appear to have serviced the Jawbone. The large warehouse lettering patiently awaiting noir photography.

You are now on the Jawbone branch of the Southern Pacific railroad. It was built, as all railroads are, for economic reasons. Los Angeles was planning its aqueduct. The planners figured that 14 million tons of freight would need to be hauled to an ever-advancing building site. A bid was put out to the wagon freighters. They came back with an amount. Then the Los Angeles number crunchers calculated what it would cost to build a railroad to move all that freight. The railroad came in at less than half the price demanded by the wagon freighters. An easy decision.

In 1907, Los Angeles solicited bids for the project and Southern Pacific won the contract. In 1908, Southern Pacific began railroad construction from its existing line in Mojave. The goal, Lone Pine. It was to be a standard gauge line and reach 143.5 miles in total. You will be hiking roughly half of it. Eventually, tracks reached past Lone Pine to Owenyo in 1910. This allowed a connection with the C&C.

Along the way, the line acquired the nickname "Jawbone." Some say the nickname is derived from Jawbone Canyon, which it passes along the way. Others are of the opinion that the railroad is so named because it resembled the shape of a jawbone. The final group to weigh in claim the railroad is named for a saber-toothed tiger jaw that was dug up by a rail grading crew. Regardless of its source, the name stuck.

The arrival of the Jawbone was met with great fanfare in Lone Pine. Which had always felt slighted by the C&C placing itself on the eastern side of the valley. The Jawbone proved an initial boon to residents of Owens Valley. It allowed Owens Valley agricultural products to reach Los

Angeles markets. And Pullman sleeper car services allowed ease of travel to and from the coast.

But while the railroad was delivering with one hand, the aqueduct was taking away with the other. Without water, farming and ranching suffered. As crops transitioned to fields of dust, demand for the railroad services decreased. Then the Depression cut rail traffic of all types off at the knees. The desire to drive automobiles did not help either. Passenger service was ended in 1942. Freight service slowed to a crawl.

Then, in 1981, fire in the rail tunnel at Searles cut off the northern section of the Jawbone for a year and a half. The Southern Pacific had been losing money on this section for a number of years. The powers that be decided that disaster was an opportunity. They seized that opportunity and abandoned the 90 miles of line north of Searles in 1982. The southern section from Searles to Mojave is still in use. At Searles, the Jawbone connects with a branch line to Trona, where mining is ongoing. From 1996 to 1998, the northern Jawbone's rails and ties were salvaged. What is left is there to support your hike.

Hike south toward the big cut in the hills ahead. You are now on the Rolls Royce of abandoned railroads. Smooth, flat, and intact. With real bridges. Due to its fairly recent abandonment. Though, for how long those bridges will withstand Mother Nature's will is an open question. For she is back on the offensive and bent on recapturing previously lost territory. Some bridges have already been washed away. By all accounts, the maintenance of the Jawbone Railroad was an ongoing migraine, due to flash floods pouring out of the often-angry Sierra Nevadas. As numerous trains derailing in washed out sections attested to.

Walking along this section brought to mind a story I heard in Zaire (now the Democratic Republic of the Congo) years ago. It seems there was a transportation director in charge of the road between Kinsasha and Kisangani. A distance of roughly 1,600 miles. The road director was Belgian, as Zaire was a Belgian Colony at the time. He had a cruel streak. When the director was ready to inspect his road, he would place a two-thirds full cup of water on the dash of his convertible Cadillac. Then he would set off from Kinsasha. Driving the speed limit. Expecting to arrive in Kisangani, some five days later, with that glass still two-thirds full. Spaced along the way were villages. The chief of each village was responsible for maintaining the section of road adjacent to their village. Sometimes the road director hit a pothole on the dirt road, and water spilled from the glass. When this happened, he would stop at the relevant village and physically assault the chief. This insured that road maintenance was a local priority.

By the time I made it to Zaire, that same road through the jungle had been consumed by the calamities of Mother Nature. A short section of it took weeks plowing through mud in a large truck. One pothole was filled by abandoning an 18-wheeler in it. The truck was covered and became part of the road. To actually drive the entire length of the road from Kinsasha to Kisangani was considered impossible. Maintenance was all but abandoned. So, I salute the people, however they were motivated, who maintain the thoroughfares of this world. It's not an easy job, especially where Mother Nature often turns resentful. And let's hope karma met that road director on a blind turn. His last visual, spilling water.

Continue walking toward the cut. Note the neat culvert bridges that direct floodwater over the aqueduct rather than underneath it. Eventually, the Jawbone returns to the 395 to intersect it. Cross four lanes of light traffic by passing through the chain link gates. Quite civilized. Pass a mountain of reclaimed Jawbone ties. Then march through the stone gravel of the former Loco Station, 4.8 miles from Olancha. Loco is a Shoshone word which means "Unknown." Which is possibly where the station got its name. The Spanish version of the word, meaning "Crazy," a second alternative. What is certain is that Loco Station was closed in 1953.

Hike through a series of extensive cuts and subsequent infills. All the while staying flat. Begin a pass of Haiwee Reservoir on your left. The more you hike, the more the reservoir strays away from the railbed. Haiwee Reservoir is part of the aqueduct system and is owned by LADWP. A second aqueduct, built in 1970, originates at Haiwee Reservoir. The two aqueducts combined deliver 430 million gallons of water a day to LA. Which hydrates a city that has grown to be the second largest in the U.S. The reservoir itself holds 80 days of aqueduct flow. Since the 1990s, the reservoir has been on again/off again closed, due to the possibility of terrorism. Much to the annoyance of local fisherman. Haiwee comes from the

Shoshone language and means "Dove." As you run out of steam, find a place of solitude.

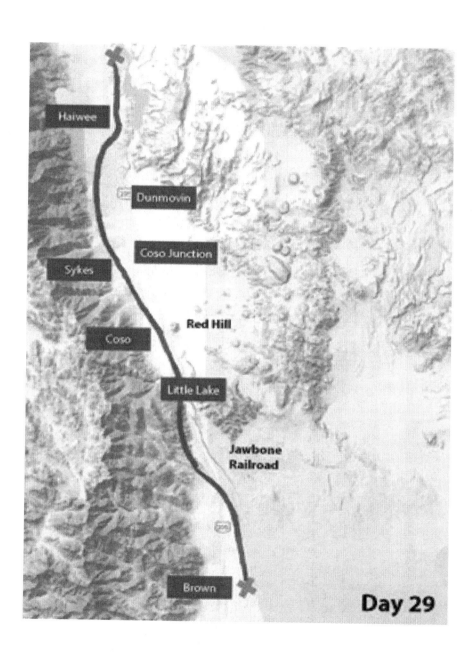

Haiwee

Dunmovin

Coso Junction

Sykes

Red Hill

Coso

Little Lake

Jawbone
Railroad

Brown

Day 29

361

Day 29

Mabel-Little Lake-Brown

Arise from your night and get on the Jawbone in the direction of Dunmovin and Coso Junction. Both south. After the end of the reservoir, the railbed moves back across the 395. Somewhere in this section you pass Haiwee Station. We found no evidence of it. Though its history is still worthy of telling.

Haiwee was a water stop until 1954. At various times, it was called Hawaii to the confusion of all involved. For a number of years, starting in 1884, there was a settlement here. Before that, Haiwee served as a rest stop for travelers passing up the Owens Valley. On New Year's Day in 1865, Indians killed the son and wife of the man who ran the rest stop. This resulted in retaliatory acts on local Indians. When the railroad arrived in 1910, the settlement moved to align with the railroad. The former town site is submerged under the Haiwee Reservoir.

As you cross the 395, note the old junction boxes for the crossing guards. Then some of the old crossing guards themselves lying in the brush. (Boards, not bodies.) Begin a big swing to the west. Pass an old blockhouse with no identifiable use. At this point, you are paralleling the aqueduct, which is underground. Capped by a cement covering.

At another time, on another trail, I once camped on top of a similar section of the LA aqueduct. On that night, the wind was ferocious. A guess would be 70-80 mph. In an effort to shelter, I placed my sleeping bag behind a small concrete pump house. Which was about two feet high. Setting up a tent was out of the question. During the night, came the urge that eventually became unignorable. I loaded down my bag with rocks, while impure words escaped. Then stood up to face the gale.

Immediately, I began sliding downwind. Somehow, I was able to swivel and dig in. And begin the urination process. Then it began to rain. I looked to the starless heavens and shouted about injustice. As the drops splattered my face. How could I set up my tent in a hurricane? The visual of a night spent laying in the rain passed through my imagination. Then a miracle. The rain stopped. It took a remarkably short time to figure out the rain was actually urine. Pushed by the wind, passing between my legs and updrafted into my face. The relief I felt at having been pissing on my face was disturbing. Anything not to have to set up that tent.

Far down in the valley, on the left, is a small group of buildings. This is Dunmovin. A visible road leaves there and heads to a mine in the east. Dunmovin is a ghost town. All 155 acres of Dunmovin, including several buildings, could be yours for $500,000. Or at least that was the price the last time I checked. The name is a mystery. But a fair guess would be somebody found heaven here and decided this is where they'd stay for the remainder of their years. Thus, the town's statement name.

Pass isolated ranches and eventually come to a dirt road that cuts across the railbed. This road leads to Coso Junction. Coso has a convenience store with all the usual amenities. It is also a big detour. Inyokern, and its much better facilities, is 29 miles to the south. Occasionally, there are LADWP maintenance crews in the area.

As you walk along this and other sections of the aqueduct, the scale of the engineering becomes apparent. This first and original section of aqueduct is 233 miles long. Amazingly, no pumps are used to transport the water. Gravity does all the work, as LA is much lower than the Owens Valley. The water even generates electricity as it flows downhill toward the Angelenos. But building an aqueduct requires a lot more than just digging a ditch. In five years, 215 miles of road, 230 miles of pipeline, 218 miles of power transmission lines and 377 miles of telegraph and telephone lines were built or installed. As well as one railroad.

Fifty-seven work camps were constructed along the way. A cement plant was built. It supplied 10,000 barrels of cement a day and almost one million barrels overall. One hundred and forty tunnels were drilled through the mountainsides. The total length of those tunnels extended 43 miles. The project planners estimated that eight feet of tunnel per day was possible. They then offered the drillers a bonus for anything over that. The drillers nearly tripled it. In fact, the tunnel drillers become so adept that they won several worldwide competitions. And a few went on to supervise other tunnel projects across the globe.

Much of the aqueduct was created by casting concrete trenches. Steel piping was also used and was considered preferable by engineers. But its cost was prohibitive, as it had to be brought from the east coast by ship. In those days, before the Panama Canal (opened in 1914), this meant a trip around Cape Horn. A daunting journey of thousands of miles, that could take weeks depending on conditions.

At its height, there were 3,900 laborers building the Aqueduct. Many were from the Balkans. Fifteen hundred of whom deserted their work and went home in 1912 to fight in the First Balkan War. The pull of patriotism too strong. (The war resulted in the Ottoman Empire losing all their European territory.) The wage at the time was $2.25 a day. Which was considered quite high. Health insurance was available for between 50 cents and $1 a month. (Imagine, in current times, paying a non-subsidized, monthly insurance premium on a half day laborer's wage.) In all, 43 men died building the aqueduct. It was finished on time and under the $24.6 million budget. Which was Mr. Mulholland's natural inclination and tendency.

Where the dirt road crosses the railbed was once Sykes. Also known as Mabel. Yet another stop on the Jawbone. Your swing through the valley begins a return to the east. At this point, you are moving through volcanic deposits. The source of which is the red, Red Hill (3,952 feet) to the east. Pass a raised ferry bridge loading dock, near an abandoned house. The Jawbone is drawn toward the 395. But when it reaches the 395, the Jawbone turns fickle and refuses to cross it. Instead, it chooses to track the 395 for a while. Feel good about yourself because you are towering above the road. And igniting conversation after conversation.

Climb out of the valley to the pass at Little Lake. As you approach the pass, there is a wet lake to the left and a dry one to the right. Brush thickens on the railbed. If you need water, you can get it out of Little Lake. Little Lake started its life as a stage stop. It stayed a stop for the rest of its life. Subsequently, as a rail stop in 1910. And then a rest stop for automobile bound travelers on the 395.

The lake itself was created when the LADWP built a dam in the former Owens riverbed. The "former" refers to a very long time ago. As in the last Ice Age, over 10,000 years ago. When melting glaciers swelled

Owens Lake to over 200 square miles. Which caused it to overflow its southern banks and create a southern section of the Owens River.

The newly formed river explored its way southward from Owens Lake, through the volcanic fields around Red Hill. Whose lava ranged in age from 10,000 to 400,000 years old. Eventually, the river created the spectacular Fossil Falls. (Which are one mile northeast of Little Lake and can still be visited.) At Fossil Falls, the Owens River poured over polished lava and fell 75 feet. Upon landing, the river continued on past Little Lake. Before finally ending its escape in China Lake. But then, the climate warmed up and the glaciers retreated. Which returned Owens Lake to its original boundaries. Changed China Lake from wet to dry. And ended the second act of the Owens River. Leaving Fossil Falls without water and its flow/fall to the imagination.

At one point, there was a hotel, restaurant, gas station and post office in Little Lake. All developed by the race car driver Bill Bramlette. Who, in 1920, set the Los Angeles to Bishop driving speed record. Covering the 203-mile route in an off-the-lot Lincoln touring car. The time of seven hours and 24 minutes setting the course record. At a blazing average speed of 27.4 mph, which must have felt like ground flying in those days. (Seven hours and 24 minutes is still a respectable time if departing during LA's rush-hour traffic on the way to Bishop during ski season.) After the feat, he used the fame created to publicize Little Lake. These days, the descendants of Mr. Bramlette run Benton Hot Springs.

Little Lake was one of those neat little towns, spaced out along highways, that provided a cool drink and a meal. While the radiator cooled down. But as technology improved, the distance a car could travel increased. Radiators stopped overheating and air conditioning improved. As did speed and gas mileage.

With these developments, people didn't need to stop in Little Lake anymore. Which forced the town to accept its obsolescence. An avalanche of bad luck followed the acceptance. One by one the businesses closed. Then the 395 was expanded to four lanes and bypassed the town. In 1981, the Jawbone gave up. In 1989, the hotel burned. The funds and will to rebuild were insufficient. In 1997, the post office closed. Finally, in 2001, what was left of the town was bulldozed. And Little Lake returned to just being a body of water.

But the bulldozers missed the post office. Which is where you can take a nice break, leaning against its green-shingled walls and sipping Little Lake water. After the break, stay to the right of the 395 with the railbed. For its part, the 395 drops down into the Indian Wells Valley below. But you stay high on the mountainside. As trains inherently dislike rapid dropping. Pass an impressive wall of lava flow in arrested development. The lava pulling up just short of the railbed. (A perhaps romantic interpretation of events.) Slowly, the railbed descends with dignity, as do you, to the valley floor.

There, the railbed eventually crosses the 395 and begins a swing to the east. If you're hiking in March and the rains are kind, the wildflowers are soul affecting. Your footprints memorialized in multicolored outlines. Pass over functioning bridges with proper wooden guardrails and around bridges taken by floodwaters. Now you are skirting China Lake Naval Weapons Testing land. The all-business fence to your east, backed by an impressive lava ridge, establishes the boundary.

China Lake became a Naval Weapons Center in 1943. It is named for the Chinese that used to mine borax from a dry lake, that is now part of the weapons range. It is huge. In all, 1,718 square miles. Which dwarfs Rhode Island. (Poor Rhode Island, always sucked into comparisons.) China Lake represents 38% of all the land the Navy owns. What do they do out there? Fly really fast. You might hear your first sonic boom, its shockwaves unforgettable. As a kid growing up near Edwards Air Force Base, we blamed every window broken with a baseball on sonic booms. The Air Force on the hook for the repair. The Navy also develops weapons and tests them out at China Lake. Usually, by blowing up the desert.

Regardless of your politics, it must also be noted that, by denying entry to the general public, the unbombed areas have attained a higher level of preservation. Three hundred and forty species of wildlife live within China Lake. As well, China Lake contain the 99-square mile Coso Rock Art District. Where 50,000 petroglyphs reside. Some up to 16,000 years old. The highest concentration of rock art in the Northern Hemisphere. In all, 95% of China Lake has been left undeveloped.

366

But my favorite part of China Lake comes, once again, from my child-hood. In the 1970s, we would convince my science teacher, Jim O'Donnell, to drive us out to the China Lake bombing range. There, we would wait by the border fence, as the helicopters shot up the ground with dum-dum bullets. Anything that drifted over the fence we considered ours by obtaining. Best of all, were the giant, silk flare parachutes. Which we would use to blindly pull our skateboards down roads on windy days. Our youth assuring us that no cars were coming from the opposite direction.

Head south. Observe your straight railbed shot across the valley. No mysteries where you're headed. The sun is probably getting tired by now. Walk until you come to a round alfalfa field on your right. Round for ease of rotating irrigation drip lines. Just before the field are telephone poles leading west, with an accompanying dirt road. You are now about 10 miles out of Inyokern, probably near Brown Station.

Brown was a large aqueduct camp and supply base. Corrals here held hundreds of burros, mules and horses. Also on-site, was a hotel, restaurant and post office. So many post offices. But, I guess they were the internet of their day. The Brown Station of those days does not appear to be present. Choose an appropriate creosote wind block for the night. Then, either settle down into the dark and revel in your self-sufficiency. Or, hop on that dirt road and walk over to the 395. Then turn right and stroll to the lonely Shell/Subway convenience store loyally awaiting your patronage. Life is an endless string of choices. You have made it 37 miles from Olancha.

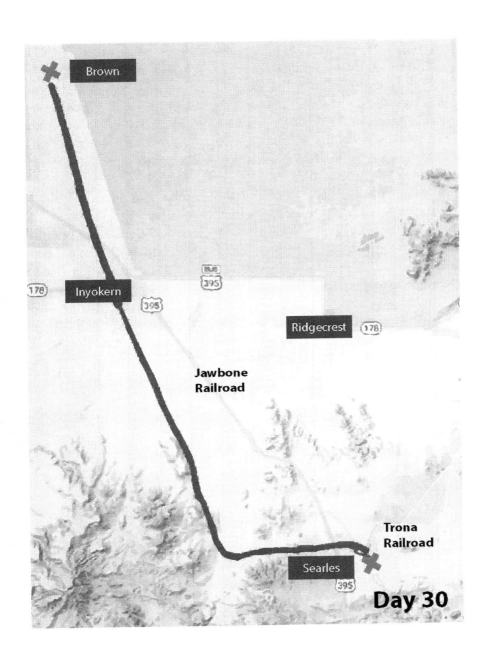

Brown

178

Inyokern

395

BUS
395

Ridgecrest   178

Jawbone
Railroad

Trona
Railroad

Searles

395

Day 30

Day 30

Inyokern-Code-Rademacher-Searles Tunnel

Continue into Inyokern, past alfalfa fields, orchards, and thickening homes. The Jawbone right-of-way cleaves the valley in two. The town of Ridgecrest and the entrance to China Lake are eight miles to the east. It's interesting to be walking through a scattered residential area while on a railbed. Remnants of rail gates and crossing signs are still in place. I imagine this neighborhood became instantly more tranquil after the railroad shut down in 1982. Dogs seem the most fascinated with your passing.

Pass under the 395 bridge and enter Inyokern. The perfect hiking town, as all you need is right next to the Jawbone. When you arrive at the intersection of Brown Road, (which you have been paralleling) and Inyokern Road, it is time to resupply. A plaque here honors the Jawbone for creating Inyokern in 1909.

Inyokern has all the required hiker support facilities within a block of each other.

INYOKERN		
1.	Food Supply	Yes
2.	Restaurant	Yes
3.	Water	Yes
4.	Hotel	Yes
5.	Beer	Yes
6.	Pool Table	Yes
7.	ATM	Yes
8.	Post Office	Yes
9.	Casino	No

The Inyokern Market is on the same intersection as the plaque (1353 Brown Road, 760-377-3298, 6:30 a.m. - 9:30 p.m., seven days a week).

The next resupply is in Johannesburg, 29 miles away. An ATM is onsite. A short walk up Inyokern Road brings you to the Mayfair Motel (760-377-5700, 1352 2nd St.), the Five Fingers Pub with pool tables, and a fine Mexican restaurant called Bernardinos (6601 W. Inyokern Road, 760-377-4012, M-Sa 7 a.m. - 8 p.m., Su 7 a.m. - 2 p.m.). Yet, further up the road is a Dollar General store (6764 Mountain View Ave., 760-377-0037, 8 a.m. – 9 p.m., seven days a week).

The name Inyokern is reached by combining the names of Inyo and Kern counties. Inyo County is the second largest county in California. And includes much of Death Valley. At 10,227 square miles, it is larger than six states. Including, of course, beleaguered Rhode Island. Though only 18,260 souls call those 10,227 square miles home. Which is what I call elbow room.

Inyo comes from a misinterpretation. It seems that when Anglos showed up in the area, they asked the local Paiutes what the name of the nearby mountain range was. The Paiutes heard, "What's the name of your leader?" Their answer, "His name is Inyo." The Anglos heard the mountains were the Inyo Mountains. So, they named the county after the mountains. And Chief Inyo was forever and unknowingly enshrined.

Inyokern was known as Magnolia on early Jawbone schedules. Its telegraph call letter was a delightfully foresightful "Q." The town is also the sunshine capital of America. Well, that's what the sign says. Who can find complaint in claiming that? A population of 1,099 people call it home.

You are now at 2,434 feet. The very good Indian Wells Brewery is nearby. The large Inyokern airport on your right, was the original Naval Air Station, before it moved eight miles east. In 1944, the Southern Pacific built a spur line from Inyokern out to China Lake. The Navy operated its own railroad on that spur line. Weapons and materials that had arrived in Inyokern on the Jawbone Railroad were brought out to China Lake on the spur line. The Navy stopped using the spur line in the mid 1960s.

Today, Inyokern is a quiet bedroom community of Ridgecrest. To leave the quiet, return to the Jawbone and turn south. The town falls away quickly, returning you to the deeper peace of the desert. Almost. Pass a shooting range and then begin to climb using the side of an old volcano. If spring is smiling at you, this is a great purple and yellow flower stretch, that would have forced Van Gogh to gush. The Jawbone keeps reaching for altitude.

Come to the murdered former stop/siding of Code. You'll understand. Just before it, try to spot the stacked stone stairwell leaving over the berm to your right. Check out the sharp little bridge leading nowhere. Someone followed their dreams of the moment. Only to be turned back. Begin a big turn back toward 395 in the distance. Look for Fred in the Flintstone formations.

Note as you get closer to the road, the mass variety of items people have brought from home to kill in the desert. Then leave there as testaments to their accuracy and the Second Amendment's right to bear arms. Keep your eyes peeled for executed garden trolls. Which forced me to spend the next hour trying to solve the mystery of what could possibly drive anyone to shoot harmless garden trolls? The scenario continues to elude me. Though I'm certain a short story resides somewhere just past my imagination. Any ideas?

Veer to the right, above the tiny burg of Rademacher. There are no services here. Nearby mines caused the creation of the village in the late 1880s. The train station here operated from 1909 to 1943, when it was abandoned. The station house sold for $26.50. You have now hiked 60 miles from Olancha.

Continue climbing and cross the 395. At the crossing, note the Rails to Trails signboard and rail. Follow the railbed onward once you've crossed the quiet 395. Then a fine surprise. An intact, abandoned railroad in place. Now you get to see how all those parts you've been stepping over actually function. As well as what their role is. Give it some study.

Follow the rails to Searles, where the still-functioning Trona Railroad joins the still-functioning lower branch of the Jawbone. The short upper Jawbone branch that you've been hiking on, that is still railed, is used as a storage line. The lower Jawbone branch is now operated by the Union Pacific, which took over the Southern Pacific in 1996. Before all this connection, choose your quarters for the night.

As you lay down to your thoughts, how about a true story of obsession or perseverance? Yours to decide by the end. It all happened not too far from where you find yourself at this moment. In the El Paso Mountains to your west. From high above the Fremont Valley, which you will cross tomorrow.

Without further ado, allow me to introduce you to William Schmidt and his stubborn tale.

William Schmidt was born in 1871, in the city of Providence, Rhode Island. Pretty much right away, he didn't like fate the way he saw it. Six siblings, the reaper even at three brothers and three sisters, died of tuberculosis around him. It was a logical decision for William to go away to a drier place. Which is how he found himself in the Mojave Desert in 1900. More decisions were necessary. What to do in the Mojave Desert, alive and free of the east coast? William settled on becoming a hard-rock miner. The enthusiasm of youth trumping zero experience.

The new miner got to it. He staked a claim at the base of Copper Mountain and began the search for wealth. For a couple of years, he mined and gathered ore. Teaching himself experience as he went. Semi-alone and determined. But William had a problem. At least in his eyes. Which are the only eyes that matter in this story.

And that problem was Copper Mountain. All 4,400 feet of it. For you see, William was mining on the wrong side of it. When it came to transport anyway. The road to the ore mills, railroad (the Jawbone, which would come in 1908) and the towns were all on the other side of Copper Mountain. In the long length of the Fremont Valley. And, unfortunately, the road/trail around Copper Mountain to the Fremont Valley was a mess. William despised risking his precious burros, Jack and Jenny, on every journey along it.

William, who was now going by "Burro," thanks to the other two story participants, called a meeting with his camp mates. By the end of that meeting a resolution was reached. A completely rational resolution at the time. Resolved: Dig a shortcut tunnel through the heart of Copper Mountain to the Fremont Valley. Knock it off in short order. Eliminate the headache of going around or over Copper Mountain. Everybody happy.

In 1902, Burro, Jack, and Jenny got started. Burro was 32 years old when he picked up his tools that day. Quickly, he ran into a problem. Copper Mountain was solid granite. Progress was measured in inches. But inches are progressive inches, when it comes to a fixed destination. Burro plowed ahead. The weeks turned into months. A simple routine developed. Dig, eat, sleep, repeat.

Funds were short. Always. So, Burro used simple hand tools. A pick, hammer, wheelbarrow and shovel. The more modern digging implements available but unaffordable. And thus ignored. His hole began to reach into Copper Mountain. Enough so, that darkness became an issue. But, kerosene for lighting was expensive. So, a single candle a day was allotted. Which translated into sometimes digging in the dark. The hole became a tunnel.

Another meeting was held. It was decided to focus on the tunnel, rather than mining for gold. Mining outside the tunnel was abandoned. And promising mineral veins inside the tunnel were ignored. Their potential value inconsequential. Months turned into years. With funds exhausted, Burro began taking summer work as a ranch hand in the Kern Valley. At the end of each summer, the tunnel was refinanced. Burro would swing by the general store in Johannesburg for supplies, then hightail it back to the one that waited.

More years passed. Burro was now a tunnel man. His mining days over. At the end of each tunneling day, a return to his one room cabin and potbellied stove. Cooking one of the thousands of meals he prepared solo on the stove's surface. Studying the newspapered walls for entertainment. Jenny and Jack to their meals outside. In 1920, a good road was pushed up through Last Chance Canyon. This road went past Copper Mountain. The three were now well connected to the Fremont Valley and its associated outside world.

Yet another meeting was held. It was decided to ignore this intrusive development. The tunnel was all that mattered. Burro stayed with the routine. By now, locals had taken to calling him, "Jackass" Schmidt. For his pursuit of perceived nonsense. The impact of this on Burro appears to have been nonexistent. At this point in the story, the tunnel was far into Copper Mountain. The ceiling was high enough for a person to walk through standing up. To keep the tunnel level, Burro used a bowl of water for measuring angles. And for convenience, he installed an ore cart and rails to haul out the rubble. After so many years of hauling it out on his back to the waiting Jenny and Jack.

But the biggest development was Burro started using dynamite. Though his hesitancy to waste funds spilled over into even this. Why waste fuse length? So, Burro cut his fuses short. Very short. Though maybe it wasn't miserliness at all. Maybe Burro just liked the thrill of a run to life.

He wasn't always successful. A number of times he had to dig himself out from rockfalls caused by the explosions. On several occasions, he was seriously injured. After which, he would have to self-mend or drag himself to another mining camp for repair. More years passed. Burro's abdominal muscles became so strong that they curved his spine painfully forward. But the tunnel also moved forward. What else mattered? Past 1,000 feet, then 1,500 feet. Dig and blast, dig and blast. His thoughts, his own. His words drying up.

In 1938, after 36 years of tunneling, Burro Schmidt came to the light. He stepped into it and gazed down upon the Fremont Valley. At last. His thoughts inconceivable to every other person in the world. He was 68 years old. After a good look, Burro turned and walked back through his half-mile of tunnel. Soon thereafter, selling his quest to another miner. Without ever having transported an ounce of ore through his tunnel. For you see, his tunnel exited high on the flanks of Copper Mountain. Much too high above the Fremont Valley floor to be of any use. But use wasn't the point, was it?

Burro moved to a nearby town and lived out his years. When asked why he dug his tunnel, Burro didn't waste conversation. "Shortcut," was about all anyone got out of him. William "Burro" Schmidt died in 1954, at the age of 82. Taking the secrets of the depths of his tunnel motivation with him. And long outliving the fate Rhode Island had in store for him. His funeral was held at the entrance to his, perhaps beloved, shortcut.

Today it is possible to reach, on the edge of Red Rock State Park, Burro Schmidt's life's work. Or art? The first visual is the still-standing cabins of the various miners who once resided here. Nearby is the mine entrance itself, where you can replicate Burro's billions of boot prints through his tunnel. The view out and over Fremont Valley, on the other side, is broad and deeply satisfying. It takes in the Koehn Dry Lake, as well as the ghost towns of Saltdale and Garlock. To the left, the Death Q is imaginable as it makes its way to Johannesburg and Randsburg. But best of all, is the attempt to channel Burro's moment. What did he do as he stepped out of his tunnel that first time? The world will just never know. And that is the best kind of mystery. For it forces us into imagining the unanswerable.

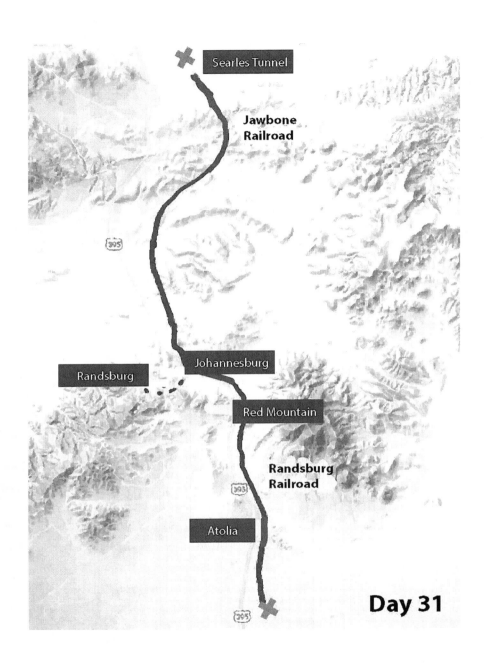

Searles Tunnel

Jawbone
Railroad

Randsburg

Johannesburg

Red Mountain

Randsburg
Railroad

Atolia

Day 31

376

Day 31

Johannesburg-Randsburg-Red Mountain-Atolia

Approach where the rail Y becomes one. Now you are on an active line. There are possibly trains being switched here. Keep your wits about you and look both ways, like your mom told you. The rail line coming from the west is the Trona Railway, which is a privately-owned railroad. Generally, whoever is doing the mining in Trona, also owns the railroad. Most of that mining in Trona is conducted on Searles Dry Lake. And what is produced is shipped on the Trona Railway to the point where you are standing, where it then joins the Jawbone Railroad. The standard gauge Trona Railway is 30.5 miles long. It is exclusively a freight railroad, as passenger service was discontinued in 1937. The Trona Railway connected with the Jawbone in 1913 and remains a profitable venture to this day.

The town of Trona is named for the mineral that is the source for soda ash. The town itself is an interesting place. The interest begins as you drive into town. Suddenly, the smell of rotten eggs is a constant companion. It permeates the town. The smell comes from the chemical plants that operate on the edge of the dry lake. It takes a lot of getting used to. Though residents claim they have. And they recognize the chemical plants keep the town of 1,800 afloat. But there are some side effects. Like the grassless football field, as grass doesn't grow in Trona. Or new residents sobbing for their first few weeks.

These days, Trona seems to be going through a rough stretch. Many homes and buildings are abandoned, And the population is down thousands from the highs of better times. Regardless, Trona soldiers on and always will. As residents like to say, "There is beauty here in the Siberia of the High Desert. You just have to look hard."

Trona has been around a long time by Mojave Desert town standards. Mining on Searles Dry Lake was started by the Searles Brothers in 1874.

But it took an educational encounter with Borax Smith for them to figure out they were sitting on a pile of borax. Smith either regretted or appreciated his tutoring, as he bought Searles Dry Lake from the Searles in 1895. At that time, Smith was trying to corner the world borax market. An attempt that ultimately failed.

Mining plodded along until 1910, when someone figured out that most of the mineral wealth was under the surface of Searles Dry Lake, not on it. Suddenly, prospects became promising. Wyatt Earp even showed up. He arrived with a large group and tried to jump (illegally take over) an extensive mining claim. Mr. Earp truly got around. In the end, Earp's effort failed and he soon moved on. In 1913, a company with deep pockets appeared on the scene. With their support, the railroad got built and the town of Trona prospered.

Eventually, it was discovered that 98 of the 104 known chemical elements are located under the Searles Dry Lake surface. The dry lake's value has been estimated at $150 billion. Another claim is that more value has been removed from the lake, than all the gold mined in California since the 1849 gold rush.

If you ever make it to Trona, be sure to visit the Trona Pinnacles, which are located at the southern end of Searles Dry Lake. The Pinnacles are basically a group of needle-like tufa rock formations that formed at the bottom of an inland sea. There are over 500 pinnacles in total, some reaching 140 feet in height. The forming took place in the range of 10,000 to 100,000 years ago. Now they appear naked and lonely without their protective sea. And are probably most appreciative of company.

From the beginning, Trona was a company town. The workers were originally paid in company script, rather than cash. The script only accepted in company stores. Which created a company-controlled economy, as well as a form of employee bondage. In return for this enforced loyalty, the company provided services, health care, and facilities. To this day, the company plant, though ownership has changed multiple times, remains the main employer in town. And to this same day, Trona struggles on, subject to the whims of the mineral and commodities markets. But still seeing the beauty.

One final bit of trivia. Charlie Manson and some of his "family" were arrested on the Barker Ranch, not far from Trona. Initially, for vandalism of a U.S. Government earthmover in Death Valley. And not for murder. Charlie was actually discovered by a highway patrolman, who was using the toilet during a raid on the ranch. The patrolman happened to look down and see some of Charlie's hair sticking out from the sink cabinet. Where Charlie was hiding out.

The Manson Family was living at the ranch, while searching for the "bottomless pit." An elusive hole on the floor of Death Valley, that Charlie believed would lead to an underground cavern and the waters of the Amargosa River. There, the family could live free of harassment from the authorities. The bottomless pit apparently appeared to Charlie during one of his acid trips. It remains undiscovered and yet another botfly.

The ruins of the Barker ranch are located in Goler Wash, which lies within Death Valley National Park. A visit to the site is possible. For the truly curious, the outlines of the bathroom vanity, where Charlie was captured, are still visible. Though much of the ranch has been torched by vandals. Not long ago, the authorities were back out at the Barker Ranch. Searching for some more of Charlie's victims. Their digging around for bodies turned up nothing.

Cross the Searles Station Cutoff Road and walk toward Searles Tunnel. Check out the switching mechanisms. Searles Station was once here. Prior to that, a stage line ran past. The stage operated from the 1890s, all the way up until 1913. When it was replaced by a Model T auto stage. Searles Station lasted from 1908 until 1953. The agent/telegrapher, at this lonely outpost, made $85 a month in 1913. The station house was removed in 1960.

Approach Searles Tunnel, built in 1908. You can see light at the end of the proverbial tunnel. But, it's a long one at 3,980 feet or over two-thirds of a mile. That's an eternity on an active line. I know what you're thinking, but it isn't worth the risk. "Stay out, stay alive," applies here as well. Back away from the tunnel for the alternate route. And a contemplation of the biggest disaster to befall the Jawbone.

379

The Searles Summit Pass presented a steep challenge for the builders of the Jawbone. So much so, that it was decided a tunnel was needed. Accordingly, work was commenced on the Searles Tunnel. Which was projected to be a long-term construction endeavor. In the meantime, a temporary bypass line was built up and over the hill that was being tunneled. That way, progress was ongoing to the north, as trains could continue bringing construction supplies in that direction. A bypass, such as this, was known as a "shoofly." Which, in railroad vernacular, probably meant having to build around something annoying, like digging a tunnel. Once the tunnel was completed, the shoofly was forgotten. For 72 years, it stayed that way.

Then, on February 22, 1981, the Searles Tunnel caught fire. The fire's origin was suspicious. Unhappy workers in Trona the main suspects. The dry wood beams of the tunnel quickly spread the blaze. Firefighters were unable to put out the fire using water, so both ends of the tunnel were sealed. When the tunnel was reopened, the fresh air reignited the fire. Products that needed to be shipped were building up in Trona and on both sides of the Jawbone. Alternative trucking was expensive. Pressure for a solution built.

Finally, it was decided to rediscover the shoofly. The railbed turned out to be in good shape, and the four miles of track needed were quickly laid. Everyone was back in business. In all, it took a year-and-a-half for the tunnel to regain functionality. Which it did in 1982. By then, though, the owners of the Jawbone decided they were no longer interested in any part of the Jawbone north of here. Fire served up the requisite excuse for abandonment. As well, the shoofly returned to historical slumber. Its rails and ties pulled up once again. The railbed left to await its next call to duty.

Turn away from the tunnel and backtrack toward the paved road. If you're walking north, you will see the shoofly rail to your left. It is marked by a sign with the letter "D," or at least it was when we passed. Turn left and follow the tracks, which still function. The tracks circle around, gaining altitude to climb over the Searles Tunnel hill. Eventually, the track ends and the railbed begins. Follow the shoofly railbed over the hill and then continue along it as it bears away to the right. Say "shoofly" real loud. It's a

pleasurable word. Especially if you drag it out. Apparently, "shoofly" originated in the south, where it was used to address an annoying fly.

From the top of the hill, the views are good. Though the destruction
caused by off-roaders mars the landscape. Continue along an extended
boomerang that brings you back to the original Jawbone. As you rejoin the
tracks, look to your right, out across the valley. There, you will spot a large
hole. The hole was carved out of solid rock by a WWI veteran. His motivation unclear. Perhaps yet another shortcut attempt.

Rejoin the tracks and chug south. A caution: You are on an active
railroad. With trains moving in both directions. Pass a lovely, little mining
camp/getaway topped by an American flag. Pass through the Summit
Range. Keep going until you start spotting RVs baking in the sun. This is
Duisenburg, a.k.a., The Lost Dutchman Mine Association. It is private
property and members only. Many of its members are also part-time prospectors. Just before the camp, beware of the harmless shark. One of the
finer pieces of pop art you're likely to encounter. I dare you to pass up the
photo.

Just as you're leaving Duisenburg, look for a well-defined dirt bike
trail that leads off to your left. The trail beelines straight toward the large
mountain in the distance. The mountain is topped with antennas and
scarred by mining. That is your direction of destination. This route saves
you continuing down the Jawbone to the 395, followed by a four-mile uphill road walk into Johannesburg. So, tap the Jawbone goodbye and hit the
trail.

The dirt bike trails you will be following are numbered. Generally,
you will be moving south. The 395 slowly curves in front of you and proceeds into Johannesburg. As long as you keep going south, you will bump
into the 395, eventually. Which would take you into Johannesburg, by
turning left, should you become confused. Now that you're confident you
can't get lost, continue on the above-mentioned dirt track off the Jawbone.
Signs indicate that this is the RM 7. Turn right when you reach RM 178.
RM 178 will lead you to the RM 19. Turn left on RM 19 and follow it as
it parallels the 395 into Johannesburg. Soon, you will see signs indicating
the direction toward Johannesburg Gas. Follow these signs.

Eventually, the buildings of Johannesburg come into view. A mine presents on your left. Its entrance welded shut, like all the mines in the area. But the relatively recent barriers don't prevent the good memories of the 1970s. When Jim O'Donnell, my friends, and I, spent hours exploring these mines with flashlights. Taking risks that would ensure parental litigation in the present day. The Johannesburg Gas ATV Road takes a hard left. Leave the road and stay straight, moving up the large wash. Stick with the wash, as it brings you into Johannesburg. The wash narrows, then becomes a dirt road. Follow the road into town. When it hits pavement, turn right and walk out to the 395. Turn left and walk two blocks to the Texaco Station and resupply.

Johannesburg and its sister city, Randsburg, have the following:

JOHANNESBURG & RANDSBURG			
1.	Food Supply	Yes	Both
2.	Restaurant	Yes	R'burg
3.	Water	Yes	Both
4.	Hotel	Yes	R'burg
5.	Beer	Yes	Both
6.	Pool Table	Yes	R'burg
7.	ATM	No	
8.	Post Office	Yes	Both
9.	Casino	No	

The Texaco has a fairly-well stocked convenience store. Enough to resupply you onward. It is located at 575 Broadway Avenue (760-374-2120, open 24 hours). The post office is right next door (M-F, 12 p.m. – 4 p.m., 760-374-2216). The next resupply and water is 28.5 miles away in Kramer Junction. For anything else, you need to go over the hill to Randsburg.

Johannesburg, "Joburg," has a population of 172. It began life as a mining center, starting in 1870. Slowly, it developed into an organized, family-oriented, residential town for nearby mines. The streets were laid out on a grid. And a water system was installed. There were banks, churches, saloons and a music hall. For both recreation and prestige, a sandy nine-hole golf course was installed. Joburg, as well as Randsburg, were named by miners who had once worked in South Africa. Joburg became a transport center with the arrival of the Randsburg Railway in 1898. Its pleasure to be the northern hub of that railroad.

Randsburg, over the ridge, went for the wilder reputation. If Joburg was for families, Randsburg was for the miners. Gold was discovered in 1894, and it set off a rush to the town that was yet to be built. Construction started immediately. At its height, there were 3,500 residents with various appetites. To service these appetites were the usual accompanying saloons, chow houses, brothels and dance halls.

Fire was a constant threat. Water was scarce and the buildings mostly made of wood. Making the spread of fire rapidly contagious. So, the fire department developed a sensible approach. When a building was on fire and spread imminent, they would detonate that building with dynamite. Which quickly extinguished the fuel source. When the fire department blew up the hardware store, during one such fire, the falling tools, pots and pans were said to be a sight for a lifetime.

Randsburg was not a short-lived boom, but stretched out over the years. In the first half of the 20th Century, the area around Randsburg produced more gold than anywhere else in California. The main gold mine in town was known as the Yellow Aster. It started up in 1894 and operated for many years. Though constant litigation hampered its productivity. In 1919, silver was discovered in the area. The Rand Silver Mine went on to produce more silver than any other mine in California. All told, it is estimated that over $25 million was taken out of area mines. These days, both towns are much quieter. Reliant mainly on tourists and passing traffic. Local mines do start up now and again, depending on demand from mineral markets. But their existence tends to be short-lived.

Present day Randsburg, population 69, is a mandatory side trip. You won't regret the walk or hitch. If for no other reason than the root beer floats, chocolate malts, and regionally-famous burgers at the soda fountain. Complete with marble countertops and spinning bar stools for your nostalgic pleasure. To get to Randsburg, simply backtrack the way you came in on the 395, for two blocks. Until a paved street called The Rand. Turn left and hike uphill.

Note the red caboose as you walk up The Rand. Originally, the house next to the red caboose and the one directly across the street, were the first and second stories of the Joburg Rail Depot. Where you are standing, was the northern terminus for the Randsburg Railway. In the 1930s, after the demise of the railroad, it was decided to turn one depot into two houses. So, the second story was removed and placed on the other side of the street. Viola!

At the top of the hill, turn left on Rand Loop/Sunset Road. Follow Rand Loop. Roller coaster over the hill, until you reach Butte Street. Turn right and walk into Randsburg, where Butte Street is the main drag. Welcome.

Be sure to have a good tour around, as there is much for the eyes to take in. It becomes quickly obvious why a number of films have been made here. Photogenic is a proper description. Major sights include an opera house, jail and various churches. Those malts are located in the Randsburg General Store, as are some groceries (35 Butte Ave., 760-374-2143, M, Th, F 11 a.m. - 4 p.m., Sa, Su, 10 a.m. - 5 p.m., Tu, W closed). It has been the general store since the 1930s. The soda fountain itself is over 100 years old and traveled here all the way from Boston. There is a breakfast and lunch menu.

The Rand Desert Museum is open Saturday and Sunday, 10 a.m. - 4 p.m. (161 Butte Ave., 760-371-0965). Even if it is closed, you can have a look at all the outside mining equipment on display. The Randsburg Inn has rooms (166 Butte Ave., 760-374-2143). The Inn is built on the site of a former brothel called "My Place Dance Hall." There is even an attached horse hotel. Also with rooms is The Cottage Hotel (130 Butte Ave., 760-374-2285). The Cottage Hotel has pizza available on the weekends (Sa-Su, 11 a.m. - 6 p.m.). The Opera House Café also serves up food.

There's a perfect bar in town called, "The Joint" (165 Butte Ave., M-W closed, except holidays, Th-Su 11 to roughly 11, depending on if it's a ghost town out there, 760-608-9421). Two pool tables are in residence. On one of my last visits, the bartender was 96 years old. She plied her craft expertly. On that visit, I played pool with a drone pilot from a nearby base.

"Yep, I sit in a seat and play a video game all day. I fly around over there and target what they tell me to target. If they say blow it up, I blow it up. Then I come here for a beer. Your shot." The post office is at 26741 Butte Avenue (760-374-2337, M-F 8:30 a.m. - 11:30 a.m.). It has been in continuous operation since the 1870s.

When you're gorged and ready to move on, retrace your steps back to the Texaco Station in Joburg. Then cross the street to the advertised knife shop. Walk to the edge of the parking lot, while paralleling the 395 south toward Red Mountain. Follow the dirt road that leaves the parking lot and tracks the 395. Quickly, you will bump into the Randsburg Railway railbed. Introduce yourself. Then step onto a new railbed and walk about a mile.

Just when the railbed is becoming quite distinct, you enter the small village of Red Mountain. A fence blocks the railbed. Simply turn right and walk out to the 395. Turn left. Follow the 395 for a few blocks, past the shuttered saloon. Look around and realize that anything business related is shuttered. Red Mountain was formerly known as Osdick. Now it is known for the large red mountain behind it, appropriately christened Red Mountain (5,261 feet). There are about 125 people in town.

With all the shutters, the town feels sleepy but it wasn't always so. Back in 1919, the town came into being, thanks to the Rand Silver mine opening on Red Mountain. The Rand Silver was an absurdly wealthy mine from which $12,000,000 of silver was extracted. The town of Red Mountain catered to the Rand's miners and their newfound wealth. The town's nickname, easily beating Vegas to it, was "Sin City." During Prohibition (a nationwide ban on the sale of alcohol, that was in effect from 1920 to 1933), there wasn't an establishment in Red Mountain that didn't serve liquor.

To go along with the liquor, there were at least 10 brothels. Gambling filled out the triumvirate. Even the KKK was offended by the moral climate of Red Mountain. The town's slogan captured it all, "Where every night is Saturday night and Saturday night is the Fourth of July." Today, the Rand Silver mine lies quiet. And in Red Mountain proper, the past seems very, very buried.

Your tolerance for a recollection of a miner I knew as a kid. The kind that are no longer around. Ted Bruener called my father his friend. And sometimes business partner. Though as a kid, I could never quite put my finger on what business they were exactly up to. I just knew it was something to do with mining. For Ted was a hard-rock miner of the old school. Who lived alone, high on the slopes of the Fremont Valley, without vehicles, electricity or running water. Not too far from Randsburg and quite close to Burro Schmidt's tunneling. The nearest neighbor, not for many walkable miles. His simple hand-built home pristine in its severe orderliness. Perhaps attributable to his Swiss birth.

It was a magical place for a child. For Ted's home was constantly enveloped in a swarm of bees. Attracted to the only bowl of water available to every horizon. A bowl Ted refilled every day. The bees all the more magical because they never stung. The image forever with me. Us kids piling out of Dad's van, battling to be the first to greet tiny Ted, with his years-long gray beard and halo of bees.

My father had a mining claim near Ted's homestead. Really, a picnic ground. But once a year, the federal inspectors would come snooping for evidence of mandated mining operations. Their visits pre-announced by letter. A week before the inspection, Ted would meet us at Dad's claim. The anticipation under our skin, bouncing us around. For my sisters and I knew what was to come.

Ted inching us downhill, as we inched back up. Distracting him from placing the dynamite. Then Ted unspooling the blasting wire with little caution. We kids, mad with an excitement that is still palpable, even after the passage of decades. "Now kids!" shouted in that distant Germanic accent. "Fire in the hole!!!" we would scream back. The words smashing into the explosion's chest thump rolling downhill. Then the race to our new mine. The inspectors none the wiser to our lack of mining effort. My father and Ted's partnership solid for another year.

Ted's own gold mine was a mile up into the mountains behind his home. Having made my first track team, I was very much impressed with my physical capabilities. Occasionally, Ted could be lured into a race to its entrance. Though in his 70s, it seemed up to him the extent of my humiliation and defeat. About his gold mine, Ted was secretive. But he did freely tell three stories with regularity.

One involved his time as a pilot with the Flying Tigers in World War II. His narrative of dog fights with Japanese Zero fighter planes mesmerizing to my wide eyes. (The Flying Tigers were a volunteer U.S. air squadron that flew for the Chinese Air Force during the early years of WWII. The distinctive nose art of their fighter planes was a shark with its mouth open. The Flying Tigers shot down 296 Japanese aircraft, while losing only 14 of its pilots in combat.)

Another Ted tale was of the Federal government arriving at his homestead in helicopters. Obviously searching for aliens, his belief. The bees quite bitter, for days afterwards, at the disturbance caused by the flying machines.

And the third, was a recounting of the discovery of a lost vertical mineshaft on Red Mountain during the Depression. Ted's slow explanation of the descent into the moonlit shaft on an old braided rope, harrowing to us youngsters. His landing uncertain. But at the bottom of the shaft, finding enough gemstones lying about to fill every one of his pockets. Then the 30-minute hand-over-hand climb upward, racing against the rope snapping, due to the 100 pounds added. Followed with lying exhausted at the lip, bathed by the moon and loud laughter. Then his face falling, as he told of hiding the entrance so well that he never found it again. The light right back to his face as he recounted paying for his kid's college with all that found wealth.

All the stories wonderful, but perceptively and patently untrue, to kids and adults alike. A lonely life in the sun will play with the imagination. Or so it was suggested. And so, the years went by. Audiences continued to wink. While Ted steadfastly retold his tales.

Then one day, a last visit. It had been decided that my family was to live in another state. I was trying out the early high school cynicism that I had recently become acquainted with. Convinced that it suited me, I dished it up to Ted and his Federal helicopter invasion. Calling him out with early youthful wisdom. Wisdom that I suspected Ted was already too old to keep up with. I interrogated, "Why would Federal helicopters come here, of all places? Tell me that, will you?"

It took him a while to make up his mind. But when he did, he did. Grabbing me swiftly by the shirt, he silently marched me uphill about 50 yards. There, embedded in cement behind some rocks, was a plaque. It read "United States Air Force: Station Bruener." "There you are boy," he said without smiling. It was our farewell.

A few years later, I returned to California. Some of the first news I learned, from my teacher and friend Jim O'Donnell, was that Ted had died. His body waiting a number of days to be discovered. Mr. O'D had gone up, after the funeral, to pay his respects at the homestead itself. The bees were already departed. As Mr. O'D wandered the dirt floors of the home, he tried to take in the years of Ted's life. Then he opened a closet door. And beheld a neatly pressed Flying Tigers pilot's uniform.

Back in downtown Red Mountain, I stopped for a while. Hanging back and staring up the slopes of the namesake Red Mountain. Orbit on ahead, tracking the railbed. Alone to myself. Awash in the sentimentality that is one of the few pleasures of aging. Hello, Red Mountain and hello, Ted. I know your mineshaft is up there. Somewhere. I damn well know it. Let it never be found.

Walking out of Red Mountain on the 395, you will come to an old Atlantic Richfield garage. The sign is probably from the 1960s, before Atlantic Richfield became ARCO. Just past the garage, rejoin the dirt trail on your left, signposted toward Cuddleback. Cuddleback Dry Lake is far to your left. The dirt road stays just to the left of the 395, then climbs to a railroad cut right next to the 395. You're back on the Randsburg Railway. The railbed stays near the 395 until you reach the ruins of Atolia.

Atolia is a lesson in the need for the occasional second look. For years, gold miners in the area had cursed a creamy, white substance in their gold pans. The substance, nicknamed "Heavy spar," made it difficult to remove the real gold. It was a classic shoofly situation. Then somebody figured out, around 1905, that the white stuff was scheelite. Which is critical to making tungsten. Tungsten is used to harden steel. Heavy spar was suddenly a valuable commodity. An example of the local lack of knowledge concerning scheelite. Workers building the Randsburg Railway cut through a shelf of high-grade scheelite in 1897 and ignored it. To their future financial peril.

Once the value of scheelite was established, a very quiet boom started. Far sexier gold and silver strikes were going on in Tonopah, Goldfield and Rhyolite. And that is where the focus traveled. But Atolia was on a below-the-radar roll. By 1908, it was the largest producer of scheelite in the world. Some of Atolia's scheelite even made it to Germany, which was gearing up for WWI. Still, the boom remained quiet. Then WWI broke out. Demand for tungsten, which is used to manufacture weapons, sky-rocketed. Suddenly, Atolia was on everyone's map.

By 1916, two thousand people were living there. The Randsburg Railway was kept busy hauling away all the scheelite. And returning with water from not-so-distant Hinkley. A movie theater opened up. The Bucket of Blood Saloon was thick with customers. Four restaurants were doing business. There was even an ice-cream parlor. Children rooted around in tailings for pieces of scheelite to sell. High-grading was a big problem. Over 100 miners were caught smuggling and arrested or fired. The future beckoned. And then it didn't. The war ended. Cheap scheelite was found in China. Demand and prices, jumped hand in hand, off a cliff.

By 1919, most had moved out and on. Many to up-and-coming Trona. The railroad also began bypassing Atolia in 1919. By 1922, there were only 79 souls left in town. Imagine living in a town where 96% of the residents decided to move out in a short period of time. Your morning stroll might turn eerie. Since 1922, mining has started up sporadically, with the last effort ending in 2007.

Continue south past various ruins. The sun, on most days, holds the possibility of warmth, even in deep winter. Note the mines that look like wells on both sides of the road. Looking down their throats reveals the perilous nature of scheelite mining. Arrive at two derelict white water towers. Skirt out to the road for 100 feet, then rejoin the dirt trail. Note the arrival of the raised railbed on your left. The dirt trail you are on leaps on top. Now you are officially on 5155. A designated desert trail, as well as the Randsburg railbed. Immediately, the railbed begins a turn east away from the 395.

Pass what little remains of St. Elmo. A stop on the Randsburg Railway. A grid was laid out for a town, and scheelite was discovered here. But a lack of water haunted plans, and the town never really took off. The railbed is in very good condition in this stretch. Nine miles out of Joburg, come to a dirt road cutting across the railbed and heading east across the valley. This is the old 20 Mule Team borax road from Mojave to Death Valley. Invite the mules into your visual.

Continue on, as the railbed pulls toward the 395 and then changes its mind. To the left, is Fremont Peak at 4,584 feet. Once home to the wealthy Monarch Mine. Time to claim a patch of sand.

The following is a bedtime story for you, loosely based on an actual event that took place along this stretch of Randsburg Railway.

The Ballad of Walt and Webster

In the beginning, it was a whispered conversation that pushed them toward Atolia. The words soaked in truth and much saloon whiskey. To 19-year-old Walt's worldview, the latter begot the former. The conversation one-sided, which Webster had taught Walt was the easiest way to learn. The drunk found his conversation again. And continued. Walt all ears.

"To hell with gold, Son, scheelite is where it's at."

"And where is scheelite?" Walt's words rushed as the drunk was sliding toward head to bar.

"You won't tell any soul?"

Walt considered rightness. "I'll tell Webster. He's my partner. But it will stop there."

The drunk squeezed his eyes hard, causing lines to reach out across the temple Walt could see. The drunk's right hand left its glass and slid off the bar. Walt recognized the gesture and shook the hand on an upswing. "Atolia youngin', get your ass there and get rich."

The conversation was over for Walt's purposes. He lifted the bar's tent flap and walked out into the street. The drunk already part of the past. A bright sun triggered a sneeze. And a word from a classroom long ago. "Destiny." Finally have it, Walt thought, as he hurried back to camp.

Webster more than doubled Walt's age. The math itself, had never been discussed. Webster surveyed the exploratory diggings around camp and considered the wasted weeks. Looking where others had already looked, found and took. The only good thing was this sitting rock. Webster would miss it. But the future wasn't here. From his sit he could see Walt coming hard up the hill. The boy was bringing obvious excitement. Webster leaned back and let anticipation occupy the moment.

Walt arrived lathered. Webster gifted time with his silence. A minute at most, "We got to go if we want to be rich. Gotta go now. It's our destiny."

Webster did enjoy the boy. "Where and how?"

"Atolia. Something called shitlite."

"Never heard of neither. Though the second doesn't sound promising. Who told you?"

"Some guy the whiskey had a hold of. But we can't tell anyone. I shook on it."

Webster allowed himself a smile. "Did the guy have any money?"

"Yeah, he bought at least three rounds that I saw." Impatience chased the end of the sentence.

"Did he work the rock?"

"How do I know?"

"His hands, Walt."

"I didn't look at his hands."

"But you felt them."

Walt went back to the shake. "Yeah, he's a digger."

"What are we waiting for?"

For days, Walt savored the ease of his victory and the warmth of fate.

A day out from Atolia, Walt explained to Webster that although he had responsibility for their newfound wealth, the partnership would stay at 50-50. Webster grinned and accepted the kindness.

But the next day and Atolia, brought reality. Conversations had been taking place elsewhere, as well. The boom was long in full swing. Organized even, as the mine bosses had moved in. The diggers, employees. Walt put his head in the dirt and wept words not heard. Webster just kept looking. Unmoved anymore by Walt's big reactions. When Walt could get up, they made their way past the town and set up camp. There, Webster left Walt to the darkness of his day and returned to town. Where he listened. And looked a bit more. Learning what he could.

The sun was gone when Webster got back. He decided to speak to the dark. "The earth looks different where they're digging this rock up. It's pale on top, like an ass that ain't seen sun. I say we ride downwash and look for a patch of ass."

Nothing. "They call the rock scheelite, not shitlight."

The same nothing.

Webster was rolling out his bedroll when the night finally responded, "I'm done looking."

"Then how you going to find anything?"

392

More nothing.

"Sleep on your options."

After that, the conversation, such that it was, gave up.

When Webster caught the day, Walt was already up and about. Webster busied himself with moving out. Walt was looking away when he spoke. "I'm coming, but I don't want to talk much." Which turned out to be the last words of the day.

The men moved south. Then zigzagged east and west. Webster pushing his ass image at the ground. Waiting for a match. Walt simply followed. This kind of company, Webster wasn't entirely against. He kept up the east/west swings throughout the day. Knowing his chances were best near the Atolia diggings. The reasons he was moving downwash were nothing he had an explanation for.

At four miles out, they camped. The night themed with silence. Webster's "Morning" unanswered.

The day repeated, until it didn't.

Webster's hat was pulled down low for the sun, on a westward swing, when he saw it. It was a small ass and Webster would have preferred a bigger one. But it was what Webster was looking for. He allowed a grin for the ass joke. But decided not to pass it on. Webster guessed they were about seven miles out of town. "Here, son."

"Here, what?"

"That's what I've been looking for."

Walt looked at the pale patch of earth in the same way he felt about Atolia. "Are you sure?"

"You want sure when it comes to rock?" Walt's answer was to sit down.

"Fifty-fifty, like you said Walt. You know the hour when the digging starts. We'll go straight down."

The next morning the men skipped breakfast and joined the predawn. Webster placed his shovel blade into the softness. Walt kept his in hand. Webster winked, and Walt allowed his first Atolia smile. It was ceremony enough. Webster leaned on learned digging rhythm. Walt attacked the soil with his excess of youth. The end of the day saw both men done. Their shallow progress shaming.

On the third day, Webster knew a decision could not be put off. "Walt, we need supplies, wood for a ladder and a pulley. What we have left in pocket is enough for the mining stuff but not much else. You want to throw it all at this? No proof of rock yet."

"Yes, Sir." The answer too quick but right. Where else and what else looked near as promising?

"I'll head into town then. While I'm there, I'll start the paperwork for our claim. What should we name it?"

"Destiny."

"But of course. Keep at it."

"Yes, Sir, again." The boy was coming around. Webster thought Walt enthused might be better for company after all. The straight shot back to town, boots to ground, took 2½ hours.

The rented wagon, loaded with supplies, took a slightly longer route back. The teamster on in years. "Just a matter of a month or two I've heard."

"What?"

"The railroad."

"What railroad?"

"How's the sand feel in your head?"

From Webster's experience, silence will often drag out an answer. After time, the horse letting loose stirred the teamster.

"The Randsburg Railway. It'll put Atolia on the map. The markers we passed are the route. They're coming from Kramer. And they're coming hard. Them graders should be to Atolia in a week or so."

Webster cut out the rest of the driver's words for his own thoughts. Damn, if the train will stop, we can load the rock straight on. Cut out the middleman and pockets get heavy with coin. Webster let the excitement get into him. And arrived that way. He didn't see the shininess in Walt's eyes. Both men held words until the back of the teamster's head.

Unusually, Webster ended the silence. "The railroad's coming, Walter."

"Not anymore."

Webster didn't want these words. "I chased them off."

Webster looked to the sand. He didn't have to ask for the story.

394

"A fellow showed up with two workers. They were putting up little red sticks about seven feet across. When they saw me, the fella rode over and said, 'There can't be a mine here'."

"I picked up the pistol and explained. This says it can."

That flustered him. He said, "Everyone knows the railroad is coming through here. The markers have been out for months. The rails go right over your diggings. Rails cannot be undermined."

I shut him down right there. "My partner and me aren't everyone. We were here first."

"And hell, Webster, he just turned around and rode away. I beat me a railroad."

Webster longed for a good sitting rock. "I need to see some things over there. Cook us up a big dinner."

"What's wrong, Webster?"

"I'll be back." He walked the markers for a long while. The food was chilled when Webster got back.

"Are you going to tell me what's going on, old man?"

Webster let that go. "We need to start digging hard and get the ladder in. Make it look like we've been at this a long time. If they see it, maybe they'll be straight with us and offer to buy us out. It's our best shot." Then quiet. "It's the only one, too."

"They ain't coming back Web, I'm telling you."

"Sure son. Let's call it early."

Three days on, the rail graders at work were visible. The pair pushed on, as even Walt knew they were all in. The ladder lengthened. They took turns digging and pullying. The mine became real and sometimes took them away from the future. Though still no sign of scheelite.

On the fourth day, during lunch, the horizon dust meant the future had lost its patience. Walt took the pistol to the hole, while Webster stood with the rifle. He stopped counting at ten riders, though he didn't have far to go. To pass the time, he tried to still the pump of blood in his chest by counting backwards. His practiced speech he left alone.

Webster grabbed the reins of the conversation. "Afternoon, Sir."

"Afternoon. I'm going to ask you two to clear off. You're in the path of the Randsburg Railway."

The speaker had authority. Webster gave him that before he started. "There are two options. You can move your railroad one way or the other just a bit, or you can be straight and buy us out."

"The railroad is fated to its course. You stand in the way. Trespassing against fate is not wise."

"Fate is a prison I don't like." Where had Webster heard that?

The speaker looked at Webster, for a time, in a different way. The interest took a while to pass. "That may be so, but you have twenty-four hours to clear off. If not, these men will do it another way. Words are over."

"Another option is, you can go to hell." The hole had its say.

"Twenty-four hours." And they turned and rode.

Walt came out of the hole. Looking wrong. His face slack. Webster watched him raise the pistol and take aim. Waiting was all there was. "Goddamn it all." Walt's voice was dull. His hand dropping, as the shot went off into the sand, three feet to his right. The riders wheeled at the sound, then wheeled away again.

It was not a time for words, the railroad man was right, but what else was there? "Easy, Walt." Webster knew not to move. He thought hard for some kind of magic.

"It's so goddamn unfair, every last bit." Walt's words seemed from somewhere far off.

"It always will be, Son. Life is about the most unfair thing I've come across. Especially the best parts. Whiskey, women, the rock, all of them damned unfair. And fair they never will be. Get a hold of that. And while you're at it, give that pistol to the ground."

Walt's eyes weren't following the words. Webster watched for a while. Watched the boy's thoughts drop away. All except for escape. Walt's pistol arm was already curving inward, when Webster turned his eyes. The boy standing dead. His second shot no surprise.

Webster leaned the rifle against a creosote. Then sat down on the bright sand and finished his lunch. After, he ate what was left of the boy's.

By the end, he could see his way. He went over to Walt and gave him a long look. Then he pulled the boy's boots off and dragged him to the hole's edge. Along the way, a bush tugged the pistol out of the boy's hand.

By way of prayer Webster murmured, "The railroad owes you a burial, Son." With that he gently slid him in. The thud took a lot out of Webster, and he sat down on the lip.

Some time passed but not too much. "God damn it all, indeed," whispered Webster. "And while I'm at it, to hell with you, Destiny."

Then he stood and looked toward Atolia and his own. A short walk away, to finish the longer one, toward becoming an employee.

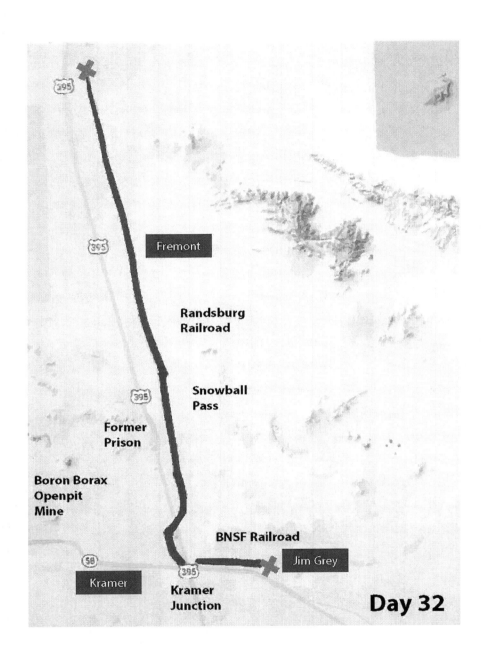

Fremont

Randsburg
Railroad

Snowball
Pass

Former
Prison

Boron Borax
Openpit
Mine

BNSF Railroad

Jim Grey

Kramer

Kramer
Junction

Day 32

398

Day 32

Fremont-Kramer Junction

Wake up and find yourself with a railway. The Randsburg Railway, to be exact. The Randsburg Railway, ironically, never reached Randsburg. As with many railroads in the area, the naming seems to have been goal focused, rather than reality based. Instead, the Randsburg Railway connected Johannesburg with Kramer, a distance of 28.5 miles. How did the railway come to be? Well, the answer to this morning's breakfast question goes something like this.

The rich mining strikes around Randsburg convinced a group of businessmen that there was profit in connecting the area with Kramer to the south. Kramer was on the Santa Fe Railroad, which connected Los Angeles to points east. From Kramer, the Randsburg ore could be transported east or west, depending on market dictates. Also, Kramer was 1,150 feet below Randsburg in terms of altitude. Gravity would assist the transport of heavy ore from the mines. The businessmen decided to roll the dice.

And so, the building of a railroad began in 1897 and finished in 1898. Passing over a mineshaft dug by a couple of miners along the way. The armed standoff, that took place during that passing, inspiration for last night's bedtime story. As in the story, the railway came out on top. Randsburg Railway provided both freight and passenger service. A 50 stamp mill was up and running in Barstow by 1898. The transport of ore, from Randsburg to Barstow, brought that desired profit. But in 1901, the construction of a 100 stamp mill at the Yellow Astor mine in Randsburg meant ore no longer needed to be shipped to Barstow. Those same profits took a dive.

In that same year, a smallpox epidemic broke out in Randsburg. Five hundred people were struck down with the disease. Attempts were made to stop the spread. Before trains could leave, a doctor walked the aisles, checking all departing passengers for signs of smallpox. If symptoms were detected, the passenger was removed and placed in quarantine.

By 1903, the Randsburg Railway was struggling. Fearing closure, the Santa Fe Railroad stepped in, and bought the Randsburg Railway for $300,000. Immediately, freight charges went up, eliciting much local complaint. The complaints were ignored, and the Randsburg Railway kept chugging along. Until the inevitable decline in mining. Which meant people left the area. The dominos leading to a corresponding decline in passenger traffic.

By the late 1920s, the Santa Fe could easily read the writing on the wall. Then came the stock market collapse and the follow-up Depression. On December 30, 1933, the Randsburg Railway surrendered to the dire economic times. In 1934, it was unceremoniously stripped of rails and ties. Leaving only its railbed to direct your way.

Continue south on the railbed to the remains of Fremont. Whistle as you come into town, as there were once whistle boards on both sides of Fremont. I had the same question. A whistle board is basically a sign with a "W" on it. Train engineers are required to blow their whistle whenever they see a whistle board.

Fremont is a few woeful foundations now, nothing more. Sufficient for a bench. You are approximately halfway between Joburg and Kramer Junction.

It was March 19 on our hike, and spring had declared early. That day, we saw desert iguanas, zebra tails, utas, horned toads and a desert tortoise. I even danced with a reptile. An early Mojave green rattlesnake was waiting right on the railbed. As discussed earlier, I heard him before I saw him. And naturally, went straight to air. On the descent, my adrenaline-soaked brain informed me the snake was to the left. So, when I landed, I performed the Texas two-step to the right. The king of the trail was content to remain coiled, bobbing and loaded. His rattles sizzled. For a long while after, I was minutely fascinated with shadows on the railbed.

Hike through a 600-foot hill cut, followed by a 400-foot infill. Pass Snowball Pass. (You'll get it.) To the right is the former Boron Air Force Station, which morphed into a Federal prison. The prison had no walls and was minimum security. Very minimum security. In 1992, Rueben Sturman, a well-known pornographer and free-speech advocate, walked away from a 10-year sentence by simply walking away. In all, a half-mile over to the 395. Where he grabbed a ride to freedom.

It didn't take too long to recapture him. But he did make it as far as Anaheim, California, where, presumably, he had some wide-ranging fun. Mr. Sturman died in a Federal prison in 1997. His life makes interesting reading. The prison closed in 2000. Though, the FAA radar site there is still active. The entire complex of modern ruins is, quite technically, off limits to explorers.

Next up is Pitchfork Corner. (Once again, you'll get it.) Then pass an array of bizarre signs, including one ordering you to, "Empty your ashtray before proceeding." The desert often leans toward the unexplained. To your southwest is Edwards Air Force Base. Home to a variety of flight speed and height records set since World War II. This base was the origin of my youth's supposed window breakers. As I lived in nearby California City. Their sonic booms our great joy. Especially when first-time visitors hit the deck, after a sky explosion went off.

Also at Edwards, the Space Shuttle flew freely for the first time. After it left its piggyback position on the back of a 747. That first space shuttle was the Enterprise, named so after a write-in campaign by fans of Star Trek. The date was August 12, 1977. It was an event us locals were allowed on base to see. And which I did see, because the action was straight up. Then the shuttle came back down to earth and landed on the base's dry lake. An event I did not see, because multiple adult heads were now in the way.

On April 14, 1981, Columbia, the first space shuttle to actually go into space, landed on that same dry lake. That landing took place after Columbia had orbited the Earth an astounding 36 times. The Columbia went on to successfully complete 27 missions, before disintegrating during re-entry to Earth's atmosphere on February 1, 2003. All seven crew members aboard were killed.

The ridge you can see to your right, covered in antennas and buildings, has been an Air Force missile launch site since 1947. Over the years, many test missiles have been launched into the night sky. Rarely with warning. Always a rush-out-of-the-house moment for locals. To see the night tricked into day.

Eventually, the railbed returns to the 395. Cross it and continue toward the solar plant in front of you. Along this stretch of railbed, on February 17, 1898, at 11:30 p.m., two trains collided. The engineer and fireman in both trains were killed. No passengers were seriously injured. Apparently, the train coming from Kramer was backing up without its locomotive headlights on. Possibly, it had left early and was trying to get back to Kramer. But truth be told, the exact cause remains a cold-case mystery. Regardless of explanations, the southbound train plowed into a surprise. The last of a lifetime for both crews. Stamp the railbed hard to see if the sands can summon up the pain of that long-ago night.

The Randsburg Railway originally continued another three miles to the settlement of Kramer. But Kramer pulled up stakes a long time ago. Kramer Junction, however, two miles south of you, does exist. And has facilities that serve giant lemonades.

The other landmark that turns you south toward Kramer Junction, is the large solar plant plopped rudely on top of the Randsburg Railway's remains. The plop blocks your trail. It's an unfortunate place to steal the sun. In its defense, the plant does generate enough electricity to power 30-40 thousand homes. Whatever your feelings, the plant forces a separation.

Say goodbye to the Randsburg Railway by turning left at the telephone pole road, just before the plant fence. Hike through the reflected glare and follow the dirt road south. Walk past the amazing antique store and cross the active railroad tracks. Note the location, as you will be following this line east. Continue into Kramer Junction, a.k.a., Four Corners.

Kramer Junction is basically a small cluster of businesses for travelers. The Junction referred to is where the 395 and the 58 cross each other. Just seven miles to the west is Boron, home of the largest borax mine in the world. Almost half of the world's borax originates from the enormous open-pit mine there. Which, at 500 feet deep, is the largest open-pit mine in California.

The Boron mine appears to be the rare mine that ignores historical precedent and goes on forever. Its borax supply apparently inexhaustible. The accidental discovery of borax here, in 1925, spelled doom for Borax Smith's borax operations in far flung Death Valley. Which, in turn, contributed to the death of the Tonopah and Tidewater Railroad.

A 20 Mule Team museum is also in Boron.

Kramer Junction has most of the facilities you will need located on one of four corners.

KRAMER JUNCTION		
1.	Food Supply	Yes
2.	Restaurant	Yes
3.	Water	Yes
4.	Hotel	Yes
5.	Beer	Yes
6.	Pool Table	No
7.	ATM	Yes
8.	Post Office	No
9.	Casino	No

The Pilot Travel Center and Gas Station provides the best option for food resupply. Showers there are $12. Your smell awaits you a few miles down the tracks, should you decide to splurge. The Pilot is 24/7 (760-762-0041). The next resupply is at a Vons supermarket in Barstow, 30 miles down the tracks. The next drinkable water is also in Barstow. Across the street from the Pilot is the Roadhouse Restaurant. A popular place open every day 8 a.m. - 9 p.m. Back by the tracks is the Astro Burger, with those giant lemonades (M-F 8 a.m. - 8 p.m., Sa 8 a.m. - 4 p.m., Su Closed, 760-762-5720). For sleeping, the Relax Inn is available (760-762-6379).

While in Kramer Junction, we met a couple and their dog, who were making their way across the country by hopping trains. The trains I watched go by Kramer Junction were flying, and I admired their convictions. They, on the other hand, thought we were nuts for having walked 725 miles to arrive at Kramer Junction. A place everyone was fine about leaving. Good laughs were had by all. And allow me to congratulate you on your 725 miles, if you're both walking and reading. There are only 86 miles left of the Q. The descender within grasp.

To leave Kramer Junction, return to the tracks. Go to the far (northern) side of the tracks and turn right. Follow the dirt road that parallels the tracks toward Barstow. The berm shields you from the acoustics and aesthetics of the 58. Both of which are unpleasant. Do not walk on the tracks, as the trains sneak up fast. The dirt road also accompanies an old telegraph line. Follow the tracks, as they mercifully start to pull away from the 58. Take a break inside a culvert and have a read about your new railroad.

Perhaps you noticed the trains that occasionally pass you? ("Bearing down like a freight train" now makes sense.) The railcars are from one of two major railroads that currently dominate transcontinental freight in the United States. The two being the Union Pacific (UP) and the Burlington Northern Santa Fe (BNSF). They represent the culminations of the incredible array of mergers and acquisitions that have marked modern railroad history. It is beyond this book and myself, to chart all the detail.

For a limited understanding, suffice it to say, the BNSF owns this line into Barstow. They continue to own this line as it leaves Barstow, passes Ludlow, and continues onto Needles, CA. As well, they own and operate the massive freight yard in Barstow. The BNSF has 40,000 employees, 1,000 in Barstow alone. One of the railroads they swallowed was the Santa Fe, which owned the Randsburg Railway back in the day.

The UP, with 50,000 employees, owns the tracks between Las Vegas and just outside Barstow. There, the UP line joins the BNSF line and together they continue on into Los Angeles. An agreement, negotiated more than 100 years ago between the two, allows this sharing. The meeting point between the two railroads is at Daggett, just outside Barstow. It resembles a large "Y."

You'll hike right by it. The UP absorbed the Southern Pacific in 1996. The same SP that owned the Carson and Colorado Railroad as well as the Jawbone Railroad. Railroads that you, by now, have hopefully developed a fondness for.

Return to hiking for a while. A short while. After that while, the sun is probably losing interest. Accept dinner and sleep for the gifts they are. Your dreams disturbed by night trains. Tossing and turning, as hobos have, down through the age of railroads.

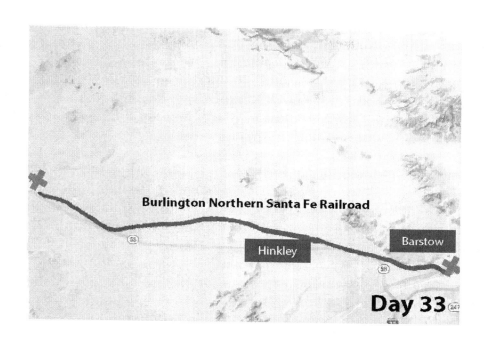

Day 33

Hinkley-Barstow

Continue the long pull away from the 58. The modern state of affairs and its accompanying noise, recede. Though this takes a while in the sound-amplifying desert. Slowly, tranquility re-embraces. Curve around the hills ahead. Which provide a great opportunity to find out what's around the corner. Try to figure out the mystery of the clear marbles you occasionally pass. Give up? (I later learned, in the Barstow Railroad Museum, that marbles are how bulk glass is transported to its destination. There to be transformed into what is needed.)

The dirt road, on the left side of the tracks, continues to tag along amicably with its big brother. You pass the old stops of Jim Grey, Hawes and Eads. (Please pronounce the latter out loud.) All former stops lost to history's strategic use of sand. Feel the power of the trains as they pass. Understand a hobo's desire to ride, rather than walk. At some point, you cross over the 1870s Panamint (Death Valley)-San Bernardino stage route.

The tracks begin a turn back towards the 58. Then you arrive in West Hinkley. Just off the tracks, on your right, is the Hinkley Market and Gas. It is across from the now-closed school. You can't miss it. And we didn't want to miss it, as by late March it was already getting hot in the day. A drink sounded good. And it was good. An entire six-pack of root beer never had a chance.

Unfortunately, the market, as well as the post office next door, closed in 2015. Not very long after our visit. The root beer almost an epilogue. All victims of an exodus from a town trending toward a ghost town. Reminiscent of the mining boom and bust towns of a hundred years ago. Only this time, the problem is water and its corruption. And that root beer? It now has to wait until Barstow. As there are no other stores in Hinkley.

Hinkley might ring a bell. It was made famous by the 2000 movie, "Erin Brockovich," which starred Julia Roberts. But Hinkley was around long before the film and, thus, is not defined by it. Beginning in the late 1800s, it was a rail stop. Ironically known for exporting water. Atolia and Ludlow both relied on water brought from Hinkley by rail. The first half of the 20th Century saw much agriculture and ranching. A strong community formed on the backs of these two industries.

Unfortunately, Hinkley also happened to be right next to Pacific Gas and Electric's (PG&E) natural gas transmission pipeline. As gas travels along this line, it has to be recompressed after a certain distance. The compressors are cooled by cooling towers. Starting in 1952, a form of chromium was added to the water that was cooling these towers. The chromium kept the mechanized parts of the towers from rusting.

When the water wasn't being used, it was stored in unlined ponds. Problem was, this form of chromium causes cancer. The use of chromium continued until 1966. During those 14 years, it seeped into the ground water/drinking water of Hinkley from the unlined ponds. Some estimates put the seepage at 370 million gallons. Where it continues to spread as you read.

The rest of the story makes for sad reading. Cancer started showing up in Hinkley. A law firm got involved. PG&E tried to cover up the problem. Only admitting the contamination in 1987. Erin Brockovich, who was a law clerk at the time, identified clusters of cancer in Hinkley. Eventually, a class action suit was filed and settled for $333 million in 1996. A record class-action settlement at the time.

After the settlement, hundreds moved out of town. The population spiraled downward to 1,915 in 2000. By 2012, an estimated 1,200 called Hinkley home. Since then, many more have left. Houses have reactively plummeted in value, as there are no buyers. So, PG&E has been forced to purchase affected homes at disputed market values. After purchase, PG&E immediately demolishes each home to discourage squatters and erase a little more of Hinkley history.

More chromium-related lawsuits have been brought and settled, both here and throughout PG&E's domain. PG&E has also spent hundreds of millions of dollars trying to stem the chromium bloom and clean up the mess. That underground bloom is now estimated to be two and a half miles wide and seven miles long. PG&E predicts it will take 45 years to fully remove all the chromium from the water supply. Though most seem to believe that Hinkley will be abandoned long before then. And that same "most" don't believe PG&E is capable of ever effectively removing all that chromium from Hinkley's aquifer.

The only school, the one visible from the tracks, closed in 2013. Ending a 111-year educational presence. The whole mess has torn Hinkley apart and poisoned more than just the water. It's a subject best not broached during your brief visit. As to filling up your water containers...

Stay with the tracks for the not always beautiful seven-mile hike into Barstow. Pass fields still being irrigated by sprinklers. A cause for thought. The tracks parallel the 58 for a while. Then the 58 peels off to the right and takes the active tracks with it. Instead of following, jump on the abandoned railbed covered in cinders that continues straight (east). Follow it through ranches and past abandoned buildings for the four miles to the Barstow Depot. Cross the new irrigation ditch when you come to it.

Continue until you come to a "Y." Take the right branch toward the Mojave River. (Probably very dry, underground and un-river like.) Cross the river of sand where there used to be a bridge. If for some interesting reason the Mojave River is actually flowing, don't try to cross it. Make your way to the bridge visible to the east and cross there. Then backtrack west to the rail depot. Assuming the Mojave River is dry, head for the active tracks on the other side of the river.

Climb up out of the riverbed and turn left at the tracks. Follow the dirt road you find, passing under the old-style auto bridge, to Casa Desierto. This is Barstow's train depot. And it is beautiful. In front of it lies a large marshalling yard for the BNSF, with trains often on the move. As stated in an earlier chapter, there is a daily train service to Los Angeles from here.

The Casa Desierto was built in 1911. It was once a "Harvey House," as well as Barstow's rail depot. Some say it was designed by Mary Coulter, who was responsible for so many amazing buildings at the Grand Canyon. Others claim Francis Wilson of Santa Barbara. Regardless, to stare at it brings back a slower time in American history. When rail was king. And tourists took their time. Staying at rail hotels, such as this one. And dressing for a proper meal.

Along this Santa Fe line, the Fred Harvey Company provided the dining experience. And that dining took place in their famous and much loved Harvey Houses. The Harvey Houses were the brainchild of Fred Harvey. Who immigrated to the States at the age of 15 from England.

At first, he tried his hand at the restaurant business. Then, after the Civil War, he became involved with railroads. In 1870, he providentially met the President of the Atchison, Topeka and Santa Fe Railroad (ATSF). Hands were shook, and Fred Harvey started providing dining services for the ATSF. He did it with style. The food was good and reasonably priced. The dining rooms elegant. And the wait service was provided by Harvey Girls. Who were women hired from the east coast to come out west and work.

The job advertisement for Harvey Girls went something like this, "Needed: Young women, 18 to 30 years of age, of good character, attractive and intelligent." An inconceivable classified in this current age. The women would live onsite at the Harvey Houses. Their room and board free. The salary decent at $17.50 a month. The Harvey Girls wore a black and white uniform and had a strict code of conduct. It was a coveted position, mainly for the adventure out west it promised. In 1942, a movie starring Judy Garland was made about the Harvey Girls. The position grew large in the public's imagination. Becoming something of a cultural phenomenon. In all, more than 100,000 Harvey Girls worked at Harvey Houses. Twenty thousand of whom ended up married to their customers. As Will Rogers once said, "Harvey Houses kept the west in food and wives."

At their height, there were 84 Harvey Houses operating along Santa Fe Lines. Business slowed, when dining cars began operating in trains. And dived with the Depression. Still, the company held on until the 1960s, before finally folding. A victim of the industry-wide decline in rail passenger travel.

Casa Desierto was a jewel in the Harvey House chain. It was also the center of social activity for Barstow. But it followed the railroading industry downhill. In 1973, the Santa Fe closed the Barstow rail depot altogether. It succumbed to ruin and vandalism. In the late 80s, the Santa Fe decided demolition was the best option for their Casa. But the city of Barstow wisely stepped in and took over the depot. They dropped a few million restoring Casa Desierto, and her reopening was planned for 1992. But unsentimental pressure was building under the earth. The day before the ceremony, it released. The 7.3 earthquake, centered in nearby Landers, set the Casa's restoration back years.

Can an earthquake bring good fortune? Every once in a great while, yes. The Casa's damage was caused by an earthquake. This qualified it for state and federal grants. To the tune of $8 million. Suddenly, there was all kinds of money to properly return the depot to glory. Casa Desierto grandly debuted her present form in 1999.

The Casa currently houses the Barstow city offices, as well as the Route 66 museum (F-Su 10 to 4, 760-255-1890). Also of great interest, is the Railroad Museum (F-Su 11 to 4, 760-256-WARM). Be sure to check out the room focusing on date nails for railroad ties. As well, have a close look at the rail bicycle. If time permits, ask the rail museum staff if it is possible to take you on a tour of the luxury railcar outside.

Now it's time to head into Barstow for resupply. Climb onto the road behind Casa Desierto and cross over the large iron bridge into Barstow. Pause on the bridge and take in the marshaling yard and Casa. It's easy to imagine an earlier time. Once across the bridge, continue straight uphill on First Street. The bar you pass on your right has pool tables and liquid refreshment. If your willpower is strong, continue uphill. Turn left when you get to Main Street. Which also happens to be Route 66.

Note the El Rancho Motel on the south side of Main Street. The El Rancho was built entirely with railroad ties, reclaimed from the TTR in 1943. Marilyn Monroe is said to have stayed there. If you look closely, you can see the tie outlines under the plaster. The Vons supermarket is a medium walk up Main Street. On the way, you will pass a multitude of hotels. If you plan to spend the night in Barstow, take your pick. They're all affordable. To camp would require a return to BLM land. Barstow is the biggest town, at 22,000, on the Death Q. So, it has all the resupply a hiker could need.

BARSTOW		
1.	Food Supply	Yes
2.	Restaurant	Yes
3.	Water	Yes
4.	Hotel	Yes
5.	Beer	Yes
6.	Pool Table	Yes
7.	ATM	Yes
8.	Post Office	Yes
9.	Casino	Yes

The Vons supermarket is at 1270 E. Main Street (760-256-8105, 6 a.m. - 11p.m., seven days a week). No more cup of noodles for you, as the selection is extensive. Leaving Barstow, there are convenience stores in 8.5 miles in Daggett, 19 and 24 miles in Newberry Springs and 53 miles in Ludlow. Which translates into reliable access to food and water for the remainder of the Q. Almost across the street from Vons is Jenny's Grill Steak & Mariscos for excellent Mexican food (1231 E. Main Street, 760-255-1500, M-F 6:30 a.m. - 9 p.m., Sa/Su 6:30 a.m. - 10 p.m.). The post office is at 425 S. 2nd Avenue (760-256-9304, M-F 9-5, Saturday 10-1).

Barstow is old by out-west standards. It began as a settlement on the Mojave River in the 1830s. Various trails to and from the west coast followed the course of the Mojave River. Preeminent among them was the Mojave Trail, which Native Americans had been using for 4,000 years. Primarily to trade, but also to raid the Spanish. And then, the Americans that followed on the Spaniard's heels. Barstow was a trail stopping point for all who came through. Wagons of settlers, as well as herds of cattle, were all attracted to Barstow's water. Or Grapevine, as it was then called.

When gold, silver and borax were discovered in nearby Calico, during the 1860s and 70s, Barstow's development took off. In 1883, the SP railroad arrived to support the mining. Within a year, they sold out to the Santa Fe. Inevitably, the mining exhausted itself, but travelers never stopped coming. First by rail. Then along the novelty of Route 66. Which was followed by Interstates 40 and 15, as well as Route 58. People continue their passing through. So, there are always service jobs. But getting industry to build so far from anywhere has proven to be Barstow's challenge.

Day 34

413

Day 34

East Barstow-Dagget-Newberry Springs-Punjab, India

Out of the soft, or not, bed. Return to First Street. Grab some donuts at the corner, if so inclined. Retrace your previous day's steps back across the bridge. And return to Casa Desierto. If the doors are open, have a wander through the building. Which is, reportedly, not haunted, but considered active. As, occasionally, a long-dead, uniformed Harvey Girl is still spotted. Explore both museums, if your visit is timed fortuitously.

When ready, make your way out of civilization by following the tracks toward the rising sun. Stay on the left side and off of the active tracks. Pass through the hill cut, then under a bridge heading east. Pass Barstow Station, off to the right, which is one of the busiest McDonalds in the States. Supposedly, this McDonalds was won in a high stakes card game. The game was between the future owner, who won, and Ray Kroc, who cofounded the McDonalds chain, but lost the critical hand. The name "Barstow Station" comes from the original building, which was created by stringing 16 railcars together.

Continue out of town until you reach the 15 Freeway. Leave the tracks by turning left and walking over to the freeway bridge. Cross the bridge. Stay east on the road (Riverside Drive) for a couple of blocks. Walk past the Paradise Inn Club, "Open Since 1959." Soon the road rejoins the tracks. Follow the joint UP/BNSF tracks past this gritty section and on out of Barstow.

The tracks split the Marine Corps Logistics Base, passing their golf course in the process. Stay close to the tracks and watch out for duffers, as there are a lot of errant golf balls on the tracks. The base has been around since WWII. It is charged with the maintenance of combat equipment the Marine Corps uses in battle.

On the other side of the base, after a few manmade ponds, habitations fall away. With time, you enter West Daggett. There is a two-story ruin on the other side of the tracks. And that is all that can be written about West Daggett. Continue on to East Daggett, where more is going on. Note the orphaned Route 66 silently matching the tracks. Take a break at East Daggett's Desert Market (760-254-2774, 35596 Santa Fe Street, M-Sa 8 a.m. - 8 p.m., Su 9 a.m. - 7 p.m.). It's just to the left of the tracks.

This market building replaced a previous wooden building that was destroyed by fire in 1908. It is made of cement and is considered to be the first fireproof building built in the Mojave Desert. Here, through the years, miners would bring in gold and exchange it for currency and goods. In 1953, a burglar was able to crack the safe and make off with $1,000 in gold. Have a cold whatever and read about Daggett from under the market's generous shade.

Today, Daggett is a sleepy village of 200. But in her past, she was a contender. A past where the boom was on and the future huge. Until greed and miscalculation waylaid that future. Daggett came into being in the 1860s. When it became the transport center for the huge mining strikes in nearby Calico. In all, $90 million was taken out of Calico's 500 mines. In comparison, a miner during that time earned 20 cents an hour. At first, Calico's ore was brought to Daggett for processing by wagon. Then the wagons were displaced by a steam tractor. Finally, a narrow gauge railroad was built in 1880 to connect the two towns. It was compromisingly known as the Calico-Daggett Railroad.

Calico is a familiar-to-you story by now. In 1881, four prospectors went out looking. And found what they were looking for. Which was silver. They founded the Silver King Mine. Which attracted a stampede. Soon there were 3,500 people, from all over the world, wandering the fresh streets of Calico. The smell of wealth hung heavy. Buildings started going up. Inhabiting them were the businesses associated with extracting that new-found wealth from miners.

On the one side of Calico were stores, hotels, restaurants, blacksmith shops, a church, and so on. On the flip side, dancing halls, 24 saloons, gambling dens, lawyers, and brothels. There was a "Boot Hill" Cemetery. (A common term of the day implying graves for men who died with their boots on. In other words, men who had died violently.) After a few years had passed, there was talk of permanence. A sheriff was appointed. A Literary Society was formed. And a school district created.

But the permanence proved temporary. For a while, Calico rode out the roller coaster of the silver markets. Then the discovery of borax lent a hand to the town's promise. But the mid 1890s saw a collapse of silver prices. Then, better borax was found elsewhere. Calico had run out of reasons to be, and the Literary Society put down their books. Calico sat alone and silent, until the 1950s, when Walter Knott came along and bought the bones. It wasn't the first time Mr. Knott had come along. For he spent time in Calico as a youth. With an uncle who called it home.

Mr. Knott set about restoring Calico to its 1880s look. As owner of the popular Knott's Berry Farm Amusement Park, he had disposable funds to throw at the project. By 1966, the restoration was complete, and Mr. Knott donated Calico to San Bernardino County. Who currently operate it as a historical ghost town monument and theme park. Worth a trip when the opportunity presents. If for no better reason than the multiple ghosts still in residence. Including what must be the only mail carrying ghost dog in nonexistence.

With all this uncovered wealth, railroads began building toward the area. The Santa Fe Railroad (prior to 1897, the Atlantic and Pacific Railroad) planned to make Daggett the main station on their new line. As well as build a large maintenance and marshaling yard there. But details of the plan leaked out.

Speculators rushed to buy up all the railroad targeted acreage. They did so at prices that were already inflated by the silver boom. After their purchases, the speculators sat back and waited for their richly deserved windfall.

When the president of the Santa Fe Railroad learned the asking prices, he figured out the game quickly enough. His reaction was unfortunate for both Daggett's future and its speculators. The following pretty much summed it up. "Who needs Daggett? Put the main station in Barstow." And that is why Barstow has 22,000 residents and Daggett 200. Greed, a tricky business.

But Daggett wasn't quite finished. By 1896, there was no more silver in Calico. With loss of purpose, the Calico-Daggett Railroad shut down.

But, back in 1883, borax was discovered in another part of those same Calico hills. In 1888, who other than Borax Smith rode into town. The guy was everywhere. The scent of borax identifiable to him from miles off. Soon after arrival, he owned the local borax mine and put a lot of people to work.

Right away, transportation identified itself as his biggest problem. The 20-mule teams operating between the mine and Daggett were too slow. Taking a day and a half each way. A steam tractor was brought in to replace the mules. But it kept breaking down and needing to be humiliatingly rescued by the replaced mules.

So, Borax Smith came up with a novel idea. To him anyway. He built a narrow gauge railroad 11 miles to his mine at Borate. Which lay a few miles east from Calico. The Borate and Daggett Railroad (B&D) quickly proved to be a success. It reduced transport costs from $2.50 a ton to 12 cents a ton. As well, a one-way trip went from a-day-and-a-half to three hours.

Construction on the B&D began in 1898 and took one year to complete. The building crew consisted of Indian and Mexican workers, who were paid ten cents an hour. More than anything, the B&D proved to Borax Smith that a borax-hauling railroad was possible. And from there on out, Borax Smith had railroads on the brain. The B&D was, in the end, just another botfly. Its legacy, the construction of the TTR.

The terminus of the B&D was Fouts Garage. That would be the sweet, wooden building close to the tracks and just slightly east of you. From there, the borax ore was loaded on to Santa Fe boxcars. Then hauled to Borax Smith's refinery at Alameda, CA. Which is located on San Francisco Bay. Borax ore caused Daggett to boom again. In 1902, the population had grown significantly. Facilities included three general stores, the Stone Hotel, three saloons and two Chinese restaurants. Nine million dollars in borax was taken out of the Calico hills.

The good times lasted for half a decade. But in 1907, better borax deposits were found in Death Valley at Old Ryan. The discovery was fatal to borax operations in Daggett. In 1914, the B&D's rails and ties were pulled up and shipped to Death Valley Junction. Where they were recycled into use on the Death Valley Railroad.

Daggett began a shrinking process. Though passing traffic kept it from flatlining. Many a dust bowl refugee passed through on Route 66 during the Depression. Headed west for greener pastures. Parts of the classic 1940 movie, "Grapes of Wrath," starring Henry Fonda, were filmed here. But when the new 40 freeway bypassed Route 66 and Daggett, the town went through a final reduction. Which brought it to its present-day size.

Stroll through town. There are some interesting buildings, including the ones right next to the Desert Market. The small Daggett Museum is at 37703 Second Street (760-254-2649, Sa/Su 1 p.m. - 5 p.m.). There is also a post office in town (619-254-2693, 33530 C St., M-F 9:15 - 12:30, 1:30 - 4:15). When knowledgeable enough about Daggett, move out along the tracks past Fouts Garage. A historical marker is in place, explaining the various exploits of the building.

Head east along the left side of the tracks. Immediately come to a rail Y. This is the fabled UP/BNSF split. The left UP branch heads off to Las Vegas. Along the way, it cuts the TTR at Crucero. Which you may remember. The right BNSF branch makes its way to Ludlow and then on to Needles, CA. Take the right branch by crossing, with care, the UP branch. Leave the Mojave River, often called the "Upside-Down River" for obvious reasons.

Head on out into the desert. Pass an enormous NRG energy generation plant that is seemingly abandoned. March on to Newberry Springs. Pass Gale Station, long lost to the drifts. Next up is the Barstow-Daggett Airport to your left. This was a military base back in WWII. After the war, it reverted to civilian use. Though, curiously, there are still some military grade Blackhawk helicopters on the tarmac. From appearances, a spur rail line once ran over to the base.

Strangely, as you approach Newberry Springs, you begin to pass ponds. This makes sense when you learn that the original name of Newberry Springs was Water. For it sits on top of the Mojave Aquifer, which is the largest aquifer in the western U.S. Geology has decided that the water table is to be very near the surface here. Jim O'Donnell, my teacher who took us out to China Lake, lived out here in a train caboose for a while. When he wanted a pond, he simply had someone come dig a hole with a tractor. It naturally filled up with water.

Today, the water supports a variety of agriculture and ranches. From pistachios and almonds to buffalo and carp. It also supports hundreds of mini oases. Which might be oval water ski courses, nudist camps, or just the family getaway/sugar shack. You've now walked past Mineola Station. Don't worry, nobody sees it anymore.

Newberry Springs is very spread out. But coming up on your right, across the 40, is a cluster of convenience stores servicing passing motorists. An underpass is provided for your ease of traverse. Near the convenience stores, just a bit east, is Immigrant Point. For your purposes, it is the large hill at the base of the Newberry Mountains that you can see sticking out from a long way off.

Immigrant Point was a beacon for very thirsty settlers and livestock coming west, on wagons, along the old Mormon Trail. When they could begin to see the Point, it had been a long time since water or forage had been available. But at the Point, there was an artesian well where water rose naturally to the surface. As well, there was plenty of pasture and shade trees. It's not difficult to imagine a quickening of the pace by man and beast.

The ruins of the old well are still somewhat there. Though the water, trees and pasture are departed. Victims of a falling water table, due to the thirst of agriculture. If you climb around on Immigrant Point, you will find seed-grinding holes and petroglyphs. Proof that Native Americans also hung out here for centuries. From the top of the Point, black circles are visible on the valley floor. These are the ground burns of fires that warmed the long-ago buried.

Always to the east on your tracks. Slowly, the hill sized Black Butte comes into your vision on the left. Here, a bubble of black lava wormed its way through the Earth's crust to have a look at things. Not seeing any other lava around, it receded back under that protective crust. Leaving the small butte as a marker. Native Americans lived around Black Butte for centuries. Before them, pre-historic man. There is scientific thought that man may have inhabited the area for 500,000 years. At the nearby Calico Early Man Site, a human skull fragment was dated at 19,000 years old.

More recently, the last area shootout between Indians and settlers took place at Black Butte. In the appropriately named "Battle of Black

Butte." More steps east. Arrive at a mill. For us, at this point, the dark was winning. We decided to push on another five miles for dinner. An earlier billboard, suggesting the possibility of Indian food, spurred the decision to keep going into the night.

If you decide to push those five miles, you will come to Fort Cody Road. Where Fort Cody Road crosses the BNSF tracks, turn right. In fact, though, you can turn right much earlier, when you see your destination Mobil station. Just cut across the desert. This will save you some back-tracking. There you will find, snuggled against the 40, a Circle K / Mobil Station (48157 Memorial Drive, 760-257 -3098, Open 24/7). From the outside, it looks like any other of the millions of such enterprises. But inside, is the most surreal stop on the Q.

For you walk in from Newberry Springs, and then you sit down in the Punjab, India. A genuine Punjabi Dhaba. As I've spent a bit of time in the Punjab, I was immediately transported. The bare bones dining. The silver segmented tray. Water pitchers on the table. Dal, roti, kheer, lassi and chai on the menu. The cooks arguing in Punjabi. Turbaned truck drivers wandering in. Hindi music floating about. "Every Sikh is a Singh, but not every Singh is a Sikh," kept running through my head. (Singh is a common surname throughout the various ethnic groups of India. It means lion. Every Sikh male shares the surname. Which was mandated by a 16th Century religious proclamation.) The first question, of course, from the cook, "Veg or non-veg?" I looked at Orbit and laughed. She just kept repeating, "Where the hell are we?"

The food was "pinch the dream" good. We ate 'till we couldn't. Then we had dessert. They also have Mexican food, but you've got to be kidding me. To top it off, the restaurant is open 24/7, and the food is inexpensive. Resupply is possible here if needed. You're about 28 miles from Ludlow and the final convenience store. As well as the end of your dance with the Q. After gorging, Orbit and I struggled back to near the tracks and told stories we both had heard many times before. Then drifted off contentedly to dreams of the Golden Temple in Amritsar.

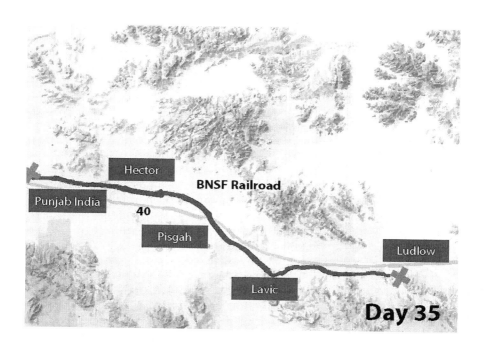

Day 35

Hector-Pisgah-Ludlow

We opened our eyes and immediately dragged ourselves back to India for more. Then it was a return to the business at hand and the final day. Return to the left side of the tracks and begin a slow climb out of the valley. Cross Troy Dry Lake. The tracks continue to pull away from the 40. The Cady Mountains are to your left. The Rodman Mountains to the right. The desert returns to a pristine state. Note the small hill to your left that seems to have been crowned by a yurt.

By now, the passing locomotive engineers will wave at you and give you the horn. They've already passed you a few times and are used to your three mph. They've also possibly bonded with your slide from sanity. Give a wave back. Along this line, probably 20 to 25 trains a day will pass you in either direction. Never once did we see a stowaway riding the rails. Sometimes, the trains are flying. Top speeds of 85 mph are reached on this stretch. Most of the ties you see are concrete.

Come to a long line of tamarisks and cottonwoods that were once irrigated. Most are still hanging on and make for nice shade. I believe this to be a former train stop known as Hector. In 2006, three days before Christmas, a train derailed here. The mountain in front of you is the 3,980 foot Sleeping Beauty Mountain. So named because that is what it looks like from the air. Not far from here, in 1964, a Navy F4 jet decided it no longer wanted to be airborne. The pilot safely ejected and landed well. The plane, not so much. Its wreckage is said to cover a large area.

The railroad begins a turn to the right. Eventually, it arrives at a big water tank (no access), then dips under the 40. Here you might pass millions of dollars of highly specialized rail equipment. Left out here unguarded, as it probably has zero value to anyone but a railroad.

Pisgah Crater, with its expansive lava flows, comes into view. Its growth spurts have caused three different eruptions. The crater itself is too young to accurately date. At one time, Pisgah was 2,638 feet high. But since the arrival of settlers, the Pisgah has been mined. Much of the ballast under the old Santa Fe tracks were Pisgah cinders. Mining is ongoing. Black sand from Pisgah was used to create black beaches in the Clint Eastwood film, "Letters from Iwo Jima." After all the mining, the Pisgah Crater is down to 2,545 feet.

Lava fields spread out before you. They are pocketed with lava tubes. Lava tubes are created when new lava flows beneath hardened lava. Once the flow ceases, a hollow tube or cave remains. The longest lava tube discovered here is 1,300 feet long. In 2011, there was a brief internet sensation when a video was posted on YouTube showing Pisgah Crater erupting. It died down quickly, after authorities confirmed that Pisgah was still fast asleep.

As kids, we used to come out to the crater on field trips with Jim O'Donnell, my junior high science teacher. He was the perfect chaperone because he didn't chaperone. Preferring to let us run wild, as the nature of youth pleads for. One particularly hot day, we were climbing around on the lava flows looking for chuckwallas, when we stumbled upon an ancient, wooden crate of dynamite. There was also a burlap sack of blasting caps. Mr. O'Donnell was back at the Pisgah Hilton, probably reading Kierkegaard or some such character. The Pisgah Hilton was an old miner's dugout we slept in on field trips to the crater. Being bright kids, we figured Mr. O'D would want to see our discovery.

The only curiosity was why the dynamite was sweating. (Later, I learned that water drops on dynamite are actually nitroglycerine, which indicate the dynamite is in an advanced state of instability.) We just figured the dynamite was sweating because it was hot like us. So, we picked up the crate and took turns lugging it. Quickly, we figured out that balancing the crate on our head was the best method of carrying it. And that is the way we stumbled the few miles back to the Hilton. Those not hauling the crate, threw blasting caps at each other, trying to get them to explode.

When we got back to the Hilton, Mr. O'Donnell had a good look at our discovery and didn't say much. Finally, and quietly, "Come on boys, let's move base over to the dunes and look for fringe-toed lizards." We packed up our stuff and left.

Later, while out on the dunes, we saw Mr. O'D flag down a passing highway patrol officer. Much later, we heard that a Marine ordnance disposal team was called in. Apparently, they took one look at our treasure and declared it too unstable to move. At all. Out came the C-4 plastic explosive. And that is how the Pisgah Hilton came to be blown up.

Hiking on, you are in the final stretch. The mother road, Route 66, appears to your right. Go ahead. It's right there. Walk out to the middle of the road and let loose with dance and song. "I get my kicks on Route Sixty-Six!" How can you not? It is the last day after all. And your audience is nonexistent.

After a bit, the rails pass over Route 66. Which is in bad enough condition that cars quickly lose their nostalgia for a drive on it and return to the 40. Pass Lavic, yet another invisible rail stop. A low valley, with Lavic Dry Lake at its bottom, opens up to your right.

Dirt roads continue to convey you along next to the rails. Completely possessing all desert south of you is the very large Marine Corps Air Ground Combat Center. Centered at Twentynine Palms, CA. From which an explosive thud can occasionally be heard. The base is 931 square miles and was created in 1949. The rails have pulled away south from the 40 at this point. Then they begin a push back. Come over a rise and spot Ludlow, where it all began. Dance. As a survivor of the Holocaust once demanded I do when life warrants celebrating.

The rails then turn back toward the Bullion Mountains to your south. This section of rail was to bring home an example of the synchronicities that flow through one's life. Many unobserved. This particular synchronicity arrived on the back of a breakfast offer. It went something like this.

Just as I was finishing this book, I found myself attempting to kayak from Hoover Dam, near Las Vegas, to the Mexican border. A distance of around 350 miles. About a week in, I was making good time paddling through a serene section of the Colorado River known as the Topock Gorge.

It was an early December morning and I had the river to myself. Until I didn't. There was plenty of time to adjust, as any motorized boat breaks into a river's quiet from a long way off. As the boat closed, it thoughtfully slowed to reduce its wake from tsunami to gentle roll. Then the boat came to a stop.

"Where you headed?"

"Mexico."

"God damn! You hungry?"

"Always."

"Let me give you what I got."

And that is how I met Gerald and his dog, Nick. "Nick," because he was rescued in the nick of time from the pound. His date with the death chamber being the very next day. I latched onto Gerald's boat, and we floated companionably along at two mph. That being the speed the Colorado chose to flow at. Over the next hour, we swapped a story or two, maybe 50. Mostly his, as I was chewing.

Eventually, the conversation turned to work. I learned he had been a train engineer for 39 years.

"Ever wreck one?"

"Just once."

Ever a taste for the macabre. "What happened?"

"Well, I was coming around the bend into Ludlow…"

I closed my eyes. Where else could it have been? A lifelong partnership, Ludlow and I.

"… And I was about to meet God."

He had all the attention I possessed. "Say more."

"Well, I'm coming around the bend into Ludlow, just me in the locomotive. Hauling freight. It was back in the day, so a caboose was attached at the rear of the train. I didn't know it at the time, but a maintenance crew had been working on the curve. They had removed most of the ties, leaving a few in place to hold the rails. What I found out was, they didn't leave enough. Not nearly. The rails widened, and my train derailed. Off we went. Smashing through the sand. Every damn car but the caboose. Which managed to hold on. The goddamn dust was everywhere. And I couldn't see a thing. I just knew I wanted to get out and away from that locomotive, before there was a fire or some such thing. And that is when God spoke to me from heaven."

"What did he say?"

"Well first off, God is loud. Real loud. That threw me for a bit. And all he asked me was if I was ok. I looked all around for him, but I couldn't

425

see nothing for the dust. Then he asked me again. 'Are you OK?' Straight above me and real loud again. So, I answered, 'Yeah, God, I'm fine.' Real loud, straight up and right back at him. What else was I supposed to do?"

"And what did he say back?"

"Well, apparently, I didn't answer loud enough because he asked me the same thing again. But by now, I had made it away from the locomotive. I looked straight up into the sky for God. There, I was able to see the cross of God with the sun blazing behind it. I couldn't believe it. Then I stared a little harder. And started to figure things out. The cross was a Piper Cub airplane. And God was a highway patrolman in that airplane. Yelling at me through a microphone hooked up to a loudspeaker. The officer just happened to be flying by when I went off the rails. So, once I realized who God was, I felt okay going back to my sinful ways."

Gerald could tell one hell of a story. Back to your Q.

As you approach the base of the mountains, a big wash cuts you off. Cross it and stay with the dirt road/railroad through the hills. Follow the railroad curve into the high part of Ludlow. Keep your eyes peeled to the left for the TTR railbed. Month old nostalgia washes over you when you spot your old friend curving out to the tractor-trailer advertiser on the 40. Cue the orchestra. And walk back into recent memories.

You have reached the end at the beginning. Your personal Q now complete. Eight hundred eleven miles in the bag. A word. Congratulations! Hopefully the 35-day long conversation with yourself was memorable. And you have a stock of trail stories that can be handed out like gifts upon return to your formal existence.

Now hustle. The café closes at 5:30 p.m. The Dairy Queen, on the other side of the 40, stays open until 9ish. Certainly, a reward shake or two awaits you there.

Dance some more. You've earned it well. For, if this is your 35th day, you've averaged 23.17 miles a day.

What next? Well, it's your turn to create your own thru hike. Preferably one I can take a shot at. Less ambitious is to hold on to this euphoria as long as it will allow you to. Swap it for your backpack. Lug your euphoria back into regular life. It is the best kind of gear, for it weighs not an ounce. And it will bring a shine to all you perceive.

And if you've just been reading all this time without the attendant hiking? Listen closely.

You may or may not hear it yet. But, assuredly, your botfly is on its way. Heed its unsolicited advice to pursue the untried. Whether it be the Q, a different hike, or some other ambitious pursuit.

For aren't we all waiting somewhere in the title of this book? Why not live a big life before you get to the front of death's queue?

A Very Long Walk

The PCT and the Death Q reflect each other
down the length of the Owens Valley.
The PCT high in the Sierras on the western edge of the valley.
The Death Q hugging its eastern contours.
For the ambitious, both could be hiked in a year.
A possible scenario: Tackle the Death Q in March
and finish it in early April.
Take a week or so off. Then head to Campo, California,
for a mid-April northbound start on the PCT.
If you make it to Canada, that would be an impressive 3,461 miles.
Just a thought. And perhaps another pesky botfly.

BIBLIOGRAPHY

Patera, Alan. Rhyolite: The Boom Years. Western Places: Volume 3, Number 2, Whole Number 10, 2014

Patera, Alan. Goldfield's Fabulous Boom. Western Places: Volume 9, Number 4, 2013

Mann, William. Guide to 50 Interesting and Mysterious Sites in the Mojave. Barstow: Shortfuse Publishing Company, 1999

McCraken, Robert. A History of Beatty Nevada. Tonopah: Nye County Press, 1992

Sharp, Robert., Glazner, Alan. Geology Underfoot in Death Valley and Owens Valley. Missoula: Mountain Press Publishing Company, 1997

Zdon, Andy. Desert Summits. Bishop: Spotted Dog Press, 2000
Gower, Harry. 50 years in Death Valley: Memoirs of a Borax Man. San Bernardino: Inland Printing, Inc., 1969

Lengner, Ken., Ross, George. Tecopa Mines: Operating During 82 years of the Death Valley Region Mining Boom. Self-Published, 2006

Serpico, Phil. A Road to Riches: The Randsburg Railway Company and Mining District. Palmdale: Omni Publications, 2004

Serpico, Phil. Tonopah and Tidewater Railroad: The Nevada Shortline. Palmdale: Omni Publications, 2013

Serpico, Phil. Jawbone: Sunset on the Lone Pine, Palmdale: Omni Publications, 2006

Paher, Stanley. Nevada Ghost Towns and Desert Atlas, Reno: Nevada Publications, 2012

"Botflies, a.k.a. Torsalo or Dermatobia Hominis." Casado Internet Group, Belize. ambergriscaye.com Web. No date.

The New Reference Atlas of the World, New York: C.S. Hammond & Company, Inc., 1929

McCulloch, John. "Tonopah & Tidewater Railroad." ttrr.org Web. No date.

Mulqueen, Stephen. "Borax Smith and the Tonopah and Tidewater Railroad." http://bit.ly/2AsOvc6 Web. No date

Ludlow, California. In Wikipedia http://bit.ly/2BFoYwL No date

"Scotland's Brick Industry." scottishbrickhistory.co.uk Web. 5 June 2014

Vanderlin, John. "This Brick's No Ordinary Brick." Web. 26 November 2008

"Plowshare Program." U.S. Department of Energy. http://bit.ly/2nohb3f Web. No date.

Route 66. In Wikipedia. http://bit.ly/2Byn4wO No date.

Rockett, Jack. "The Great Bunion Derby: Across the U.S. on Foot 1927." http://bit.ly/2kiwzgD Web. 7 November, 2006

"Cerro Gordo: Mining Town Turned Ghost Town." Friends of Cerro Gordo. Pamphlet. No date.

"World War II Desert Training Center, California Arizona Maneuver Area." https://on.doi.gov/2AoanaI Web. No date

Mizpah Review: 1907 to Today, A Look Back at Life in Tonopah. Pamphlet. No date.

Goldfield Nevada: Goldfield Historic Walking Tour Booklet. The Goldfield Historical Society, 2013.

Woodruff, David., Woodruff, Gayle. Tales Along El Camino Sierra. Independence: Independence Press, 2017

Death Valley National Park. In Wikipedia. http://bit.ly/2iY4j2D No date.

"Death Valley." National Park Service. http://bit.ly/29tdjDa Web. No date

"Death Valley Geology." National Park Service, http://bit.ly/2jimeOp Web. No date.

"Chuckwalla." http://bit.ly/2n29v2I Web. No date.

"Rattlesnakes in California." California Department of Fish and Game, http://bit.ly/1ONEOGI Web. No date.

Juckett, Gregory., Hancox, John. "Venomous Snakebites in the United States: Management Review and Update." 1 April 2002

"Gopher Snakes." Desert USA, http://bit.ly/2jVB0d5 Web. No date.

"Red Racer." http://bit.ly/2BBBqNl Web. No date.

"Common Kingsnake." Desert USA, http://bit.ly/2g0pZE0 Web. No date.

Sahagun, Louis. "A Variety of California Kingsnake Is Wreaking Havoc in Canary Islands." Los Angeles Times, Web. 27 April 2014

"Tarantulas." Desert USA. http://bit.ly/2BB1Fn2 Web. No date.

"Desert Kit Fox." National Park Service, Joshua Tree National Park. http://bit.ly/2jUqGSF Web. No date.

Oliver, Dexter. "Gray Foxes." http://bit.ly/2nuv2oU Web. No date.

Kangaroo rat. In Wikipedia. http://bit.ly/2jgp5Hq No date.

"Jackrabbit." National Geographic. http://on.natgeo.com/2jgpqKc Web. No date.

"Desert Cottontail." Desert USA. http://bit.ly/2zSKZHf Web. No date.

"Jackrabbit." Desert USA. http://bit.ly/2cGWbjG Web. No date.

Pronghorn. In Wikipedia. http://bit.ly/2uTqLyq Web. No date.

"Wild burro (Feral Ass)." Digital Desert: Mojave Desert. http://bit.ly/2AT7Ztl Web. No date.

Stillman, Deanne. "The Last Burros of Mojave Desert: A Christmas Story that Needs a Happy Ending." Huffington Post. Web. 24 December 2006, Updated 25 May 2011

Hurt, Suzanne. "The Wild Horses of the Mojave." Mammoth Monthly. http://bit.ly/2jTGMw9 Web. September/October 2007

"Coyotes." Desert USA. http://bit.ly/PxBc0O Web. No date

"Bats in the Desert and the Southwest." Desert USA. http://bit.ly/2jhPvbV Web. No date.

"Desert Tortoise." Desert USA. http://bit.ly/1NHQLNU Web. No date.

"The Roadrunner-Bird." Desert USA. http://bit.ly/2ekt6KZ Web. No date.

"Scorpions." Desert USA. http://bit.ly/2B078Yj Web. No date.

"The Turkey Vulture." Desert USA. http://bit.ly/2AuH6eH Web. No date.

"Red-Tailed Hawk." Desert USA. http://bit.ly/2Au7WU1 Web. No date.

"Joshua Trees." National Park Service. http://bit.ly/22ETSQx Web. No date.

"Creosote." National Park Service. http://bit.ly/2A769Fv Web. No date.

"Mojave Yucca." Digital-Desert: Mojave. http://bit.ly/2AsjAyV Web. No date.

"What is a Jumping Cholla?" Jumping Cholla Enterprises. http://bit.ly/2jV0zuU Web. 5 December 2013

"Cholla Cactus." Desert USA. http://bit.ly/2nwkky2 Web. No date.

"Barrel Cactus." Desert USA. http://bit.ly/2bmqmuz Web. No date.

"Tamarisk: Frequently Asked Questions." http://bit.ly/2kpGqRE Web. No date.

"Fremont's Cottonwood." Digital-Desert: Mojave Desert. http://bit.ly/2iY4CKq Web. No date.

Paher, Stanley. Death Valley Ghost Towns Las Vegas: Nevada Publications, Volume Two, 1981

"Railroad History, An Overview of the Past." http://bit.ly/2BCVlvj Web. No date.

Strong, Mary Francis. "The Town Too Dry to Die." Desert Magazine, February 1974, Pages 8-11.

"Bagdad Chase Mine." http://bit.ly/2krkVjz Web. No date.

Ross, Delmer. "Ludlow and Southern Railway." http://bit.ly/2jhSW2j Web. 2000

Ross, Delmer. "The Bagdad Chase Mine." http://bit.ly/2jSIPAs Web. 2001

"The History of Route 66." http://bit.ly/2nuzofz Web. No date.

Powell, Devon. "Operation Plowshare." Stanford University. http://stanford.io/2nvaEnD 5 March 2014

"Amboy Area and the Mojave Desert." http://bit.ly/2zSIEf5 Web. No date.

"The Tonopah and Tidewater Railroad." http://bit.ly/2AT9Ez5 Web. No date.

"Borax Smith and the Tonopah and Tidewater Railroad." http://bit.ly/2AsOvc6 Web. No date.

Zentner, Joe. "Borax and the 20 Mule Team." http://bit.ly/2BLssxO Web. No date.

Twenty mule team. In Wikipedia. http://bit.ly/2ipXClY Web. No date.

Silver, Mike. "Fight of the Century"---Then...And Now. boxingoverbroadway.com May 17, 2015

"Zzyzx Quack - Founded Town, Last Name in the Atlas." http://bit.ly/1p9av55 Web. No date.

Danger, Tatiana. "Welcome to Zzyzx: California's Most Mysterious Weird Little Town." http://bit.ly/2ioGHzV 6 January 2016

"Embezzlement Blamed on Heat and Gas Engine." Los Angeles Times. 9 October 1932, Page 32.

"Armargosa River Natural Area." https://on.doi.gov/2iqUFkS Web. No date.

"The Amargosa River: Retracing an 1849 Journey." Cannundrum. http://bit.ly/2AtQ8Z7 16 May 2009

"Death Valley Ghost Towns: Lila C. Mine." http://bit.ly/2AyoyYT No date. Page 7.

"Ryan, Death Valley, California." http://bit.ly/2zSSiyF Web. No date.

Muckenfuss, Mark. "Death Valley: New Ballerina to Fill Toe Shoes of Legendary Dancer." The Press Enterprise. http://bit.ly/2jhFfQI 20 April 2015

"Amargosa Opera House: Marta Becket's Death Valley Art Oasis." KCET Link. http://bit.ly/2A9OZHc 5 January 2016

"Ash Meadows." U.S. Fish & Wildlife Service. http://bit.ly/2BLjEYF Web. No date.

Henle, Mike. "Jim Marsh." http://bit.ly/2zQyxHU Web. No date.

"Jack Longstreet, A Nevada Frontier Character." Miscellaneous Ramblings of a Happy Wanderer. http://bit.ly/2iXyGpN Web. 14 May 2012

"T and T Ranch." http://bit.ly/2AuW2td Web. No date.

"Carrara." http://bit.ly/2A9GCeY Web. No date.

"Gold Center." http://bit.ly/2Ato4Fu Web. No date.

McCoy, Suzy. "History of Beatty." http://bit.ly/2B0JWcm Web. No date.

"Nevada Test Site." http://bit.ly/2kqD9RZ Web. No date.

Tophan, Laurence. Jha, Alok., Franklin, Will. "Building the Atom Bomb: The Full Story of the Nevada Test Site." The Guardian. http://bit.ly/2nx0PVZ 22 September 2015

Schimel, Kate. "Is Yucca Mountain Back on the Table?" High Country News. http:// bit.ly/2A8L39M 30 August 2015

Rhyolite, Nevada. In Wikipedia. http://bit.ly/2kq7vEj No date.

"Frank Shorty Harris." National Park Service. http://bit.ly/2iqzSOB Web. No date.

Wilcox, Len. "Shorty Harris from Beatty to Ballarat." http://bit.ly/2kqEUP3 Web. No date.

Las Vegas and Tonopah Railroad. In Wikipedia. http://bit.ly/2Ay1Tfb No date.

"William A Clark." http://bit.ly/2B0oDHS Web. No date.

Dedman, Bill. "The Clarks: An American Story of Wealth, Scandal and Mystery." NBC News. http://nbcnews.to/2BLLDaH 29 June 2010

Biographical Notes "Walter Edward Scott – Death Valley Scotty." Wandering Lizard History. http://www.wanderinglizard.com/

Blitz, Matt. "The St. Francis Dam Disaster." http://bit.ly/2jjckfh Web. 12 December 2013

Intellicast, The Authority in Expert Weather. Intellicast. Web. No date.

Harfield, Dave. "How Far Can We See if Unobstructed?" How it works. http://bit.ly/2io4ZKm 27 April 2012

"Greasewood." Desert USA. http://bit.ly/2zR5eF4 Web. no date.

Cottontail Ranch. In Wikipedia. http://bit.ly/2jiSd0C No date.

"Stonewall." http://bit.ly/2AUAyGz Web. No date.

"Ralston." http://bit.ly/2iZvFFj Web. No date.

"The History of Goldfield." The Goldfield Historical Society. http://bit.ly/2BCD3tQ Web. No date.

Hall, Shawn. "History of Tonopah." http://bit.ly/2jUmAKl Web. No date.

"The Anti-Chinese Riot in Tonopah, Nevada, 1903." The Free Library. http://bit.ly/2jWpizb Web. No date.

Clarke, Chris. "Scores of Birds Killed during Test of Solar Project in Nevada." KCET. http://bit.ly/1SLTU0R Web.18 February 2015

Danko, Pete. "Crescent Dunes Solar Tower Will Power Up in March – Without Ivanpah's Woes." Breaking Energy. http://bit.ly/1y8TRiv 10 February 2015

"A Rarely Seen Shortline – Nevada Silver Peak Railroad Web. No date.

Silverpeak, Nevada. In Wikipedia. http://bit.ly/2nwaPPv No date.

"Columbus, Nevada." In Wikipedia. http://bit.ly/2ktyqz2 Web. No date.

"Coaldale, Nevada." http://bit.ly/2AV1Qg5 Web. No date.

"Candelaria." http://bit.ly/2A9nuO8 Web. No date.

"Carson and Colorado Railway." carsoncolorado.com Web. No date.

"Marietta, Nevada." In Wikipedia. http://bit.ly/2AfXVuH Web. No date.

"Historic Benton Hot Springs." historicbentonhotsprings.com Web. No date.

Chalfant, California. In Wikipedia. http://bit.ly/2ipEmEY No date.

"Laws Railroad Museum and Historic Site." lawsmuseum.org Web. No date.

"Laws, California." http://bit.ly/2BzQmvh Web. No date.

"Bishop, California." bishopvisitor.com Web. No date.

"Los Angeles Aqueduct." Department of Water and Power. http://bit.ly/2zSdSD8 Web. No date.

"Los Angeles Aqueduct." http://bit.ly/2iWHiNk Web. No date.

"William Mulholland." New Perspectives on the West. http://to.pbs.org/1hzlgTF Web. No date.

Blitz, Matt. "On Occasions Like This, I Envy the Dead: The St. Francis Dam Disaster." Smithsonian. http://bit.ly/2kp5Hvk 12 March 2015

"The Lower Owens Valley River Project (LORP)." The Owens Valley Committee. http://bit.ly/2zQIRiU Web. No date.

Owens Valley. In Wikipedia. http://bit.ly/2ASCSy1 Web. No date.

Wright, David. "Greenwater, Furnace, Kunze and Ramsey." http://bit.ly/2AAdZoi Web. No date.

Marshall, Cohen. "The Owens Valley Radio Observatory: Early Years. Engineering and Science." Caltech Office of Strategic Communications. http://bit.ly/2ASEiIV Web. 1994

"About Soda Ash." http://bit.ly/2nAcuDM Web. No date.

Klusmire, Jon. "Palisade Glacier." http://bit.ly/2kmB8X1 Web. No date.

"Pumice." http://bit.ly/1TPkvwv Web. No date.

Goldbaum, Kate. "What is the Oldest Tree in the World?" http://bit.ly/1ocFjia Web. 23 August 2016

"Tule Elk History in the Owens Valley." http://bit.ly/2Ah76Lr Web. No date.

Meares, Hadley. "The Flood: St. Francis Dam Disaster, William Mulholland and the Casualties of LA Imperialism." KCET. http://bit.ly/2nBHHGC 26 July 2013

"Owenyo, California." http://bit.ly/2kuPuEL Web. No date.

"Lone Pine, California." Lone Pine History 1860 – Today. http://bit.ly/2kuPXXx Web. No date.

1872 Lonepine Earthquake. In Wikipedia. http://bit.ly/2Aga96O
No date.

"Manzanar." National Park Service. http://bit.ly/1YYcAfN Web.
No date.

"442nd Regimental Combat Team." Densho Encyclopedia.
http://bit.ly/20yMKEr Web. No date.

"The Tribe's History and Culture." Clear Lake's First People – Ha-
bematolel Pomo of Upper Lake. http://bit.ly/2BGGPTg Web.
No date.

"Tule: A Multipurpose Plant of the California Indians." Cabrillo
College.
http://bit.ly/2jn8UZ0 Web. No date.

"Saline Valley Saltworks." Owens Valley History.
http://bit.ly/2jo9dma Web. No date.

Fretheim, Paul. "The Incredible Saline to Swansea Salt Tram."
http://bit.ly/2AV6F9n Web. No date.

Cerro Gordo. http://bit.ly/2jjUdmw Web. No date.

Swansea. In Wikipedia. http://bit.ly/2BIlGIq No date.

Keeler, California. In Wikipedia. http://bit.ly/2BFn4Ly Web. No
date.

Olancha/Grant/Cartago. http://bit.ly/2jlFM4r Web. No date.

Haiwee, California. In Wikipedia. http://bit.ly/2Axmv9v Web. No
date.

"Little Lake." http://bit.ly/2nBu4XQ Web. No date.

Dimmick, Pamela. "Fossil Falls." http://bit.ly/2zVMqV0 Web. No
date

"Naval Air Weapons Station China Lake." https://ti-
nyurl.com/y9phsp6p Web. No date.

Inyokern. In Wikipedia. http://bit.ly/2zVtl5m No date.

Schwartz, Scott. "Burro Schmidt's Tunnel, Miners Shortcut to Nowhere." http://bit.ly/2BFoR3e Web. No date.

Langley, Christopher. Refetoff, Osceola. "William "Burro"
Schmidt and his Tunnel to Nowhere." High & Dry. KCET.
http://bit.ly/2jocmT2 12 June 2014

"Trona Railway." http://bit.ly/2zXbs6v Web. No date.

Mattern, Jim. "Trona, California." http://bit.ly/2jmr4tM 13 August
2012

Antonson, Julie. "Death Valley National Park Barker Ranch."
http://bit.ly/2ADKLoc Web. 6 April 2016

"Randsburg, California." History of Randsburg Mining District.
http://bit.ly/2B9J1WT Web. No date.

"Atolia – Randsburg Tungsten Boom." http://bit.ly/2BcQ69k Web.
No date.

"Johannesburg." http://bit.ly/2zURoSe Web. No date.

Mattern, Jim. "Red Mountain (Osdick) California."
http://bit.ly/2iYaZgX Web. 25 January 2012

"Randsburg Railway." Rand Desert Museum. http://bit.ly/2k2nPap
Web. No date.

"Reuben Sturman." digplanet.com Web. No date.

"Boron, California." http://bit.ly/2k0Z5iU Web. No date.

Howell, Elizabeth. "Columbia: First Shuttle in Space."
http://bit.ly/1RyiYrw Web. 16 January 2013

Howell, Elizabeth. "Enterprise: The Test Shuttle."
http://bit.ly/1hyntpg Web. 9 October 2012

BNSF Railway. In Wikipedia. http://bit.ly/2ivTzEz Web. No date.

UP. In Wikipedia. http://bit.ly/2ABzJSq Web. No date.

Steinberry, Jim. "Hinkley: A Ghost Town in the Making." The Sun.
http://www.sbsun.com/arti-
cle/LG/99999999/NEWS/130809937 Web. 9 October 2016

"Harvey Houses." harveyhouses.net Web. 9 September 2009

Carrole, Anne. "How Waitresses Fed the Western Expansion: The
Harvey Girls." http://bit.ly/2jodlTc Web. 7 August 2011

"Casa Del Desierto." http://bit.ly/2BQNKtO Web. No date.

"Barstow, California." http://bit.ly/2BHS5Pf Web. No date.

"Barstow Station." http://bit.ly/2nBxDxc Web. No date.

"Daggett Museum – Daggett, California." http://bit.ly/2BR3ey7
Web. No date.

Borate and Daggett Railroad. In Wikipedia. http://bit.ly/2j1l90w
Web. No date.

Newberry Springs California. In Wikipedia. http://bit.ly/2ADbDoH
Web. No date.

Pisgah Crater. In Wikipedia.. http://bit.ly/2ktc9S5 Web. No date.

Clarke, Chris. "Breaking: Dormant Mojave Desert Volcano is
Dormant." KCET. http://bit.ly/2BHhHvy Web. 3 August 2011

Harris, Selwyn. "Pahrumpians Overrun Small Railroad Town Seeking Fortune." Pahrump Valley Times. http://bit.ly/2j1jJ6c 13 January 2016

Caruthers, William. "Loafing Along Death Valley Trails; A Personal Narrative of People and Places." Palm Desert: Desert Magazine Press, 1951

ACKNOWLEDGEMENTS

Some thank you's need to be spread around. In no particular order:

My gratitude to my lovely daughter, Fumiko, who, though motivated by purchasing power, diligently typed away on significant portions of this manuscript. As well as provided multiple inspirations for labeling stops along the trail.

To Orbit, a.k.a. Jessica Mencel, for sharing the trail, encouraging the project and translating my hieroglyphic scrawls into a readable format.

And to Lia Smaka, who turned out to have a unique ability to be able to decipher those hieroglyphics, out loud, to the ever-typing Orbit.

To Cirina Catania, who once again held my hand and led me through the digital age and all its daunting pitfalls. Then repeatedly grabbed my wrist, when I was about push the technological panic button and begin throwing things. And who, in the end, answered her draft notice/begging and consented to be my editor. In and of itself, a heroic task that consumed years.

To Marie Klaire Chichi Odumody Taylor, who made me pick up the pen when I wanted to put it down, who brought wisdom where there was none, who typed parts of the book even in her sleep and who proofread the manuscript while climbing stairs to nowhere. But more than any of that, she patiently explained to me how everything could always be better. Everything.

To Riley, who typed, and Kilian, who didn't. But who then cleaned up all my hopeless math. Any math mistakes contained herein, can now be laid squarely at Kilian's 11-year-old feet.

To Ashley Hubbard, who providentially appeared on a river in the Yukon. And went on to make things like maps and book covers, move from an idea to something you could see.

To Phee Sherline, who was generous with her husband's legacy.

To Phil Serpico, who wrote about railroads in a way that made me want to go and find them.

To sisters Jennifer, Jill and Beth for being interested, for providing insight and for transportation when called.

To Otter, who hiked away.

To Ronnie Gagnon, for reading the fiction and making it much, much better. Or at least comprehensible.

To Walter Menck, who took time out from a rough stretch to make very helpful suggestions.

To Aunt Pat, who inadvertently introduced the term, "fucktuation," into my life, on a Sunday of all days.

To Nick and Courtney Rowley, who kindly and generously provided the financial foundation from which such explorations are launched.

To Henry Peacor, for having only positive things to say about suffering. Whether it be marching toward uncertain destinations or trying to make sense of a story in its early stages.

To Leslie Chapin, who gifted that atlas, that eventually shifted victory to the botfly. And then drove hours and suffered unimaginably bad meals, to deliver us to a waiting Ludlow.

To Jim and Joanne Price, for their generosity and instant ability to turn strangers into friends.

To Madison, my niece, who took time from her studies to try and figure out what her uncle was up to.

To Dr. Bal Raj, who performed double knee surgery on me with such skill that three weeks later I was able to hike from Ludlow to Beatty on the Death Q without issues.

To Brittan Cortney, who battled through some early fiction and was generous with suggestions.

To my fellow PCT'ers Red Beard, Slack, Veggie, Ole, Track Meat, Ube and Doc who each, in their own way, managed to increase my passion for any hike.

To the good folks at the Pacific Crest Trail Association for all the fine work they do to keep the PCT functioning.

To George Benton Halteman, whose contributions would fill a book all by themselves.

To Ralf Schellscheidt, who encouraged the international angle of some of the side stories.

And finally, to all the others who contributed to the success of the hike in ways big and small. Whether it be a friendly smile, an offer of water, a conversation that filled in blanks, or any number of a thousand kind things. Humble thanks and deep appreciation are all I can offer.

ABOUT THE AUTHOR

Steven "Blast" Halteman is currently a Jury Consultant and Trial Strategist, and the co-author of a book on legal strategy, "Trail by Human." In his personal life, he is an avid adventurer, traveling the world seeking new horizons and blogging about them at, "Stories From Steve." (http://www.storiesfromsteve.org)

Halteman's career history is decidedly eclectic and unorthodox. He's been, among other things, a house designer, college professor, wilderness skills instructor, night court judge, bartender, roofer, cabinet maker and lumberjack.

Always a fervent hiker and a lover of history, he has spent much of his life exploring more than 100 countries by walking, hitching, backpacking, riding his bike, using public transportation or meandering by boat.

Occasionally, he has settled down and called a number of countries home, including Turkey, Japan and Costa Rica.

Once a competitive runner, he has completed multiple marathons and a couple of ultramarathons. These days, he enjoys taking life more slowly, savoring the small details in the world around him, and indulging his new-found interest in thru hiking. This book, "The Death Q," is the result of that desire.

Halteman hiked the entire Pacific Crest Trail, starting in Mexico and finishing at the Canadian border on his 50th birthday. Over the years, he has completed multiple overseas long-distance hiking trails. In 2018, Halteman will attempt the 2,700-mile Continental Divide Trail from Mexico to Canada through the middle of the United States. He has a teenage daughter, whom he is relentlessly trying to convince to hike the Appalachian Trail with him. A project without success so far.

Halteman recently relocated from Costa Rica and settled in California. He is working on his third book, a novel.

Made in the USA
San Bernardino, CA
05 December 2018